Eugene Lesser's

Sports
Birthdays

Portions of the text and photographs of SPORTS BIRTHDAYS *appeared in the* San Francisco Examiner *in the author's daily columns from November 14, 1983 to July 5, 1985.*

Published by: Ed Buryn
P.O. Box 31123
San Francisco CA 94131

Computer Support:	Howard Fallon
Production Assistance:	Sierra Buryn
	Valerie Valdez
Thanks also to:	Josephine Buryn
	Mary Greer
	Mike Bass

Note

The information in this book has been carefully researched from many sources. However, the accuracy of every individual item cannot be guaranteed. Readers are encouraged to submit corrections and comments; refer to the form provided on the last page.

LCCN: 85-071054
ISBN: 0-916804-03-8

Manufactured in the United States of America

for Pamela Nittolo
who gave me the strength

The main theme of *Sports Birthdays* is homage. A birthday gives us an occasion to focus for a moment on the greats, near-greats, and not-so-greats. It's only a moment, but a moment we rarely take. Though I am an opinionated type, and have my say from time to time, I have tried primarily to emphasize the noble, ignoble, human accomplishments of men and women in sport.

My affinity for birthdays began as the classic sexually repressed eleven-year old who memorized every ballplayer's batting average. Baseball, the most documented sport, provided me with a universe in which everything was significant–the ballplayer, his stats, and such exotica as his birthdate and birthplace. It all went together: **JACKIE ROBINSON (January 31, 1919), Cairo, Georgia.** This isn't trivia.

NOTES

■ **HANK GREENBERG (1911)** — The original "Hammerin' Hank," one of the awesome hitters in baseball history. A big (6-3½, 210) right-handed outfielder-first baseman for the Detroit Tigers, he hit 331 home runs in a career that came to less than 10 full seasons (a tremendous home run average), shortened because of injury and four-plus seasons in World War II (from age 30 to 34). The year before he went into the service, in 1940, Greenberg hit .340 and led the league in homers, RBI, doubles, and slugging. He carried the Tigers to three pennants (1934, '35, and '40) and had some incredible years — he hit his fabled 58 homers in 1938 (no

Hank Greenberg

righty hitter has ever hit more), knocked in an unbelievable 183 runs in 1937 (one fewer than Gehrig's AL record), and hit 63 doubles in 1934 (four fewer than Earl Webb's ML record). In 1946, his first full year back from the service (and final one for Detroit), Greenberg — at age 35 — led the league in homers (44) and RBI (127). Greenberg worked as an exec alongside Bill Veeck at Cleveland and Chicago during the years those teams won pennants in the 1950s. He was also known as one of the top senior tennis players in the country.

■ Also born today: **DOAK WALKER (1927)**, Heisman Trophy winner from SMU in 1948, played with the Detroit Lions in early 1950s and twice led league in scoring ... **PIERRE DE COUBERTIN (1862)**, a baron and French educator, the main force behind the establishment of the modern Olympic Games, first staged in Athens in 1896 with only 13 nations participating ... **CHARLES COOPER (1943)**, S.F. Examiner sports editor... **EARL TORGESON (1924)**, bespectacled pugnacious Braves-etc first baseman ... **GEORGE CONNOR (1925)**, college and pro Hall of Fame lineman with Notre Dame and Chicago Bears ... Padres righty **LAMARR HOYT (1955)**, AL Cy Young Award winner in 1983... the **McKEEVER** twins, **MIKE** and **MARLIN**, born in 1940, both football stars at USC ... basketball player, coach, announcer **HORACE "BONES" McKINNEY (1919)**.

*Rocky Graziano (1922) NYC
Middleweight champ 1947-48*

Xmas ('84) gift from Chisox

NOTES

■**GINO MARCHETTI (1927)** — Marchetti, named the best defensive end of the NFL's first 50 years. He was born in Kayford, W.Va., and grew up in Antioch,

California. He starred on the awesome USF team of 1951 that went undefeated, a team that is considered one of the greatest college teams of all-time. In 1952 he was drafted by the New York Yanks, who before the season started became the Dallas Texans. One year later they left Texas and became the Baltimore Colts. In his 13 years with them he went to the Pro Bowl 11 times and was considered the best

Gino Marchetti

pass rusher in the league during his prime. Marchetti is remembered for stopping Frank Gifford inches short of a first down late in the 1958 NFL title game against the N.Y. Giants. That forced the Giants to punt with two minutes left. Baltimore tied it up and won in a sudden-death overtime.

■Also born today: **GEORGE "TEX" RICKARD (1870)**, impresario who made boxing a million-dollar event by promoting Jack Dempsey's fights; his bout against Georges Carpentier in 1921 was the first million-dollar gate ... **BOB FEERICK (1920)**, S.F.-born basketball star at Santa Clara, then with the Washington Capitols of the old BAA in the late 1940s, later coached the Capitols, then Santa Clara, and the Warriors, worked in Warrior front office until his death in 1981 ... **MARV FLEMING (1942)**, tight end who played in Super Bowls with the Packers and Dolphins... **PAT FISCHER (1940)**, the gutsy defensive back for 17 years with the Cardinals and George Allen's over-the-hill gang in Washington ... ... Cowboys/Browns running back **CALVIN HILL (1947)**.

■ **BOBBY HULL (1939)** — "The Golden Jet," one of the great scorers in hockey history, Hull skated with the Chicago Black Hawks from 1957 to 1972. He won two MVP awards (1965, 1966), three scoring titles (1960, '62, and '66), and led the league in goals seven times. He startled the hockey world in 1972 by jumping from the established NHL to the fledgling WHA, giving it instant credibility. He finished the second phase of his career with the Winnipeg Jets from 1972 until he retired in 1980. He won two more MVP awards in the new league (1973, 1975). Hull was considered a perfect physical specimen, with "the shoulders of a wrestler, the waist of a swimmer, and the legs of a fullback." Bobby's younger brother, Dennis Hull, was also a left-winger, also with the Black Hawks.

■ **HANK STRAM (1924)** — Ex-football coach and radio announcer. Stram was the guiding genius of the Kansas City Chiefs from their inception in the AFL in 1960 until 1975. He created one of the dynasties of modern football in Kansas City, culminating in the Chiefs' decisive win over the Vikings in Super Bowl IV. Stram and partner Jack Buck have been a successful broadcasting duo.

Hank Stram

Many Monday Night Football viewers have been so turned off by Howard Cosell's personality that they turned off the TV sound and listened to Stram's insightful commentary on the radio.

■ Also born today: **JOE FALCARO (1896)**, Italian-born bowler who defeated the world champion at age 15 and was considered the world's best bowler at age 50 ... Oriole OF-1B **JIM DWYER (1950)**, a good ballplayer that the Giants virtually gave away in 1979 ... **WILLIAM RENSHAW** and **JAMES RENSHAW (1861)**, the twins from England considered creators of modern lawn tennis,

NOTES

■ **DON SHULA (1930)** — Shula, one of the greatest football coaches of all time, An Ohio native, he went

Don Shula

to little John Carroll there and was drafted by the Cleveland Browns as a defensive back in 1951. He played two years there, tour years with the Colts, and retired after the 1957 season with the Redskins. Shula replaced Weeb Ewbank in 1963 as the Colts' coach and stayed through the 1969 season, taking the Colts to the NFL title in 1968. In 1970 Shula went over to the Miami Dolphins, where he created a dynasty in his first few years. He has since directed one of the most consistently winning franchises in pro sports. Shula established himself as one of the all-time coaching greats by winning more than 100 games in his first 10 years as a pro coach.

■ **FLOYD PATTERSON (1935)** — Patterson, heavyweight champion (1956- 59, 1960-62). Born in Waco, N.C., he won the Olympic middleweight gold medal, becoming the first Olympic winner to win the world heavyweight title. He was also the youngest ever to become heavyweight champion (21 years, 11 months). In 1959, Patterson was upset by Ingemar Johansson via a third-round knockout. A year later Patterson achieved yet another distinction — he became the first heavyweight champion to lose and then regain his crown. He knocked Johansson out in five rounds and — a year later, 1961 — knocked him out again (in six rounds). Patterson is currently head of the New York State Boxing Commission.

■ Also born today: **GEORGE SELKIRK (1908)**, known as "Twinkletoes," he replaced Babe Ruth in right field for the Yankees in late 1934 ... **TOMMY CORCORAN (1869)**, still holds the record for most assists (14) by a shortstop in a nine-inning game — set in 1903. ... **TITO FUENTES (1944)**, Former Giant second baseman. ... **DAVE MAGGARD (1940)**, UC athletic director.

NOTES

■ **CHUCK NOLL (1932)** — Noll, one of the best and least-heralded coaches in NFL history, was born in Ohio (Cleveland), went to a small Ohio College (Dayton) and played pro ball with the Cleveland Browns (offensive guard, 1953-59). He became head coach of the Pittsburgh Steelers in 1969, inheriting a team that had not even been near a .500 season for five years. Building rapidly, mostly through the draft (Terry Bradshaw, Franco Harris, Lynn Swann, Joe Greene, Mel Blount, Jack Lambert—virtually every key play-

Chuck Noll

er on the Steeler dynasty of the '70s was drafted in '69, '70 and '71), Pittsburgh won four Super Bowls, in 1975, 1976, 1979 and 1980. In 1984, he took a so-so Steeler team to the AFC title game, defeating along the way the 49ers, Raiders and Broncos (all on the road).

■ **CLAUDE 'BUDDY' YOUNG (1926)** — A brilliant 5'-4" scatback from the University of Illinois, he became the first black player to score a touchdown in the Rose Bowl when, in his last college game (four days before his 21st birthday), he led Illinois in a 45- 14 drubbing of UCLA. He had a nine-year pro career with the New York Yankees of the All- American Football Conference and the Baltimore Colts. He was the NFL's director of player relations at the time of his death in 1984.

■ Also born today: **BYRON "BAN" JOHNSON (1864)**, American League president, 1900-27, originator of the "Cincinnati Agreement," establishing the two major leagues in 1903, also born in Ohio (Norwalk) ... **ALEX ENGLISH (1954)**, high-scoring forward with the Denver Nuggets ... **JIM OTTO (1938)**, great center with the Oakland Raiders from 1960 to 1974, played in every game in the history of the club to that point — never missing a game in his career! ... **SAM WYCHE (1945)**, coach of the Bengals, speaking of Ohio and Cincinnati ... **EUGENE 'MERCURY' MORRIS (1947)**, the former Miami Dolphin running back is doing 20 years in prison on cocaine trafficking charges.

■ **KID GAVILAN (1926)** — Welterweight champ, 1951 to 1954 (a long tenure for that division). Known as "The Hawk" 30 years before Aaron Pryor, Gavilan was born Gerardo Gonzales in Cuba. He fought around Havana until 1947 when he went to New York City and began his climb to the top, which he achieved via a 15-round decision over Billy Graham for Ray Robinson's vacated title after having earlier defeated pretender Johnny Bratton in another 15-round decision. Gavilan had an aggressive, flashy style featuring his famed "bolo punch," an uppercut

Kid Gavilan

that he wound up and threw. Early in 1954 he challenged Bobo Olson for his middleweight title and lost a 15-round decision. Later that year Gavilan lost his welter title to Johnny Saxton via yet another 15-round decision. In fact, all of Gavilan's 30 losses were by decision. He won 106 fights, only 27 by KO. His crowd-pleasing style made him a natural for TV, which helped make him one of the most popular fighters of the 1950s.

■ **KID CHOCOLATE (1910)** — Another boxing champion, also from Cuba, and with the same nickname (Kid), was born on this day. Featherweight champ in 1932, Chocolate was an inspiration to many blacks to enter boxing as a career, including the great three-division champion, Hammerin' Henry Armstrong.

■ Also born today: **EARLY WYNN (1920)**, one of a handful of pitchers to win 300 games, he's one of only six whose career spanned four decades (1939-63, with Senators, Indians, and White Sox) ...

golfer **NANCY LOPEZ (1957)**, in 1978 she won an unprecedented five straight LPGA tournaments, married to Mets infielder Ray Knight ... another righty pitcher: **RALPH BRANCA (1926)**, threw high inside fastball to Bobby Thomson on Oct. 3, 1951, giving up the "shot heard 'round the world"; he should have walked him intentionally with first base open and pitched to the rookie, Willie Mays.

NOTES

■ **JOHNNY MIZE (1913)** — "The Big Cat," power-hitting first baseman inducted into the Hall of Fame in 1981. Mize played for the Cardinals, Giants and Yankees from 1936 to 1953, less three years lost to World War II. Mize won the batting title in 1939 while with the Cardinals, and also led the league in slugging percentage that season, a rare achievement. Mize was truly a great hitter. He hit for power (359 homers), average (.312 lifetime BA), and no doubt struck out less than any power-hitter in baseball history. In

Johnny Mize

1947, while with the NY Giants, "Big Jawn" hit 51 home runs (an NL record for a left-handed hitter) while striking out only 42 times. Mize spent his twilight years with the Yankees as a pinch-hitter deluxe and played in the World Series in each of the five years he was with them (1949-53). In the 1952 Series, Mize homered in games three, four and five. In his last year, at age 40, he was 19-for-61 as a pinch-hitter, the best in the league. Mize, who holds the major league record for hitting three home runs in a game six times, is currently retired, living in his birthplace, Demorest, Ga.

■ **ALVIN DARK (1923)** — Born in Comanche, Oklahoma 61 years ago, Dark started as QB at Louisiana State University but chose baseball and broke in with the Boston Braves in 1948, winning the rookie-of-the-year award and leading them to the pennant. He was also on the pennant-winning Giants team in 1951. A .289 lifetime hitter, Dark was a great clutch performer. He also managed the Indians, A's and S.F. Giants, who in 1962 under his leadership won their only pennant.

■ Also born today: **EDDIE LeBARON (1930)**, pocket lefty quarterback at the College of Pacific, then the Redskins and Cowboys in an 11-year pro career; currently the general manager of the Atlanta Falcons ... tennis immortal **MAURICE E. McLOUGHLIN (1890)**, "The California Comet," U.S. singles champion 1912 and 1913 ... **TONY CONIGLIARO (1945)**, ex-Bosox outfielder (won home run title in 1965), still suffering from a 1982 heart attack ... **CHILI DAVIS (1960)**, S.F. Giants right fielder.

NOTES

■DWIGHT CLARK (1957) —

49ers wide receiver, born in Kinston, N.C., 10th round

draft choice out of Clemson in 1978 (one of the many drafting coups in Bill Walsh's career). Clark developed into one of the most dependable receivers in the NFL — strong, good hands, good instincts, the bread-and-butter guy. He and Joe Montana compare with the greatest passing duos in pro-football history, and The Catch, the play that beat the Cowboys in the 1981 NFC title game, stands among football's greatest single plays. It also epito-

Dwight Clark

mizes Clark's and Montana's individual and collective brilliance. In our memory Clark will always remain fixed — arms outstretched, hands around the football, above it all.

■BRUCE SUTTER (1953) —

Ace reliever for the Atlanta Braves. After 9 seasons in the majors (with the Cubs and Cardinals), Sutter has a sub-500 lifetime won-loss record (60-62) and (though he led the majors with a 1.54 ERA in 1984) entered last season with a lifetime ERA of 2.71, not that good for a short reliever. Up to 1979 with the Cubs he struck out more batters than innings pitched (with his fabled split-finger fastball, a sinking pitch) but hasn't been near that pace since. Like most relievers, he is overrated and overused, despite being one of the better ones in the game. He signed a $44 million contract for 30 years with the Braves.

■Also born today: former Raider fullback **HEWRITT DIXON (1940)** ... centerfielder **JIM BUSBY (1927)**, a great glove mostly with the White Sox and Washington Senators ... **JACQUES ANQUETIL (1934)**, pronounced ankh-TEEL, legendary French long-distance bicyclist ... **WALKER COOPER (1915)**, power-hitting catcher with the Cardinals and New York Giants and brother of pitcher Mort Cooper who was MVP in 1942 ... **DOREEN WILBUR (1930)**, a famous United States woman archer ... English golfer **PERCY ALLISS (1897)**.

NOTES

■ **BART STARR (1934)** — The great quarterback of the Green Bay Packers (1956 to 1971). Born in Birmingham, Ala., he played college ball at the University of Alabama and, because he sat out his senior year with a back injury, was drafted by the Packers in the 17th round. Starr was a methodical performer who never lost his cool and hardly ever made mistakes. He still owns the NFL record of 294 consecutive passes without an interception, a record that is not in great danger of being equalled. When he retired in

Bart Starr

1971 he had a pass completion percentage of 57.4, the best all-time mark up to that time. Starr led the Packers to rather easy victories in Super Bowls I and II, and was named the MVP in each game. Unfortunately, this magnificent QB with the magnificent name decided to become head coach of the Packers in 1975. His last few years, culminating in his ouster in 1982, were painful. It's true in most sports: great players don't make great coaches.

■ Also born today: **RALPH TERRY (1936)**, righty pitcher with the Yankees in the early 1960s, won 23 games in 1962; he gave up Bill Mazeroski's ninth-inning homer to win Series for Pittsburgh in 1960; he also served pitch to Willie McCovey in 1962 Series final game that was lined right at Bobby Richardson (even though Terry should have walked him with first base open) . . . former Cowboy fullback **ROBERT NEWHOUSE (1950)** . . . **M.L. CARR (1951)**, Celtics swingman who played college basketball at little Guilford with World Free . . . **DICK ENBERG**, the best all-around (basketball, football, boxing) sports announcer on TV . . . **JOHN KIBLER (1929)**, NL umpire since 1963.

■ **WILLIE McCOVEY (1938)** —
The great slugger who holds the National League record for career home runs by a left-handed hitter

Willie McCovey

(521) "Stretch" broke in with the S.F. Giants on July 30, 1959, going 4-for-4 against Robin Roberts. Except for three seasons with the Padres (to whom he was ignominiously traded for Mike Caldwell) and a brief stint with the A's, McCovey spent the rest of his 22-year career with the Giants before retiring in 1980, one of only six players whose career spanned four decades. He won the MVP award in 1969, the Comeback Award in 1977 (after his return to the Giants), finishing with a .270 BA and several major league records, including most years by a first baseman and 45 intentional walks in 1969, and set such National League records as most grand slam homers (18) and most homers by a first baseman. It was McCovey who hit into one of the most famous outs in baseball history when, in Game Seven of the 1962 World Series, he lined a game-ending shot into the glove of Bobby Richardson with the winning runs on base. McCovey deserved a break, too, because they never should have pitched to him with first base open and a righty pitcher going (Ralph Terry, whose birthday is one day before Willie's.)

■ **GEORGE FOREMAN (1949)** — Born in Marshall, Texas (Y.A. Tittle's birthplace). In 1973, Foreman became heavyweight champion and drove Joe Frazier into retirement with a second- round KO. The following year, he lost the title to Muhammad Ali, a victim of the great one's "rope- a- dope." Since then, George has become involved in evangelical work and found inner peace.

■ Also born today: **WALTER J. TRAVIS (1862)**, Australian golfer who settled in U.S., took up golf rather late in life and became one of the greatest ever as well as one of the most unpopular ... **BILL TOOMEY (1939)**, won the decathlon in the 1968 Olympics ... lefty **CLIFF CHAMBERS (1922)**, lifetime 48-53 pitcher but he threw a no-hitter in 1951 (and was traded the following <u>month</u> by Pirates to Cardinals).

NOTES

■FREDDIE SOLOMON (1953) – 49er wide receiver, one of the elite of his trade. Born in Sumter, S.C., Solomon was a tremendous athlete at Tampa University, where he played quarterback and ran for more than 3,000 yards with trackman speed. In 1975, the Dolphins drafted him in the second round and made him a receiver. Four years later (on the brink of greatness) he was traded to the 49ers for Delvin Williams. Under Bill Walsh, Solomon's career took off and he stands today at the top of his game, among the all-time best.

Freddie Solomon

■LYNWOOD "SCHOOLBOY" ROWE (1910) — A big right-hander with the Detroit Tigers (1933-42) and the Phillies (1943, 1946-49), born in Waco, Texas. In his second season, Rowe went 24-8 and led the Tigers to the pennant. The next year Rowe won 19 games and the Tigers won the pennant again. Rowe followed that act with another 19-game season in 1936. In 1940 he was on his third pennant-winning Tigers team and led the league with an .842 percentage, going 16-3. After losing two years in World War II, Rowe had some good seasons with the Phillies before retiring with an excellent 158-101 won-loss record. Rowe was the first player to appear in All-Star competition for both leagues — in 1936 with the Tigers and in 1947 when, as a Phillie, he pinch-hit for Warren Spahn (that's obscure).

■TRACY CAULKINS (1963) — Born in Winona, Minn., Caulkins is the greatest swimmer in American history. In 1982 she won her 36th national title, breaking Johnny Weissmuller's mark. Her 15 American records include the 100 and 200-m breaststroke and 500-m free-style.

■DARRYL DAWKINS (1957) — Double D, Dr. Dunk, Chocolate Thunder, with the Nets. In 1975 he was the 76ers' first-round draft choice out of an Orlando, Fla., high school.

■JOHN "PADDY" DRISCOLL (1896) — A triple-threat running back of the 1920s with the Chicago Cardinals and Chicago Bears (died in 1968).

NOTES

■**FRITZ CRISLER (1899)** — This legendary coach of the University of Michigan (1938-48) was born Herbert Orin Crisler in Earlville, Ill.

Fritz Crisler

He played football at Chicago University under Amos Alonzo Stagg (who gave him his nickname) but was going to be a doctor. Unfortunately (depending how you look at it), he couldn't afford medical school after graduating from college in 1921 and Stagg asked him to become his assistant coach. He spent a valuable apprenticeship with Stagg for eight years, becoming a head coach first at Minnesota (1930-31), then Princeton (1932-37), including two undefeated seasons, and finally Michigan, where he built a dynasty with a state-of-the-art single wing, winning 71 games and losing 17. A friend of Crisler's described his coaching attitude thusly: "The best was expected of you, and you needn't be congratulated for trying." He was the father of two-platoon football (though he later tried to outlaw it, seeing it as a Frankenstein monster that robbed the game of all-around athletes), and he modernized the huddle, blocking techniques, the stances of linemen and backs, and other aspects of football. His monument is his 1947 Michigan team that won the national title and defeated USC in the Rose Bowl, 49-0. 45 years earlier, in the first Rose Bowl game, Michigan (under Fielding "Hurry Up" Yost, another legendary Michigan coach) defeated Stanford by the same score.

■Also born today: **TOM DEMPSEY (1947)**, born with part of his right foot missing, kicked 63-yard field goal while with New Orleans Saints to beat the Detroit Lions, 19-17, on last play of game, shattering previous record of 56 yards by Bert Rechichar in 1953 ... **JOE FRAZIER (1944)**, heavyweight champion, 1968-73, defeated Ali in 1971 in the greatest fight of his career ... boxer **GEORGES CARPENTIER (1894)**, light-heavy champion, 1920-22, who lost to Jack Dempsey in 1921 in the first bout with a million-dollar gate ... **RAY HARROUN (1879)**, won the first Indy 500 in 1911, averaging 75 mph ... **BILL MADLOCK (1951)** — perennial MVP candidate with the Pirates since 1979.

NOTES

Sports birthdays / Jan. 13

■**TOM GOLA (1933)** — Gola, one of the greatest college basketball players, was born in Philadelphia. One of seven children of a policeman, he learned to play on asphalt courts in the tough playgrounds of his lower middle-class neighborhood. He was a high school phenom there, selected to the first-string high school All-American team and leader of the North victory over the South in the North-South high school all-star game. He went to LaSalle College in Philly and broke into the starting lineup as a freshman, a 6-foot-6,

Tom Gola

210-pound forward. All he did was lead them to the NIT championship and be named co-MVP of the tourney. It must be remembered that the NIT was even more prestigious than the NCAA tournament at that time. Gola got better over the next three years. As a senior he averaged 24.1 points a game. Again, in 1954, that was burning the nets. A player like Gola had hardly ever been seen before. Usually, only 5-10 playmates had Gola's fluidity, floor savvy, passing and ball-hawking ability. The Philadelphia Warriors took him as a territorial draft selection in 1955 and converted him to guard, one of the first big guards in the NBA. He became the glue for that Paul Arizin/Neil Johnston-led Warrior team, and they won the NBA title. As a college freshman and as a pro rookie, Gola played on championship teams. He played his last three seasons with the N.Y. Knicks and retired in 1966.

■Also born today: **A.H. "ART" ROSS (1886)**, best known as architect of Boston Bruins dynasty in late 1920s and later, and inventor of the modern puck and goal net; the Art Ross Trophy (for the leading scorer of the year) is named for him ... **PAT HADEN (1953)**, USC QB who led them to 1975 Rose Bowl win over Ohio State, later Rhodes Scholar, later QB with L.A. Rams ... **RUSSELL ERXLEBEN (1957)**, who set NCAA kicking records at Texas ... Cardinal righty **BOB FORSCH (1950)**, born in Sacramento, pitched no-hitter in 1978 (his brother Ken, currently with the Angels, also has tossed a no-hitter).

■ **RUBEN OLIVARES (1947)** — Bantamweight champion (1969-72) and featherweight champion (1973, 1974).

Ruben Olivares

Olivares was born in Mexico City but, unlike the normal script, did not go into boxing to escape his life of poverty. His father was a successful businessman. Olivares took up boxing because he loved it. He didn't lose a fight in his first 51 bouts and is considered the hardest-hitting bantam of modern times. Of his 87 victories, 77 were by a knockout. Olivares' best-known fights include his five-round KO of Lionel Rose to win the bantam title in 1969, his three bouts with Jesus (Chucho) Castillo (in which Olivares won, lost, and regained the title), the loss of his featherweight title to Alexis Arguello via a 13th-round KO in 1974, and his second round TKO over Bobby Chacon in 1975 to regain the vacant featherweight crown.

■ Also born today: **FRED ARBANAS (1939)**, tight end for the Kansas City Chiefs dynasty of the 1960s, one of the many obscure greats on that team, who had vision in only one eye ... two famous Sieberts were born today, unrelated: **ALBERT "BABE" SIEBERT (1904)**, hockey immortal with the Montreal Canadiens, MVP in 1936-37, in 1939 he was captain of the Canadiens and was signed to coach them the next season but he drowned that summer at age 35 ... and **WILFRED "SONNY" SIEBERT (1937)**, in 1966 pitched no-hitter, went 16-8 (with a .500 Cleveland team), led the AL in percentage; 140-114 lifetime pitcher (also with Bosox and Rangers) with solid 3.13 ERA ... **GENE WASHINGTON (1947)**, Nureyev-like wide receiver for Stanford and 49ers during their division-winning early 1970s; not so good as a TV color man ... **WAYNE GROSS (1952)**, had a darn good year at the plate for the Orioles in 1984 despite hitting .216 — his 74 hits drove in 64 runs and he hit 22 homers (or 30 percent of his hits!)

NOTES

■ **RAY CHAPMAN (1891)** — The only player to die in a major league baseball game. He was a shortstop for Cleveland his entire career, from 1912 until that fateful day in 1920 when he was struck on the left temple by a pitch thrown by right-hander Carl Mays, a submarine pitcher who threw practically underhand. Chapman crumbled at home plate, was rushed to a hospital and died soon after. He was 31. It was a hard-luck incident in many respects. Chapman was a popular player throughout the league who was peaking as a player. He had three good years behind him and had played in 111 games until his death hitting .303 with an impressive 97 runs scored — almost one a game. The Indians went on to win the 1920 pennant, their first ever, and defeat the Brooklyn Dodgers in the World Series. Curiously, Chapman does hold one major league record, set in 1917 — most sacrifices (67) in a single season.

■ **BOB DAVIES (1920)** — Phenomenal basketball player in college and the pros. Before Bob Cousy, there was Bob Davies, the smoothest, slickest back-court player ever to play the game up to that point. He was renowned for his dribbling abilities at Seton Hall, where he led them to 43 straight wins during the war years. He was probably the first to use the behind-the-back dribble that Cousy popularized years later. He played with the Rochester Royals from 1945 to 1955 and was a strong influence on the guards that came after him. "The Harrisburg Houdini" was one of the most exciting players ever to step onto a court.

■ Also born today: **KENNY EASLEY (1959)**, free safety for the Seahawks, named the NFL's defensive player of the '84 season... **BOBBY GRICH (1949)**, California Angels veteran second baseman ... **LEO "DUTCH" MEYER (1898)**, TCU football coach, 1934-52 ... **RANDY WHITE (1953)**, Dallas Cowboys defensive tackle since 1975 ... **HOBART "HOBEY" BAKER (1892)**, hockey and football great who died at age 26, testing airplanes in World War I... **MIKE MARSHALL (1943)**, won the Cy Young Award in 1974 (the first reliever to win it) with the Dodgers, setting a few major-league records; most games by a pitcher in a season (106), most innings by a reliever (208), most consecutive games pitched (13). As a reliever, he won 43 games in three years (1972-74) with Montreal and the Dodgers.

NOTES

■ **DIZZY DEAN (1911)** —Pitching great with the Cards in the 1930s and one of the "unforgettable characters" of baseball, was born Jay Hanna Dean in Lucas, Ark.

Dizzy Dean

Dean won 18 games as a Cardinal rookie in 1932, then won 20 games a year later. The following year, 1934, Dean went 30-7 and led the Cards to the pennant and World Series victory against the Tigers. He followed that act with two more tremendous seasons, going 28-12 and 24-13, and at age 25 had won 120 major league games. In 1937, during the All-Star Game, tragedy struck Dean in the form of a line drive (by Earl Averill) that hit him on the foot. Though he pitched for three more seasons (with the Cubs), his dominance ended. Dean's career won-loss record is 150-83, a .644 percentage that is one of the best ever. During his five-year heyday (1932-36), he led the NL in strikeouts and complete games almost every year. In the World Series of 1934, Dean won two games and his brother, Paul, won the other two. Paul won 19 games that year and the next while Dizzy won 30 and 28. No brothers pitching on the same team have ever approached those figures. Dean, a folk hero, died in 1974.

■ **ERIC LIDDELL (1902)** — Liddell, Scottish Olympic sprinter portrayed in the film, Chariots of Fire, set a British record for the 100-yard dash (9.7) that stood for 35 years. A year later, at the 1924 Olympics, he caused a mild sensation by withdrawing from the 100-meter competition because the heats were on Sunday, the Sabbath. He won a bronze medal in the 200 meters and then shocked the world by winning the 400 meters, not his specialty. He died where he was born, in China, in a Japanese concentration camp in 1945. He had been doing missionary work there.

■ Also born today: **A.J. FOYT (1935)**, the only four-time winner of the Indy 500 ... black jockey **WILLIE SIMMS (1870)**, who won the 1896 Kentucky Derby on Ben Brush ... bowling Hall of Famer **JOSEPH BODIS (1897)** ... **JIMMY COLLINS (1870)**, Boston third baseman-manager, 1901-06, who managed the Red Sox to a pennant in 1903 and won the first World Series (over Pittsburgh).

NOTES

■ **MUHAMMAD ALI (1942)** — beautiful fighter ever to step into a ring. Born Cassius Marcellus Clay in Louisville, Ky., he had a tremendous amateur career, winning national Golden Gloves, AAU titles and the gold medal in the light-heavyweight division at the 1960 Olympics. A syndicate of 11 millionaires (all white) sponsored his pro career and hired trainer Angelo Dundee who wisely did not try to change Ali's natural, though unorthodox,

Probably the most

Muhammad Ali

style. So Ali was just past his 22nd birthday when, in 1964, he completely outclassed heavily favored Liston, who couldn't come out for the seventh round. After three years of utter dominance as the champion, he was stripped of his title for refusing to be drafted into the Vietnam War because of his religious beliefs. A black Muslim, he had already changed his name. After a 3½-year layoff, Ali returned to the ring in 1974 to get back his title. First Ali lost a decision to Joe Frazier but won his title back via a humiliating eighth-round KO over George Foreman, then avenged his defeat by Frazier in the "Thrilla in Manila" in 1975. Ali later avenged losses by Ken Norton and Leon Spinks. Three times Ali regained his title. In 60 fights, Ali lost only four times, the last time to Larry Holmes when Ali was 38 years old. The claim of many fans (and Ali himself) that he is the greatest is valid. Certainly no fighter ever had Ali's influence or status as a world figure.

■ Also born today: goalie **JACQUES PLANTE (1929)**, with Canadiens and others won Vezina Trophy eight times, six in a row (1955-60) and once at age 40 ... **"PHILADELPHIA" JACK O'BRIEN (1878)**, light-heavy champ, 1905-12, rated No. 2 all-time in his division ... **KIPCHOGE KEINO (1940)**, Kenyan runner won gold medals in 1968 (1,500 meters) and '72 (steeplechase) ... **DON ZIMMER (1931)**, utility infielder, 1954-65, mostly with the Dodgers (lifetime .235 hitter). Married his high school sweetheart at home plate in Elmira, N.Y.

NOTES

■ **CURT FLOOD (1938)** — St. Louis Cardinals' center fielder of the 1960s who stood up to the reserve clause. Born in Houston, Flood came up

briefly with the Reds but went over to the Cardinals and broke into their lineup as a 20-year-old rookie. For 12 years, Flood was a solid performer — a .293 lifetime hitter, a good outfielder and fast. He and leadoff man Lou Brock formed a dynamic one-two in the batting order that helped the Cardinals win pennants in 1964, '67 and '68 (including two World Series, losing only to the '68 Tigers).

Curt Flood

After the 1969 season, Flood was traded to the Phillies but refused to accept the trade and decided to challenge the constitutionality of the reserve clause (which bound players to one team) in the courts. He sat out the 1970 season and finally lost his case. After a brief 13-game stint with the Washington Senators, Flood, who once had a shot at 3,000 hits and the Hall of Fame, decided to retire. His book, "The Way It Is," is recommended reading. In the late 1970s, Flood was an Oakland A's announcer and more recently has worked in the Oakland parks department.

■ Also born today: **JOE SCHMIDT (1932)**, middle linebacker with Detroit Lions from 1953-65, the first great MLB of the 4-3 defense, somewhat in the shadow of Ray Nitschke; coached Lions (1967-72) with 43-34-7 record ... **LARRY SMITH (1958)**, rebounding forward for the Warriors ... rodeo star **PHIL LYNE (1947)** ... QB **PAT SULLIVAN (1950)**, the 1971 Heisman Trophy Award winner from Auburn, and S.F. sportswriter **PRESCOTT SULLIVAN (1906)** ... **BOB LURIE (1934)**, owner of the S.F. Giants since 1976 who has made only two major mistakes — hiring Spec Richardson and Tom Haller as his general managers.

Died in 1985.

■ **CHICK GANDIL (1888)** — Gandil, spearhead of the eight Chicago White Sox players who threw the 1919 World Series to the Cincinnati Reds, was born Charles Arnold Gandil in St. Paul Minn. Gandil was a strong first baseman who had his best years with the Washington Senators (1912-15) but was still a solid performer with the White Sox and played with the 1917 team that beat McGraw's Giants in the Series. That Chicago team was considered the greatest up to that point. Gandil, angry at owner Charles Comiskey's tight-fisted hold over the players, was the brains of the whole scheme.

Chick Gandil

Many people believe (because they read it in "The Great Gatsby") that gamblers tried to fix the Series Even Arnold Rothstein ("Wertheimer" in Gatsby), who finally did handle the deal, wouldn't have dreamed it possible. No, it was Chick Gandil who dreamed it possible and approached shocked gamblers with the plan. The players (only two of whom influenced the Series — the two best White Sox pitchers, Ed Cicotte and Lefty Williams) were banned for life. Gandil lived for many years in Calistoga Calif., and died there in 1970, the last survivor of the "eight men out."

■ Also born today: **DAN REEVES (1944)**, Denver Broncos coach ... **OTTIS ANDERSON (1957)**, St. Louis Cards' great running back. In just three seasons, Anderson became the Cardinals' career rushing leader ... Notre Dame and Steelers QB **TERRY HANRATTY (1948)** ... **MATTHEW WEBB (1848)**, British swimmer and naval officer, became the first man to swim (without life jacket) across the English Channel; eight years later, in 1883, Webb drowned trying to swim Niagara Falls.

■ **CAMILO PASQUAL (1934) —** Righty pitcher for the Senators, which became the Twins, and for the expansion Senators in the late 1960s. Born in Cuba, Pasqual broke into the majors as a 20-year-old but was a late bloomer. In his first five years, he was never near a .500 season. In fact, his 28-66 record was under .300. For the next 10 years, however, Pasqual was only under .500 once (in 1961, and led the league in strikeouts anyway). He led the AL in strikeouts, complete games and shutouts three times and twice won 20 games (in '62 and '63).

Camilo Pasqual

After a slow start, he finished his career in 1971 with an outstanding 174-170 won-loss record in 18 seasons. Not a bad hitter, Pasqual hit two grand slam homers in his career. In recent years he has been an Oakland A's scout.

■ **LOU FONTINATO (1932) —** New York Ranger defenseman (1954-61) and the NHL's chief enforcer during that period. Even as a rookie in 1954, he was considered the toughest player in the league. In 1960, however, Gordie Howe challenged Fontinato in Madison Sq Gdn and, to the horror of Ranger fans, proceeded to batter Fontinato with a flurry of punches that left the Rangers' hero in a bloody heap and with a broken nose. From that day on, Fontinato was never the same player. His flamboyance died and his playing went downhill. A year later, he was traded to the Canadiens but was forced into retirement by a serious injury that broke his neck.

■ **Also born today:** **CAROL HEISS (1940)**, won the figure skating gold medal at the 1960 Olympics after having copped a silver medal in the 1956 Games. After retirement, she became a well-known TV sportscaster. She married the figure skater Hayes Jenkins, who also won a gold medal in 1956 ... golfer **WILLIE TURNESA (1914)** ... Browns and Redskins QB **MILT PLUM (1935)**, whose 110.4 in 1960 was the highest QB rating ever ... **FRANK KUSH (1929)**, fired as head coach at Arizona State after he allegedly slapped his punter; in 1982, signed five-year coaching contract with the Baltimore Colts.

Fired '84,
Coach in USFL '85

Sports birthdays/Jan. 21

■ **GIL DOBIE (1879)** — "Gloomy Gil," one of the greatest (and least popular) coaches in college football history, was born in Hastings, Minn. He went to the Univ of Minnesota, where he was the star quarterback. In 1900, he led the Golden Gophers to their first Big Ten title. Dobie first became a head coach at North Dakota Agricultural Coll., which he led to two straight undefeated seasons. He then coached at the Univ. of Washington for nine years and never lost a game. Dobie didn't lose a single game in his first 11 years of coaching — a record not likely to be equaled. After a three-year stint at Navy, Dobie coached at Cornell (1920-35) and had three unbeaten seasons there. He finished his career at Boston College (1936-38), retiring with a 180-45 won-loss record, an awesome .800 percentage over 33 years. Dobie was "at once the finest precisionist and the toughest coach in history." A stern, Scrooge-like and pessimistic man ("a coach can only wind up two ways — dead or a failure") who read Schopenhauer for relaxation, he died Xmas Eve, 1948.

■ **JACK NICKLAUS (1940)** — "The Golden Bear," who many claim the greatest golfer ever, *is* the top money-winner. After winning two U.S. Amateur titles (1959 and '61), Nicklaus won the 1962 U.S. Open at 22 (defeating Arnold Palmer in a playoff) and won it three more times, in 1967, '72, and — 18 yrs after his first one — 1980. He won the Masters and PGA tournaments five times each, the British Open six times — 17 majors and 68 tournament wins, second only to Sam Snead.

Jack Nicklaus

■ Also born today: Ex-K.C. Chiefs tight safety **JIM KEARNEY (1943)**, who was described by retired Raider Raymond Chester as the toughest defensive back he ever faced ... **LEW FONSECA (1899)**, won batting title in 1929 as a Cleveland first baseman ... **BILLY "WHITE SHOES" JOHNSON (1952)**, Atlanta Falcons receiver who caught Steve Bartkowski's "Hail Mary" pass to beat the 49ers in 1983 ... **SAM MELE (1923)**, ex-player and manager of Minnesota Twins' only pennant in 1965.

■ **QUINTIN DAILEY (1961)** — Ex-USF basketball star, Chicago Bulls' guard. Born in Baltimore, Dailey set a

Maryland high school career scoring record. In only three years at USF, he became the school's second leading career scorer (behind Bill Cartwright). Dailey was involved in two separate scandals that brought widespread scorn upon him — he was charged with assault on a woman at USF and, later, after seeming not to express remorse, was picketed outside the Bulls' arena (and elsewhere). It was also revealed that he was receiving money as a student in violation of NCAA rules which triggered the president of USF to terminate the basketball program. Dailey has since issued statements that express remorse and compassion for his victim.

Quintin Dailey

■ **LESTER HAYES (1955)** —   One of the elite NFL cornerbacks An ex-running back from Texas A&M, he was a fifth round pick by the Raiders, the 126th player chosen in the 1977 draft (good drafting, Al). They converted him to cornerback and he was the very best in 1980, when he helped the Raiders go all the way. In 1984, on Hayes' 29th birthday, he helped the Raiders win another Super Bowl championship.

■ Also born today: **GALINA ZYBINA (1931)**, Soviet shotputter, the first woman to put the shot more than 50 feet, winning 1952 Olympic gold medal; four years later she broke 54 feet but had to settle for a silver medal... three hockey greats: Goalie **BILL DURNAN (1915)**, winner of the Vezina Trophy in all seven years of his career ('43-'49) with the Canadiens ...
ELMER LACH (1918), one-third of the Canadiens' "Punch Line" with Maurice Richard and Toe Blake....
MIKE BOSSY (1957) , one of the best scorers in hockey.   Bossy has been with the New York Islanders since 1977 when he scored an NHL record 53 goals for a rookie. He led the NHL in goals in 1978, and is the only player, other than Gretzky and Richards, to score 50 goals in 50 games.

NOTES

■ **JERRY KRAMER (1936)** — Green Bay Packers rt. guard 1958 to 1968. Born in Jordan, Mont., Kramer played college ball at the University of Idaho and was an obscure draft choice of the Packers, the worst team in the NFL at the time. With Kramer's considerable help, they became the best team and one of the greatest of all-time. Despite the Packers' five NFL titles, and despite Kramer's Pro Bowl appearances, he remained obscure until he made The Block (precursor of The Catch) that enabled Bart Starr to score on a

Jerry Kramer

quarterback sneak on the last play of the 1967 NFL title game against the Cowboys to pull it out, 21-17. Then Kramer became one of the most prominent offensive linemen in NFL history. His published journal, "Instant Replay," was one of the first and most influential journal-style football books.

■ **CHICO CARRASQUEL (1928)** — The first big-name major league baseball player from Venezuela. A shortstop from 1950 to 1959, mostly with the Chicago White Sox, he set a fielding record for shortstops in 1951: 54 consecutive games, including 297 chances, without an error — a mark that stood for two decades (Eddie Brinkman broke it). Carrasquel was named starting shortstop for the AL All-Star team five years in a row (1951-55). A national hero in Venezuela, he is the country's commissioner of amateur sports and manages the Caracas Lions, one of the country's top teams.

■ Also born today: **HORACE "NIP" ASHENFELTER (1923)**, winner of the 3,000-meter steeplechase in the 1952 Olympics, born in Collegeville, Pa.; no one gave him a chance to win the event but he beat the heavily favored Soviet and set an Olympic record... diver **GEORGIA COLEMAN (1912)**, born in Idaho (where Jerry Kramer played college football), the first woman to do 2½ forward somersaults in competition... and two pitchers who each threw no-hitters: **BOB BURKE (1907)**, 38-46 with Senators, threw his no-hitter against Boston in 1931 and **DON NOTTEBART (1936)**, 36-51 with Houston, no-hit the Mets in 1963.

NOTES

■ **MONTE CLARK (1937)** –Former coach of the Detroit Lions. Born in Fillmore, Calif., Clark played both the

Monte Clark

offensive and defensive line at USC and was team captain as a senior. He was drafted by the 49ers in 1959, three years later went to Dallas, and the following season, 1963 was dealt to the Cleveland Browns, where he came into his own as a player and was a starting offensive tackle for seven years. He apprenticed under Don Shula for a few years and, in 1976, Clark became head coach of the 49ers, bringing them to an 8-6 finish that was the team's first winning season in four years. When Joe Thomas emerged in the 49ers front office, Clark resigned and began coaching the Detroit Lions in 1978. The Lions did have a couple of 9-7 seasons (in the weak NFC Central Division) but fell badly to 4-11-1 in 1984 and his seven-year total was 43 wins, 61 losses, and one tie. Clark never did turn the Lions around.

■ Also born today: **WILLIAM G. MORGAN (1870)**, invented volleyball at the YMCA gym in Holyoke, Mass., in 1895 ... soccer star **GIORGIO CHINAGLIA (1947)**, played with the New York Cosmos and led the NASL in scoring in 1976, '78, and '79 ... **BOBBY BEATHARD (1937)**, born on the same day and year as Monte Clark, Beathard has been the Redskins general manager since 1978... ex-Viking defensive back **BOBBY BRYANT (1944)**... jockey **MANUEL YCAZA (1935)**.

NOTES

■**LOU "THE TOE" GROZA (1924)** — Cleveland Browns offensive tackle and the first great kicker of the post-World War II era. Groza was born in Mar-

tins Ferry, Ohio and, after only three games on the Ohio State freshman team, was drafted into the Army. In 1946, Groza joined the newly formed Cleveland Browns (with only three freshman games under his belt) and became a big part of one of the winningest teams in sports history. Groza was an All-NFL tackle six times and was the NFL Player of the Year in 1954. He missed the 1960 season because of injuries, but returned

Lou Groza

the following year and played seven more seasons as a kicker only. He retired in 1968 with 1,608 points, second only to George Blanda's 2,002, and owned 10 NFL records. His brother is the basketball All-American (from Kentucky in the late 1940s) Alex Groza.

■Also born today: **STEVE PREFONTAINE (1951)**, distance runner from Oregon who was killed in an auto crash in 1978 ... **DICK McGUIRE (1926)**, basketball player with St. John's and the N.Y. Knicks, and NBA coach; "Tricky Dick" is the brother of Al McGuire (who also played for St. John's and the Knicks) ... Several great wide receivers were born today: **ALFRED JENKINS (1952)** of the Falcons, **JACK SNOW (1943)** of the Rams, **GORDY SOLTAU (1925)** of the 49ers (also a kicker like Groza), **DON MAYNARD (1937)**, No. 1 in career yardage (11,834), No. 2 in TDs (88) and average per catch (18.7), and No. 3 in career receptions (633) ... And two pitchers: righty **ED HEAD (1918)**, a great name, pitched no-hitter for the Brooklyn Dodgers in 1946 (vs. Boston Braves), and lefty **WALLY BUNKER (1945)**, who won more games in one season than any teen-ager in major league history: in 1964 he was an incredible 19-5 ... **GEORGE SEIFERT (1940)**, Bill Walsh's defensive coordinator who is esteemed highly in the NFL as head coach material.

NOTES

■ **WAYNE GRETZKY (1961)** — "The Great Gretzky," who made the world hockey-conscious. Long before

Wayne Gretzky

most players enter their prime, Gretzky had broken every major hockey record (except for the longevity records of Gordie Howe). At age 21, he broke Phil Esposito's record of 76 goals in a season (taking almost half as many shots on goal). He has scored the most points in a season, most assists and is the only NHL player to win the MVP unanimously. He has won the award the last five years. He is the first to score 70 goals or more for 3 straight seasons. Beyond his individual accomplishments, Gretzky has turned Edmonton into a championship team because of his team play and tremendous versatility. Working on a 21-year contract worth more than $20 million, he is a popular, low-key guy who does a lot of charity work.

■ Also born today: **BOB NIEMAN (1927)**, St. Louis Browns outfielder who, in 1951, became the only player to hit home runs in his first two major league at-bats (his first one was a grand slam); ended his career in a pennant-winning S.F. Giants uniform in 1962 ... **HENRY JORDAN (1935)**, great defensive tackle of the 1960s Green Bay Packer dynasty; inducted into the Hall of Fame in 1983 ... **THOMAS HENRY COTTON (1907)**, considered the greatest British golfer ... Auto racer **PAUL NEWMAN (1925)**, still competing ... **WALTER MEANWELL (1884)**, "The Little Doctor," born in Leeds, England, basketball pioneer and Hall of Fame coach at Wisconsin from 1912 to 1934 (except for a three-year stint at Missouri), compiling a 290-101 record. He also wrote books on basketball and conditioning, developed the idea of clinics, and showed the value of a laceless ball.

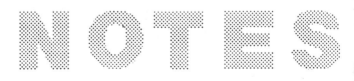

■ **JOE "THE JET" PERRY (1927)** — Perry, the great San Francisco 49er running back (1948-60, 1963), was born Fletcher Perry in Stephens, Ark. Perry never played at a four-year college, though he ran for 22 TDs at Compton JC in one season. However, it wasn't until he played for the Alameda Naval Air Station that 49ers scouts became aware of his ability and gave him a tryout. He made the team and, ultimately, the Hall of Fame. Perry, a quick fullback, rushed for 9,723 yards, including his (and the 49ers') two years in the AAFC

Joe Perry

('48 and '49), still the sixth best on the all-time list despite the expanded schedules of the modern era. His 71 career TDs is also the sixth best mark. Perry was the first NFL running back to have two straight 1000-yard seasons ('53-'54). Apart from his ability, his longevity in the league was the result of staying in tremendous shape. Lenny Moore called him "the best conditioned athlete I ever saw." And that's a mouthful.

■ **FRANKIE ALBERT (1920)** — Albert, the great pocket lefty quarterback, is yet another 49ers legend born on this day. At Stanford he was one of the first T-formation QBs, under Clark Shaughnessy who introduced the T to college ball. Albert was the 49ers' first quarterback, beginning in 1946 when they entered the AAFC. He played seven seasons, retiring after the 1952 season, and played with Joe Perry most of his career. In fact, Albert dubbed him "The Jet" (and even first called Hugh McElhenny "The King"). Albert threw 29 TD passes in 1948 which set a record that wasn't broken until Johnny Unitas threw 32 in 1959. Also a punter, he led the league in that department in 1949 with a humongous 48.2 yard average.

■ **Also born today: JACK WESTROPE (1918)**, top jockey in 1933 at age 15, riding 301 winners, killed when thrown by mount at Hollywood Park in 1958 ... Oriole outfielder-DH **JOHN LOWENSTEIN (1947)** ... Bengal wide receiver **CRIS COLLINSWORTH (1959)**, **DENISE BEBERNES (1954)**, a brilliant golfer who suffered from alcoholism, committed suicide in 1982.

■ **PARRY O'BRIEN (1932)** — Without question the most significant individual in the history of shot - putting. O'Brien revolutionized the shot-put event by introducing a technique that became common and bears his name. This technique was ridiculed at first but critics were finally silenced. O'Brien, the first man to put the shot 60 feet, dominated the event in the early 1950s. He won 116 consecutive meets from 1952 to 1956. He won the 1952 Olympic gold medal and then became the only shot-putter to

Parry O'Brien

win two consecutive gold medals when he repeated his triumph in 1956. In 1960, O'Brien was still good enough to cop the silver medal and even made the 1964 Olympic team, placing fourth. He was a tremendous athlete who ran a 10.8 100-meters in 1953 and was the U.S. discus champion in 1955.

■ **BILL WHITE (1934)** — Ex-National League first baseman and current N Y Yankees announcer. An excellent first baseman who could hit for power and average, White broke in with the New York Giants in 1956, hitting a home run in his first at-bat. He missed the 1957 season because of military service and rejoined the Giants when they moved to San Francisco the following year. By then the Giants had Orlando Cepeda as their first baseman so White was dealt to the Cardinals. He had his best years in St. Louis, hitting 20 or more homers five times and hitting more than .300 four times. In 1961, playing in back-to-back double-headers, White got 14 hits (which must be a record). He retired with a .286 lifetime BA and more than 200 homers. He has been a Yankee announcer since the mid-1970s.

■ Also born today: **CHARLIE KRUEGER (1937)**, great defensive tackle who spent his whole career (1959-73) with the 49ers ... **PAT KENNEDY (1908)**, the most famous referee in basketball history, a gate attraction because of his colorful on-court mannerisms ... **KEN BUCHANAN (1945)**, lightweight champion, 1970-72, lost title to Duran ... **PETE RUNNELS (1928)**, won two batting titles with Bosox in 1960 and '62.

NOTES

■ **BARNEY OLDFIELD (1878)** — Oldfield, the first famous auto racer, was born Berna Eli Oldfield in Wauseon, Ohio. He was a professional bicycle rider and had never driven a car when Henry Ford approached him to test-drive his first racing car. After two weeks learning how to operate the new-fangled horse-less carriage, he accepted Ford's offer. A few months later, in 1903, behind the wheel of Ford's soon-to-be-famous "999" car, Oldfield became the first to travel a mile a minute in an automobile. In 1910, he set the record at 131.7 miles per hour.

Barney Oldfield

Oldfield single-handedly popularized the automobile. He became a symbol of excitement and exploration to millions and his image behind the wheel, jauntily smoking a cigar, became known around the world. Though his name (still a part of the language) became synonymous with speed, he spent his last years as a safety adviser and campaigner for safe driving. He died in 1946.

■ Also born today: golfer **DONNA CAPONI (1945)**, won U.S. Open in '69 and '70, she was the third woman golfer (after Kathy Whitworth and JoAnne Carner) to win $1 million in prize money ... **BILL RIGNEY (1918)**, infielder with the N.Y. Giants from 1946 to 1953, managed 17 years in the bigs, including the Giants (1956-60); became assistant to the president and commentator on Oakland's TV broadcasts ... **JOE PRIMEAU (1906)**, Hall of Fame center with the Toronto Maple Leafs (1929-36), one-third of the famous "Kid Line" (with Busher Jackson and Charlie Conacher) ... **BILL NELSON (1941)**, USC quarterback, who played in the pros with the Steelers and the Browns ... **BOB FALKENBURG (1926)**, tennis ace of the '40s (brother of Jinx Falkenburg).

NOTES

■ **WALT DROPO (1923)** — 1950s, power-hitting first baseman. Known as "Moose" because of his Moosup, Conn., birthplace and his 6-foot-5, 220-pound frame, he was a three-sport star at the University of Connecticut. Outstanding in basketball and football (he was drafted by the Chicago Bears), Dropo chose baseball and broke in with the Boston Red Sox. He had one of the greatest rookie seasons ever, hitting .322 with 34 homers and 144 RBI, only one RBI behind Ted Williams' major-league rookie record. Dropo played for five other teams in a 13-year career. In 1952, only a few weeks after he was traded to the Detroit Tigers, Dropo became the 2nd major leaguer ever to hit safely in 12 consecutive at-bats. With the White Sox in 1961, Dropo hit two pinch-hit grand slam home runs within a month. He currently imports fireworks from China (where he claims to have hit a ball over the Great Wall).

Nolan Cromwell

■ **Also born today:**
NOLAN CROMWELL (1955), L.A. Rams safety since 1977. ... **BORIS SPASSKY (1937)**, Soviet chess player who was world champion from 1969 (when he defeated Mikhail Tal) until 1972 when, in the most publicized chess match in history, he lost his title to the awesome Bobby Fischer; at age 18, Spassky became the youngest grandmaster in Soviet chess history ... **DAVE JOHNSON (1943)**, Mets manager who played second base with the Orioles for eight years (1965-72), went over to Atlanta where, in his first year, he set the ML record for second basemen by hitting 43 homers; he should have been manager of the year in 1984 (over Jim Frey of the Cubs)... auto racer **RUDI CARACCIOLA (1901)** ... poet **JACK SPICER (1925-1965)**, a passionate baseball fan.

NOTES

■ **JACKIE ROBINSON (1919)** —
The first black player in the major leagues, born in Cairo, Ga. Robinson's dignity and fearlessness signaled a new age for the United States. Blacks began entering basketball, football and, increasingly, the professions, business, politics and all phases of American life. No man was ever asked to endure more abuse in order to make his living as an athlete. One of the most intense competitors in sports history, Robinson played 10 years with the Brooklyn Dodgers, coming up as a 28-year-old rookie in 1947 and retiring after the 1956 season with a .311

Jackie Robinson

lifetime BA. Robinson was the most daring base-runner of the modern era and put on a clinic every time he got on base. His running style — arms up, pigeon-toed, gyrating hips — was unique. And he batted clean-up! In 1949, he won the batting title and led the league in stolen bases, for which he earned the MVP award. After retirement, Robinson became a prosperous businessman, but was plagued by ill health (including being nearly blind in his last few years) also domestic problems (his son, Jackie Jr., after kicking his heroin addiction, died in an auto crash at age 24). Robinson died of a heart attack in 1972. Recommended is his aptly-titled autobiography, "I Never Had It Made."

■ Also born today: **JOE WALCOTT (1914)**, born Arnold Cream, heavyweight champion (1951-52). "Jersey Joe" was — at 37 years, 5 months — the oldest fighter to become heavyweight champ and he was one of only two fighters to deck Rocky Marciano (the other was Archie Moore).... **DON HUTSON (1913)**, Green Bay Packers end (1935-45), MVP in 1941 and '42, his 99 TD catches are still a record (with only 488 receptions) ... **NOLAN RYAN (1947)**, Astros righty, 231-206 career won-loss record, neck-and-neck with Steve Carlton for all-time strikeout crown.... **ERNIE BANKS (1931)**, shortstop and first baseman with the Chicago Cubs, 1953-71. He was the first NL player to win MVP twice in a row (1958-59), hit 512 career HRs (tying Eddie Mathews). Banks was known for his credo, heard daily, "It's a beautiful day for a ballgame."

Achieved 4000-strike-out plateau in 1985

■ **ALBIE BOOTH (1908)** — Yale's "Little Boy Blue" was born in New Haven, Conn., (where else?) The greatest name in the history of Yale football (unless you go for Pudge Heffelfinger), Booth was a 5-foot-6, 144-pounder who thrilled crowds with his ballet-like running prowess. Though light players were more common in those days, Booth was still usually the smallest player on the field. His fame began as a sophomore when he led Yale to a big upset over the Chris Cagle-led Army juggernaut. He was also known for his phenomenal drop-kicking, often on the run. He later became an Ivy League referee, and died in 1959.

Albie Booth

■ **CONN SMYTHE (1895)** — Like Albie Booth, Smythe achieved fame in his home town. Smythe was born in Toronto and his name is synonymous with Toronto hockey. He was coach, manager, president, and owner of the Toronto Maple Leafs. Since 1964, the Conn Smythe Trophy has been given to the MVP of the Stanley Cup playoffs.

■ Also born today: Golfers **DEBBIE AUSTIN (1948)** and **JACKIE CUPIT (1938)** ... **DICK SNYDER (1944)**, SuperSonics guard of the early '70s ... **BILLY SULLIVAN (1875)**, a catcher with the Chisox in the early 1900s. His career was undistinguished except for one fact: he was the first catcher to position himself up behind the plate, which influenced infield play and pitching itself.

NOTES

■ **WILLIE KAMM (1900)** - Considered the best defensive third baseman of his day. He also batted .281 during a 13-year career with the Chicago White Sox and Cleveland Indians, 1923-1935. He had a keen batting eye, striking out only 405 times in 5,851 career at bats, while walking 824 times. The White Sox purchased him from the San Francisco Seals of the Pacific Coast League in 1922 for the then-astronomical price of $100,000, and also sent the Seals two players. After his major league playing career ended, he managed the Mission Reds of the PCL for two seasons.

Willie Kamm

■ **GEORGE HALAS (1895)** — Born in Chicago and died in that city at age 88. The most enduring name in pro football, Halas was a co-founder of the NFL in 1920 and founder of the Chicago Bears (originally called the Decatur Staleys) in that same year. He played end for them (1920-29) and coached the Bears for 40 seasons (more than any other coach), winning seven NFL titles and a record 425 games. Halas is the only man associated with the NFL throughout its first 50 years, and the only man to be voted into the Hall of Fame as player, coach, and owner.

■ **AL "RED" SCHOENDIENST (1923)** — Schoendienst born in Germantown, Ill. had a distinguished 19-year career, mostly with the St. Louis Cardinals, though he was also with the Milwaukee Braves when they won two straight pennants in 1957 and '58. Red was an excellent glove and a career .289 hitter. He was also the Cardinal skipper from 1965 to 1976, leading them to their two straight pennants — in 1967 and '68.

■ Also born today: Cleveland Browns WR **DAVE LOGAN** (1954), drafted in the three major sports out of Colorado ... two great chess players: **SVETOZAR GLIGORIC** (1923) of Yugoslavia, and Brazilian prodigy **HENRIQUE MECKING** (1952).

NOTES

■ **EMILE GRIFFITH (1938)** —Welterweight champion (1961-65), middleweight champ (1966-68). Born in the Virgin Islands, Griffith won the welter title in 1961 with a 13th-round KO of Benny "Kid" Paret. He lost that title to Paret in a rematch (15-round decision) but regained it in 1962 in their rubber match in a 12-round KO in which Paret was badly hurt and died 10 days later. In 1963, Griffith lost his title to Luis Rodriguez and again regained it only three months later via a 15-round decision. In 1966, Griffith went up in weight and defeated Dick Tiger for the middleweight crown. He lost that title in '67 to Nino Benvenuti, once again regaining it later that year. Griffith lost his title for good in '68 in his third bout with Benvenuti. Most of Griffith's big fights went the distance. Though lacking a knockout punch, he was a tough performer and an excellent boxer. He fought until he was almost 40.

■ **FRED LYNN (1952)** —
Baltimore Orioles outfielder. Lynn had one of the greatest rookie seasons in baseball history with the Red Sox in 1975, hitting .331 with 21 homers, 105 RBI and winning the MVP award, something that rookies don't do very often. In 1981, the Red Sox infamously dealt him to the California Angels where he waited (in vain) for Gene Autry to buy a pitching staff. Lynn's career took an upswing when he was signed by the Orioles as a free agent. Lynn is one of the best all-around performers in the game.

■ Also born today: Packers wide receiver **JOHN JEFFERSON (1956)**, the great "J.J." ... **ARTHUR ARFONS (1926)**, auto racer and designer ...
Two great quarterbacks: **FRAN TARKENTON (1940)**, who, despite owning nearly every QB record, is not deemed worthy of the Hall of Fame, and **BOB GRIESE (1945)**, QB of the Dolphin dynasty of the 1970s.

NOTES

■**BYRON NELSON (1912)** — One of the greatest names in golf, born in Ft Worth, Tex. Nelson won two Masters tournaments, two PGA tournaments and the U.S. Open in 1939. He is the only athlete to win the AP Male Athlete of the Year award twice in a row (1944 and '45). In 1945, Nelson won 19 tournaments, the most ever won in a single season. Of the 19 wins, 11 were consecutive. No golfer had ever done that before — or since. Another record of Nelson's is winning prize money in 113 consecutive tournaments. In later years, Nelson became known as a golf announcer and the mentor of Tom Watson.

Byron Nelson

■**LAWRENCE TAYLOR (1959)** Probably the best linebacker in the NFL. The Giants' first pick in the 1981 draft out of No. Carolina, Taylor asserted himself as a rookie, getting the most votes for the Pro Bowl that year. Taylor was preparing to jump to the USFL (he already had signed a big contract) when the Giants decided to approximate the USFL bucks and give him a contract worth $6 million for the next six years. The Giants also gave Taylor a $1 million interest-free loan and paid the New Jersey Generals $750,000 for letting Taylor out of his contract. After all that dust settled, the Giants wound up with a mediocre team and one helluva linebacker.

■Also born today: **NEIL JOHNSTON (1929)**, Philadelphia Warriors center, won NBA scoring title three straight years ('53, '54, '55) ... **IVY WILLIAMSON (1911)**, coaching legend at Wisconsin (1948-54), went to 1953 Rose Bowl... **GERMANY SCHAEFER (1878)**, AL infielder in early 1900s; from second base he stole first base (!), umpire said it was legal.

■ **HANK AARON (1934)** — The Man Who Broke Babe Ruth's Record (for career home runs) and the first player listed in the all-time baseball register, is known as "The Hammer" and "Bad Henry".

Hank Aaron

Aaron broke in with the Braves in 1954, spent two decades with them and retired in 1976 after two seasons with the Milwaukee Brewers. He is No. 1 in career homers (755), RBI (2,297) and total bases (6,434). A .310 lifetime hitter, he won three batting titles (how many other power hitters have won three batting titles?) and won the MVP award in 1957. In 1973 — at age 39 — Aaron banged 40 home runs. Aaron, who once wanted to be baseball commissioner, became an executive with the Atlanta Braves.

■ **ROGER STAUBACH (1942)** — Elected to Hall of Fame in 1983. Staubach won the 1963 Heisman Trophy playing for Navy, served his four-year commission, and began his 13-year career with the Cowboys. Playing the way he did, after a long layoff, was an incredible feat in itself and probably unique. During the 1970s he was the NFC's leading passer five times and one of the best running QBs ever. A clutch performer who never lost his cool on the field, "The Dodger" was uncanny in the last two minutes.

■ Also born today: **CRAIG MORTON (1943)**, Staubach's rival (and finally second-string) QB on the Cowboys, won MVP award with the Denver Broncos in 1977 ... **SAMMY MANDELL (1904)**, lightweight champion (1926-30) ... **MIKE HEATH (1955)**, A's catcher-outfielder ... auto racer **DARRELL WALTRIP (1947)**, rival of Bobby Allison.

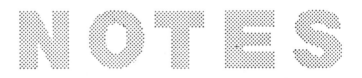

■**BABE RUTH (1895)** — The mythic "Sultan of Swat," born in Baltimore. Ruth came up as a pitcher, breaking in with the Red Sox in 1914. The next year, at age 20, he was 18-8. At age 21, he won 23 games and led the AL in ERA (1.75) and shutouts (9). He won 24 games the following season and then, at age 23, he did something rather unusual: while going 13-7, he managed to lead the AL in home runs and slugging percentage. Gradually, Ruth stopped pitching altogether, was infamously traded to the Yankees and went on to become the greatest slugger in the history of the game. At the

Babe Ruth

pace he was on, Ruth would have made the Hall of Fame as a pitcher. His .671 percentage (his career won-loss record was 94-46) is one of the top marks ever and his 2.28 lifetime ERA was one of the lowest — and almost all of this was achieved by age 24. Ruth revolutionized baseball with his home run prowess. The number 714 (his lifetime home run total) still has a magical significance. Though Hank Aaron topped that figure, it took him more than 2,000 at-bats to do it. Ruth remains No. 1 in slugging percentage (.690) and career home run percentage (8.5). All this and a lifetime batting average of .342, higher than all of the singles hitters that came after him. Ruth was a larger-than-life character, flamboyant and often outrageous, who drank and partied heavily. He died of cancer in 1948.

■Also born today: A couple of other left-handed hitters were born on this day: **DALE LONG (1926)**, the big first baseman, mostly with the Pirates and the Cubs, hit home runs in eight consecutive ball games in 1956, a major league record (even Ruth never did that), and **SMOKEY BURGESS (1927)**, a catcher with the Pirates, Reds, etc., who was the No. 1 all-time pinch-hitter (most ABs, 507, and most pinch-hits, 145) . . . ex-Raiders middle linebacker **DAN CONNERS (1941)** . . . 49ers right tackle **KEITH FAHNHORST (1952)**.

■**BUSTER CRABBE (1908)** — This Olympic swimming champion who went Hollywood was born Clarence Lindon Crabbe in Oakland, Calif.

He grew up in Hawaii as a great swimmer and all-around athlete. Crabbe won the 400-meter free-style event at the 1932 Olympic Games, breaking an Olympic record that had been broken eight years earlier by yet anoth-er swimmer who went Hollywood, Johnny Weissmuller. Crabbe was an early film Tarzan (the role that made Weissmuller famous) but later gained fame in western and adventure serials, especially Flash Gordon and Buck Rogers

Buster Crabbe

in the 1930s. He later was athletic director of a resort hotel in the Catskills and was in the swimming pool business. He wrote "Energetics" in 1970, a fitness book for older people.

■Also born today: **CARNEY LANSFORD (1957)**, hard-luck third baseman for the A's; in 1984 hit .300 or better for the fourth straight season; won batting title (.336) with the Red Sox in 1981; a tremendous competitor ... **DAN QUISENBERRY (1954)**, submarine-style righty reliever with K.C. Royals; one of the most quotable of all athletes (even he thinks relief pitchers shouldn't win MVP awards). ... **ROBERT BRAZILE** (1953), Houston Oiler linebacker ... Texas Rangers righty **BURT HOOTEN** (1950) ... skier **MARILYN COCHRAN** (1950), sister of skiers Roy and Barbara Ann Cochran.

Sports birthdays / Feb. 8

■ **JOE BLACK (1924)**—First black pitcher to win a World Series game. Born in Plainfield, N.J., Black joined the Brooklyn Dodgers in 1952 as a 28-year-old rookie. He had a phenomenal year, going 15-4 almost strictly in relief with a 2.15 ERA. His rival that year was Hoyt Wilhelm, who also began that year as a 28-year-old rookie. Wilhelm nosed out Black for the league's best percentage with his 15-3 record but Black won Rookie of the Year honors. Despite Black's experience as a reliever the Dodgers made him their starter in Game One

Joe Black

against the Yankees in the World Series. Black went all the way, beating Allie Reynolds, and became the first black pitcher to win a World Series game. He started Game Four and pitched just as well but got beat this time by Reynolds. He also started Game Seven (would you say the Dodgers were leaning on him a little bit?) but lost that one, too. Black only pitched five more seasons and was never again nearly as effective, despite his impressive 30-12 lifetime won-loss record. Roger Kahn wrote about Black in his book, "The Boys of Summer," in which several of the 1950s Brooklyn Dodgers are revisited. Black is currently an executive with the Greyhound Bus Company.

■ **CLETE BOYER (1937)**—Boyer, third baseman who anchored the Yankee infield of the early 1960s, a team that won five straight pennants. He ended his career with the Atlanta Braves, retiring in 1971. The brother of Ken Boyer and Cloyd Boyer, Clete is currently the A's third-base coach.

■ Also born today: **AD WOLGAST (1888)**, lightweight champion, 1910-12, one of the all-time best ... **HOOT EVERS (1921)**, outfielder mostly with Detroit in late '40s and early '50s; hit .323 in 1950; currently the Tigers' director of player development ... **FRITZ PETERSON (1942)**, N.Y. Yankees right-hander (1966-74), swapped wives with teammate Mike Kekich (straight up).

NOTES

■ **BILL VEECK (1914)** — The most spectacular, creative and endearing owner in major league history.

The son of a baseball writer, Veeck became president of the Cubs in 1919. He is often called "the P. T. Barnum of Baseball" because of such innovations as the exploding scoreboard, using Eddie Gaedel, a midget, to pinch-hit (he walked on four straight pitches), and various promotions. However, he was a shrewd executive who broke attendance records in Cleveland and Milwaukee by developing top teams. He

Bill Veeck

was the first executive in the American League to sign a black player, Larry Doby. Veeck also gave Satchel Paige a chance to pitch that same season; 1948. They helped the Indians win the pennant and World Series. Veeck bought the Chicago White Sox in 1959 and they won their first pennant in 40 years. Veeck lost a leg in World War II combat. He is famous for his aversion to ties (a la Ted Williams) and has written such fascinating books as "The Hustler's Handbook" and "Veeck—As In Wreck."

■ Also born today: **VIC WERTZ (1925),** good power-hitting lefty first baseman mostly with Detroit and Cleveland, best known for his tremendous World Series drive to deep center field that Willie Mays ran down, his back to the plate ... **JAKE KILRAIN (1859),** fought (and lost to) John L. Sullivan in the last bare-knuckle fight in the U.S., ending an era ... **AUBREY "DIT" CLAPPER (1907),** great Boston Bruins defenseman from 1927 to 1946 ... **BILL BERGEY (1945)** ex-middle linebacker with Bengals and Eagles ... **HEINIE ZIMMERMAN (1887),** third baseman with Cubs and Giants, a .295 lifetime hitter, banished from baseball in 1919 for throwing games, though it was never proven.

NOTES

■ **BILL TILDEN (1893)** — "Big Bill," the greatest tennis player of his era (and probably of all time), was born William Tatem Tilden II into a wealthy Philadelphia family. Tilden became a tennis prodigy (having your own tennis court helps), winning his first tournament at age 7. Like Mozart, he kept getting better. As an amateur, he won 31 national titles and won the U.S. Open six years in a row (1920-25). He was the first American to win the men's title at Wimbledon, in 1920, won it again the following year, and a third time in 1930, at age 37, also winning the U.S. Open that

Bill Tilden

year for the seventh time. Tilden put tennis on the international map. In the 1920s, his name stood alongside Babe Ruth, Jack Dempsey, and Bobby Jones in the "golden age of sports." Tilden turned pro at age 31 and toured for 20 years, playing top tennis into his 50s. At age 47, he came out of a hospital to beat 25-year-old Don Budge, the U.S. Amateur champion who had just turned pro. At the age of 52, Tilden and Vincent Richards won the pro doubles title. Tilden made many short films on tennis and wrote many books and pamphlets on the game. His autobiography, "My Story," appeared in 1948. A homosexual, Tilden twice was jailed in the late 1940s for contributing to the delinquency of a minor. Though he earned more than $1 million, he was broke in his last years. He died of a heart attack at age 60. The following day he was to travel to Cleveland to play in a tennis tournament.

■ Also born today: **ALBERT "CHALKY" WRIGHT (1912)**, featherweight champion, 1941-42, fought as a pro for 20 years and had 200 fights; the first world boxing champion from Mexico; died at age 45 after falling in the shower ... **WALTER BROWN (1905)**, organized the Boston Celtics and was a co-founder of the NBA in 1946; he was president of the Boston Garden from 1937 until his death in 1964; also president of the Boston Bruins ... **ALLIE REYNOLDS (1915)**, great (mostly) N.Y. Yankee right-hander, W-182, L-107, pitched two no-hitters ... oh yeah, **MARK SPITZ (1950)**, swimmer.

NOTES

■ **MAX BAER (1909)** — Heavyweight champion (1934-35), born in Omaha, Neb. Baer was a good fighter who might've been great but didn't want to be. Baer was big and strong with a deadly right hand but he loved partying and hated training. He was also a gentle, good-natured guy who never got over killing a fighter (Frankie Campbell) in the ring in 1930. Baer, ironically, lost his "killer instinct" from that moment on. Baer won the title in one of the most one-sided fights in boxing history. Primo Carnera was down 11 times in the fight, finally for the last time in the

Max Baer

11th round. In Baer's first title defense a year later, James J. Braddock, a hungry challenger, upset him in a unanimous 15-round decision. Baer was in 83 fights, winning 70 of them, 52 by KO. The first Jewish heavyweight champion, his boxing trunks had a Star of David sewn on them. He died at age 50 of a heart attack.

■ Also born today: **TOMMY HITCHCOCK (1900)**, the most famous polo player of all time (in fact, the only famous polo player of all time); his father, Thomas Hitchcock, was the captain of the American team in the first playing of the Westminster Cup in 1886; Tommy was a top player at age 13; a World War I flying ace at age 17, he also flew combat missions in World War II and died in a training flight at age 44 ... tennis player **BUDGE PATTY (1924)**, Wimbledon singles champion, 1950, and doubles champion (w/Gardnar Mulloy), 1957 ... **MADELINE MANNING (1948)**, won gold medal in 800-meter event at the 1968 Olympics... sportswriter and sportscaster **LARRY MERCHANT (1931)** ... **JAMES SILAS (1949)**, ABA great, played in NBA with Spurs and Cavs.

NOTES

■ **SAM LANGFORD (1880)** — A great black boxer held back by the racism that prevailed in sports (and elsewhere) in the early 20th century, born in Nova Scotia. Short (5-foot-7½) with massive shoulders and long arms, Langford (known as the "Boston Tar Baby") had to be content fighting other blacks almost exclusively. He fought Jack Johnson two years before Johnson became champion and lost a split decision, but Johnson (also black) refused to give him a rematch after he became champion. Langford, who usually gave away 20 to 30 pounds to

Sam Langford

his opponents, fought in 252 bouts and lost only 23 in a career that ended at age 44 because of failing eyesight. He went totally blind and died in 1956.

■ **BILL RUSSELL (1934)** — Basketball great who refused entrance into the Hall of Fame to protest prior exclusion of blacks. After leading USF to two straight NCAA titles in 1955 and '56, he had a 14-year career with the Boston Celtics in which he won five MVP awards, three of them in a row (1961-63). The greatest defensive center in basketball history, Russell averaged 22 rebounds a game throughout his career and revolutionized basketball with his shotblocking, rebounding technique and defensive intensity. He was the first black man to coach a major league team in any sport. After an apparent falling out with Rick Barry over a supposed racist remark, he and Barry are currently a broadcasting team on TV.

■ **Also born today: DOM DIMAGGIO (1917),** born in San Francisco, he played a great center field (almost as good as brother Joe) for the Boston Red Sox for 11 years, finishing with a .298 lifetime BA ... **JOE GARAGIOLA (1926),** childhood buddy of Yogi Berra, ex-Cardinal and Pirate catcher, TV announcer ... **DON WILSON (1945),** Astros righty pitcher who committed suicide in 1974 (he and Bill Russell were both born in Monroe, La.)

NOTES

■ **WILLIE RITCHIE (1891)** — Ritchie, lightweight champion, 1912 to 1914, was born Gerhardt Steffen in San Francisco. He didn't intend to

Willie Ritchie

be a fighter, but he was a boxing fan who hung around the gym quite a bit. He was to be a cornerman for a local boxer whose opponent didn't show up. The opponent's name was Willie Ritchie, so Steffen became Ritchie — pressed into service at age 15 with no ring experience outside of the gym. In 1912, in Daly City, Ritchie defeated Ad Wolgast for the lightweight title. Two years later, Ritchie lost the title to the British champion, Freddie Welsh, on a one-point decision (they fought in London). He was never given a chance to regain the title. In 1919, Ritche was KO'd by Benny Leonard, the first time Ritchie had ever been knocked out, and retired (though he did fight a few more times several years later). Ritchie was a boxing instructor for the U.S. Army during World War I and later was appointed a boxing inspector by the California State Commission. Ritchie died in 1975.

■ Also born today: **PATTY BERG (1918)**, great golfer, won over 80 tournaments and was AP Female Athlete of the Year three times (1938, 1943, and 1955) ... **JAN-EGIL STORHOLT (1949)**, Norwegian speed skater who predicted he'd win a gold medal in the 1,500-meter event and he did — on his birthday at the 1976 Olympics ... **HOUSTON McTEAR (1957)**, co-record holder of the 100-yard dash (9.0 seconds) ... **SAL BANDO (1944)**, Captain Sal of the Oakland A's dynasty of the early 1970s, currently an executive with the Milwaukee Brewers.

■ **WOODY HAYES (1913)** — Wayne Woodrow Hayes, born in Clifton, Ohio, became football coach at Ohio State in 1951 and went to the Rose Bowl eight times, winning four and losing four, though it's the four times that he lost (in 1971, '73, '75 and '76) that tend to be remembered on the West Coast. Ohio State dominated the Big Ten in the mid-1970s, winning four years in a row (1973-76). A run-oriented disciplinarian, Hayes was a dinosaur who couldn't adapt to the modern game or the modern athlete. His end came in 1979 on national TV when he punched a Clemson player during the Fiesta Bowl. He was fired shortly afterward.

Woody Hayes

■ **MEL ALLEN (1913)** — Born on the same day and year as Woody Hayes is the "Voice of the Yankees," the most famous of all radio baseball announcers. Born in Birmingham, Ala., Allen exuded a warmth and geniality for 25 years, retiring in 1964. His "How about that!" is the most famous phrase in the history of sports announcing. His voice also adorned the "Movietone News" sports highlights from 1946 to 1964.

■ **JOHNNY LONGDEN (1906)** — Great jockey, born in England. His 6,032 winners total is second only to Willie Shoemaker. He rode until age 60, winning the last race of his career at Santa Anita in 1966. He won the Triple Crown in 1943 aboard Count Fleet. Since retiring as a jockey he has worked as a trainer, and is the only jockey also to win the Kentucky Derby as a trainer — with Majestic Prince in 1969.

■ Also born today: **MICKEY WRIGHT (1935)**, great golfer, female athlete of the year in 1963 and '64 . . . two figure skaters: **DONNA ATWOOD (1923)** and **JOJO STARBUCK (1951)**, Terry Bradshaw's ex . . . hockey immortal **BERNIE "BOOM-BOOM" GEOFFRION (1931)**, of the Montreal Canadiens . . . **CHARLES "RED" BARRETT (1915)**, righty pitcher mostly with Boston Braves (69-69 lifetime); one day in 1944 he won a game on 58 pitches, the fewest ever thrown in a nine-inning game (great outing, Red) . . . **ROLANDO NAVERETTE (1957)**, WBC junior lightweight champion (1981-82), born in Philippines, currently doing time for murder.

NOTES

■ **GEORGE EARNSHAW (1900)** — Earnshaw, righty mainstay of the Philadelphia A's dynasty of the 1930s, was born in New York City. A big (6-4, 210 pounds) late-blooming 28-year-old rookie nicknamed "Moose", Earnshaw was 7-7 but won 20 games or more for the next three years (1929-31), the A's winning the pennant each year (losing only one of those World Series, in 1931). He and teammate Lefty Grove rate as one of the best righty-lefty duos in major league history. From 1928 to 1933, Earnshaw and Grove won 250 and lost 99.

George Earnshaw

Probably no other duo had a better percentage for a comparable period of time. Earnshaw was the pitching hero of the 1930 World Series against the Cardinals. He won Game Two with a complete-game six-hitter. In Game Five he pitched seven brilliant scoreless innings, but Grove, who threw the last two innings in relief, got the win (on Jimmie Foxx's two-run ninth inning homer to break the scoreless tie). With one day's rest, Earnshaw came back in Game Six to throw another complete game, a five-hitter, to nail down the Series.

■ **EARL 'RED' BLAIK (1897)** — One of the greatest college football coaches of all-time, was born on this day in Detroit. He coached at West Point for 25 years — from 1927 to 1933. After an interlude at Dartmouth (1934-40), he returned to West Point in 1941 and remained there until he retired in 1958. Blaik created an awesome dynasty in the 1940s, ushering in a new era — modern, potent offenses that stimulated more interest in football throughout the country.

■ Also born today: Auto racer **GRAHAM HILL (1929)**, won the 1966 Indy 500 and 14 Grand Prix events before dying in a plane crash in 1975 (trying to land his private plane in dense fog north of London) ... three quarterbacks: **KEN ANDERSON (1949)**, of the Bengals, **JOHN HADL (1940)**, of Chargers/Rams, and **MARC WILSON (1957)**, Raider QB, one of Al Davis' rare mistakes . ... **RON CEY (1948)**, veteran third-baseman with Cubs, great RBI man, giving up "The Penguin" was another egregious Dodger mistake.

NOTES

■ **JOHN McENROE (1959)** — Born in Wiesbaden, Germany. Your basic *enfant terrible*, McEnroe does not strive to ingratiate himself to fans, officials or (to his credit) media. A prodigy at age 18, he became the youngest player in 100 years to reach the men's semifinals at Wimbledon. Three years later, in 1980, he was rated No. 1 in the world. And that's the way it stood in 1985 too. Now McEnroe can truly say, 'Do you know any other games?."

John McEnroe

■ **"SLIDING BILLY" HAMILTON (1866)** — The Ty Cobb of the pre-Cobb era, born in Newark, N.J. An outfielder with Philadelphia and Boston in the NL, 1888-1901, his .344 lifetime batting average is the eighth best all-time mark. His 912 career stolen bases was eclipsed by Lou Brock. Hamilton was a genius at getting on base and then scoring runs. His 192 runs scored in 1894 is an all-time major league record, his combined hits (220) and walks (126) in that same year is still a National League record and his consecutive-game hitting streak of 36 is the eighth longest in major league history. He died in 1940 and was elected to the Hall of Fame in 1961.

■ Also Born Today: **BOBBY BAUER (1915)**, one-third of the Boston Bruins' famous "Kraut Line" with Woody Dumart and Milt Schmidt; in 1940, they finished 1-2-3 in the NHL in scoring ... Skier **JILL KINMONT (1936)**, broke neck rendering her a quadriplegic; her life story, "The Other Side of the Mountain," was a book and film ... **LAURENCE "LON" MYERS (1858)**, the greatest runner of the 19th century, he once held every U.S. running record —from 50 yards to a mile ... San Francisco sports curmudgeon **GLENN DICKEY (1936)** ... **DICK MODZELEWSKI (1931)**, "Big Mo," the great offensive tackle with the N.Y. Giants, etc., 1953-66 (brother of Ed Modzelewski, "Little Mo.").

NOTES

Jim Brown

■ **JIM BROWN (1936)** — Called the greatest running back of all time. He had no weakness. He would've been an all-pro linebacker. Did he ever miss a game because of injury? His rushing record, 12,312 yards, was broken by Walter Payton, but Brown is No. 1 in yards per carry (5.2) and his 106 rushing TDs is going to be around for a while. After nine seasons with the Cleveland Browns (1957-65), in which he led the league in rushing eight times, Brown retired at the top of his game, rivalling Jim Thorpe as the greatest football player ever.

■ **RED BARBER (1908)** — Probably the best baseball announcer ever, Walter Lanier Barber started in Cincinnati in 1934 (doing only three commercials in nine innings) but made his name with the Brooklyn Dodgers. He called himself "the 'ol Redhead" and referred to his broadcasting perch as "the catbird seat." When the Dodgers had the bases loaded, he'd say the bases were "F.O.B." — full of Brooklyn. Homeruns were usually accompanied by his "Oh, doctor!" He broadcast N.Y. Yankee games from 1954 to 1966. A literate and sensitive presence with a laid-back southern drawl, Barber and playwright Tennessee Williams have a couple things in common—both were both in Columbus, Miss., and both had the middle name Lanier, after the southern poet, Sidney Lanier. Barber lives in Florida, writes a Sunday sports column, and does a Friday radio spot on PBS.

■ **ROBERT NEYLAND (1892)** — Neyland (pronounced Nee-land), the legendary Tennessee football coach from 1926 to 1952, except for 1935 and the World War II years, was born in Greenville, Texas. An army general who went to West Point, Neyland at one time was an aide to General Douglas MacArthur His record (171 wins, 27 losses, 12 ties) rates with the best of all time. Playing single-wing (long after the T-formation became fashionable), Neyland produced nine unbeaten teams and a national championship in 1951. Neyland introduced many innovations to southern football — the stopwatch, low-cut shoes, zone defense, the press box-to-bench telephone.

■ Also born today: St Louis Cardinals QB **NEIL LOMAX** (1959). _Alan Wiggins (1958), O's 2nd basem bounced by Padres in '85 because of drug problems._

■**LEN FORD (1926)** — Defensive end with the Cleveland Browns during the 1950s, born in Washington, D.C. He was a two-way All-American from Michigan under the legendary Fritz Crisler. Ford was a senior on the 1947 team, one of the greatest college teams of all time. He spent two years as an offensive end with the Los Angeles Dons of the AAFC. When the Cleveland Browns left the AAFC for the NFL, Paul Brown acquired Ford and made him a strictly defensive player — the prototype of the big (6'5", 260 lbs.), yet quick, defensive end of the modern era. He

Len Ford

was All-Pro for five straight seasons (1951-55) and recovered 20 fumbles. He spent his last year, 1958, with the Green Bay Packers. Ford died at age 46 of a heart attack. In 1976 he was elected to the Hall of Fame.

■**GEORGE GIPP (1895)** — Laurium, Mich. He was a phenomenal running back and kicker at Notre Dame under Knute Rockne. As a freshman he kicked a 63-yard field goal. In the final game of his tremendous college career, Gipp played with a sore throat. He died three weeks later of infection. Several years later, Rockne, trailing Army at the half, inspired his team to "win one for the Gipper."

■**Also born today: JOE "FLASH" GORDON (1915)**, N.Y. Yankee second baseman (traded to Cleveland in 1947 for Allie Reynolds) ... golfer **JUDY RANKIN (1945)**, in '76 became first woman golfer to earn more than $100-thousand in a season ... auto racer/manufacturer **ENZO FERRARI (1898)** ... **BATTLING BATTALINO (1908)**, lightweight champion, (1929-32) ... **MAURICE LUCAS (1952)** one of the top power forwards of all time ... **LUIS ARROYO (1927)**, Arroyo, lefty relief ace for the 1961 N.Y. Yankees... **MANNY MOTA (1938)**, ex-Dodger, has the most career pinch hits (150), currently Dodger coach.

NOTES

■**EDDIE ARCARO (1916)** — This great jockey was born George Edward Arcaro in Cincinnati, Ohio.

Arcaro grew up in Kentucky and took to horses as a youngster, though his apprenticeship as a jockey was slow and difficult. In his first race he supposedly finished last, lost his cap and whip, and almost fell off his mount. He wasn't even close to bringing home a winner in his first 100 races. Despite years of frustration and near-poverty Arcaro survived to become probably the most famous jockey of all time. He was the first American jockey to win 3,000 races. Of his 4,779 winners, he rode five Kentucky Derby winners (later equalled by Bill Hartack): Lawrin, 1938; Whirlaway, 1941; Hoop, Jr., 1945; Citation, 1948; and Hill Gail, 1952. He is the only jockey ever to win the Triple Crown twice (on Whirlaway and Citation) and he also won six Preaknesses and six Belmont Stakes. Arcaro — one of the golden names in sport.

Eddie Arcaro

■Also Born Today: **RUSS NIXON (1935)**, Red Sox catcher of early 1960s, never stole a base in over 900 games, holds record for hitting three sacrifice flies in one game; managed Reds and became a coach with the Expos ... **FOREST EVASHEVSKI (1918)**, single-wing quarterback at Michigan known as "The Ape," who threw many a great block for tailback Tom Harmon; later coached at Iowa and Washington ... **HANA MANDLIKOVA (1962)**, Czech tennis player, one of the world's best, beat Martina Navratilova in 1984 in Oakland, ending her streak of winning 54 consecutive matches ... **PAUL KRAUSE (1942)**, holds NFL record for most career interceptions (81), erasing record long held by Emlen Tunnell.

■ **BOB RICHARDS (1926)** — "The Vaulting Vicar," the the greatest figure in the history of pole vaulting. Born in Champaign, Illinois, where he was a star high school quarterback in football, Richards focused on the pole vault while at the University of Illinois. An ordained minister in the Church of the Brethren, Richards was not the first to clear fifteen feet (Cornelius Warmerdam was, using a bamboo pole) but he cleared that height more times than any vaulter in the era of the aluminum pole (later eclipsed by the fiberglass pole). He finished third in the 1948 Olympics, then won gold medals in 1952 and 1956, the only vaulter

Bob Richards

to win the event twice, and the only vaulter to place in three straight Olympic Games. Richards later became well-known on Wheaties' boxes and was a leader of a national physical fitness program in the 1960s.

■ **ELROY FACE (1928)** — One of the greatest relief pitchers in baseball. He played in 802 games with the Pittsburgh Pirates (1953, 1955-68) tying him with Walter Johnson for the most games pitched with one team. In his first five seasons, Face's won-loss record was 32-36. In his sixth season he went 18-1, the best single-season percentage (.947) for pitchers with at least 15 decisions. It was also the most wins by a reliever in a season. In the 1960 World Series against the Yankees, he appeared in four of the seven games and had three saves. Since retirement, Face has been a carpenter and a member of the Pennsylvania civil service commission.

■ Also born today: **PHIL ESPOSITO (1942)** — "Espo," great hockey player with the Black Hawks, Bruins and N.Y. Rangers, the league MVP in 1969 and 1974 ... financier and horseman **CORNELIUS V. WHITNEY (1899)**, founder of the C.V. Whitney stables ... N.Y. Yankees' "Old Reliable" **TOMMY HENRICH (1913)** ... two auto racers: **ROGER PENSKE (1937)**, and **BOBBY UNSER (1934)**, brother of Al Unser.

NOTES

■ **DUMMY TAYLOR (1875)** — Turn-of-the-century righty pitcher who was a deaf mute, born Luther Haden Taylor in Oskaloosa, Kansas. He played his nine-year career (1900-1908) with the New York Giants. Taylor was probably the only baseball player who could not speak or hear. His teammates learned the hand alphabet in order to communicate with him, and manager John McGraw often used it to give his signs. His first four years were hard-luck ones, consistently under .500 — but pitching well despite the losses. In 1901, Taylor was 17-27 but he started 43 games (to lead the league), and had a 3.18 ERA. The next year he went 8-18 with the unlikely ERA of 2.19 (22 complete games out of 29 starts), laboring for the cellar-dwelling Giants. For the rest of his career, however, Taylor had only one sub-.500 year (1906) and never had an ERA over 2.66. Only five teams have had three 20-game winners on their staff in National League history (the last one in 1923). One of them was the 1904 New York Giants. Taylor won 27 games, Mathewson won 32 and Red Ames won 22. Taylor died in 1958.

■ Also born today: **ALAN TRAMMELL (1958)**, too good to be true — tremendous glove, solid .300 hitter with more than occasional power — who with second-baseman Lou Whitaker forms the best keystone combo in the bigs ...

Jack Ramsay

JACK RAMSAY (1925), coach of the Trail Blazers, with best record among active coaches, had his day, but drafting Sam Bowie over Michael Jordan was less than brilliant and he gave too much away to get Kiki Vandeweghe ... **TOM YAWKEY (1903)**, owner of Boston Red Sox from 1935 until his death in 1976 ... **MARSHALL CASSIDY (1892)**, horse racing pioneer, invented the stall starting gate and perfected the use of the photo-finishing camera ... **GEORGE W. MAY (1889)**, horseshoes champion, developed so-called open-style of pitching.

NOTES

■ **ABE ATTELL (1884)** — Attell, featherweight champion (1901-12) and the third ranking featherweight of all time, was born in San Francisco. Known

Abe Attell

as "The Little Hebrew," Attell was one of the first Jewish world boxing champions. He was only 17 when he won the vacant title (though it was disputed for three years) and held it until Johnny Kilbane (also one of the all-time top ten rated featherweights) decisioned him in 1912. He and Kilbane are the only featherweights to hold their title for over a decade. Attell had 165 bouts in his career, losing only ten times and just three times by KO. After retirement, he was known to associate with gamblers and mobsters and played a prominent role in the fixing of the 1919 World Series. He was one of the key middlemen of the whole deal, who actually made the initial payment of money while hatching plots to exploit both the rebellious White Sox players and the big tuna, Arnold Rothstein, who bankrolled the fix. Attell died in 1970.

■ **RYNE DUREN (1929)** — Fire-balling ace reliever with the New York Yankees in the late 1950s. The pride of Cazenovia, Wisconsin, he played for several teams in his ten-year career but peaked with the Yankees in 1958 (leading AL in saves) and 1959 (with a 1.88 ERA and 96 strikeouts in 76 innings). Duren, who was also one of the worst-hitting pitchers of all time (seven bingles in 114 at-bats for a .061 lifetime BA), had a severe drinking problem which he finally kicked and wrote about in his book, "The Comeback." The Cubs' Ryne Sandberg was named after Duren.

■ Also born today: **SPARKY ANDERSON (1934)**, the Detroit Tigers' manager... basketball twins **TOM** and **DICK VAN ARSDALE (1943)** ... **CHARLES O. FINLEY (1918)** and **CONNIE MACK (1862)** the only owners of the A's until the Haas family bought it in 1980, were both born on this day.

■ **DANTE LAVELLI (1923)**—Hall of Fame end with the Cleveland Browns. Born in Hudson, Ohio, he went to Ohio State because he knew of Paul Brown's reputation

there. Injuries and World War II interrupted his college career but, after the war, Lavelli got (as a favor — no one expected him to make it) a tryout for Brown's new pro football franchise, the Cleveland Browns. He became an instant star of the new league (the AAFC), leading the league in receptions and catching the winning TD pass in the first AAFC title game. After four straight titles, the Browns merged with the NFL and continued to dominate. In Lavelli's 11-year career

Dante Lavelli

with Cleveland (1946-56), he played in the championship game every season except his last. He still has the record for most receptions (24) in title games. Lavelli caught 386 passes in his career for 6,488 yards (a very good 16.7 a catch) and 62 TDs (a phenomenal one TD for about every six catches).

■ **BARNEY DREYFUSS (1865)** — Born in Freiburg, Germany (birthplace of Freud), Dreyfuss became the owner of the Pittsburgh Pirates and built Forbes Field, the first steel stadium. He is also credited with originating the idea for the World Series.

■ Also born today: **ELSTON HOWARD (1930)**, Catcher-outfielder with Yankees (1955-66), MVP in 1963, the first black to play with the Yankees and the first black coach in the American League (with Yanks, from 1968 to '79); invented the weighted donut used in on-deck circles; he died in 1980 ... **FRED BILETNIKOFF (1943)**, another fabulous wide receiver born today, caught 589 passes (fifth best) with the Raiders (1965-78), one of the toughest competitors ever and now on the Invaders' coaching staff ... **RON HUNT (1941)**, second baseman with Mets, Giants, and Expos, who was great at getting hit with pitches (he and Elston Howard were born in St. Louis) ... **LEE CALHOUN (1933)** won gold medals for 110-meter hurdles in the 1956 and '60 Olympics ... **ED "TOO TALL" JONES (1951)**, Cowboys defensive end.

NOTES

■**EDDIE MURRAY (1956)** –The most devastating hitter in baseball today, born in Los Angeles. A 21-year-old rookie in 1977, he played in 160 games, hit 27 homers and drove in 88 runs. He got better — now he averages .300, hits over 30 homers and drives in over 110 runs. He could have been chosen MVP in every year he has played. Murray, also a good glove, is that rarity — a power-hitter who switch-hits. Before he's through, Murray will be rated second only to Mickey Mantle in that department. He's got a good shot at 400 home runs and — as always — is my early pick for MVP.

Eddie Murray

■**HONUS WAGNER (1874)** —Shortstop on the all-time All-Star team, born John Peter Wagner in Carnegie, Pa. A late bloomer for an immortal, Wagner was a 26-yr-old rookie with Pittsburgh and played there his entire career (1900-17). He retired — at age 43 — with a .329 lifetime batting average, 3,430 hits (sixth best mark), 252 triples (an NL record), and 2,426 singles (an NL record for 65 years until Pete Rose broke it in 1981). His 722 stolen bases were topped only by Brock, Cobb, Collins and Max Carey. Wagner hit .300 or better for 17 consecutive years. He won eight batting titles. Bowlegged, with huge hands, Wagner was considered the best player in the National League throughout his career. He coached the Pirates from 1933 until his death in 1955.

■Also born today: **BENNY OOSTERBAAN (1906)**, great end from Michigan who formed one-half of famous passing duo —with QB Benny Friedman; the first receiver to make All-American three straight years; later coached at Michigan ... **FRED SINGTON (1910)**, also a college football hall of famer, a tackle from Alabama (1928-30). ... auto racer and playboy **LANCE REVENTLOW (1936)**, son of Barbara Hutton, died in a 1972 plane crash.

NOTES

■ **MONTE IRVIN (1919)** — N.Y. Giants outfielder of the early 1950s. Born Monford Merrill Irvin in Columbia, Ala., he was a star of the Negro Leagues who broke into

baseball with the Giants as a 30-year-old rookie. Irvin excelled at every aspect of the game — he could hit for power and average, he could run, and was a good outfielder with a strong arm. Because he was also an exceptional human being he was being groomed as the first black player in the majors, a distinction that fell to Jackie Robinson instead. An indication of Irvin's ability in his prime is the fact that he led the National League in RBI in

Monte Irvin

1951, in his first full season in the majors — at age 32! He finished his abbreviated eight-year career with a .293 lifetime BA and a ticket to the Hall of Fame. Irvin is a long-time public relations executive for the baseball commissioner.

■ Also born today: **"CHAMPAGNE TONY" LEMA (1934)**, golfer who died (at age 32) in a plane crash in 1964 (with his wife); earlier that year he won the British Open ... three Olympic champions: **HERB ELLIOTT (1938)**, winner of the 1,500 meters in 1960; **LEE EVANS (1943)**, winner of the 400 meters in 1968; and **DON QUARRIE (1951)**, winner of the 200 meters in 1976 ... **BERT BELL (1895)**, founder (and coach) of the Philadelphia Eagles in 1933 and NFL commissioner from 1946 until his death (at a football game) in 1959. It was Bell who coined the phrase, "On any given Sunday ..." ... Reds outfielder **CESAR CEDENO (1951)** ... ex-Viking defensive great **CARL ELLER (1942)**.

NOTES

■ **GROVER CLEVELAND ALEXANDER (1887)** — Hall of Fame righty pitcher (known as "Pete"), for the Phillies, Cubs, and Cardinals (1911-30), born in Elba, Nebraska. Alexander broke into the majors as a mature 24-year-

old pitching sensation, winning 28 games, a rookie record. He wound up with 373 wins (tied for third with Christy Mathewson) and 90 shutouts (second only to Walter Johnson's 113) and the single season shutout record of 16 (in 1916). For six straight years (1915-20), Alexander's ERA was under 2.00. His winningest years were with the Phillies (climaxed by winning thirty or more for three years in a row,

'Pete' Alexander

1915-17) though he also had big years with the Cubs. He enjoyed a third incarnation as the aging veteran who helped the Cardinals win the pennant in 1926 (after the Cubs dealt him to the Cards in June) and then performed heroically in the Series against the Yankees, beating them in Game Six and then nailing down Game Seven with clutch relief pitching (which included striking out Tony Lazzeri with the bases loaded). He followed that by winning 21 games in 1927 and, in '28, going 16-9 — at age 41 — and helping the Cards win another pennant. Alexander was a fun-lover who consistently flouted curfews and training rules, which hurt him later when he found it difficult to land jobs as a coach or executive with a club. He worked at odd jobs and knew hard times, though when his situation became known a fund was created to assist him. He died in 1950.

■ Also born today: **VIC JANOWICZ (1930)**, Ohio State running back and baseball star, won 1950 Heisman Trophy, led Buckeyes to Rose Bowl win over Cal and Jackie Jensen, another pretty good two-sport athlete ... **ELWIN "PREACHER" ROE (1915)**, Dodger lefty (and spitballer) who was 22-3 in '51 ... **JOHNNY BLANCHARD (1933)**, slugging catcher with the Yankees (1955-65) ... **PHIL VILLAPIANO (1949)**, ex-Raider linebacker, currently with Buffalo Bills ... **WALLACE "BUDDY" WERNER (1936)**, American skier in two Olympics, killed in 1964 avalanche while filming sports fashion film.

NOTES

■ **RAYMOND BERRY (1933)** —Great clutch receiver for the Baltimore Colts (1955-67), born in Corpus Christi, Texas, played college ball at SMU and did not impress

Ray Berry

the pro scouts. He was drafted by the Colts in the 20th round and retired thirteen years later with 631 receptions, at that time an NFL record though currently fourth on the all-time list. He and QB Johnny Unitas formed a passing duo for the ages. No other combo produced the same excitement for so long. Berry was rather small and considered slow for a wide receiver. He had poor eyesight and one leg was shorter than the other. However, no one was greater in the clutch. He was master of the sideline pattern, and he had great hands. Not only did he rarely drop a pass but he fumbled only once in his career after a reception. In the famous sudden death title game in 1958 against the New York Giants, Berry caught 12 passes for 178 yards and one TD in the Colts' 23-17 win. After retiring, he was an assistant coach with the Dallas Cowboys and Detroit Lions before being named head coach of the New England Patriots during the 1984 season.

■ Also born today: golfer **GENE SARAZEN (1902)**, twice won U.S. Open (in 1922 and '32), thrice won the PGA title (1922-23, 1933); developed the sand wedge and wrote "Thirty Years of Championship Golf" ... **ALLISON DANZIG (1898)**, tennis writer for the New York Times, the first writer to enter the tennis hall of fame ... auto racer **PETER REVSON (1939)**, son of cosmetics magnate, finished second in 1971 Indy 500 and won the '73 British Grand Prix, died racing in South Africa in 1974.

NOTES

■**FRED DEAN (1952)** – S.F. 49ers' fabulous defensive end. Born in Arcadia, La., Dean was a linebacker four years at Louisiana Tech and was drafted in 1975 by the Chargers in the second round. In 1981 Dean was dealt to the 49ers for a second-round draft pick — after having been named defensive lineman-of-the-year by the NFL Players Association in 1980! Dean's arrival in early October turned the 49ers' 2-3 beginning into its first ever NFL title, and for the second straight year — but with a different team — was named defensive lineman-of-the-

Fred Dean

year. In 1983 Dean's 17½ sacks led the league and broke the Niners' team record of 16 by Tommy Hart. In 1984 Dean held out for most of the regular season, then was great in helping vault the 49ers over the Miami Dolphins in the Super Bowl.

■**M.J. "JOE" MALONE (1880)** — The NHL's first superstar, skated with the Montreal Canadiens and played in the first NHL game on Dec. 19, 1917. He scored five goals that night and scored 44 goals in his 21 games that season, a per game percentage that is still a record. Malone also holds the record for most goals in one game (7), set in 1920.

■Also born today: **FRANK MALZONE (1930)**, Red Sox third baseman from 1955 to 1965, voted to the all-time Red Sox team in 1969 (Wade Boggs will succeed him); Malzone is currently a Red Sox superscout ... **CHARLES BLONDIN (1924)**, French gymnast who walked on a wire across the Seine in Paris, the Thames in London, and Niagara Falls, which he crossed on a 1,100 foot wire, suspended 160 feet over the falls ... auto racing titan **MARIO ANDRETTI (1940)**, won Indy 500 in 1969; in 1984 broke the all-time one lap track record at Indianapolis, doing the 2½ mile oval in 210 mph. ... **BILL HALLER (1935)**, AL umpire since 1963, brother of Giants' GM Tom Haller ... and another great defensive end: **CHARLES "BUBBA" SMITH (1945)**.

NOTES

■ **AL ROSEN (1924)**— Power-hitting third baseman for the Cleveland Indians who played only seven full seasons, but had 192 career HRs and a .285 lifetime BA. His 37 HRs led the American League in his rookie year (1950), 2nd most ever by a rookie. In 1953, Rosen led the AL in HRs and RBIs, missed the Triple Crown by one point when Mickey Vernon nosed him out for the batting title. Rosen, former president of the Yankees, currently is president and general manager of the Houston Astros.

Al Rosen

■ **PEPPER MARTIN (1904)** — "Wild Hoss of The Osage" was born in Temple, Okla. Martin was the fastest and scrappiest of the Gas House Gang of the St. Louis Cardinals in the 1930s. A third baseman and outfielder, Martin was a .298 lifetime hitter and led the league in stolen bases three times. He's still remembered for batting .500 and running wild against Mickey Cochrane and the Philadelphia A's in the 1931 World Series.

■ Also born on Leap Year Day: **HENRI RICHARD (1936)**, Canadiens hockey star, brother of Maurice "The Rocket" Richard. Henri was known as "The Pocket Rocket" ... and **JOHN NILAND (1944)**, ex-Cowboy offensive guard.

NOTES

■ **MAX BENTLEY (1920)** — Bentley, the best of a great hockey family, was born in Delisle, Saskatchewan (and known as the "Dipsey Doodle Dandy from Delisle.") Max was one of six brothers who played big-league hockey. Doug Bentley, like Max, was a Hall of Famer who played with Max on the Black Hawks and the Rangers. Before Wayne Gretzky, Max Bentley was considered by many to be the greatest center of all time, known for his prowess as a stick-handler and playmaker. He was one-third (with brother Doug and Bill Mosienko) of the Black Hawks' Pony Line (a trio of

Max Bentley

diminutive finesse skaters). He twice won the Art Ross Trophy (most points), in 1945 and '46, and won the Lady Byng Trophy (sportsmanship and ability) in 1942. Max was traded to the Toronto Maple Leafs in 1947 and led them to four Stanley Cup victories in five years and an unprecedented three consecutive cups (1947-49). After retiring in 1954, Max and brother Doug went back home and helped operate the family wheat farm.

■ Also born today: **PETE ROZELLE (1926)**, NFL commissioner since 1959 ... **RILEY ODOMS (1950)** one of the great tight ends in NFL history, had brilliant 13-year career with the Denver Broncos ... **TOM "HOLLYWOOD" HENDERSON (1953)**, ex-linebacker with the Cowboys and 49ers; imprisoned for molesting two teen-age girls and then trying to bribe them not to testify ... **ERNIE PADGETT (1899)**, turned one of baseball's seven unassisted triple plays in 1923 as Braves shortstop; not only did he appear in a scant 271 major league games in his career but that game in 1923 was one of only four that he appeared in all season (on Oct. 6, possibly the last game of the year for a Braves team that went 54-100) ... **BRIAN WINTERS (1952)**, ex-Bucks shooting guard, one of the best ... **TOM CLARK (1941)**, poet and baseball aficionado.

NOTES

Mel Ott

■ **MEL OTT (1909)** — Great NY Giants outfielder from 1926 to 1947, was born in Gretna, La., He never played in the minors, breaking into the bigs at age 17. The first National League player to hit 500 home runs (finishing with 511), he was also a .304 lifetime hitter and managed the Giants through most of the 1940s while still an active player. The great Ott, with his famed front leg lifted as he swung, died of injuries in a 1958 auto accident.

■ **CLAIR BEE (1900)** — Born in Grafton, W.Va., a pioneering basketball coach at Long Island University He created and coached the Baltimore Bullets from the NBA's inception in 1946 until the Bullets folded in 1954. His innovations include the 1-3-1 zone defense, and helping develop the 3-second lane and the 24-second clock in the NBA. Bee also wrote more than 50 books on basketball as well as sports fiction for children, including the popular Chip Hilton series. His 357-79 won-loss college record, for an .819 percentage, is the best ever for a college coach.

■ Also born today: **PETE JOHNSON (1954)**, the Bengals, Chargers, and Dolphins 270-pound fullback ... **HOWARD "HOPALONG" CASSADY (1934)**, Ohio State running back and Heisman Trophy winner in 1955 ... **MOE BERG (1902)**, baseball player (1923-39), lawyer, WWII spy, linguist, goodwill ambassador to Latin America ... two pitchers who won MVPs in the NL: **MORT COOPER (1913)**, brother of Walker Cooper, and **JIM KONSTANTY (1917)**, relief pitcher for Phillies who started Game One in the 1950 World Series against the Yankees.

NOTES

■**WILLIE KEELER (1872)** — "Wee Willie" (5-feet-4½, 140 pounds), the baseball player who invented (and practiced) the slogan, "hit 'em where they ain't," born in Brooklyn. His .345 lifetime batting average is fifth on the all-time list. He played from 1892 to 1910 with several teams and twice led the league in hitting. It was Keeler's 44-game consecutive hitting streak, set in 1897, that Pete Rose eclipsed three seasons ago. Keeler choked up on the bat and could place the ball anywhere he wanted.

Wee Willie Keeler

■**JACK SCOTT (1942)** — Radical sports activist, born Scranton, Pa., wrote "The Athletic Revolution" and a biography of Bill Walton, with whom he had intimate association. Scott also headed the influential Institute of Sports and Society in Berkeley and drove Patty Hearst across country in 1975 while she was still a fugitive.

■**KENNY KING (1957)** — L.A. Raider running back. A blocking back for Billy Sims at Oklahoma, he had a similar role with the Oilers, knocking down linebackers for Earl Campbell. He came to the Raiders before the 1980 season and helped them go to the Super Bowl as a running back and was part of the longest rushing play from scrimmage in Super Bowl history.

■Also born today: **JULIUS BOROS (1920)**, two-time (1952 and '63) winner of the U.S. Open .... High-jumper **JOHN THOMAS (1941)** ... Broncos linebacker **RANDY GRADISHAR (1952).** Herschel Walker (1962), NJ Generals RB, broke rushing record in '85 (2411 yards).

NOTES

■**DAZZY VANCE (1891)** — Right-handed strike-out artist for the Brooklyn Dodgers in the 1920s, born

Arthur Charles Vance in Orient, Iowa. Vance was the latest bloomer ever to make it into the Hall of Fame. He toiled in the minors for a decade but did not make it to the big leagues until 1922 — at age 31. In 11 years with the Dodgers he won 187 of his 197 wins. He holds the NL record for leading the league in strikeouts seven straight times (1922-28). Vance peaked in 1924, when he went 28-6 and led the league in ERA, complete games, and shutouts. He was named the MVP. Vance, a fastball pitcher with excellent control, was also a fun-lover who helped give the Dodgers a reputation as a team with zany, eccentric types. He died in 1961.

Dazzy Vance

■**KNUTE ROCKNE (1888)** — The most successful coach in college football history was born in Norway. His record at Notre Dame (1918 to 1930) was 105-12-5. He also had five undefeated seasons. As a player, he and quarterback Gus Dorais formed the first famous passing combo in 1913 and put Notre Dame on the map. It was Rockne who said, "When the going gets tough, the tough get going." Less known is this nugget: "Most men, when they think they are thinking, are merely re-arranging their prejudices." "The Bald Eagle," as he was known, died in a 1931 plane crash.

■Also born today: **FRANCIS JOSEPH "LEFTY" O'DOUL (1897)**, .349 lifetime hitter (fourth best after Cobb, Hornsby, and Joe Jackson), won two batting titles, one of them in 1929 with a .398 average and 254 hits (second best after George Sisler's 257), born in S.F. .... **MARGARET OSBORNE DUPONT (1918)**, she and tennis partner, Louise Brough, won U.S. doubles title twelve times, including nine years in a row (1942-50) ... **PASCUAL PEREZ (1926)**, flyweight champion, 1955-60, the first Argentinian to win a world boxing title ... **"SUNNY" JIM FITZSIMMONS (1885)**, who trained many great horses, including Nashua ... Scottish auto racer **JIM CLARK (1936)**, in 1963 became the youngest Grand Prix champion in history, winning it again in '65 the year he won the Indy 500; died in a 1968 auto race collision

NOTES

■ **FREDDIE WELSH (1886)** — Lightweight champion (1914-17) and one of the five highest-rated lightweights of all time, born in Pontypridd, Wales. His real name was Frederick Hall Thomas but he assumed another name to keep his boxing career a secret from his mother. Previous champions Joe Gans, Battling Nelson and Ad Wolgast refused to give him a title shot because he had beaten the best fighters in that division. Finally, Willie Ritchie went to London in 1914 to give him his chance and Welsh got his title by a fraction of a point in a 20-round decision

Freddie Welsh

(shades of Mike McTigue winning a split decision over Battling Siki in Dublin on St. Patrick's Day). Welsh lost his title to Benny Leonard by a ninth-round KO, the only time he had ever been knocked out and only the fourth loss in 167 fights. Welsh, one of the best pure boxers in the history of the lightweight division — quick and clever — was also a vegetarian, and probably the only one to become world champion. He put all of his savings into a health resort that failed. He died broke in 1927 at age 41.

■ Also born today: **DEL CRANDALL (1930)**, 19-year-old rookie for Braves in 1949 and played for them until 1963, "the greatest catcher in Braves' history," recently managed Mariners ... **RANDY MATSON (1945)**, the first shot-putter to reach 70 feet, won in 1968 Olympics ... **PAUL CHRISTMAN (1918)**, one-fourth of the Chicago Cardinals' "$100,000 Backfield" (with Charley Trippi, Pat Harder, and Marshall Goldberg), later TV football announcer ... **MILT SCHMIDT (1918)**, the center of the renowned "Kraut Line" of the Boston Bruins (the wingmen were Bobby Bauer and Woody Dumart) .... **CARROLL ROSENBLOOM (1907)**, owner of Colts (born in Baltimore), then traded franchises with L.A. Rams in mid-1970s and owned Rams until his death in 1979 (succeeded by his wife, now Georgia Frontiere).

Willie Stargell

■**WILLIE STARGELL (1941)** — Pirates' first baseman of the 1960s and '70s and one of the great sluggers in baseball history. He was born Wilver Dornel Stargell in Earlsboro, Okla., (first-baseman on the All-Okie team, edging out Randy Bass). He broke in with the Pirates as a 21-year-old rookie in 1962 and (like Honus Wagner, Pie Traynor and Roberto Clemente) played with the Pirates for his whole career, retiring after the 1982 season — at age 41. Only 15 players hit more than his 475 home runs. He was a star on the Pittsburgh teams that won pennants in 1971 and 1979 and came from behind in both years to win both World Series. Stargell hit 48 homers in 1971 (only six NL players have hit more) and, in 1979, was named co-MVP (with Keith Hernandez).

■**LEFTY GROVE (1900)** — Robert Moses Grove, the great A's (1925-33) and Red Sox (1934-41) pitcher, was born in Lonaconing, Md. He won the first MVP ever (1931) and won 300 games in his career, sixth among modern-era pitchers. His .680 percentage is 4th best all-time. He led the league in strikeouts in his first seven years, (1925-31), won 20 games seven straight times (1927-33), and led the league in ERA an incredible nine times. In 1931, he had a 31-4 record with a 2.06 ERA, one of the greatest single seasons any pitcher has ever had.

■**CLARK SHAUGHNESSY (1892)** —The "Father of the modern T-formation," born St. Cloud, Minn. coached at Chicago U., 1933-39, until they dropped football. He became an adviser for the Chicago Bears, developing the T, experimenting with the man in motion and using a split end. These innovations resulted in the Bears' 73-0 rout of the Redskins for the 1940 NFL title game. The next year, he took Stanford to an undefeated season and victory in the Rose Bowl, establishing the T as THE modern offense.

■ Also born today: Sportswriter **RING LARDNER (1885)**, wrote for Chicago Tribune, also known for letters from a fictitious baseball player, first written for the Saturday Evening Post and compiled as "You Know Me, Al." ... **ANN CURTIS CUNEO (1926)**, Olympic swimming champion in 1948, San Francisco -born swimming teacher.

NOTES

Sports birthdays/March 7

■ **ANDY PHILLIP (1922)** — Phillip, basketball luminary at Illinois and in the NBA, was born in Granite City, Ill. He was a high-school phenom in his native town and went to the University of Illinois where, in 1941, he and four other sopho-mores were starters on a quick and poised team that went 18-5 and earned the nickname, "The Whiz Kids." Phillip was the best of those kids. A tremendous shooter, ballhandler, and defend-er, he had quick hands and played very intensely — though he never changed the expression on his face. His college career was interrupted by two years of Marine Corps duty during WW II. He returned to Illinois with only one of the original "Whiz Kids" missing and they continued their winning ways. Phillip was drafted by the fledgling Chicago Stags in the (also fledgling) Basketball Association of America in 1947 and for a decade was one of the pros' best playmaking guards.

Andy Phillip

■ Also born today: **FRANCO HARRIS (1950)**, one of the greatest all-time fullbacks ...
LYNN SWANN (1952), Franco's Steeler teammate, a clutch and acrobatic performer, he was the best wide receiver in football until he retired in 1981 to pursue a career in TV sportscasting.   ... auto racer **JANET GUTHRIE (1938)**, in '77 became the first woman to qualify for, and race in, the Indianapolis 500 ... **BOBO HOLLOMAN (1924)**, in 1953 pitched no-hitter in first major league start (only pitched one year and was 3-7).

Ivan Lendl (1960), Czech tennis player, won 1985 Wimbledon.

NOTES

■ **JIM BOUTON (1939)**—A true baseball nut who pitched for the N.Y. Yankees (1962-68), attempted several comebacks, the last time in 1978 with the Braves, and even beat the bushes in Class A and semipro leagues until finally retiring. He was 21-7 in 1963 (and took a heartbreaking 1-0 loss to Drysdale in Game Three of the Series) and 18-13 the following year (with two World Series wins). He wrote about those Yankee years in *Ball Four,* a tell-all journal in 1970 that made him wealthy and unpopular with many players

Jim Bouton

mentioned in the book. He has written several other books, including an up-dated *Ball Five.*

■ **JIM RICE (1953)**—Red Sox slugger In 1975, he broke in with a tremendous season (.309, 22 HRs, 102 RBI) only to be obscured by teammate Fred Lynn, also a rookie, who won MVP. He won his own MVP award in 1978 after hitting .315, 46 HRs, and 139 RBI.

■ **CARL FURILLO (1922)**—Brooklyn (and L.A. Dodgers) right-fielder from 1946 to 1960. "The Reading Rifle" (he was born in nearby Stony Creek Mills, Pa.) played many a line drive off that right-field wall in Ebbetts Field, then gunned down the runner at second base. His lifetime batting average was .299 and he won the 1953 battting title with a .344 mark. Roger Kahn wrote about him (and other ex- Dodgers) in the 1971 book, *The Boys of Summer,* in which he talks about his long struggle with the Players Association and his (unsuccessful) attempts to receive pension benefits.

■ **RICHARD ANTHONY "DON'T CALL ME 'RICHIE'" ALLEN (1942)** — A tremendous right-hand hitter and one of the most underrated and maligned athletes of the modern era, Allen (born in Wampum, Pa.) came up with the Phillies as a 22-year-old third baseman in 1964 and had what is probably the best rookie season any third baseman has ever had. In 1969, Allen played for the Phillies; in 1970, he played for the Cardinals; in 1971, the Dodgers; in 1972, the White Sox. How many players would have four good years in a row for four different teams? Allen did, peaking with the MVP award. In his 13-year career, Allen wound up with a .298 lifetime BA and 331 home runs, hit more than .300 seven times.

NOTES

■**TERRY McGOVERN (1880)** — McGovern, bantamweight (1899) and featherweight (1900-01) champion, was born in Johnstown, Pa. "Terrible Terry" became world bantamweight champion at age 19 via a first-round KO but vacated that title a few months later to challenge the great George Dixon for his feather title. McGovern won on an 8th round KO and held the crown for almost two years, defeating six challengers, all by knockouts. He was riding high when he met Young Corbett in November of 1901 but Corbett upset him with a second-round KO. In 77 bouts, McGovern

Terry McGovern

lost only four times and is rated the greatest all time featherweight. He died days before his 38th birthday.

■**BOBBY FISCHER (1943)** — Perhaps the greatest chess player of all. Fischer, a Chicago-born prodigy, became U.S. champion at age 15 and, in that same year, became the youngest international grandmaster in the history of chess. He defeated Boris Spassky in 1972 for the world championship but resigned his title two years later in a dispute over international match rules. A religious fundamentalist and political conservative, he has remained incognito for the last decade.

■Also born today: **ARKY VAUGHAN (1912)**, born Joseph Vaughn in Swifty, Ark., (hence his nickname), shortstop with Pittsburgh (1932-41) and Brooklyn (1942-43, 1947-48), lifetime .318 hitter, he and a friend drowned in a fishing accident at age 40; after years of neglect, he was elected to the Hall of Fame in 1985 ...
GERRY LINDGREN (1946), distance runner who set world record (27:11.6) in six-mile run in 1965; he was the first American high school distance runner to break nine minutes ... **JACK BRANT (1881)**, jockey honored on 103rd birthday at Golden Gate Fields...
JACKIE JENSEN (1927), born in San Francisco, "The greatest all-round athlete Cal ever produced" was the only athlete ever to be a football first-string All-American and a baseball MVP, with the Red Sox in 1958. Jensen died of a heart attack in 1982...
BILLY SOUTHWORTH (1893), managed Cardinals to 3 straight pennants (1942-44), Boston Braves to one (1948).
.... golfer Andy North (1950), won 1985 us open.

■ MIKE JACOBS (1880) — Fight promoter who had exclusive control of Joe Louis' career, born in New York . Jacobs struggled up from poverty on the lower west side of New York — a crusty, crafty, self-educated man who became the foremost boxing promoter in the world. In 1933, he and three Hearst journalists (including Damon Runyan) organized the 20th Century Sporting Club which challenged Madison Square Garden's monopoly on boxing — and won, finally merging with it in 1938. Jacobs' leverage was in his contract to handle Louis. He had earlier achieved a

Mike Jacobs

reputation as a resourceful ticket speculator in New York's theater district, and made even more money in boxing. Louis alone earned $4.6 million in his career. From 1937 to 1947, he promoted 61 world championship fights and more than 1,500 boxing cards, selling over $30 million worth of tickets. Jacobs died in 1953.

■ Also born today: CURLEY CULP (1946), defensive tackle with the K.C. Chiefs during their dynasty in the late '60s and early '70s; named the NFL's outstanding defensive player in 1973 ... **MARQUES HAYNES (1926)**, dribbling and ball-handling wizard for the Harlem Globetrotters in the 1950s who later split from them to form his own team (as did Goose Tatum) ... **SANDRA PALMER (1941)**, golfer who won the women's U.S. Open in 1975 (only 5-feet-1½) ... **IRINA PRESS (1939)**, Soviet track and field star who won the 80-meter hurdles event at the 1960 Olympics and the women's pentathlon at the 1964 Olympics; her sister, Tamara Press, was also a great track and field performer. .... **TONY GALENTO (1910)**, heavyweight who fought Joe Louis in 1939, losing by fourth-round KO; later Hollywood bit actor.

NOTES

Bernie Bierman

■ **BERNIE BIERMAN (1894)** — One of the great college football coaches, Bierman coached at Tulane (after being an assistant there under Clark Shaughnessy) from 1927 to 1932, and brought them to prominence, including a trip to the Rose Bowl in 1932. He returned to Minnesota (where he was born and where he had been a football star) and coached the Golden Gophers to five national titles (1934, '35, '36, '40, '41), including three in row, a feat never equalled before or since. His record at Minnesota was 93 wins, 35 losses, and six ties. A single-wing coach who developed the buck-lateral series, Bierman was a systematic, uncomprising and unsentimental coach who once said, "I never made an emotional speech in my life."

■ **SIR MALCOLM CAMPBELL (1885)** — English auto and boat racer, first to reach 300 miles per hour in an auto. Four years later, in 1939, he set the speedboat record of 141 mph. He also set speed records for motorcycles and airplanes. Sir Malcolm's speedboat records were broken by his son, Donald Campbell, who died racing in 1967. Malcolm died in 1949.

■ Also born today: **VINCE BORYLA (1927)**, set-shot artist ("Boryla with a bomb") with the N.Y. Knicks in early 1950s . . . two tennis greats (both doubles champions): **LOUISE BROUGH (1923)**, she and Margaret Osborne DuPont won U.S. doubles title 12 times (1942-50, 1955-57) and **JACQUES BRUGNON (1895)**, he and his French compatriots, Jean Borotra, Rene Lacoste and Henri Cochet, won many doubles titles and dominated the Davis Cup for 1927 to 1932.

Became Denver Nugget GM.

NOTES

■ **JOHNNY CALLISON (1939)** —Left-hand hitting out fielder, mostly with the Phillies (1960-69). He came up

with the White Sox at age 19 but soon moved over to the Phillies, peaking out from 1962 to 1965 during which he hit 112 homers, averaged about 90 RBI a season and fielded brilliantly. During that same four-year period, Callison led the league in assists every year, establishing a major league record. Callison was the hero of the 1964 All-Star game, hitting the game-winning home run in the bottom of the ninth inning. He was given the first MVP award for the All-Star game. He retired in 1973 with a .264 lifetime BA. Callison has been a car salesman in Glenside, Pa.

Johnny Callison

■ **TOMMY FARR (1914)** —British heavyweight champ in the late 1930s who fought Joe Louis, born in Wales. Farr started fighting at age 13 in traveling exhibitions. He became a quick, tough boxer who had a difficult style, always crouching and weaving. His big moment came in 1937 in Joe Louis' first title defense after having defeated Braddock earlier in the year. Farr gave Louis one of the toughest fights the champion would ever have, but lost the 15-round decision. After 10 years out of the ring and at the age of 36, Farr made an impressive comeback to the ring, fighting his way back — three years later — to earn a title fight against Don Cockell but he lost via a seventh round KO and retired.

■ Also born today: **DALE MURPHY (1956)**, phenomenal Atlanta Braves outfielder, the 3rd (and youngest) NL player to win back-to-back MVPs... **ED DIDDLE (1895)**, basketball coach at Western Kentucky (1922-64), his 759 wins is fourth after Rupp, Allen, and Iba. . . **VERN LAW (1930)**, pitched 16 years for the Pittsburgh Pirates, the last to pitch 18 or more innings in one game (in 1955). His son is second baseman Vance Law ... kicker **MARK MOSELEY (1948)**, of Washington Redskins, MVP in 1982 ... two auto racing greats: **E.G. "CANNONBALL" BAKER (1882)** and **JOHNNY RUTHERFORD (1938)**, won Indy 500 in 1974, '76 and '80. . . outfielder **JIMMY WYNN (1938)**, the "Toy Cannon."

NOTES

■ **JOE WALCOTT** (1873) -Welterweight champ (1901-06), No. 1-rated all time welterweight, born in Barbados, W. I. Walcott came to the U.S. in 1887, settled in Boston and had his first pro fight at age 16. One of the shortest welterweights ever (5-1½), he was a furious puncher who also had the advantage of a manager like Tom O'Rourke, who handled such champions as Jimmy Wilde and George Dixon, the all-time No. 1 flyweight and bantamweight, respectively. In 150 fights, Walcott lost 24 times, though many of them were questionable. For example, in 1895 he was declared the loser because he failed to knock out the lightweight champion, Kid Lavigne, as had been stipulated. Walcott lost his title at age 33 to Honey Mellody (whose name alone deserves immortality) and should have retired, but fought for five more years, losing more than half of the time. Speaking of names, Walcott's was used in homage by an outstanding heavyweight years later whose real name was Arnold Cream, born in New Jersey. The original Walcott, "The Barbados Demon," died in an auto accident in 1935.

Joe Bellino

■ Also born today: **JOHN "HOME RUN" BAKER** (1886), premier HR hitter of the dead ball era; third baseman on Connie Mack's "$100,000 Infield" (with Stuffy McInnis, Eddie Collins and Jack Barry) ... **JOE BELLINO** (1939), running back with Navy, won 1960 Heisman Trophy ... **GEORGE McAFEE** (1918), versatile back with the Chicago Bears in the 1940s, now runs McAfee Oil in Durham, N.C., where he played college ball (at Duke).

NOTES

■ **WES UNSELD (1946)** –Tower of strength on the front line of the Baltimore (later Washington) Bullets, 1968 to 1979, born in Louisville, Ky.

Played college ball at Louisville U., where he was a three-time All-American. Unseld was the second player chosen in the 1968 draft, though many doubted his future as a center at only 6-feet-7. Unseld erased all doubts by winning the MVP award as a rookie, a rare feat in any sport. He was especially effective under the basket, where he knew how to use his 250 pounds. A tremendous rebounder and defender, he

Wes Unseld

was also a master of the outlet pass.

■ **BENNY "KID" PARET (1938)** — Two-time welterweight champion, born in Cuba. He first won the title in 1960, then lost it in 1961 to Emile Griffith. Later that year Paret regained his title from Griffith but in their third meeting Paret lost both his title and his life, dying of injuries suffered in that fight at age 23.

■ Also born today: **TIM ROSSOVICH (1946)**, linebacker out of USC, played for the Eagles and others, known for his stunts on and off gridiron, currently an actor ... Two golfers, **BOB GOALBY (1931)**, who won the 1968 Masters, also a broadcaster; and **BOB CHARLES (1936)**, who won British Open in 1963, the only lefty ever to win it ... Auto racer **LEE PETTY (1914)**, three-time NASCAR champion (only three drivers have won more titles, one of whom is son Richard) ... Two basketball players, **CHARLIE SHARE (1927)**, All-American center from Bowling Green, played in 1950s with Fort Wayne and St. Louis Hawks; and **CLYDE LEE (1944)**, power forward with the Warriors from the mid-'60s to the mid-'70s ... **SAMUEL J. PERLMAN (1900)**, publisher and editor of the Daily Racing form and New York Morning Telegraph from 1947 to 1965 ... Yankee catcher **BUTCH WYNEGAR (1956)**, played in the 1976 All-Star Game (as a Minnesota Twin) at age 20 ... English bridge expert **ALGERNON BLACKWOOD (1869)**.

NOTES

■ NORM VAN BROCKLIN (1926)
—

Quarterback with the Rams and Eagles, born 58 years ago today in Eagle Butte, S.D. An All-American at Oregon in 1948, he played with the Rams for nine of his 12 NFL seasons (1949-57), twice leading the league in passing and twice in punting. Despite the inflated yardage of today's QBs, that is still an all-time professional record. In 1960 he led the

Norm Van Brocklin

Eagles to an NFL title and won the MVP award. He retired at the end of that season and began an unsuccessful career coaching at Minnesota (1961-66) and Atlanta (1968-74), where he was also general manager. An irascible man who fought with players, fans, and reporters, he also had a likeable side and away from football was quite genial. Plagued with poor health, he died of a heart attack in 1983.

■ Also born today: outfielder **BOBBY BONDS (1946)**, formerly with the Giants, Yankees, Angels, White Sox, Rangers, Indians, and Cardinals — a home run hitter who also stole 40 or more bases seven times ... sprinter **JACKSON SCHOLZ (1897)**, of "Chariots of Fire" fame, who won the 200 meter dash at the 1924 Olympics ... **OZZIE NEWSOME (1956)**, Cleveland Browns wide receiver ... running back **DICK BASS (1937)**, of College of Pacific and Rams fame ... **PADDY RYAN (1853)**, born in ireland, won American heavyweight title (bare-knuckle), lost to John L. Sullivan; later Sullivan knocked Ryan out after 50 seconds of the first round.

Lloyd Waner

■ **LLOYD WANER (1906)** — Born in Harrah, Okla., played for the Pittsburgh Pirates from 1927 to 1940. In his rookie year (when Pittsburgh won the pennant) he hit .355 and scored a league-leading 133 runs — on only two homers and 14 stolen bases. He and his brother Paul, known respectively as "Little Poison" and "Big Poison," were teammates on the Pirates during those years. Lloyd had a .316 lifetime batting average and struck out only 173 times in 7,772 career at bats — or once in every 45 at bats. Both Waners are in the Hall of Fame.

■ **LOU NOVA (1915)** –Boxer, actor and devotee of yoga, born in Los Angeles. Nova twice knocked out Max Baer,(1939 and 1941),driving Baer into retirement Later that year, Nova challenged champion Joe Louis. Nova was a excellent boxer but only a fair puncher. Louis decked him in the 6th round. Nova was a student of the occult and hyped the Louis fight with talk of his "cosmic punch." It attracted almost 60,000 fans. Nova also acted in several plays and films.

■ Also born today: **JOE DELAMIELLEURE (1951)**, All-Pro offensive guard of the 1970s with the Buffalo Bills ... **CLINT COURTNEY (1927)**, one of the few catchers to wear glasses, he was also pugnacious, as were most ballplayers who wore glasses ... ex-running back **MacARTHUR LANE (1942)**, born in Oakland, played with Packers, Cardinals, and Chiefs; good runner, receiver, and blocker ... **TOM GORMAN (1919)**, NL umpire from 1951 to 1976.

■**BOBBY JONES (1902)** — Immortal golfer born in Atlanta, Georgia. In 1930, he became the only golfer to win the Grand Slam, the four major tournmaments (U.S. and British Opens and U.S. and British Amateurs), a feat considered unlikely to be achieved again. He also won four U.S. Opens (1923 '26, '29, and '30). He died in 1971.

Bobby Jones

■**SAMMY BAUGH (1914)** — "Slingin' Sammy," Washington Redskins quarterback from 1937 to 1952, was born near Temple, Texas. After an All-American career at TCU, Baugh signed a baseball contract with the St. Louis Cardinals, but finally chose football. He led the Redskins to the NFL title in his rookie year. Baugh is simply one of the best football players who ever lived. A tremendous passer, he also was a skilled defensive back who led the NFL in interceptions in 1943 and also led the league in punting for four straight years (1940-43). He still holds the record for the best punting average for a season (51 yards a punt), established in 1940.

■**PETE REISER (1919)** — Brilliant hard-luck baseball player, St. Louis born. In his first full season with the Brooklyn Dodgers (1942), Reiser won the batting title and led the league in doubles, triples, runs scored, and slugging. He spent the next three years in World War II (a tragic interruption of his career) and played until 1952, though never a full season after 1947 because of recurring injuries sustained crashing into outfield walls. In 1946 he stole home seven times, a record he shares with Rod Carew. He died in 1981.

■**HANK SAUER (1919)** — Home run hitter deluxe in the late 1940s and early 1950s. In his 15-year career (mostly with the Cubs) Sauer hit 288 home runs and was a .266 lifetime hitter. He retired at 40 and has been a long-time Giants scout and roving batting instructor.

NOTES

■ **BENNY FRIEDMAN (1905)** —Great Michigan quarterback, born in Cleveland. He and receiver Benny Oosterbaan formed a legendary passing duo, both making All-America in 1925 and '26. Friedman was the finest passer up to that time, the first QB to use the pass on first down and as a consistent weapon instead of a mere adjunct to the running game.

Dwayne Murphy

■ **DWAYNE MURPHY (1955)** — Oakland A's center fielder. Murphy, probably the best defensive outfielder in the league, and impressive home run hitter. He has played in the bigs since 1976, all with the A's. He is the soul of the team.

■ Also born today: auto racer **MARK DONOHUE** (1937), won 1972 Indy 500, died at Austria's Grand Prix in 1975 a few days after his 221 mph single lap was the fastest ever traveled on a closed, or "oval" track ... racing car designer **ANDY GRANATELLI (1923)**, whose autobio is "They Call Me Mr. 500" ... two literary types: **JOHN UPDIKE (1932)**, for Rabbit Angstrom, who broke the Penn. high school scoring record in his junior year, and **GEORGE PLIMPTON (1927)**, author of "Paper Lion," "Out Of My League," and godfather of the Fantasy Camp craze.

NOTES

Joe Kapp

■ JOE KAPP (1938) — Univ of Calif. football coach since 1982. He is the only QB to lead his team to the Rose Bowl (with Cal in 1959), the Grey Cup (with the British Columbia Lions in 1963 and '64), and the Super Bowl (with the Vikings in 1970). When the Vikes traded him to the Patriots in 1971, Kapp quit — still in his prime — to challenge the NFL in court about the reserve clause. In 1969, he equalled an NFL record by throwing seven TD passes in one game.

■ "IRON MAN" JOE McGINNITY (1871) — Born in Rock Island Ill., known for his feats of endurance. He pitched five complete game double-headers—three times in the month of August 1903, winning all six games. He started 381 games in his career, completing 335, and though he pitched for only 10 years (he was a 28-year-old rookie), he won 247 games. His 434 innings pitched in 1903 is still an NL record. After his major-league career, the "Iron man" pitched for 17 more seasons in the minors, winning 204 more games. He won six games in his final season — with Dubuque, at age 54.

■ Also born today: BILL WAMBSGANSS (1894) , "Wamby," Cleveland second baseman, made the only unassisted triple-play in World Series history (in 1920) ... JAY BERWANGER (1914), Univ. of Chicago running back, the first Heisman Trophy winner (in 1935) ... RICHIE ASHBURN (1927), Phillies center fielder (1948-59), winning two batting titles (in 1955 and '58) ... sprinter and track coach PAYTON JORDAN (1917), ... A's pitcher MIKE NORRIS (1955), best righty in the AL in 1981 ... ex-Warrior guard JEFF MULLINS (1942).

out of baseball, victim of fast-lane-itis.

NOTES

Bobby Orr

■ **BOBBY ORR (1948)** —Great defenseman with the Boston Bruins (1967-76) and Chicago Black Hawks (1977-79), NHL's MVP three straight yrs (1970, '71, and '72) and won the James Norris Trophy (for best defenseman) an incredible eight years in a row (1968-75). Orr, whose career was shortened by five knee operations, was the first defenseman to lead the NHL in scoring (in 1970 and 1975), and holds the record for most goals (46) by a defenseman in a season.

■ **VINCENT RICHARDS (1903)** — tennis great, born in New York City. He won four U.S. doubles title, twice with Bill Tilden (in 1921 - '22) when only 18 - 19 years old. Richards was the first well-known tennis player to turn pro and later became the first commissioner of the World Professional Tennis League.

■ Also born today: **GEORGE GODFREY (1853)**, the first black American heavyweight boxer ... **DERRICK DICKEY (1951)**, "Double D," ex-Warrior forward ... L.A. Laker coach **PAT RILEY (1945)**.

NOTES

■**TOMMY DAVIS (1939)** — Line-drive hitter extraordinaire in both leagues from 1960 to 1975. Born in Brooklyn, N.Y., Davis came up as a Dodger, but in L.A. in 1960. Two years later, Davis won his first batting title (.346) and won it a second straight time in '63 (.326). In '62, Davis had one of the best offensive years in recent memory. Aside from the batting title, he led the league with 153 RBI (no one has topped that figure since) and 230 hits, and he hit 27 home runs. He also played in all the Dodgers' 163 games that year. After eight seasons with the Dodgers, Davis bounced from team to team, including the A's, and was traded eight times in the

Tommy Davis

last nine years of his career — hitting well everywhere he went. He spent his last three years as a designated hitter with the Baltimore Orioles and finished with a .294 lifetime average. Davis later was a coach with the Seattle Mariners.

■Also born today: sprinter **CHARLIE GREEN (1945)**, won a bronze medal in 100 meters in 1968 Olympics, later held world record ... two football coaches: **JOCK SUTHERLAND (1889)**, played at Pitt under Pop Warner, coached Pitt (1924-38) and even the Pittsburgh Steelers in 1946 and '47, and **TOM FLORES (1937)**, head coach of the Raiders since 1979 ... **SHANTY HOGAN (1906)**, catcher mostly with N.Y. Giants and Boston Braves from 1925 to 1937; he set an NL record for catchers with 121 consecutive errorless games. ...

catcher **MANNY SANGUILLAN (1944)**, a lifetime .295 hitter with the Pirates, one of the great bad-ball hitters.

■ **ED MACAULEY (1928)** — "Easy Ed," one of the greatest centers in basketball history, college and pro.

Ed Macauley

Ed Macauley was born in St. Louis and put St. Louis University on the map with his brilliant play, earning All-America honors as a junior and senior and leading the Billikins to NIT glory in 1948. He won the tournament's MVP award as he led St. Louis to a decisive 65-52 win over a Dolph Schayes-led NYU team that had not lost in 19 games. Macauley continued to stay at home in the pros as he signed with the St. Louis Bombers. He was the fifth leading scorer as a rookie. The Bombers folded after that season and Macauley wound up on the Boston Celtics. In his six years with them, he finished among the top scorers every year. In 1956, the St. Louis Hawks had the first selection in the draft. Red Auerbach didn't have to do much to convince Hawks owner Ben Kerner that Macauley, a home-town idol, could help the Hawks in more ways than one. So the Hawks wound up with Macauley (and Cliff Hagan) and the Celtics selected a center out of USF — Bill Russell. Brilliant move by the redhead but the Hawks did pretty well themselves, winning two straight Western Division titles (on the shoulders of Macauley, Hagan, and let's not forget Bob Pettit) and even defeating the Celtics in the finals for the NBA title in 1957-58. Ed retired with a 17.5 average. Agile, effortless, "Easy Ed" was beautiful to behold. At 6'8" and only 190 lbs, he relied on finesse.

■ Also born today: **BILLY VESSELS (1931)**, Oklahoma running back, Heisman Trophy winner in 1952 ... **BILLY GOODMAN (1926)**, only utility player ever to win a batting title (in 1950 w/Bosox) ... ex-Warrior **SONNY PARKER (1952)**, he could really fill that lane. ...N.Y. City chess player **LARRY EVANS (1932)** ...
TOMMY GIBBONS (1891), one of the top all-time light-heavyweight boxers, known for his heavyweight title bout with Jack Dempsey, who won 15-round decision. That fight today is used as an example of corruption and greed among promoters and politicans ...
ARTHUR POE (1879), early Princeton football great and great nephew of — that's right — Edgar Allen Poe.

NOTES

■ **MOSES MALONE (1955)** — The great Moses, born in Petersburg, Va., (not far from Ralph Sampson's birthplace). A national basketball hero at Petersburg High School, he was recruited by every major college but chose the pros instead as an 18-year-old. After two years in the ABA, Moses broke the all-time offensive rebounding record in his first NBA season (1976). He is still the dominating big man in the NBA.

Moses Malone

■ **ARNIE WEINMEISTER (1923)**–Great Canadian-born fullback at the Univ. of Washington, he spent only six years as a pro — with the New York Yankees of the AAFC in 1948-49, and with the New York Giants, 1950-53, where he was All-Pro as a converted tackle. Despite his brief career, he was the dominant player at his position while he was in the league and was rewarded in 1984 with induction in the Hall of Fame.

■ Also born today: Eagles quarterback **RON JAWOR-SKI (1951)** ... two speed racers: one on land, **CRAIG BREEDLOVE (1938)**, set world land speed record in 1965, going 614 mph in a jet-engined car (his wife, Lee, set the same record — for women — a few days earlier), and **DONALD CAMPBELL (1921)**, broke water speed record, just as his father, Sir Malcolm Campbell, had done, attaining speed of more than 300 mph before his boat, like his father's boat, exploded, killing him (in 1967)

■ **LARRY WILSON (1938)** —Hall of Fame safety for St. Louis Cardinals from 1960 to 1972

Born in Rigby, Idaho, he was a running back at Utah but the Cards converted him to defensive back — a cornerback at first but after nearly getting cut was shifted to safety, where he thrived. Wilson, known to his teammates as "Wildcat," was a scrappy go-for-it performer who was the first to unveil the safety blitz, a tactic that offenses found difficult to deal with and one that strongly influenced the game. Wilson's 52 career interceptions are a St. Louis Cardinals record, and he was named to eight Pro Bowls. When Wilson retired after the 1972 season, the Cardinals retired his jersey, No. 8.

Larry Wilson

■ Also born today: **JACK McAULIFFE (1866)**, lightweight champion, 1887-97, one of the few boxers never to lose a fight in his career (52 bouts) ... **RENALDO NEHEMIAH (1959)**, 49ers wide receiver, Bill Walsh's pet project, a tremendous athlete but not quite an NFL receiver; in 1985 his world record for the 110 meter hurdles was broken by Greg Foster ... **ROGER BANNISTER (1929)**, English miler was the first to run the mile in under four minutes (three decades later it's down around 3:48) ... **LEIGH STEINBERG**, Berkeley-based agent who represents Steve Bartkowski, Mark Gastineau, Bill Ring, and others ... **GEORGE SISLER (1893)**, second-string first baseman on the all-time all-star team; holds record for most hits in a season (257 — in 631 at-bats for a .407 average; that season he hit 19 homers and struck out 19 times!).

NOTES

■**EMLEN TUNNELL** (1925) —Great defensive back and punt returner born in Bryn Mawr, Pa. Undrafted out of Iowa in 1943, Tunnell had to talk the New York Giants into a tryout in 1948. He played with them for 11 seasons and helped establish the Giants' "umbrella defense." In 1967, he became the first black elected to the Pro Hall of Fame. He was also the first black to play for the Giants and the first hired to a coaching position (assistant with the Giants) in the modern NFL. The 6-foot-3, 210-pound Tunnell, whom many consider the best safety ever (he was

Emlen Tunnell

named to the 50th anniversary All-NFL team), still holds the record for most punt returns and most yardage on punt returns and interceptions. His 79 career interceptions stood as a record for almost two decades until it was broken by Paul Krause of the Vikings (who also went to Iowa). Tunnell died in 1975 of a heart attack.

■**HOWARD COSELL** (1920) — "Humble Howard," "The Mouth," was born in Winston-Salem, N.C. Howard has been accused of ruining the World Series, of babbling incoherently during fights, and of driving millions of Monday Night Football fans to turn off the volume and listen to Buck/Stram radio broadcasts. He has been called pompous, arrogant, vain — and much more. The current mood, however, is to almost venerate him — as a survivor, or something. I'll say this: he probably would make a fun father-in-law.

■ Also born today: Kansas miler **WES SANTEE** (1932) ... knuckleballer **EMIL "DUTCH" LEONARD** (1909), had 191-181 record in 20-year career with Senators, Cubs, etc.

■ **GINO CAPPELLETTI** (1934) — Born in Keewatin, Minn. One of pro football's top 10 all-time point-makers, one of the only place-kickers to also score touchdowns. A good receiver, he caught 42 touchdown passes. Cappelletti played college ball at Minnesota and had an 11-year career with the Boston Patriots (1960-70). His 155 points in 1964 and his 147 points in 1961 is the second and third best mark for a season (after Paul Hornung's 176 in 1960).

■ **DICK NOLAN** (1932) — A defensive back for the  New York Giants (1954-57, 1959-61), his mates in the "umbrella defense" were such stars as Em Tunnell, Otto Schnellbacher, Dick Lynch, Tom Landry and Jim Patton. He coached the 49ers from 1968 to 1975, winning three division titles (1970-72), and the Saints from 1978 to 1980. He later became Landry's assistant in Dallas.

Dick Nolan

■ **CHARLES "RIP" ENGLE** (1906) — Another football coach – a college legend. Born Salisbury, Pa., Engle coached at Penn State from 1950 to 1966, compiling a record of 194 wins, 48 losses and four ties. He led Penn State to its first post-season football victory — the 1959 Liberty Bowl, winning 7-0 on the last play of the game on a fake field goal. Heck of a call, coach. He coached at Brown a few years earlier and brought his quarterback there, Joe Paterno, over to State as his assistant. Paterno succeeded Engle when he retired. Engle died in 1983.

NOTES

■ **JAMES RODNEY RICHARD (1950)** — Flame- throwing 1970s righty pitcher with the Houston Astros. At 6-feet-8 and 225 pounds, Richard was an imposing figure on the mound. He and Nolan Ryan are the only two pitchers ever officially clocked at throwing faster than 100 mph. Richard was a tremendous strikeout pitcher whose 8.37 strikeouts per nine innings is the fourth best all-time mark after Ryan, Sandy Koufax and Sam McDowell. Only 11 pitchers in major league history have struck out more than 300 batters in a season. Richard is

J.R. Richard

the only righty National Leaguer ever to do it and one of only five pitchers to do it more than once (in '78 and '79). In one of the tragedies of sports, Richard suffered a stroke and partial paralysis that ended his career at its height despite a lengthy comeback attempt.

■ Also born today: auto racer **CALE YARBOROUGH (1939)**, NASCAR champion, 1976-78, the only one to do it three straight times ... **ANNEMARIE PROELL (1953)**, Austrian skier who won 1980 Olympic gold medal in the downhill and during the 1970s won World Cup championship six times, including five times in a row (1971-75) ... **MILLER HUGGINS (1879)**, N.Y. Yankees manager, 1918-29, overseeing six pennants and five World Series ... Golfer **ED FURGOL (1916)**, won U.S. Open in 1954 ... **WES COVINGTON (1932)**, lefty-swinging outfielder mostly with the Braves and Phillies from 1956 to 1966; .279 lifetime BA; made two spectacular catches against Yankees in 1957 Series; he became a sportswriter in Edmonton, Canada.

NOTES

Rick Barry

■ **RICK BARRY (1944)** — Basketball's "Golden Boy" one of the greatest forwards in basketball history (the others being Elgin Baylor, Bob Pettit, Julius Erving and Larry Bird, in case you're interested). He was No. 1 in scoring in both the NBA and the ABA. He led the N.Y. Nets to the ABA title in 1972 and led the Warriors to the NBA title in 1975. The best passing forward ever and the best foul-shooter (the last man to shoot fouls underhand), Barry was also a competitor and team leader who refused to lose. The same traits that made Barry a hardcourt genius make him often seem abrasive and arrogant as a human being. He was the league-leading ref-baiter throughout his career and the least popular basketball star of all time. —(Unless it was Elvin Hayes)

■ Also born today: **AUGUST A. BUSCH, JR. (1899)**, "Gussie," the brewer and owner of the St. Louis Cardinals ... **KEVIN LOUGHERY (1940)**, coach of the Chicago Bulls ... righty pitcher **LON WARNEKE (1909)**, w/Cubs and Cards in 1930s and early '40s, had 193-121 record with 3.18 ERA, known as "The Arkansas Hummingbird" ... **JOE FORTUNATO (1931)**, great middle linebacker w/Bears 1955-66 ... another righty pitcher: **VIC RASCHI (1919)**. "The Springfield Rifle" had great but brief career with the Yankees (1946-53) with 132-66 record for a .667 percentage, the sixth best all-time mark; he was one of the formidable triumvirate; Reynolds, Raschi and Lopat.

NOTES

■ **DENNY McLAIN (1944)** — A great pitcher for Detroit in the late 1960s. Born in Chicago, Ill. McLain broke in with the Tigers in 1963 as a 19-year-old rookie. Two years later he was 16-6 with a 2.61 ERA. In '66, McLain won 20 games, in '67 he went 17-16, and then — in 1968 — had the kind of year even good pitchers only dream about. He went 31-6 with a 1.96 ERA, and a league-leading 28 complete games. He struck out 280 while walking only 63. He was named the Cy Young award winner and the league's most valuable player. The next year he went 24-9 and again won the Cy

Denny McLain

Young award (sharing it with Mike Cuellar), becoming one of only three pitchers to win it twice in a row. From that point — a 25-year-old pitcher still in his prime — McLain's career went downhill. He had arm problems, was dealt to the Senators (where he went 10-22), and began hanging out with the wrong people. He got involved with gamblers and crooks and became one himself. In 1985, McLain was convicted of racketeering, extortion and possession of cocaine.

■ Also born today: **KURT THOMAS (1956)**, the first U.S. male gymnast to win a gold medal in world championship competition (for the floor exercise); won Sullivan award (for best amateur athlete) in 1979 ... **WALT FRAZIER (1945)**, "Clyde" played with the N.Y. Knicks from 1967 to '77, one of the five best guards ever ... N.O. Saints fullback **EARL CAMPBELL (1955)**, 1977 Heisman Trophy winner from Texas, NFL's MVP as a rookie, and the only player to win the MVP twice in a row ... **TOMMY HOLMES (1917)**, Boston Braves outfielder of the 1940s (.302 lifetime BA); he held modern NL record for hitting in consecutive games (37) that Pete Rose broke ... **FERRIS FAIN (1921)**, first baseman who won two straight batting titles in 1951 and '52 with the Philadelphia A's (great glove)... **CY YOUNG (1867)**, pitched the first perfect game of the 20th century — at age 37!; he won 511 games but never won the Cy Young award.

NOTES

Jerry Lucas

■ **JERRY LUCAS (1940)** — This great high school. college and pro basketball star was born in Middletown, Ohio He is one of only six players to win high school All-American honors for three straight years (others include Kareem, Albert King and Eugene Banks). After a tremendous college career with Ohio State, Lucas began his pro career in 1964 with the Cincinnati Royals and won Rookie-of-the-Year honors. He later played with the Knicks and, briefly, the Warriors. After retiring, Lucas became an authority in powers of memory.

■ **WILLIE GALIMORE (1935)** — Born in St. Augustine, Fla., Galimore was a brilliant running back for the Chicago Bears. Drafted out of Florida A&M in 1957, Galimore provided the broken-field running as the Bears made their way to the top, culminating in the NFL title in 1963. The following season, in training camp, Galimore and teammate Bo Farrington were killed in an auto accident. That year, the defending champion Bears plummeted to sixth place and a 5-9 record.

■ **JAMES "RIPPER" COLLINS (1904)** — The Gas House Gang's first baseman was born in Altoona, Pa. He played with the Cardinals from 1931 to 1936, then briefly with the Cubs and Pirates, finishing with a .296 lifetime BA. Despite his smallish size (5-feet-9, 165 pounds), Collins was the first power-hitting switch-hitter in the big leagues, a group that only numbers about a half-dozen in the history of the game.

NOTES

■ **TOMMY RYAN (1870)** – Welterwt champ (1894-96) and middlewt champ (1898-1904), born Redwood, N.Y., won the welter title by decisioning Mysterious Billy Smith in a bout that police stopped with Ryan ahead. In 1898 he won the middleweight title and kept it for six years until retiring in 1904 with only three losses in 109 fights. Of his 86 wins, 68 were by knockout. Ryan was knocked out only once, by the legendary Kid McCoy, who made Ryan believe he was hurt but needed the purse money. Ryan obliged by carrying him for the whole fight but in the 15th, McCoy surprised Ryan, caught him off guard, and knocked him out. Hence, the phrase "The Real McCoy," which is what Ryan saw in the 15th round. As a middleweight, only Stanley Ketchel is ranked higher than Ryan, according to the Ring Encyclopedia. He died in 1948.

Gordie Howe

■ **GORDIE HOWE (1928)**, skated with the Detroit Red Wings for an NHL-record 26 years (1946-71), winning six scoring titles and six MVP awards; holds record for most career games, goals, and points; came out of retirement at age 45 with fledgling WHA and (flanked by his sons, Mark and Marty) led the Houston Aeros to the title while copping another MVP award–at age 46; he was 52 when he finally quit.

■ **Also born today:** golfer **TOMMY BOLT (1918)**, winner of the U.S. Open in 1958 ... bowling great **ANDY VARIPAPA (1894)**, born in Italy, made many bowling films ... **ED MARI-NARO (1950)**, running back from Cornell who set NCAA rushing records, after brief pro career turned to acting on TV (*Hill Street Blues*) ... oh yeah, another pretty good fighter, **JACK JOHNSON (1878)**, heavyweight champion, 1908-15.

NOTES

■ **PHIL NIEKRO (1939)** — The oldest player in the major leagues (whose knuckleball transcends time and bats).

Phil Niekro

After 20 years with the Braves (beginning in Milwaukee in 1964) and coming off a solid 11-10 season, Niekro was given his outright release by owner Ted Turner in a move forever enshrined in the Hall of Shame. Funny, George Steinbrenner was thrilled to pick him up for only $700,000 a year on a two-year contract. Turner looked a whole lot worse at year's end when Niekro finished with a 16-8 record and a 3.00 ERA. The stats say he was one of the five best pitchers in the AL that year. Watching him work is like watching Olivier do Hamlet. Phil has won about 300 games and his brother Joe (another knuckleballer who gets better as he gets older) has won about 200. They need 530 wins between them to break the record for most combined wins by two brothers, held by Gaylord and Jim Perry.

■ Also born today: **RUSTY STAUB (1944)**, power-hitting first baseman for the Mets, Expos, Astros and others; he and Ty Cobb are the only major leaguers to hit a home run before age 20 and after age 40 ... **BEAU JACK (1921)**, born Sidney Walker, two-time lightweight champion in early 1940s; went nearly blind, had no money left from purses, and worked for 20 years as shoeblack at the Fontainebleau Hotel in Miami; in '82 removal of cataracts partially restored vision ... **HUGO BEZDEK (1884)**, the only man to manage major league baseball (Pirates, 1917-19) and major college football (Penn State in the 1920s)... **RON PERRANOSKI (1936)**, ex-reliever and Dodgers pitching coach.

■**LUKE APPLING (1907)**— "Old Aches and Pains," born in High Point, N.C., Appling played his entire career as the White Sox shortstop (1930-50), finishing with a .310 lifetime BA. He won two batting titles — in 1936 (with an extraordinary .388 mark) and again in 1943 at age 36, one of the oldest players ever to win a batting title. A master of the strike zone, his specialty (hardly ever seen anymore) was fouling off pitches at will until he drew a walk. Appling made headlines last year at an Old Timers game when he hit one out.

Luke Appling

■**CARMEN BASILIO (1927)**— Boxing champion born in Canastota, N.Y., near Syracuse. He was a two-time welterweight champion during the 1955-57 period, losing the title to Johnny Saxton and regaining it in a rematch. Basilio moved up to middleweight and won the title by defeating the great Ray Robinson in a 15-round split decision. Six months later, in 1958, Sugar Ray took back his crown, beating Basilio in another grueling split decision. Basilio, a fierce body puncher, gave away a few inches in reach to Robinson and was more than five inches shorter. Basilio won 55 fights and lost 16 but was stopped only twice and never counted out.

■Also born today: **DON SUTTON (1945)** and **REGGIE SMITH (1945)**, both born the same day, same year, within 200 miles of each other, and played for the Dodgers together ... **ARNIE HERBER (1910)**, Packer QB of the 1930s, first of the great long passers ... figure skater **DON JACKSON (1940)**, one of only three to perform a triple lutz... **DICK RADATZ (1937)**, Bosox reliever in early 1960s, won 16 games in relief in 1964, more than any AL reliever ever, second only to Elroy Face ... auto racer **JACK BRABHAM (1926)**, born in Australia, Grand Prix winner in 1959, '60, and '66.

Sutton signed with A's in '85, shooting for 300 wins

NOTES

Stella Walsh

■ **STELLA WALSH (1911)**—Great track star born in Poland as Stanislawa Walasiewicz. She won a gold medal at the 1932 Olympics in the 100 meter dash, setting a world record with her time of 11.9 seconds, and won a silver medal in the 1936 Olympics. Her track career spanned four decades, as she continued her amazing career in senior competition. At age 44 she won the pentathlon in the National AAU senior track meet. Walsh emigrated to the U.S. as a child and lived most of her life in Cleveland where she was well-known for working with children. In 1980, Walsh, a bystander at a Cleveland robbery, was shot and killed. The autopsy revealed a shocking fact about this tremendous athlete. She was a man.

■ Also born today: goalie **BERNIE PARENT (1945)**, 12 years with the Philadelphia Flyers, shared Vezina Trophy with Tony Esposito in 1974 and twice won the Conn Smythe Trophy (MVP in playoffs), retired after '79 season because of eye injury ... 49ers tight end **RUSS FRANCIS (1953)**, Oregon U. grad who sat out senior year to protest the firing of his coach ... **WALLY MOON (1930)**, named after football coach Wallace Wade, Moon was 1954 rookie of the year for the Cardinals, split career with Dodgers (1959-65), becoming the first Los Angeles Dodger to hit .300 ... **JIM PARKER (1934)**, one of the all-time all-pros at offensive tackle and guard with the Colts of the late 1950s and '60s ... **LYLE ALZADO (1949)**, Raider defensive tackle, ex-Bronco, out of minuscule Yankton College in South Dakota (his high school coach had to alter his transcript to get him admitted) ... **MIKE PRUITT (1954)**, yet another football great, Pruitt (out of Purdue) has been an outstanding runner, blocker, and receiver for the Cleveland Browns

NOTES

■ **TRIS SPEAKER (1888)** — "The Grey Eagle" (also known as "Spoke"), immortal center fielder with the Indians, Red Sox, and others, born in Hubbard, Texas. Among outfielders, only Joe DiMaggio and Willie Mays challenge Speaker's combination of offensive and defensive brilliance. A .344 lifetime hitter (the fifth best mark for 20th century players), Speaker has the most career doubles (793), and hit more than .380 five times. As a center fielder, he holds the AL season record for most assists (35) and the major league record for career assists (449). He made two unassisted

Tris Speaker

double plays in one season and led the AL in putouts nine times. In 1923, at age 35, Speaker hit .380 with 17 homers and 130 RBI — and he was managing the club at the same time. He was Cleveland's manager from 1919 to 1926 and led them to their first pennant and World Series in 1920. The great Speaker died in 1958.

■ Also born today: **JOHN LANDY (1930)**, Australian miler, the second (six weeks after Roger Bannister) to break the four-minute mile (in 1954); in the "Miracle Mile" later that year Bannister nosed out Landy in a fabulous race in which both runners ran faster than four minutes ... **GIL HODGES (1924)**, Dodger first baseman from 1947 to 1961, hit 370 career homers with .273 lifetime BA; finished out career with Mets which he managed from 1963 to '71 and led them to their amazing 1969 pennant and World Series; like Tris Speaker, Hodges managed his team to their first pennant ever ... **BILL BRIDGES (1939)**, after playing basketball for most of his career with the St. Louis (and Atlanta) Hawks, he played his last season with the Warriors championship team of 1975 ... golfer **JOANNE CARNER (1939)**, five-time U.S. Amateur champ, twice won U.S. Open (1971, '76), in 1981 she became the all-time woman golfer money winner and broke the career million-dollar barrier.

NOTES

■ **GLENN "POP" WARNER (1871)** —Football legend. He coached briefly at Georgia and Cornell (his alma mater), then at Carlisle for 15 years, where he helped develop Jim Thorpe. He then coached at Pittsburgh (1915-24), Stanford (1925-32), and Temple (1933-38). It was his record of 312 career wins that was broken by Alabama's Bear Bryant. He is considered second only to Amos Alonzo Stagg as a football innovator. He invented the double wing formation and pioneered in using the single wing.

Pop Warner

An AP poll in 1954 rated him the best coach of all time. Only Stagg had a longer continuous coaching career than Warner's 46 years.

■ **BILL DINNEEN (1876)** — Born in Syracuse, New York. Dinneen pitched in the major leagues from 1898 to 1909, winning 171 games and losing 178 with a solid 3.01 ERA. In 1904, he set an American League record by pitching 37 straight complete games (or all the games he started), 337 consecutive innings without relief. It was an awesome feat of durability (he was 23-14 that year). A year earlier, in 1903, he was the pitching hero of the first World Series for the Red Sox. He started four games, completed all of them (and won three of them).

■ Also born today: **ALVIN "DOGGIE" JULIAN (1901)**, Hall of Fame basketball coach at Dartmouth, Holy Cross (winning the national title in 1947), and Boston Celtics ... **DWIGHT HICKS (1956)**, 49ers brilliant free safety ... **RENNIE STENNETT (1951)**, Pirates hard-hitting second baseman who hurt his ankle and then became Bob Lurie's $3 million albatross ... **HENRY "DUTCH" DEHNERT (1898)**, pioneer basketball player with the original Celtics, developed the pivot play, which led to the three-second rule.

NOTES

■ **MICKEY COCHRANE (1903)** —
Born in Bridgewater, Mass., Cochrane (born Gordon Stanley Cochrane) is considered by many to be the all-time all-star catcher. He played with the A's (1925-33) and Tigers (1934-37), compiling a .320 lifetime BA and twice winning the MVP award (in 1928 and 1934). He was player-manager for the Tigers, leading them to pennants in '34 and '35. His career ended after suffering a fractured skull when hit by a pitched ball in 1937. The great "Black Mike" died in 1962.

■ **ERNIE LOMBARDI (1908)** —
another great catcher born on this day. "Schnozz" Lombardi, Oakland-born, spent his career mostly with the Cincinnati Reds (1932-41) and N.Y. Giants (1943-47). Despite being a large man (6-feet-3, 230 pounds) and a slow runner, Lombardi was a .306 lifetime hitter and even won two batting titles (in 1938 and in 1942, the one year he spent

Ernie Lombardi

with the Boston Braves). Lombardi's absence from the Hall of Fame is conspicuous. If Rick Ferrell, recently inducted, rates inclusion, then certainly the great Lombardi does, too.

■ Also born today: **BERT BLYLEVEN (1951)**, this Holland-born righty is the best curveball pitcher in the majors ... figure skater **JANET LYNN (1953)** ... QB **JOHN HUARTE (1944)**, 1964 Heisman Trophy winner ... tennis player **ART LARSEN (1925).**

NOTES

John McGraw

■ JOHN J. McGRAW (1873) — "Little Napoleon," whom many consider the greatest manager of all time, born in Truxton, N.Y. A great third baseman , 1891 to 1906, with the Baltimore Orioles and others, he compiled a .334 lifetime BA. The feisty John J. managed the New York Giants from 1902 to 1932, winning 10 pennants, including four in a row (1921-24), the only NL manager to do so. He also won three World Series, including two in a row against the Yankees, in 1921 and 1922. McGraw is second only to Connie Mack in career games and wins. He died in 1934.

■ TONY DORSETT (1954) —Running back, won the Heisman Trophy in 1976 after breaking the NCAA rushing record at Pittsburgh — 6,082 yards in four years. The Cowboys pulled a real coup in dealing for him when he was drafted by Seattle. I can't remember what they gave the Seahawks, but, whatever it was, it was a steal. One of the greatest running backs ever to put on cleats, Dorsett has an excellent chance to break Jim Brown's rushing record (but not Walter Payton's).

■ Also born today: BENNY LEONARD (1896), lightweight champion, 1917-24; became ref and died in ring at age 51 ... WALTER CAMP (1859), football player, coach, pioneer, and author, called "The father of American football," coached A. A. Stagg, originated the "daily dozen" exercises, and the All-American teams.

NOTES

■ **JOHN HAVLICEK (1940)** —
The greatest swingman in NBA history, born in Martins Ferry, Ohio. An All-American at Ohio State (also a wide receiver who was a late cut by the Cleveland Browns), Havlicek was drafted by the Boston Celtics in 1962 and spent his entire career with that team, retiring in 1978. He is fifth in career points and held the all-time record for most games until Elvin Hayes broke it in 1984.

■ **JIM "CATFISH" HUNTER (1946)** —
This great right-hander with the A's (1965-74) and Yankees (1975-79) was the ace of the A's pitching staff that won three straight World Series in 1972, '73 and '74. Free agency destroyed the awesome A's as Hunter (after the '74 season) signed with the Yankees for a then-staggering $3.5 million contract. In 1968, while still a sub-.500 pitcher, Hunter threw a perfect game. He retired with 224 wins, 166 losses, and credentials for the Hall of Fame.

Catfish Hunter

■ **SONJA HENIE (1913)** — Born in Oslo, Norway, Henie put figure skating on an international level, winning gold medals in the 1928, '32 and '36 Olympics. Her ability and beauty led to a Hollywood career in light musicals, such as "Sun Valley Serenade" in 1941. She died of leukemia in 1969.

■ Also born today: The New York Mets' **GARY CARTER (1954)**, successor to Johnny Bench as best NL catcher ... Buffalo nose guard **FRED SMERLAS (1957)**.

NOTES

■**PAUL ROBESON (1898) —**
World-famous actor and singer, and less famous early football great, was born in Princeton, N.J. He attended nearby Rutgers University and was a tremendous end who made the All-American team in

1917 and '18. Robeson played with three professional teams in the early 1920s and was one of the early pro football stars. Robeson took a rare course for a black man of that time. He was well educated (earning a law degree) and became a star in dramatic roles (O'Neill's "The Emperor Jones") and musical ones (he was a sensation in "Show Boat") but he developed a strong social conscience trav-

Paul Robeson elling throughout the world on concert tours. In 1950 he was denied a passport by the U.S. government and lived abroad until the Supreme Court reversed the decision eight years later. A great man and a great athlete, Robeson died in 1976.

PAUL ARIZIN (1928) — High-scoring forward for home town Philadelphia Warriors (1950-52, 1954-62). Arizin played college ball at Villanova (yea, Wildcats) and broke in with an impressive 17.2 points per game as a rookie. In his next nine seasons (after which he retired) Arizin never finished with less than a 21-point average. One of the most consistent scorers of his era, his patented line-drive jumper was a deadly weapon.

■Also born today: **NATE COLBERT** (1946), Padre first baseman, co-holds (with Stan Musial) record for homers in a double-header (5) and owns outright the record for most RBI in a double-header (13)...**CURLY LAMBEAU** (1898), Green Bay Packers founder (in 1919), player (1921- 29), general manager (1919-49) and coach for an NFL record 29 straight years (1921-49) . . . golfer **SEVERIANO BALLESTEROS** (1957), winner of the British, French, Dutch, Swiss, German, Japanese, Spanish and Italian Opens ... **JIM "HIPPO" VAUGHN** (1888), Chicago Cubs right-hander (1913 to 1921) pitched in major league's only double no-hitter game. He finally gave up a run in the 10th (unearned), losing on a swinging bunt by the Reds' Jim Thorpe.

■ **CLARKE HINKLE (1912)** —
Hall of Fame fullback for the Green Bay Packers (1932-41). Born in Toronto, Hinkle went to Bucknell and entered the NFL as a 20-year-old rookie. Only 5-feet-11 and 200 pounds, he was a bruising runner who made tacklers pay. Hinkle helped Green Bay establish a dynasty in the late 1930s, winning NFL titles in 1936 and 1939. Hinkle fit perfectly with a team that featured a devastating passing attack with halfbacks Arnie Herber and Cecil Isbell throwing to Don Hutson. They did a lot of play-action and burned defenses for years. Hinkle, who led the league in scoring in 1938 and was All-Pro four times, was

Clarke Hinkle

also a linebacker and both a punter and placekicker. In his 10-year career his punting average was an impressive 43.4. Many considered him the greatest all-around fullback ever when he retired in 1941.

■ Also born today: **CHUCK CONNORS (1921)**, the actor ("Rifleman" on TV) who played two sports on a big-league level — baseball with the Chicago Cubs in 1951 and basketball with the Boston Celtics (1946-48) ... sportswriter **JIMMY CANNON (1910)**, New York City all the way — hard-boiled, sentimental, terse, often writing in the second person ("You're Bobo Newsome. You've toiled 20 summers for second-division clubs and never looked back") ... **CLIFF BLANKENSHIP (1880)**, appeared in only 95 games as a catcher with the Reds and Senators in the early 1900s, but whose claim to fame was discovering and signing the great Walter Johnson.... **DON MEREDITH (1938)**, "Dandy Don," Dallas Cowboys quarterback, 1960 - 1969, then sports personality on the tube on Monday Night Football ... **ROSS YOUNGS (1897)**, Hall of Fame outfielder with the NY Giants had a .322 lifetime BA. His manager, John J. McGraw, called him the greatest outfielder he had ever seen. Youngs died in his prime of Bright's Disease. He was 30.... **JOHN MADDEN (1936)**, ex- Raider coach, 1969-78, and a hot TV commentator ... ex Steeler cornerback **MEL BLOUNT (1948)** ... bowler **MARK ROTH (1951)** ... **KEN GRIFFEY (1950)**, Yankee OF-1B, born in Donora, Pa., birthplace of Stan the Man.

NOTES

■ **DANNY FORTMANN (1916) —**
Hall of Fame lineman with the Chicago Bears (1936-43) who later became a prominent physician. Born in Pearl River, New York, he was a brilliant student at Colgate who graduated at age 19. In fact, George Halas, owner and coach of the Bears, was shocked that he had drafted anyone so young — in the first-ever NFL draft. And he was a rather small lineman even in that era. He was just 6 feet tall and never weighed more than 210 pounds. Everything was against Fortmann making it — except his exceptional ability. He played guard next to tackle Joe Stydahar and formed an awesome right side of the line. On defense he was a cat, very smart and a deadly tackler. All-Pro for six straight years, he played on three championship teams — in 1940, 1941 and 1943. He retired in his prime at age 27 and had already finished medical school.

Sam Chapman

With Halas' consent, he'd pursued both careers. After retirement, Fortmann moved to California, becoming chief of staff at St. Joseph's Hospital in Burbank.

■ **SAM CHAPMAN (1916)**, Philadelphia A's outfielder from 1938 to 1951 except for four lost years serving in WW II. After sterling baseball and football careers at Cal, he became a lifetime .266 hitter in the pros who averaged almost 20 homers a year. Born in and still living in Tiburon, Calif., he works as an inspector for the Bay Area Air Quality District.

■ **BARNEY McCOSKY (1918)**, another American League outfielder of the 1940s, mostly with the Tigers and A's, who also lost four crucial years to WW II, lefty swinger with .312 lifetime BA ... **JIM HEARN (1921)**, righty pitcher with Cardinals and N.Y. Giants who went 17-9 in '51 when Giants won pennant; bought a golf center in Atlanta.

Joe Lapchick

■ **JOE LAPCHICK (1900)** — Hall of Fame basketball player and coach, born Yonkers, N.Y. Lapchick was the first star center, and began playing for money as a 14-year-old. He was the center on the Original Celtics, the first great pro team, from 1922 to 1935, except for two years. After a 20-year playing career as a pro, he retired and began his distinguished career as a coach — at St. John's (1936-48, 1956-65), winning four NIT championships and two Coach-of-the-Year awards, and with the New York Knicks (1948-56). Lapchick died in 1970.

■ **ADDIE JOSS (1880)** — Tremendous righty pitcher for the Cleveland Indians (1902-10), born in Juneau, Wis. He won 160 games, lost 97, and is second in career ERA — a sizzling 1.88. He pitched a perfect game in 1908 and another no-hitter in 1910. He started 261 games and completed 235. While still pitching with Cleveland, he was stricken with meningitis and died two days after his 31st birthday.

■ Also born today: **CHARLIE LAU (1933)**, popular and effective batting coach, hitting mentor of George Brett, died in 1984 . . . **MIKE GARRETT (1944)**, ex-USC (Heisman Trophy, 1965) and K.C. Chiefs running back . . . lefty **JOHNNY ANTONELLI (1930)**, who pitched Giants to '54 pennant (with a win and a save in the four-game sweep of the Indians in the Series) . . . heavyweight **BILLY MISKE (1894)**, fought Dempsey for title in 1920, losing in three-round KO, one of only two losses in 47 decisions; died of Bright's Disease at age 29 . . . **VIC WILLIS (1876)**, another righty pitcher, like Joss, who has credentials for the Hall of Fame: a 248-206 won-loss record, eight 20-game seasons, and the NL record for pitching 45 complete games (in 46 starts) for Boston in 1902.

NOTES

■ **JOSE NAPOLES (1940)** — Welterwt champ (1969-70, 71-75). One of many outstanding Cuban welters, Napoles had one of the longest reigns in the history of the division. He won the title in 1969, defeating Curtis Cokes in a 13-round KO. He lost it for six months to Billy Backus before regaining it in a re-match, and kept it for four more years until he was TKO'd by Britisher John Stracey in 1975 and retired — after his 15th title defense. Earlier, he tried to go up in weight and fight Carlos Monzon for his middleweight title, but lost via a seventh-round TKO. He won 76 fights (54 by KO) and lost eight.

Jose Napoles

■ **CHARLIE SWEENEY (1863)** — S.F.-born righty pitcher of 1880s, won 41 games in 1884 and was considered one of the fastest pitchers in pro baseball. Quick-tempered, he suddenly quit baseball at age 24 in a dispute over being taken out of a game for a reliever. He later committed murder and spent his remaining years in San Quentin, where he died at age 38.

■ Also born today: Three Olympic medalists — **HAROLD OSBORN (1899)**, who became in 1924 the first Olympic athlete to win the decathlon and an individual event, the high jump; **EDWARD HAMM (1906)**, who won long jump in 1928, and **BILLY KIDD (1943)**, skier and TV commentator who won silver in slalom at '64 Olympics, losing by .14 of a second ... **JIM "BAD NEWS" BARNES (1941)**, a 6-foot-8 forward from Texas Western (now UTEP) who had a seven-year NBA career playing with six teams, notably his rookie year with the Knicks in 1964-65.

NOTES

■ **PETE ROSE (1941)** —

Pete Rose

The premier hitmaster in major league history, soon to break Ty Cobb's career mark of 4,191 hits and then the record will be his forever. Will someone ever again dedicate himself that completely to playing baseball? That same person would have to do better than get 200 hits a year for 20 years, would have to avoid injury or play hurt, and he would have to sacrifice a lot. For instance, he would (like Rose) never go to the movies because it might adversely affect his batting eye. As a player-manager, Rose needs to juggle his personal goals and his team's goals. including vows that the Reds will not finish in the cellar. Rose was born in Cincinnati, achieved his greatest glory in Cincinnati and returned home to a perfect situation for him. He deserved it. He is the only player to have 10 seasons of 200 hits or more. (And he had a couple of 198s in there, too). He has the most hits for a switch-hitter. He was Rookie-of-the-Year in 1963, MVP in 1973, won three batting titles, tied the NL record for hitting safely in 44 straight games, and had a stretch of 14 out of 15 seasons of hitting .300 or better.

■ Also born today: **JOE KUHARICH (1917)**, football coach at USF (including the immortal 1951 team), then in the NFL with the Eagles and Redskins ... **VALERIE BRUMEL (1942)**, Soviet high-jumper who broke world record (7-foot-4½) at age 18, won gold medal at 1964 Olympics, climaxing career that ended the following year when a motorcycle injury crushed his right leg. He never jumped again ... **DON MUELLER (1927)**, N.Y. Giants outfielder (1948-57) with lifetime .296 BA, hardly ever struck out, "Mandrake" was fine batsman who hit .342 in 1954 but finished second to teammate Willie Mays for batting title ... **HARRY GILMER (1926)**, one of the first in a succession of great Alabama quarterbacks (Bart Starr, Ken Stabler, Joe Namath), he played in the NFL with the 'Skins and the Lions.... legendary Spanish bullfighter and breeder **JUAN BELMONTE (1892)** ... **KEN LOEFFLER (1902)**, basketball coach at LaSalle (1949-55), winning 1954 NCAA title with Tom Gola & Co ... sprinter **EVELYN ASHFORD (1957)**.

NOTES

■ **WALT HAZZARD (1942)** — UCLA basketball coach and former court star of the UCLA teams of 1962-64 that won the national title in '64, the first of John Wooden's 10 NCAA crowns, Hazzard had a solid nine-year

NBA career, mostly with the Lakers and Hawks, playing under his former Muslim name Mahdi Abdul-Rahman. A little over a year ago, Hazzard succeeded Larry Farmer, who had resigned. UCLA basketball was in a funk. In one year, Hazzard has brought them back to respectability — and more. Like Villanova, UCLA bloomed late. A fifth-place team in the weak Pac-10, UCLA finally got it together in the last couple of weeks and won the NIT (its

Walt Hazzard

first-ever appearance in the tournament) with brilliant ball-handling, quickness and a severe man-to-man defense. When it was all over, UCLA was one of the top 10 teams in the country. I guess that makes Hazzard a genius.

■ **JAMES J. JEFFRIES (1875)** — Heavyweight champion (1899-1905), born in Carroll, Ohio. He won the title by beating the great Bob Fitzsimmons via an 11th-round KO and retired as champion because of lack of opposition. The 6-2½, 220-pounder was a hard hitter and could take a punch. Jeffries had only 21 fights in his career, winning 18 (15 by KO), drawing two and losing only once, six years after retiring. Offered a big purse, Jeffries was persuaded to return to the ring as a "white hope" to defeat the champion, Jack Johnson. Jeffries was game but the referee stopped the fight and he never fought again. He died in 1953.

■ Also born today: ex-49er and Raider tight end **TED KWALICK (1947)** ... ex-Bucks and Bullets forward **BOB DANDRIDGE (1947)** ... ex-Reds and Giants catcher **ED BAILEY (1931)**, hit 17 HRs (in only 254 at-bats) when Giants won the pennant in '62.

NOTES

■**KAREEM ABDUL-JABBAR (1947) —**
Greatest scorer in NBA history and NBA's oldest active

player, still one of the best. He averages 20 points a game, his skyhook is still unstoppable, and his passing is still sharp. The other great centers (Wilt, Russell, Malone, Walton) all had one predominant aspect to their game; Kareem is unique in his all-around ability and his durability. When Wilt was Kareem's age, he was a defensive specialist. It's unheard of for a 38-year-old center to score 20 points a game — as the NBA's oldest player! That's where Kareem's got it over all of them.

Kareem Abdul-Jabbar

The winner of six MVP awards, Kareem passed Chamberlain (they're the only two with more than 30,000 points) and is putting his record out of reach, at least in this century. Kareem has also been a team leader, a spokesman on social issues, and a significant model of dignity for a generation of athletes. (Born Lew Alcindor in New York City,)

■Also born today: **RICHARD "NIGHT TRAIN" LANE (1928)**, Hall of Fame defensive back mostly with the Chicago Cardinals (1954-59) and Detroit Lions (1960-65), third in interceptions (68), second in interception return yardage, holds record for most interceptions (14) in a season (despite playing in only 12-game season); married singer Dinah Washington . . . **PAUL WANER (1903)**, Hall of Fame outfielder for the Pirates (1926-40), won three batting titles and had .333 lifetime BA; known as "Big Poison" while his kid brother Lloyd Waner (also Hall of Famer and Pirate teammate) was called "Little Poison" . . . **SANDY HAWLEY (1949)**, the youngest jockey to win 3,000 races and the first to win 4,000 races in only 12 years . . . **JIM LONBORG (1943)**, won Cy Young Award as Bosox right-hander in 1967, leading AL in wins (22) and strikeouts (246), won two Series games that year though Cardinals won in seven games.

NOTES

■ **ALEXANDER JOY CARTWRIGHT (1820)** — The man who, more than anyone else (especially Abner Doubleday), was "The Father of Modern Baseball," born in NYC.

He organized the first baseball team (the Knickerbocker Ball Club of New York), drew up baseball's first rules, and umpired the first game (June 19, 1846). They called what he invented the "New York" game. In 1850, Cartwright trekked out to California on horseback and on foot, teaching baseball to frontiersmen and Indians along the way — a veritable preacher of the gospel Cartwright intended to sail back to New York (by way of China) but became sick in the Pacific and was put ashore on Hawaii. He liked it there (no kidding) and settled in Honolulu where he became fire chief and taught baseball to the Polynesians, setting up leagues and making a lot of money doing it. He died in Honolulu in 1892.

Alexander Cartwright

■ **Also** born today: **ADRIAN "CAP" ANSON (1851)**, baseball's first superstar, Chisox first baseman (1876-97) and manager for most of that time, hit .300 or more for 20 seasons and had lifetime .333 average. He was also a racist who did much to keep blacks out of baseball ... **KEVIN PORTER (1950)**, former guard and great assist-man with Pistons and Bullets, holds NBA's record for assists in a single game ... **DELVIN WILLIAMS (1951)**, ex-49er and Dolphin running back ... **F. MORGAN TAYLOR (1903)**, won 400 meter hurdles at 1924 Olympics and won bronze medals at the 1928 and 1932 Olympics.

... defensive end **LAMAR LUNDY (1935)**, one of the L.A. Rams "Fearsome Foursome" of the 1960s ... first baseman **JAKE DAUBERT (1884)**, .303 hitter with the Dodgers and Reds, died at age 40 while still active.

NOTES

■**ERIC WRIGHT (1959) —**
This 49er cornerback is one of the best in the NFL in man-to-man pass coverage. Born in St. Louis, Mo., he played college ball at Missouri, where he was All-American. Wright was the 40th player chosen in that unbelievable 1981 draft in which the Niners also picked up Ronnie Lott and Carlton Williamson and (with the acquisition of Dwight Hicks) formed a defensive secondary that is second to none in NFL history. Wright is a thoroughbred. He can go man-to-man with the best receivers in the league and makes open-field tackles like a free safety (which he played in college). Curiously, he is still not

Eric Wright

as well-known as he should be outside of the West Coast. Before he hangs 'em up, Wright will go down as one of the all-time best.

■Also born today: **SAM CRAWFORD (1880)**, "Wahoo Sam" was an outfielder (1899-1917) mostly with the Detroit Tigers, owns two major league records: most career triples (312) and most inside-the-park home runs (51) ... **NATE "THE SKATE" ARCHIBALD (1948)**, guard with the Kings, Celtics, etc., In the 1972-73 season, he became the first player to lead the NBA in scoring (34 points per game) and assists (910) ... German auto racer **JOCHEN RINDT (1942)** ... ex-Pittsburgh Pirate pitcher **STEVE BLASS (1942)**, who had great years in 1971 and '72, then tubed out inexplicably ...
GEORGE "DUFFY" LEWIS (1888), S.F.-born outfielder (1910-1921) mostly with the Red Sox; one-third of the noted outfield which included Tris Speaker and Harry Hooper.

NOTES

■ BUCKY WALTERS (1909) —

A third baseman converted into one of the best righty pitchers in Cincinnati Reds history, born William Henry Walters in Philadelphia. He came up with the Braves in 1931 as a third baseman and didn't start pitching until

Bucky Walters

1935 with the Phillies. He was traded to the Reds in 1938 and had his best years with them. The year after he was traded, Walters won the MVP award with a 27-11 record, leading the league in every major department and leading the Reds to only their second pennant. The next year, 1940, the Reds won their second straight pennant as Walters led the league in wins. ERA, complete games, innings and was the pitching star in the World Series, winning two

clutch games. The Reds beat the Tigers in seven games. Outside of 1919, when the White Sox threw the World Series to the Reds, their 1940 victory was their first untainted championship (and their last one for 35 years). Walters, who hit grand slam homers in both leagues, had the distinction of beating the Dodgers in the first televised major league games (in 1939). Walters finished with a 198-160 won-loss record, including 42 shutouts. He briefly managed the Reds (1948-49) and later was a pitching coach with the Braves and Giants.

■ Also born today: **MARK VAN EEGHEN (1952)**, leading rusher in Raider history, played college ball at Colgate and succeeded Marv Hubbard, who also played college ball at Colgate ... **GEORGE "WHITEY" KUROWSKI (1918)**, St. Louis Cardinal third baseman of the '40s hit 106 homers in only six and a half seasons, .286 lifetime hitter ... **ADOLPH "GERMANY" SCHULTZ (1883)**, lineman on Fielding Yost's "point-a-minute" teams of 1901-1904 — four straight undefeated seasons. He missed only 10 minutes in those four years...   and two football players and coaches: **ALEX WEBSTER (1931)**, fullback with N.Y. Giants, coached Giants in ealy 1970s and **JACK PARDEE (1936)**, linebacker with the Rams and 'Skins (1957-72), coached the Bears, the 'Skins, and USFL. _Alexis Arguello_ (1952), boxer, three world titles.

NOTES

■ **DAVE "BEAUTY" BANCROFT (1892)** —Hall of Fame shortstop with the Phillies, N.Y. Giants, Boston Braves and Brooklyn Dodgers, born in Sioux City, Iowa. Bancroft,

Dave Bancroft

a switch-hitter, came up with the Phillies in 1915, was dealt to the Giants in 1920. He played on the great 1921-23 teams that won three straight pennants and two World Series, batted .300 or better all three years. In 1920, he went 6-for-6 in one game (all singles). After the 1923 season was traded (along with Casey Stengel) to the Braves, which he also managed (1924-27) while twice hitting over .300. Bancroft retired in 1930 with a .279 lifetime batting average. He was named to the Hall of Fame in 1971 and died a year later.

■ **ERNIE STAUTNER (1925)** — Hall of Fame defensive tackle. Born in Calm, Bavaria, played college ball at Boston College and was drafted by the Steelers. For 14 years (1950-63), Stautner was the heart of the Steeler defense. Known for his mobility and desire, he played most of his career in obscurity although his nine Pro Bowl appearances indicate his peers knew him well. Stautner then became defensive line coach for the Dallas Cowboys for many years.

■ Also born today: righty **MILT WILCOX (1950)**, breaking-ball pitcher with the Detroit Tigers since 1977 ... **ROBERT BYRNE (1928)**, U.S. chess champ in 1960 and long-time chess columnist for the N.Y. Times ... **BETTY CUTHBERT (1938)**, Australian sprinter who won gold medals in the 100- and 200-meter dashes in 1956 Olympics and eight years later won a gold medal in the 400 meters in the 1964 Olympics ... **HARRY AGGANIS (1930)**, "The Golden Greek" All-American quarterback from Boston University, then Red Sox first baseman until stricken with pneumonia and dying unexpectedly at age 25.

NOTES

■ ROCKY KANSAS (1895) —

Lightweight champion (1925-26), was born Rocco Tozzo in Buffalo, New York. He is yet another "Rocky" whose name derives from Rocco and not from punching prowess (though all "Rockys" were punchers). Kansas began his pro career at age 16, but did not become champion until he was 30. Twice he challenged the great Benny Leonard for his lightweight title and lost both times. After Leonard vacated the title, Kansas won it. However, in his first

Joe McCarthy

defense six months later, he lost it to Sammy Mandell. Kansas then retired. Only 5'2", he was a two-fisted hitter who won by KO in half of his 64 victories.

■ JOE McCARTHY (1887) —

Percentage-wise the best all time major league manager, born in Philadelphia. After a 17-year career strictly in the minor leagues, managed the Cubs (1926-30, 1929 pennant), the N.Y. Yankees (1931-46), winning eight pennants and seven World Series; and the Boston Red Sox (1948-50), finishing second twice. He was the first manager to win pennants in both leagues. In 24 years of managing, McCarthy never finished in the second division — a unique achievement. "Marse Joe" died in 1978 at age 90.

■ Also born today: **STEVE OWEN (1898)**, N.Y. Giants football coach (1931-53), who won eight division titles and two NFL titles (in 1934 and '38); originated the A formation (similar to the shotgun) and the umbrella defense, which led to the 4-3-4 defense ... **AL BUMBRY (1947)**, veteran Orioles outfielder released by the O's in 1984 ... bowler **WILLIAM KNOX (1887)**, bowled the first 300 game in ABC tournament history... **DICK GREEN (1941)** A's second baseman from 1964 to 1975 ... swimmer **RICK DEMONT (1956)**, won first place in the 400 meter freestyle at the '76 Olympics but was disqualified for using a prohibited drug.

■ **SPENCER HAYWOOD (1949)** —
The enfant terrible of the ABA and NBA   Born in
Silver City, Mississippi, Haywood
attended the University of Detroit where, as a 19-year-old
freshman, he was selected to
the US Olympic team (the
youngest player on the squad).
a year later he became the first
"hardship case" in pro basketball history, playing for Denver
in the ABA, at once the youngest player in the pros and the
league's MVP. One year later, in
1970, Haywood jumped to the
NBA, the first player to enter
that league before his college

Spencer Haywood

class graduated. He was a tremendous scorer with
Seattle (29.2 average in '72-'73), later playing with the
Knicks, New Orleans Jazz, Lakers, and Bullets.
Haywood's effectiveness as a player (and person)
declined after Seattle because of injuries, misunder-
standings with management, and a rapacious press.
He retired in 1982, his brilliance as a player a dim
memory. He really was a hardship case — but only a
few could appreciate it.

■ **MICKEY VERNON (1918)** —
Born James Barton Vernon in Marcus Hook, Pa. His
20-year career, mostly with the Washington Senators,
ended with a .286 lifetime BA and two batting titles,
one in 1946 and again in 1953, becoming, at age 35,
one of the oldest players to win a batting title (tied
with, among others, Al Oliver). Another claim to fame
for this first baseman — he is one of seven whose
career spanned four decades (1939-1960).

■ Also born today: **NEAL BALL (1881)**, Cleveland
shortstop who, in 1909, made the first unassisted
triple-play in major league history ... boxer **JOHNNY
DUNDEE (1893)**, Italian-born featherweight champ,
1923-25 ... S.F.'s own **PHIL SMITH (1952)**, hoop star
at George Washington HS, USF, and Warriors ...
ex-Steeler DT **DWIGHT WHITE (1949)**.

NOTES

■**WARREN SPAHN (1921)** — The winningest (363) left-hand pitcher in ML history, born in Buffalo, N.Y.

Warren Spahn

Only Cy Young, Walter Johnson, Christy Mathewson and Grover Alexander won more games — all of them from a much earlier era. No modern era pitcher is within 40 wins of Spahn. He won 20 games or more 12 times, including a league-leading 21 wins in 1961 at age 40 and a 23-7 record, the best percentage of his career, at age 42. He pitched two no-hitters after age 39 — a doubly unbelievable feat. He led the NL in complete games every year from age 36 to age 42. Like most good pitchers, Spahn was a good hitter. In fact, one of the , with 35 career homers. He later actively ran his 2,800-acre ranch in Oklahoma for many years.

■**BUD WILKINSON (1916)** — Great college football coach, born in Minneapolis, Minnesota. He started coaching at Oklahoma in 1947 and retired with a record of 145 wins, 29 losses, and four ties. He won three national titles (1950, 1955, 1956), had four undefeated teams, and had two tremendous winning streaks — one of 31 games (1948-51) and one of 47 games (1953-57), the longest in modern football history. After two decades of retirement, except as a TV sports announcer, he became coach of the St. Louis Cardinals for two losing seasons (1978-79).

■**"SUNNY JIM" BOTTOMLEY (1900)** — Hall of Fame first baseman with the St. Louis Cardinals and others from 1922 to 1937, born in Oglesby, Ill. A lefty all the way, he was a lifetime .310 hitter with power who rarely struck out. He was the MVP in 1928, leading the league in homers, triples, RBI, and hit .325. Though Sunny Jim's career was brilliant, one day (Sept. 16, 1924) stands out. He was 6-for-6 in a nine-inning game (a rarity), and also set a major league record that still stands — 12 RBI in a single game. He died in 1959.

■Also born today: **GAIL GOODRICH (1943)**, the NBA's 12th all-time scorer, with the Suns and Lakers ... **TONY ESPOSITO (1944)**, great NHL goalie, played into his 40s, brother of Phil Esposito ... S.F. native **DOLF CAMILLI (1907)**, 1941 MVP with Dodgers.

NOTES

■ **CARROLL DALE (1938)** — Brilliant ex-Packer receiver. Born in Wise, W. Va., Dale played college ball at VPI and was drafted by the Rams in 1960. After five years of sub-.500 seasons, the Rams dealt him to the Green Bay Packers in 1965. Dale got very little ink for playing an important role in Lombardi's dynasty. He shared the spotlight with two other fine receivers — Max McGee and Boyd Dowler. His 438 receptions is 15th on the all-time list, and he's seventh in total yardage and 11th in yards per catch with a dynamic 18.9 average.

Carroll Dale

■ **AUGUST "MIKE" MICHALSKE (1903)** — Another NFL star (a Hall of Famer, in fact) who also played for the Packers. He was born in Cleveland, Oh. All-American at Penn State, he played mostly for the Green Bay Packers in an 11-year career in which he played almost every game and suffered only one injury. He was a pioneer who began the idea of converting fullbacks to guards in the pros. Michalske and teammate Cal Hubbard were the first to use what are now known as stunts, criss-crossing their rush and coming at the QB from unexpected angles. Michalske helped Green Bay win four NFL titles and was paid even more than quarterback Arnie Herber, who received most of the publicity.

■ Also born today: **HOWARD EHMKE (1894)** right-handed pitcher with Tigers, Red Sox and A's from 1916 to 1930, finished with a 167-166 career won-loss record. Connie Mack's A's won the 1929 pennant and he shocked the baseball world by naming Ehmke to pitch game one of the Series against the hard-hitting Cubs. He responded by pitching a 3-1 complete game while striking out 13 batters, a World Series record at that time. Ehmke pitched only 13 more innings in his major league career. He died in 1959 ... Canadian sportsman **MIKE RODDEN (1891)**, the first person inducted into both the Hockey Hall of Fame and the Canadian Football Hall of Fame... **BILL SINGER (1944)**, one of only a few pitchers to win 20 games in each league — with the Dodgers in '69 and the Angels in '71.

NOTES

■ **JOHN HENRY "POP" LLOYD (1884)** —
Born in Palatka, Florida , Lloyd was one of the first giants of black baseball. Known as the "Black Wagner" (Honus, that is), he was a tremendous shortstop and left-handed hitter. In fact, Wagner himself said he was honored to have Lloyd called the "Black Wagner" and that it was "a privilege to have been compared with him." He played for (and managed

Meadowlark Lemon

— even in his early 20s) such early teams as the New York Lincoln Giants.

■ **MEADOWLARK LEMON (1932)** — Another great black athlete who never played in white leagues was born Meadow George Lemon III. He was a long-time star with the Harlem Globetrotters, from the 1950s to the '70s and became world-famous for his comic basketball virtuosity. He, Goose Tatum and Marques Haynes are the Big Three in the 'Trotter pantheon.

■ **FRED HANEY (1898)** —
Born in Albuquerque, N.M., he had a 7-year AL career as a third-baseman (nicknamed "Pudge") during the 1920s, but made his name three decades later as manager of the awesome Milwaukee Braves, winning pennants in '57 and '58. He almost had four pennants in a row, losing to the Dodgers in '56 by a game and to the Dodgers again in '59 in a playoff. Haney made the rare transition from manager to general manager of the Braves in the 1960s. He died in 1977.

■ Also born today: 49er guard **RANDY CROSS (1954)** ... pole vaulter **BOB GUTOWSKI (1935)**, bronze medal at '56 Olympics ... hockey player **STEVE SHUTT (1953)**, with Montreal Canadiens ... two golfers: **JERRY BARBER (1916)** and Scotsman **FRED MCLEOD (1882)**.

NOTES

Hack Wilson

■ **HACK WILSON (1900)** – Born in Elwood City, Pa., a slugging outfielder with the Cubs, 1926 to 1931. His 190 RBI in 1930 is still the major league record. After a half century, the record seems secure. No one has even approached that figure since before World War II. In that same year, Wilson hit 56 homers, still a National League record. Wilson, a lifetime .307 hitter, was 5'6" and weighed 190 pounds. Get the idea? He wore a 5½ shoe and an 18 inch collar. Wilson was an alcoholic and died broke in 1948, saved from a pauper's grave by a $350 grant from the National League office.

■ Also born today: pitcher **SAL MAGLIE (1917)**, "The Barber," led Giants to pennant in 1951 with a 23-6 record (and how many pitchers have pitched for the Giants, Yankees, and Dodgers while all of them were in NY?) ... **EDWARD EAGAN (1898)**, the only man to win gold medals in both the summer (Lt - heavyweight boxing champ 1920) and winter (member of bobsled team in 1932) Olympics ... **BERNARD MALAMUD (1914)**, whose 1952 novel, The Natural, was filmed – with Robert Redford (who was a for-real ballplayer) ... **NINO BENVENUTI (1938)**, junior middleweight champ (1966-67) and middleweight champion (1967-70), beat Emile Griffith for title in '67 , lost it in '70 to Carlos Monzon; in 90 fights, the Italian-born Benvenuti lost only 7 times ... **FANNY BLANKERS-KOEN (1918)**, in '48 Olympics she won 100 meters, 200 meters, 80-meter hurdles and 400-meter relay: four gold medals, the most won by a woman in track and field in one Olympics.

NOTES

Rogers Hornsby

■ **ROGERS HORNSBY (1896)** — The greatest second baseman in history was born in Winters, Texas. He spent most of his 23-year career with the Cardinals (1915-26) and finished with a .358 lifetime BA, second best after Cobb's .367. He won seven batting titles, six in a row (1920-25), and three times hit more than .400, including the modern record of .424. Hornsby has 2nd most career homers (302) for a second baseman and is generally considered the greatest right-hand hitter of all time. He had a unique batting stance — feet together and as far back and away from the plate as the batter's box would allow. He managed 13 years with five teams, winning a pennant with the Cards in 1926 and beating the Yankees in the World Series. He died in 1963.

■ **GEORGE GERVIN (1952)** — The high-scoring guard for the San Antonio Spurs. Born in Detroit, he played at Eastern Michigan but was expelled for fighting and went with the ABA Virginia Squires in 1972. Since 1974, he has been with the Spurs. He came into the pros as a forward but switched to guard and, at 6'8", is almost impossible to stop. Known as "The Iceman", he has won three scoring titles and, though a bit elderly by NBA standards, is still a scoring machine.

■ Also born today: **HORACE STONEHAM (1903)**, ex-owner of Giants for decades — on both coasts ... **ENOS SLAUGHTER (1916)**, one of the hustlingest baseball players ever; Cardinal outfielder and later pinch-hitter with Yankees, made the Hall of Fame in 1984, best known for scoring decisive run from first on single to left in 1946 World Series; "Country" never stopped running (right through the third-base coach's sign to hold up) as Red Sox shortstop Johnny Pesky hesitated on throw in ... **CHUCK KNOX (1932)**, has great record as head coach, making winners out of the Rams, Bills and Seattle Seahawks ... **EARL ANTHONY (1938)**, Bowler-of-the-Year in 1974, 1975 and 1976.

NOTES

■**CHARLIE MAXWELL (1927)** — Hard-hitting outfielder with the Detroit Tigers and three other teams, 1950 to 1964. Known as "Smokey" (also "Paw Paw", after the town he grew up in) Maxwell was a lefty power-hitter (who looked a lot like ex-Yankee outfielder Charlie Keller, right down to hairy forearms) who had good years with the Tigers. In 1956 he hit .326 with 28 homers. In '59 he had his best numbers — 31 homers and 95 RBI. That year Maxwell hit home runs in four consecutive at bats in a doubleheader, the last at-bat in the first game and the first three at-bats in the second game. In 1951, playing with the

Charlie Maxwell

Red Sox, he hit three pinch-hit homers, all off future Hall of Famers — Satchel Paige, Bob Feller and Bob Lemon. Maxwell retired with a .264 batting average, later became sales manager for a die-casting company right in good old Paw Paw, Michigan.

■Also born today: **TONY PETERS (1953)**, Washington Redskins defensive back who was arrested on drug charges and, although receiving only a suspended sentence from the courts, wasn't allowed to play during the 1984 season ... **FLYNN ROBINSON (1941)**, high-scoring collegian with Wyoming basketball teams in the early '60s, had good years with the Milwaukee Bucks in 1968 and '69, then was traded to the Cincinnati Royals in a deal that sent Oscar Robertson to the Bucks (and an NBA title) and Robinson to obscurity ... **TOM STURDIVANT (1930)**, pitcher with the Yankees (and six other teams) went 16-8 in '56 and 16-6 in '57, leading the league in winning percentage ... **PEDRO "PETE" RAMOS (1935)**, Cuban-born righty with the Washington Senators and others from 1955 to 1970; led AL in losses four years in a row (1958-61); Ramos once owned a cigar manufacturing company in Cuba. He received a three-year jail sentence in 1979 for cocaine possession. ... righty pitcher **RED LUCAS (1902)**, pitched with Cincinnati Reds (1926-33) and Pirates (1934-38), winning 157 games; nicknamed "The Nashville Narcissus".

■ **JOHNNY MILLER (1947)** — Mid-1970s golf star. A San Francisco native, Miller won the U.S. Junior Championship as a 17-year-old in 1964. He won 20

world-wide tournaments from 1971 to 1976, including the U.S. Open in 1973 (clinching it with a 63 in the final round). In 1974, he was golf's biggest money winner, copping eight major tournament wins. Miller's game went drastically downhill in the late '70s, supposedly because he began spending more time with his family. In 1978 he was 111th on the list of money winners. His form returned in 1981 and in '82 he scored the biggest individual win on record —

Johnny Miller

$500,000, defeating Seve Ballesteros in a nine-hole playoff. Miller is a protege of Billy Casper. They're both Mormons.

■ Also born today: **EMIL "DUTCH" LEVSEN (1898)**, righty pitcher with Cleveland for his whole six-year big-league career, he was the last to pitch two complete-game wins in a double-header (in 1926, his best year, he went 16-13); not to be confused with Emil "Dutch" Leonard (another — and better — righty pitcher), nor with lefty pitcher Hubert "Dutch" Leonard ... **GEORGE ALLEN (1922)**, football coach of the NFL Rams and Redskins, the CFL Montreal Alouettes, and the USFL Arizona Wranglers ... **JIM RYUN (1947)**, born on the same day and year as Johnny Miller, Ryun was the greatest schoolboy runner in history and the best middle-distance runner ever ... **LUIS APARICIO (1934)**, "Little Looie", born in Venezuela. Considered the best defensive shortstop of his era (1956-73), he led the American League in fielding percentage for eight straight years, and also led the league in stealing a record nine times — in his first nine seasons! Aparicio was a steady, durable performer, one of a handful to play in over 10,000 games.

NOTES

■ ISIAH THOMAS (1961) —Great Detroit Pistons guard. Thomas was born in Chicago and led Indiana to the NCAA title as a junior. He then went hardship and was the second player chosen in the draft. This rather small and very young court general not only "made it in the pros" but became an instant star with immediate impact on the league. In 1985, Thomas broke Kevin Porter's record for most assists in a season. Thomas is the happening guard in the league. Thomas' all-around floor game is impeccable. He can penetrate or stop-'n'-pop, he runs the offense with a cool hand, and his passing is second to none. He deserves to play on a winner.

Isiah Thomas

■ FIELDING "HURRY UP" YOST (1871) — Born in Fairview, W. Va. He coached innovative football at Michigan from 1901 to 1928, had eight unbeaten teams, including the "point-a-minute" teams of 1901 to 1904, juggernauts that won 55 games in a row before an epic 2-0 loss to A. A. Stagg's University of Chicago team in 1905. His Michigan team played Stanford in the first Rose Bowl in 1902, winning 49-0 and gaining almost 1,500 yards rushing. He was the first to use the tailback formation and the run-pass option, and he introduced the Statue-Of-Liberty play. Like many football coaches, he was a military history buff. He died in 1946.

■ Also born today: DON SCHOLLANDER (1946), in 1964 he became the first swimmer to win four gold medals in one Olympics — in the 100- and 400-meter races and the 400- and 800-meter relays ... PHIL GARNER (1949), "Scrap Iron" gives veteran leadership to the Astros; got 12 hits in 1979 World Series while with the Pirates, tying a Series record.

NOTES

■ **CHUCK BEDNARIK (1925)** — Hall of Fame center and linebacker for the Philadelphia Eagles (1949-62), Pennsylvania all the way, he was born in the tough steel

town of Bethlehem, went to Penn and played his entire pro career with the Eagles. George Trafton was the definitive center of the 1920s, Mel Hein of the '30s and Bulldog Turner of the '40s. Bednarik dominated the center position during the following decade, playing both ways for half of his career but used as a center exclusively for the other half (except for 1960 when, because of a teammate's injury, Bednarik

Chuck Bednarik

played two ways again and helped the Eagles win the NFL title). Bednarik was the last 60-minute football player. A fierce performer, Bednarik is known as the man who, in 1960, shortened Frank Gifford's career (and nearly shortened Gifford) with a bruising but legal tackle. In 1969 Bednarik was chosen as the center on the NFL's all-time team.

■ Also born today: jockey **STEVE CAUTHEN (1960)**, in '76 his mounts won more than $6 million, shattering the record; at age 16 he became the youngest jockey ever to win the Triple Crown — on Affirmed ... **OLLIE MATSON (1930)**, another Hall of Fame football player born on this day; he played on the 1951 USF juggernaut, won a bronze medal in the 400 meters and a silver medal in the 1,600-meter relay at the 1952 Olympics, had a brilliant 15-year NFL career with Chicago Cardinals and later the Rams, traded for nine players ... **JOHNNY BERADINO (1917)**, utility infielder with Browns, Indians and Pirates (1939-52), .249 lifetime batting average; made it bigger acting on TV as Dr. Steve Hardy on soap opera General Hospital (as actor changed spelling of last name from Berardino) ... **ALBERT D. LASKER (1880)**, "The Father of Modern Advertising, he was co-owner of Chicago Cubs and built the first 18-hole public golf course with grass greens ... **CLIFF BATTLES (1910)**, running back for the Wash. Redskins from 1932 to 1937. He broke the NFL season rushing record in 1937, became the first to repeat as rushing leader, and the first player from a small college — West Virginia Wesleyan —to be named to the college football Hall of Fame.

■ **JOHN C. HEENAN** (1833) —
The bare-knuckle heavyweight champion of the U.S. (1860-63), was born John Camel Heenan in West Troy, N.Y. At age 17 Heenan went to California (where he became known as "The Benicia Boy") and made his reputation as a tremendous puncher. In 1860 after he had disposed of the competition (and the fighter who beat him refused to give him a rematch), Heenan went to England to fight the British champion Tom Sayers in what was going to be called a world title. This event caused a sensation on both sides of the Atlantic and is a milestone in the art of fisticuffs — the first boxing match to create international interest. Volumes have been written about this fight. In the 42nd round, Heenan (who outweighed Sayers by about 40 pounds) had his man caught in the ropes and was about to win the fight when the crowd went wild and started tearing the ring apart. The ref stopped the show and called it a draw. Celebrities, royalty, members of the clergy even, and the many far-flung correspondents in attendance got their money's worth. Even Dickens and Thackeray made the scene. Boxing, as an international sport, took a quantum leap. Heenan was married to the flamboyant actress and poet, Adah Isaacs Menken, whose marriages and liaisons were well-known. She had a strong influence on Heenan's career and, as much as anyone, was responsible for producing the historical Sayers bout. Heenan died in 1873 at age 40.

■ Also born today: **GATES BROWN** (1939), outfielder and pinch-hitter deluxe with the Tigers (1973-73); hit 16 career pinch-hit homers, topped only by Cliff Johnson (19) and Jerry Lynch (18) ... **EDDIE COLLINS** (1887), one-fourth (and the best) of Connie Mack's "$100,000 Infield" the best second baseman in American League history, his 25 years in the league is a longevity record ... **JAMAAL WILKES** (1953), "Silk," ignominiously allowed to leave the Warriors in 1977, has been brilliant since then with the Lakers.   ... reliever **CLAY CARROLL** (1941), whose 37 saves for the Reds in 1972 set an NL record ... **ANDY FARKAS** (1916), Redskins running back, 1938-44, led NFL in scoring in 1939.

NOTES

Sports birthdays / May 3

■**RAY ROBINSON (1920)** — The great welterweight (1946-51) and middleweight (on and off from 1951 to 1960) champion, considered by many to be the greatest fighter, pound for pound, of all time. Born Walker Smith

in Detroit, he used to idolize Joe Louis, carrying the champion's bag to and from the gym. Walker Smith went to a fight as a spectator and subbed for a fighter named Ray Robinson who failed to pass the physical. He won his first 40 fights, lost to Jake LaMotta on decision (which he avenged four times), and then won 90 more in succession before losing (eight years after his loss to LaMotta) a

Ray Robinson decision and his title to Randy Turpin. Sixty-four days later, Robinson won his title back via a 10th-round TKO. Robinson fought as a pro for 25 years and fought 22 world title fights. He was never knocked out in his more than 200 fights. Outside the ring he was known for his fuschia Cadillacs and flashy style, and had a career as a singer, dancer and actor. Also has devoted himself to his Sugar Ray Youth Foundation.

■**REECE "GOOSE" TATUM (1921)** — "The Clown Prince of Basketball" was the star and main showman of the Harlem Globetrotters from 1942 until 1954. He then formed his own barnstorming team, the Harlem Roadkings (later the Magicians). Only 6-feet-3, he had an 84-inch arm span and used it well as a dazzling ballhandler. Tatum died in 1967.

■Also born today: Hall of Fame lefty pitcher **EPPA RIXEY (1891)**, won 266 games with Reds and Phillies ... two more boxers: **JOSE TORRES (1936)**, light-heavy champion, 1965-66, and **HENRY COOPER (1934)**, British heavyweight champion, 1959-70 ... **DAN BANKHEAD (1947)**, the first black pitcher in the major leagues (with Dodgers in 1947) ... **RED RUFFING (1905)**, a righty pitcher with the Boston Red Sox (1924-30) and Yankees (1930-46). He won 273 games, was one of the best hitting pitchers ever with a .269 lifetime average. He always used the on-deck circle before batting instead of waiting on the bench.

■ **BETSY RAWLS (1928)** — One of the great woman golfers, born in Spartanburg, S.C. Rawls was one of the 12 founders of the LPGA (Ladies Professional Golf Association) formed in 1950 by luminaries that included Babe Didrikson Zaharias, Patty Berg and Louise Suggs. Among Rawls' many tournament wins are four U.S. Opens (1951, '53, '57 and '60), a feat equalled only by Mary "Mickey" Wright. Rawls was also named Woman Golfer of the Year in 1953 and '60.

Betsy Rawls

■ **MARCEL THIL (1904)** — Middleweight champion 1932-37), born in Saint-Dizier, France. Thil had a slow climb to the top, losing as many times as he won in his first 25 bouts. In his 66th fight he took on the American "Gorilla" Jones in Paris and won the world title when Jones was disqualified for fouling in the 11th round. Thil was an aggressive body puncher, with little finesse who could take a punch — he was stopped only twice in 97 fights. In 1937 Thil was beaten by Fred Apostoli and suffered a badly cut eye. That was his last fight. Thil, who married his manager's daughter, died in 1968.

■ Also born today: **EL CORDOBÉS (1936)**, great Spanish bullfighter, the highest paid in history, born Manuel Benitez Perez ... sportswriter **JOHN LARDNER (1912)**, wrote for Newsweek (1939-60), died in 1960 at age 47, son of sportswriter/short story writer Ring Lardner ... **ELMER LAYDEN (1903)**, fullback of the legendary Notre Dame backfield known as the Four Horseman, later coached at Duquesne and Notre Dame, and was NFL commissioner (1941-46). ... German auto racer **WOLFGANG VON TRIPS (1928)**, great name ... **HARLON HILL (1932)**, Chicago Bears receiver, 1954-61, All-Pro his first three seasons.

NOTES

Chief Bender

■ **CHIEF BENDER (1883)** — Great right-handed pitcher, born Charles Albert Bender in Brainerd, Minn. In a 16-year career, mostly with the Philadelphia A's, Bender was 212-128 for a brilliant .624 percentage, with an equally impressive 2.45 lifetime ERA. His father was Dutch and his mother was half-Chippewa. Thus he was dubbed "Chief," but Connie Mack, manager of the A's, always called him Albert. He learned his baseball at Carlisle Indian School in Pennsylvania (which Jim Thorpe attended) and after graduation joined the A's at age 19. He entered the Hall of Fame in 1953, died one year later.

■ Also born today: **GORDON RICHARDS (1904)**, English jockey who rode into his 50s ... **BOB CERV (1926)**, hard-hitting outfielder with the Yankees, Kansas City A's, etc.; had best year in '58 with A's hitting 38 homers and 104 RBI; later was baseball coach at Sioux-Empire College in Hawarden, Iowa ... ... **TONY CANADEO (1919)**, "The Gray Ghost of Gonzaga," Green Bay Packer fullback of the 1940s ... rodeo star **PETE KNIGHT (1903)**, world champion saddle bronc rider four times; died in 1937, thrown from a horse in competition ... **BILL BUNTIN (1942)**, basketball star at Michigan (he and Cazzie Russell led team to NCAA final, losing to UCLA), drafted by Pistons but died of heart attack at age 26 ... **STEVE SCOTT (1956)**, the U.S.'s best miler whose 3:51.2 is one of the fastest times ever for the mile... **JOSE PAGAN (1935)**, ex-Giants SS.

NOTES

■ **WILLIE MAYS (1931)** — The greatest baseball player of all time. In 1951, after his 20th birthday, Mays was called up to the Giants and helped them win their miracle pennant. He retired in 1973 (ignominiously traded to the Mets) with 660 home runs (third after Aaron and Ruth). Not too shabby for the most spectacular outfielder of all time. And how many power hitters were brilliant base-runners? Mays was a living clinic on how to play this darn game. The consummate artist, he also played gracefully and joyfully.

Willie Mays

No National League player has hit 20 triples in a season since he did it in 1957, and he is one of only five players in the 20th century to hit four home runs in a nine-inning game.

■ Also born today: **MARLIN "PAT" HARDER (1922),** running back on the Chicago Cardinals' "$100,000 backfield" of the late 1940s (with Charlie Trippi, Paul Christman and Marshall Goldberg), still an NFL referee after all these years ... **FREDDIE "RED" COCHRANE (1915),** welterweight champion, 1941-46, a hard-luck champ who won the title via decision against Fritzie Zivic, but had to serve in World War II (while his title was frozen). When he returned five years later, he was 30 years old and couldn't regain his form. He was knocked out twice by Rocky Graziano in two non-title bouts, then in his first title defense, four years after winning the crown, he was knocked out in the fourth round by Marty Servo. He then retired ... **NED IRISH (1905),** pioneer sports promoter and executive, long-time president of Madison Square Garden, founder of the New York Knicks, died in 1983 ... **WEEB EWBANK (1907),** the only football coach to win championships in the AFL (N.Y. Jets, 1969) and the NFL (Baltimore Colts, 1971) ... **PERRY JONES (1888),** developed junior tennis on the West Coast.

NOTES

■ **JOHNNY UNITAS (1933)** — Voted "1960s Player of the Decade". The Steelers drafted him in the 9th round out of Louisville in 1955 and cut him in the preseason. He kicked around for about a year, playing semi-pro and wondering about his career. The Colts took a chance and signed him in 1956 to a $7,000 contract. That chance paid off. Unitas played 17 seasons for the Colts, led them to three NFL titles (1958, '59, '70) and broke virtually every quarterback record of his time. The last player to wear high black shoes in the NFL, Unitas still owns one record — he threw a TD pass in 47 consecutive games. Sid Luckman, the great Hall of Fame QB, said: "Johnny Unitas is the greatest quarterback in the history of the game. He's better than Sammy Baugh, better than me, better than anybody."

Johnny Unitas

■ Also born today: **JOE JACOBS (1897)**, boxing manager who handled many fighters, including Max Schmeling, Tony Galento and Mike McTigue. He's semi-famous for having uttered "I shoulda stood in bed," and "We wuz robbed" (after Jack Sharkey regained the heavyweight title in a disputed decision over Schmeling) ... for you Colgate fans, **MARV HUBBARD (1946)**, former Oakland Raider fullback who attended college at Colgate and was replaced by another Colgate grad, Mark van Eeghen ... **D. BELFORD WEST (1896)**, college Hall of Famer from Colgate who was a two-time All-America tackle ... **TOM ZACHARY (1896)**, lefty pitcher for several teams. He had his best years for the Washington Senators, and in 1927 served up the pitch that Babe Ruth hit for his 60th homer ... **DICK WILLIAMS (1929)**, Padres manager, achieved fame by managing the Red Sox to a pennant in 1967 and then managing the Oakland A's to three straight pennants (and World Series) in 1972, '73 and '74 ... **VITO "BABE" PARILLI (1930)**, NFL QB for two decades with the Packers, Browns, Raiders, Jets and mostly the Boston Patriots (1961-67); later a QB coach.

NOTES

■ **SONNY LISTON (1932)** — Liston, heavyweight champion (1962-64), was born Charles Liston in St. Francis County, Arkansas. Born poor, he spent much of his youth (and some of his adulthood) on the wrong side of the law. In 1962, at age 30, Liston finally got his title shot against champ Floyd Patterson and knocked him out in the first round. In their return match, Liston scored another sensational one-round KO. At this point Liston was considered invincible. His brooding, hard-hitting style (and his brushes with the law) instilled fear in everyone — except the young and brash Cassius Clay,

Sonny Liston

who shocked the ring world and everyone else by scoring a seven-round TKO (as a whopping 7-1 underdog) and then taking Liston out in round one of their return match. Except for a few more fights, Liston's career was finished. His record was impressive — 50 wins in 54 fights (39 KOs). He probably would have been champ for quite a while if he never had to deal with the awesome Ali. Liston died in 1970 at age 38 under mysterious circumstances. The coroner's report said he expired of "lung congestion brought on by poor oxygen and nutrient supply to the heart muscle."

■ Also born today: Jockey **ANGEL CORDERO Jr. (1942)**, in 1985 rode Spend A Buck to his third Kentucky Derby victory, also won on Cannonade in '74 and Bold Forbes in '76 ... **MIKE CUELLAR (1937)**, great Cuban lefty curveballer with Astros and Orioles ... **FRANCIS OUIMET (1893)**, whose international success marks the beginning of golf as a popular sport in America. ... bullfighter **JOSELITO (1895)**, rival of Juan Belmonte in the Golden Age of Bullfighting (1914-20), fatally gored in ring at age 25 ...
RONNIE LOTT (1959), the Niners' brilliant cornerback, still the hardest hitting defensive back in the NFL ... **EDD ROUSH (1893)**, Hall of Fame outfielder (1913-31), mostly with the Cincinnati Reds, won two batting titles (1917 and 1919), lefty swinger had .323 lifetime BA.

NOTES

■ BURL TOLER (1928)—
Football star, pioneer NFL official, and noted educator. Born in Memphis, Tennessee, Toler attended USF and played on their final football team in 1951. That team went

Burl Toler

undefeated and is ranked among the greatest college teams of all time. It included such Hall of Famers as Gino Marchetti and Ollie Matson but Toler was considered one of the stars of the team and was an honorable mention All-American. He was drafted by the Rams but broke his leg in the College All-Star game that year, thwarting a pro career as a player but beginning a multifaceted career as an NFL head linesman, a position he's had for two decades. In fact, Toler was the first black major league official in any pro sport. He is also the first black ever to become an assistant junior high school principal in San Francisco. He later became principal and administrator of The City's community colleges, has also been police commissioner since 1978.

■ Also born today: **BOB ASKIN (1900)**, "the best rodeo cowboy of all time"... two defensive backs who both played for the Packers in the 1960s: **BOB JETER (1937)** and **JESS WHITTENTON (1934)** ... two golfers: **HARRY VARDON (1870)**, pioneer Englishman who won six British Opens, and **JOHN MAHAFFEY (1948)**, peaked in 1978, winning PGA championship ... **CALVIN MURPHY (1948)**, the smallest and toughest NBA guard during his career (1970-82) with the Houston (and San Diego) Rockets; one of the three or four best foul-shooters ever and a virtuoso baton-twirler ... tennis great **PANCHO GONZALES (1928)**, U.S. singles champion in 1948 and '49.... long jumper **RALPH BOSTON (1939)**, won gold medal in 1960 Olympics ... **HY TURKIN (1915)**, N.Y. Daily News sportswriter and author of "The Official Encyclopedia of Baseball," died at age 40. _Tony Gwynn (1960), Padres RF and '84 NL Batting Champion._

NOTES

■ **JIMMY DEMARET (1910) —**
One of the best and most beloved golfers ever to play the game. Demaret, one of the first to wear colorful and flamboyant golf attire, was also the first golfer to win three Masters tournaments (in 1940, '47, and '50). He and his partner (another great player, Jack Burke Jr.) built the Champions Golf Club, a now-famous course in Houston, where he was born and, in 1983, died.

Jimmy Demaret

■ **TAMARA PRESS (1937) —**
Soviet track and field luminary, set world records in her two specialties, shot put and discus. She is the only woman ever to win two consecutive Olympic gold medals in the shot put in 1960 and 1964 and almost had the same distinction in the discus throw, winning a silver medal in '60 and a gold medal in '64. Her sister is Irina Press, another track and field great who won the penthalon at the '64 Olympics.

■ **EDWARD G. BARROW (1868) —**
Barrow, the man who converted Babe Ruth into an outfielder, was born in Springfield, Ill. Barrow is less well-known for discovering Honus Wagner in the early years of his wide-ranging career. He managed Ruth and the Red Sox to the 1918 pennant and began Ruth's conversion from pitching. In 1920, shortly after Ruth was dealt to the Yankees, Barrows became Yankee GM and completed the conversion, a change that brought baseball into the Golden Age of the 1920s. An innovative executive, Barrow died in 1953.

■ Also born today: **THOMAS LIPTON (1850)**, yachtsman and tea merchant ... **MANUEL SANTANA (1937)**, tennis player who won the U.S. national singles title in 1965 and the British title at Wimbledon in 1966 ... **JIM ZORN (1953)**, lefty QB for Seattle Seahawks; now backup to Dave Krieg.... **PAT SUMMERALL (1930)**, the Walter Cronkite of TV sports, receiver and kicker with N.Y. Giants, among others ... French-born **CHIQUITO DE CAMEO (1881)**, real name was Joseph Apesteguy, long dominating as No. 1 jai-lai player.... **PHIL AND STEVE MAHRE (1957)**, twin brothers, both outstanding Alpine skiers, won the gold and silver medals in the Winter Olympics (1984) – an incredible achievement for twin brothers.

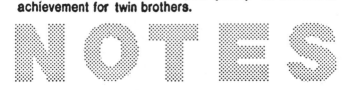

Charlie Gehringer

■ **CHARLIE GEHRINGER (1903)** One of the great second basemen in AL history. He had a 19-year career (1924-42) — all with the Detroit Tigers, probably the longest career with one team for a second baseman. A lifetime .320 hitter with more than occasional power, Gehringer won the batting title in 1937 and the MVP award in the same year. Eighth in career doubles (574), he hit 60 doubles in 1936, one of only a handful to hit 60 or more in a season. He was known as "The Mechanical Man" for his quiet efficiency.

■ Also born today: **MILT PAPPAS (1939)**, righty pitcher who almost won 100 games in each league (110 with Orioles, 99 in NL with three teams) and was involved in an infamous trade: The Orioles sent him to the Reds for Frank Robinson (who was the MVP the following year) ... **JACK TWYMAN (1934)**, one of NBA's top all-time scorers (19.2 career average per game) with the Cincinnati Royals, teammate and later guardian of paralyzed Maurice Stokes ... skier **NANCY GREENE (1943)**, 1968 gold medal winner has been called "the greatest woman competitor in North American history" ... **GENE HERMANSKI (1920)**, Brooklyn Dodgers outfielder in the late 1940s ... **RIP SEWELL (1907)**, righty pitcher for Pittsburgh (1938-40), with lifetime 143-97 won-loss record; known for his high-arc blooper ball, known as the "eephus pitch," which Ted Williams dramatically hit out of the park in the 1946 All-Star Game.

NOTES

■**YOGI BERRA (1925)** — One of baseball's beloved figures, the former great Yankee catcher and Yankee manager. He played with the Yankees from 1946 to 1963 and finished with a .285 lifetime BA. His 358 homers stood as a record for a catcher until Johnny Bench broke it in his last year. Berra was named MVP three times — 1951, '54 and '55 — and his best year was 1950. An incongruous looking athlete, Berra was 5-feet-7½ and 185 pounds and had a simian gait. Unortho-

Yogi Berra

dox at the plate, he was a free-swinging bad-ball hitter who nevertheless rarely struck out (in 1950 he hit 28 homers and struck out 12 times — now that's awesome). Yogi's record as a manager is pretty solid. He managed the Yankees one other time — in 1964 — and won. He managed the Mets for two years — 1972 and '73 — and won once. Berra was only the second manager whose son played for him — (Connie Mack managed his son Earle).

■Also born today: **HAROLD OLSEN (1895)**, Hall of Fame basketball coach at Ohio State (1922-46) and ABA's Chicago Stags (1946-49) ... diver **PATRICIA MCCORMICK (1930)**, won gold medals in springboard diving and platform diving in 1952 and 1956 Olympics ... **LOU WHITAKER (1957)**, of the Tigers, the best second baseman in the majors, an MVP possiblity ... **FELIPE ALOU (1935)**, outfielder with Giants (1958-63) and others; the oldest of the three Alou brothers (including Jesus and Matty) who all played major league ball. In fact, they all played for the Giants at one time. In one game (on Sept 5, 1963), the Giants featured an All-Alou outfield, the first brothers trio to play in the same outfield. When Matty won the NL batting title in 1966, Felipe's .327 was second. It was the only time that brothers finished one-two. ... Another great Olympian woman, **RENATE STECHER (1950)**, sprinter from East Germany who won the 100 meters and 200 meters at the 1972 Olympics; she co-held the world record for the 100 meters (11.0) ... **HANK BOROWY (1916)**, righty pitcher who, in 1945, pulled a Rick Sutcliffe by moving from an AL team (Yanks) to the Cubs, going 11-2 and leading them to the pennant.

■ **JOE LOUIS (1914)** — "The Brown Bomber" was born Joseph Louis Barrow, Jr. near Lafayette, Ala. His 12-year reign (1937-49) as heavyweight champion was the longest reign as champion in any division. He defended his title 25 times. Louis thrived in an era that could not accept blacks in the public eye, even as athletes. He wasn't called "The Black Bomber." However, his ability (possibly the greatest heavyweight ever) and his longevity, not to mention his patriotism or his humility, made him a beloved figure. Jackie Robinson said that Louis paved the way for the black man in professional sports.

Joe Louis

After his ring career, Louis was broke (despite the millions he earned) and owed the government in back taxes. This great champion, who made many tours and appearances for the U.S. troops and helped sell bonds, etc. was forced to appear in shabby wrestling spectacles in order to pay his tax debt. Louis suffered from nervous breakdowns in the 1970s and died in 1981.

■ Also born today: **WAYNE ESTES (1943)**, Utah State basketball star, accidentally electrocuted helping people in auto accident; he was the first player from that school to score more than 2,000 points, was second leading scorer in U.S. (after Rick Barry), and had scored 48 points the night he died ... **DUSTY RHODES (1927)**, Giants pinch-hitter extraordinaire whose pinch-hits won three of four Series games in 1954. A fascinating portrait of Rhodes, who rarely played while sober, can be found in Leo Durocher's autobiography, "Nice Guys Finish Last.". . . **LEON WAGNER (1934)**, "Daddy Wags," the flamboyant hard-hitting outfielder of the 1960s, with the Giants, Cardinals, Angels, Indians. Wagner resides in S.F., has been active as an actor and businessman. . . . Hall of Fame hockey player **CECIL "BABE" DYE (1898)**, NHL star of the 1920s, twice led the league in scoring (1923 & '25).

NOTES

■ EARLE COMBS (1899) —

Hall of Fame outfielder with N.Y. Yankees from 1924 to 1935, born in Pebworth (that's right, Pebworth), Ky. It would have been difficult to play for a team with Babe Ruth and Lou Gehrig and not be in their shadows. In Combs' case, it was difficult but he did it, anyway, finishing with a magnificent .325 lifetime batting average, one of the top 20 averages in history. Combs was the center fielder and leadoff batter on the Murderers Row juggernaut of the 1920s. Even teams with guys like Ruth and Gehrig need guys like Combs, who was fast, a brilliant defensive player and a heady all-around performer who was especially

Earle Combs

adept at stealing signs. He hit over .340 four times, led the league in triples three times and hit 30 or more doubles eight straight times. Combs was a lefty swinger who played his whole career with the Yankees. He was a Yankee coach for another decade, then coached the St. Louis Browns, Red Sox and Phillies. He died in 1976.

■ Also born today: **TONY PEREZ (1942)**, the Reds' younger first baseman (he platoons with Pete Rose), entered the 1985 season 18th on the all-time RBI list and has a shot at 15th; his 371 home runs isn't chopped liver, either ... **LORNE "GUMP" WORSLEY (1929)**, great goalie with the New York Rangers, Canadiens and Minnesota North Stars, three-time winner of the Vezina Trophy, retired at age 45 ... **"BIG ED" WALSH (1881)**, righty pitcher with the White Sox (1904-16), owns the lowest career ERA (1.82) of all time.

NOTES

■ **GEORGE BRETT (1953)** — The great Kansas City Royals third baseman, whose lifetime batting average (.314) is exceeded only by Rod Carew's among active players.

George Brett

In 1979, Brett became one of only five players to hit 20 homers, 20 triples, and 20 doubles in the same season (he almost had 20 stolen bases, too). The next year he topped himself, electrifying the sports world with his quest for .400. He ended with .390, the closest to .400 since Ted Williams did it in 1941. Brett's level stroke is beautiful. His tremendous shot off of Goose Gossage in the 1980 AL playoffs still lives vibrantly in our memory. George is the brother of ex-pitcher Ken Brett.

■ **HARRY WILLS (1889)** — Born in New Orleans, a great heavyweight contender in the early 1920s, but — because he was black — never got his chance to fight for Jack Dempsey's title. In fact, after Wills and Dempsey signed a contract to fight (because of popular demand), the governor of New York canceled the bout and compensated Wills with $50,000. Wills weighed 220 and stood 6-feet-4. He fought mostly other black fighters, losing only eight fights of 102. He still boxed at age 40 and died in 1958.

■ Also born today: another heavyweight: **JERRY QUARRY (1945)** ... **DON SHINNICK (1935)**, ex-Colt who is one of the all-time leaders in interceptions among linebackers; later a Raider coach (wore his cap backwards on the sidelines) ... **DON NELSON (1940)**, ex-Celtic, later was coach of the Milwaukee Bucks (lousy dresser) ... golfer **KEN VENTURI (1931)**, won 1964 U.S. Open, born in San Francisco ... pole vaulter **DON BRAGG (1935)**, won gold medal at the 1960 Olympics ... **WALTER "TURK" BRODA (1914)**, goalie with Toronto Maple Leafs (1936-43, 1945-52), won two Vezina Trophies (in 1941 and '48) and helped the Leafs win four Stanley Cups.

NOTES

■ **BILLY MARTIN (1928)** — Five-time manager of the N. Y. Yankees. Born Alfred Manuel Pesano in Berkeley, he was a favorite of Casey Stengel when Casey managed the Oakland Oaks and he was brought up to the Yankees in 1950 when Stengel started managing in New York. Billy played parts of seven seasons from 1950 to 1957 (missing 1954), having only one full season. Still, he made a name for himself (and not just for partying with Mickey Mantle and Whitey Ford). In

Billy Martin

1953, he had a record 12 hits for a six-game World Series, but is best-known for his hustling catch of a high infield fly in the 1952 Series against Brooklyn. That one play captured his essence as a player, manager, and person — never say die. Martin managed successfully with the Twins, Tigers, Rangers, Yankees, and A's — but was fired each time (three times w/the Yanks) because of personal differences as well as his penchant for violent scenes. Difficult to assess him as a manager. He hurt teams with personal vendettas and paranoid outbursts (as well as burning out a pitching staff because of his old-school insistence on complete games) but he did know how to win. Most managers don't.

■ Also born today: **JACK MORRIS (1955)**, pitching workhorse of the Detroit Tigers ... figure skater **HAIG B. OUNDJIAN (1949)**, one of only three to perform a triple lutz ... **OLGA KORBUT (1955)**, revolutionized gymnastics by winning three gold medals and one silver medal at the 1972 Olympics ... **DONNY ANDERSON (1943)**, All-American running back from Texas Tech, drafted no. 1 by the Green Bay Packers ... **RUBE WALKER (1926)**, back-up catcher for Roy Campanella during the 1950s. ex-pitching coach with the Mets and Braves.... **DAVE PHILLEY (1920)**, pinch-hitter deluxe w/eight teams; had the AL record for 24 pinch hits (for the 1961 Orioles) and holds the major league record for consecutive pinch hits (9).

NOTES

Sports birthdays / May 17

■ SUGAR RAY LEONARD (1956) —

The un-retired, re-retired ex-champion, born in Wilming-

Sugar Ray Leonard

ton, N.C. The Olympic sensation of 1976 won the WBC welterweight title by defeating Wilfred Benitez and won the WBA version by beating Thomas Hearns (both on late-round KOs). He also won the WBA junior middleweight title by knocking out Ayub Kalule. The only loss of his career was to Roberto Duran (by decision) in 1980, which he avenged later that year in the infamous "no mas" fight. A 1982 detached retina operation led to his retirement with a 32-1 record with 23 knockouts. A year and a half later, despite many contrary opinions, the great "Sugar Ray" attempted a comeback against Kevin Howard. Howard put Leonard to the canvas for the first time in his pro career, but Leonard still won the fight, announcing after that he was retiring for good.

■ JAMES "COOL PAPA" BELL (1903) —

One of the titans of the Negro Leagues, an outfielder with great speed who could hit (.332 lifetime average), known as the "black Ty Cobb". He later became a scout and discovered Ernie Banks (for which Bell received a basket of fruit). Bell was named to the Hall of Fame in 1974 and thanked Ted Williams for helping to pave the way by bringing up the plight of early blacks in the Negro Leagues in Williams' acceptance speech when he entered the Hall in 1966.

■ Also born today: **EARL MORRALL** (1934), QB for 49ers, Dolphins, Colts and others; won MVP in 1968, leading Colts to title after obscurity as back-up to Unitas; played into his 40s (loved that crew cut). ... **WILHELM STEINITZ** (1836), world chess champion, 1872-94, 22 straight years.

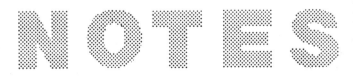

■ **REGGIE JACKSON (1946)** — Home run hitter deluxe (with the California Angels et al), in 1985 was in his 19th major league season and beyond the 500-homer plateau. Jackson has attained living legend status and it couldn't have happened to a guy who wanted it — or deserved it — more. He has passed Mel Ott (511), Ernie Banks and Ed Mathews (tied throughout a stormy career at 512) on the all-time home run list and before this season ends he will probably soar past Ted Williams and Willie McCovey (tied at 521). Then, he would only need about 15 more

Reggie Jackson

homers to climb over Jimmy Foxx (534) and Mickey Mantle (536) and own the No. 5 position in the all-time home run sweepstakes. Not too shabby, Reggie.

■ **BROOKS ROBINSON (1937)** — The greatest third baseman of his era. He was with the Orioles from 1955 until 1977, and is one of only a handful of players to spend more than two decades with one club. A lifetime .267 hitter with power (251 homers), he won 16 Gold Glove awards, won the MVP award in 1964 and helped the O's win four pennants and two World Series.

■ Also born today: **CHARLIE "CHOO CHOO" JUSTICE (1924)**, All-American running back from North Carolina in late 1940s, college Hall of Fame ... **CARROLL HARDY (1933)**, football star at Colorado, then a one-year halfback for the 49ers (1965); had brief baseball career, became the only player to pinch-hit for Ted Williams (after Ted fouled one off his ankle and had to leave the game) ... **JACK SANFORD (1929)**, rookie-of-the-year with the Phillies in 1957, had best year with pennant-winning Giants in 1962, going 24-7, including a phenomenal 16 wins in a row, later an Orioles scout ... hurdler **ROD MILBURN (1950)**, won gold medal at '72 Olympics in 110 meter hurdles ... **CHARLES "BABE" ADAMS (1882)**, righty pitcher with Pittsburgh (1909-26), won three complete games in 1909 Series, defeating Cobb and the Tigers in seven games ... **FRED PERRY (1909)**, English tennis player, one of the all-time greats.

NOTES

■ **DOLPH SCHAYES (1928)** –Great NBA forward, born NYC. He played college ball at NYU when it was a powerhouse. He then went pro with the Syracuse Nationals and moved with them to Philadelphia when they became the 76ers in 1964. His 16-season mark is equaled only by John Havlicek and Elvin Hayes. He is the 11th leading scorer in NBA history, and one of only a dozen to play in more than 1,000 games. Schayes, a 6-8 forward, could shoot, rebound and play defense. He is one of the six or seven greatest forwards of all-time. His son, Dan Schayes, is a seven-foot center with the Utah Jazz.

■ **GIL MCDOUGALD (1928)** —
McDougald played for the New York Yankees for 10 seasons (1951-60), compiling a .276 career batting average. He was named rookie of the year in 1951 over Minnie Minoso (whose stats were better) in a decision that still elicits controversy. For the last time, then: yes, Minoso had a brilliant year but for a fourth-place club, while McDougald led a great team in hitting and helped them win the pennant and World Series. McDougald was one of the most versatile infielders of the 1950s. His career was about split between second base and third base and he played a lot of shortstop. He also had the most exaggerated open stance of all time, and held the bat low, his right elbow pointing down. He was born in San Francisco.

■ Also born today: **ARCHIE MANNING (1949)**, veteran NFL quarterback ... **DEORMOND "TUSS" MCLAUGHRY (1893)**, football coach at Brown (1928-40) and Dartmouth (1941-42, 1945-52) ... sprinter **PERCY WILLIAMS (1908)**, who won gold medals for the 100 meter and 200 meter dash in the 1928 Olympics.

NOTES

■ **WENDELL TYLER (1955)** —
Brilliant San Francisco 49er running back. Born in Shreveport, La., Tyler moved to Los Angeles, where he was a star at Crenshaw High School, an All-American at UCLA, and a two-time 1,000-yard running back with the L.A. Rams. Then a curious thing happened on the day before the 1983 college draft. The Rams traded their great running back (along with Cody Jones and a third-round choice) to the S.F. 49ers (their traditional and divisional rival) for the Niners' second and fourth choices in that draft. Unbelievable, you say? Next year Tyler broke the 49ers' single-season rushing record and helped his team win it all while the

Wendell Tyler

Rams struggled for respectability. Tyler and backfield partner Roger Craig make a formidable, and unique, tandem.

■ Also born today: **BUD GRANT (1927)**, longtime (1967-83) Viking coach with brilliant 151-87 won-loss record and 15 divisional titles, retired, then un-retired in 1984 to resume coaching bummer Vikings — why, Bud, why? ... **KEN BOYER (1931)**, Cardinals third baseman (1955-65), .287 lifetime hitter, 282 home runs, MVP in 1964; brother of major leaguers Clete Boyer (currently A's coach) and pitcher Cloyd Boyer ... **BOBBY MURCER (1946)**, like Mickey Mantle, he was born in Oklahoma and came up to the Yankees as a 19-year-old shortstop who was converted to a center fielder ... hockey great **STAN MIKITA (1940)**, center with the Chicago Black Hawks from 1959 to 1980, won Hart Trophy (most points), Art Ross Trophy (MVP), and Lady Byng Trophy (sportsmanship and ability) twice each.... **SADAHARU OH (1940)**, world's home run record-holder. Playing for the Yomiuri Giants, Oh hit 868 home runs in a fabled career and became the most celebrated performer in Japanese baseball. **LEROY KELLY (1942)**, Cleveland Browns running back, 1964-73, his 74 TDs is third after Jim Brown and Jim Taylor ... Detroit southpaw pitcher **HAL NEWHOUSER (1921)**, MVP in 1944 and '45.

NOTES

■EDDIE GRANT (1883) — This big-league baseball player, killed in World War I and whose monument stood in the old Polo Grounds, was born in Franklin, Mass. A National League infielder for 10 years with a .249 life time BA, he graduated from Harvard and was called "Harvard Eddie." At age 28, he retired from baseball and entered law practice. When the U.S. entered the war in 1917, Grant enlisted and in 1918, just a month before the end of the war, he was killed in the Argonne Forest in France at age 35. In 1921, Grant's two sisters unveiled a plaque on a granite slab in deep center field of the Polo Grounds in New York City (Grant played with the Giants in his last two years). The plaque stood until the Giants vacated the premises after the 1957 season.

■MONTY STRATTON (1912) — This hard-luck right-handed pitcher was born Monty Franklin Pierce Stratton in Celeste, Texas. Like Averill (below), Stratton also played in the 30s and in the AL (Chisox) but Stratton's career was brief. During three partial seasons, he went 15-5 with a 2.40 ERA, and in 1938, at age 26, he was 15-9. After the '38 season, Stratton, on a hunting trip, was shot accidently in the right leg. It had to be amputated. With an artificial leg, Stratton did pitch again, but not in the major leagues. His courageous rehabilitation is the subject of his 1949 film autobio, "The Stratton Story," with James Stewart (and June Allyson, of course).

Earl Averill

■Also born today:
EARL AVERILL (1902), Hall of Fame outfielder with Cleveland in 1930s, .318 lifetime hitter, 238 homers, born in Snohomish, WA ... KENT HRBEK (1960), first baseman with the Minn. Twins since 1981; outside of Harmon Killebrew, he's the best thing to ever happen to the Twins; a great hitter (for power and average), a fine glove, born in Minneapolis, grew up in area of Metropolitan Stadium, the Twins' original park ... BOBBY COX (1941), manager of the Toronto Blue Jays since 1982, managed Braves from '78 to '81. ... golfer HAROLD 'JUG' MCSPADEN (1908)...ARA PARSEGHIAN (1923), Notre Dame football coach and TV commentator.

NOTES

■ **AL SIMMONS (1902)** — The Hall of Fame outfielder who hit with his "foot in the bucket", born Aloysius Harry Szymanski in Milwaukee. One of the elite hitters in baseball history, Simmons was a lifetime .334 hitter with 307 home runs in a 20-year career, the glory ones spent with the Philadelphia A's (1924-32). His 1,827 career RBI is the 11th best mark, sandwiched between Ted Williams and Frank Robinson. In 1929 he won the batting title, hitting .381 with 165 RBI and 34 homers. The next year he hit .390 for his second straight title. Though Simmons put his foot in the

Al Simmons

bucket, he didn't necessarily pull the ball. He kept his front leg free to hit to any field. He was named to the Hall of Fame in 1953 and died three years later.

■ Also born today: **GEORGE BEST (1946)**, playboy soccer star from England and briefly with the San Jose Earthquakes ... golfer **HORTON SMITH (1908)**, winner of the first Masters title in 1934 ... **LARRY SIEGFRIED (1939)**, played college ball with awesome Ohio State teams in 1959 and '60 with teammates John Havlicek, Jerry Lucas (and, off the bench, Bobby Knight); later a fine defensive guard for the Celtics in the 1960s ... Angels lefty **TOMMY JOHN (1943)**, 23rd season in 1985 **EDWARD J. HART (1887)**, college Hall of Fame tackle from Princeton ... two centers (both natives of Nebraska who went to the state university): **MICK TINGLEHOFF (1940)**, later with the Vikings for many years, and **DAVE RIMINGTON (1960)**, two-time winner ('81 and '82) of the Outland Trophy.

Signed by A's mid-season '85

■ **MARVELOUS MARVIN HAGLER (1952)** —
Middleweight champ since 1980. Despite his record (only

two losses in more than 60 fights), Hagler still had something to prove, which he did against Tommy Hearns. Hagler has earned his niche in history. He says he'll fight until he breaks Carlos Monzon's record 15 title defenses. Money motives aside , Hagler should fight John "The Beast" Mugabi right now and retire. Hagler's almost religious devotion to his craft showed against Hearns. Tho an impressive win for the champ, the fight took its toll on him.

Marvelous Marvin

■ **DUMMY HOY (1862)** — Late 1800s outfielder, a deaf mute, was born Ellsworth Hoy in Houckstown, Ohio. He was a .288 lifetime hitter during 14 seasons (1888-1902) and scored more than 100 runs nine times. Hoy once threw out three runners at the plate in one game. At 5-feet-4 and 148 pounds, he was one of the smallest players ever. Because of his deafness, Hoy encouraged umpires to use hand signs for balls and strikes. Hoy was also one of the oldest ex-ballplayers. He died in 1961, five months shy of his 100th birthday.

■ Also born today: **LAWRENCE S. RITTER (1922)**, distinguished NYU economics professor who wrote "The Glory of Their Times," an oral history of the early days of baseball, the first book of its kind ... **ROD THORN (1941)**, GM of the Chicago Bulls, ex-NBA guard with Seattle and others ... tennis player **JOHN NEWCOMBE (1943)**, won two U.S. singles titles (in '67 and '73) and three Wimbledon titles ... Australian golfer **DAVID GRAHAM (1946)**, won U.S. Open in 1981.

NOTES

Sports birthdays / May 24

■ **SUZANNE LENGLEN (1899) —**
Considered to be the greatest woman tennis player of all time, born in Paris. She was untouchable on the courts in the early 1920s, one of the most colorful and tempermental ever to play the game. In 1926, she strained Anglo-French relations by refusing to play in a match that Queen Mary attended — just to watch her play. After winning five consecutive Wimbledon titles she became the first amateur to turn pro, and was the star performer in the first touring troupe. However, the hectic touring schedule caused her to die at age 39 of pernicious anemia.

Suzanne Lenglen

■ **JOE OESCHGER (1891) —**
Pitched in record-setting 26-inning game. A right-hander with an undistinguished lifetime record of 83-116, he pitched mostly for the Braves and Phillies. On May 1, 1920, while pitching for the Braves, Oeschger and Leon Cadore hooked up in the longest game ever played — with both pitchers going the distance! Yes, Oeschger gave up a run in the fifth inning but pitched the remaining 21 innings until it was called because of darkness — a 1-1 tie after all that. Oeschger gave up nine hits and walked only three batters in what might be the greatest pitched game ever.

■ **Also born today:**
BILL WAKEFIELD (1941), another righty pitcher involved in a marathon game. In his one big-league season (with the Mets in 1964), he started the longest game in Giants history, a 23-inning affair.... **TONY STRATTA (1930),** S.F.-resident authority on tennis and long-distance running (and no doubt a few other things)... **LIONEL CONACHER (1901),** had outstanding career in five pro sports, brother of hockey greats Charlie and Roy Conacher ... **MIKE REID (1948),** 1969 Outland Trophy winner from Penn State, later a defensive tackle for the Bengals, had separate identity as concert pianist(!) ... **WILLIE MIRANDA (1926),** Cuban-born, the definitive good field-no hit shortstop.

NOTES

■ **GENE TUNNEY (1898)** —
"The Fighting Marine", born New York City. Born into wealth, he overcame family opposition to box as a pro.

Gene Tunney

He is best known for twice outpointing Jack Dempsey in two title fights. The first, in 1926, drew the biggest crowd ever to attend a fight — 120,757. The re-match, featuring the famous "long count," had the biggest gate receipts ever — more than $2.5 million. He also received the biggest purse — $1 million — of the pre-TV era. In 1928 Tunney retired at age 30 — undefeated as a heavyweight. The only loss of his 10-year career was as a light-heavyweight, to Harry Greb — which he avenged no less than four times. Disdaining all offers to make a comeback, Tunney became a wealthy businessman and even a literary type whose intimates included George Bernard Shaw. Tunney died in 1978. His son, John V. Tunney, was a U.S. Senator from California.

■ Also born today: **COOKIE GILCHRIST (1935)**, Buffalo Bills fullback, one of the early AFL stars ... two great Boston Celtics guards. **K.C. JONES (1932)**, became Celtics coach and one of the best in the NBA; was the NBA's first black coach, with the Bullets in '73 (born in S.F.) and **BILL SHARMAN (1926)**, formed great tandem with Cousy, terrific foul shooter ... two ex-Giants pitchers: **JOHN MONTEFUSCO (1950)**, with the Yankees, and **BOB KNEPPER (1954)** of the Astros ... outfielder **AUGIE GALAN (1912)**, .287 switch-hitter, the first player to homer from both sides of the plate in one game (born in Berkeley, Ca.).

NOTES

■**JACK ROOT (1876)** —
The first light-heavyweight champion (1903), born Janos Ruthaly in Austria. The newly-created light-heavy title was an inspiration of Root's manager in order to make his fighter a champion. It worked. He defeated Kid McCoy on a decision but lost it only three months later. Root was part of another piece of history. After James J. Jeffries retired as undefeated heavyweight champion, Jeffries selected the two contenders, Root and Marvin Hart, to clear up the title's vacancy, and refereed the bout. Hart knocked out Root in the 12th round and Root retired within a year. Root lost only three of his 55 fights.

■Also born today: **DARRELL EVANS (1947)**, helped the Tigers win it all in 1984 ... Two baseball managers: **JOE ALTOBELLI (1932)** of the Orioles, who, as Giants manager, folded in the stretch in 1978 — and was still named manager of the Year, and **JIM FREY (1931)** of the Cubs ... **WESLEY WALKER (1955)**, N.Y. Jets wide receiver, out of Cal ... **BRENT MUSBURGER (1939)**, after signing a $10 million contract for five years, had better not talk about players being overpaid ... **DAN ROUNDFIELD (1953)**, longtime Atlana Hawks forward, currently with Pistons, who should've been with a contender during his prime ... **DAN PASTORINI (1949)**, ex-Santa Clara, Oilers, Raiders, Rams QB.

Dealt to
Bullets in May '85

■ SAM SNEAD (1912) —

"Slammin' Sammy," golf's first big money-winner, He was born in Hot Springs, Va., and was a fine high

school athlete, starring in baseball, football, and basketball. He turned down college scholarships to pursue golf and had a legendary career, winning a record 84 major tournaments on the American tour — in parts of six decades, from the 1930s to 1980 when, at age 68, he shot a 69-67 at a Pro-Am tourney with the same sweet swing he's famous for, a swing Jack Nicklaus says is still good as any on the tour. A highly competitive person, Snead was well-known for his golf hustling in the 1930's, playing matches for $10,000. Snead's biggest rival was Ben Hogan and the victory that is most dear to him, and one of the most famous in golf, is the 1954 Masters which Snead won in a playoff. His last Masters (and his 44th consecutive one) was in 1983. His retirement ended an era.

Sam Snead

■ MIKE "PINKY" HIGGINS (1909) —

Hard-hitting third-baseman for the Philadelphia A's (1933-36), Red Sox (1937-38), and Tigers (1939-46), was born in Red Oak, Texas. He owns the major league record for twelve straight hits. Walt Dropo also had a 12-for-12 streak but some walks were thrown in. Higgins got consecutive hits in 12 at-bats (in 1938). A little piece of the rock for Pinky Higgins that's a half-century old and more of an achievement each year. Higgins died in 1969.

■ Also born today:

ex-heavyweight **ZORA FOLLEY (1942)**, who got his payday with Ali in 1967 (losing by 7th round KO) ... **FRANK ELKINS (1910)**, ski editor, N.Y. Times, 1929-54... **TERRY MOORE (1912)**, Cardinals center-fielder (1935-42, 1946-48), .280 lifetime hitter and one of the best defensive outfielders ever ... **MIKE SIANI (1950)**, ex-Raider wide receiver out of Villanova ... **DICK SCHNITTKER (1928)**, All-American basketball player from Ohio State who played with the Minneapolis Lakers from 1953 to '58 ... **GARY NOLAN (1948)**, baby-faced right-hander with the Reds in late '60s and early '70s; best years were as 19-year-old rookie in '67 (14-8), in 1970 (18-7) and in 1972 (15-5 and 1.99 ERA).

NOTES

■ **JIM THORPE (1886)** —The greatest American athlete. A Sac and Fox Indian, he grew up on a reservation in Oklahoma. He was "discovered" and coached by Pop Warner at the Carlisle Indian School in Pennsylvania. Incredibly, that school defeated such college titans as Harvard, Army, and Penn. Thorpe won the pentathlon and decathlon in the 1912 Olympics but was stripped of his medals and records because of his brief stint as a semi-pro baseball player. He played in the majors for parts of six seasons and in 1917, in one of the 77 games he played for the

Jim Thorpe

Reds, got the winning hit in the 10th inning of the major leagues' only double no-hitter. In a 1950 AP poll, he was voted the greatest football player and the best all-around athlete of the 20th century. Thorpe died in poverty and neglect in his small trailer in 1953.

■ **JERRY WEST (1938)** — Fabulous Lakers guard for 15 seasons. Born in Cheylan, W.Va., West went to the state university and in his senior year took that school to the NCAA finals (where they lost to Cal, 71-70). He spent his whole pro career with the Lakers (1960-74), was named first-string All-NBA 10 times, and is one of only six players to score more than 25,000 points. His 27.0 points per game for a career is topped only by Wilt Chamberlain and Elgin Baylor (all three were Laker teammates — and fourth on the list, Kareem Abdul-Jabbar, is also a Laker). West and Oscar Robertson must be considered the greatest guards of all time. West coached the Lakers (unsuccessfully) from 1976 to '79, then became the Lakers' general manager.

■ Also born today: **KIRK GIBSON (1957)**, Tigers right-fielder, MVP in the '84 World Series, ex-wide receiver at Michigan State ... **WARD "PIGGY" LAMBERT (1888)**, Hall of Fame basketball coach at Purdue (1916-46), a pioneer of the fast-break offense, coached many All-Americans, including John Wooden ... **JAMES DWIGHT (1862)**, "the father of American lawn tennis" ... **RICHARD RETI (1889)**, Czechoslovakian chess player and theoretician ... **BRUCE TAYLOR (1948)**, ex-49er cornerback and punt returner, brother of ex-NBA guard Brian Taylor.

NOTES

■TONY ZALE (1913) —

Tough middleweight champion (1941, 1945-47, 1948) born in the steel town of Gary, Ind., could punch and take a punch. He's famous for his three brutal title fights with Rocky Graziano. Zale won the first (getting off the floor to win a 6th round KO), and won the third on a 3rd round KO. Zale finally lost his title in 1948 — at age 35 — to Marcel Cerdan. Zale's record was 70 wins (46 KOs), 18 losses, two draws.

Tony Zale

■ AL UNSER (1933) —

One of the auto racing greats was born in Albuquerque, N.M., Unser has won three Indy 500s — in 1970, '71, and '78. He also has three second-place finishes, most recently in 1983. He and brother Bobby Unser are the only brothers to win the Indy 500.

■RALPH METCALFE (1910) —

Brilliant sprinter, was born in Atlanta, Ga. In the 1936 Olympics, he won a silver medal in the 100 meters, finishing one-tenth of a second behind Jesse Owens, Metcalfe also won bronze in the 200 meters in '36. He was later a long-time congressman from Illinois.

■Also born today: **JOE ROTH (1954)**, Cal QB of the mid-1970s, great passer who currently would be an NFL star if not for his tragic death at age 22 of Hodgkin's Disease ... **JOHN HENCKEN (1954)**, U.S. swimmer who won the 200-meter breaststroke at the 1972 Olympics and came in third in the 100-meter breaststroke ... **GEORGE "RED" HORNER (1909)**, Hall of Fame defenseman with the Toronto maple Leafs (1928-40) ... **GEORGE MCQUINN (1909)**, slick-fielding first-baseman mostly with the St. Louis Browns from 1938 to 1945; he played for the championship Yankees in 1947; a .276 lifetime hitter.... **MELVIN DURSLAG (1921)**, long-time sports columnist with the L.A. Herald-Examiner, contributor to TV Guide ... *ED BURYN (1934)*, "Vagabond Ed", publisher of **SPORTS BIRTHDAYS**.

NOTES

■ **GALE SAYERS (1943)** —One of football's greatest broken-field runners. Born in Wichita, Kan., he played college ball at the University of Kansas and was drafted by the Chicago Bears in 1965. He was an instant sensation, equaling the record of six TDs in a single game (at Wrigley Field against the 49ers) and setting the record of 22 TDs in a rookie season — broken in 1983 by Eric Dickerson. Sayers' 30.6 average makes him the leading all-time kickoff returner. After twice leading the NFL in

Gale Sayers

rushing (1966 and '69), he was plagued by knee injuries until, in 1971, he was forced to retire at age 28 and was enshrined in the Hall of Fame in his first year of eligibility.

■ **AMOS RUSIE (1871)** —
This iron-man righty pitcher was born in Mooresville, Ind., and was known as "The Indiana Thunderbolt." His fastball and slider made him the best pitcher in the National League, along with Cy Young. Rusie pitched for the pre-McGraw Giants in the 1890s, winning 230 games in only eight seasons — that's right, an average of almost 29 wins a year. The strikeout artist with the flaming red hair semi-retired from baseball after a 20-11 season in 1898 to fight the reserve clause and earn more money. It was a losing battle. Except for 22 innings with the Reds three years later, Rusie never played again and wound up working as a laborer for a buck-and-a-half a day.

■ Also born today: **HAROLD "BUD" FOSTER (1906)**, Hall of Fame basketball player at Wisconsin (1928-30), later coach there ... **LYDELL MITCHELL (1949)**, Colts running back, played at Penn State with Franco Harris ... **LARRY KELLEY (1915)**, Yale end who won the second Heisman Trophy award in 1936 — actually, it was the first time that the award (originally known as the Downtown Athletic Club Trophy) was called the Heisman Trophy ... **ROBERT PECK (1891)**, college Hall of Fame football player (a center) who was a two-time All-American at Pitt ... **OMAR "TURK" LOWN (1924)**, righty pitcher with Cubs and Chisox; only 55-61 lifetime but was bullpen ace when Sox won pennant in 1959 (led AL in saves), Turk became a post office worker in Pueblo, Colo.

■ **JOE NAMATH (1943)** — "Broadway Joe," the guy who put the American Football League on the map. A

Joe Namath
—on Monday night football in '85.

great quarterback from Alabama, he signed a much-publicized $400,000 contract with the N.Y. Jets in 1965 that gave the struggling AFL credibility. The prediction (and fact) of victory over the Colts in the 1969 Super Bowl made Namath an instant legend. He was one of the greatest, if not the greatest, pure passers in football history. Until Dan Fouts did it in 1979, Namath was the only quarterback to throw for more than 4,000 yards in one season. Namath pursued an acting career in theater and films.

■ **EDWARD BENNETT WILLIAMS (1920)** — Born in Hartford, Conn., he made his name as an ACLU lawyer who defended unpopular figures such as Joe McCarthy, Jimmy Hoffa, Frank Costello and Polly Adler. He was president of the Washington Redskins from 1965 to 1979, but had to relinquish control to buy the Baltimore Orioles in 1979.

■ Also born today: **BOB FERRY (1937)**, ex-NBA forward, later GM of the Washington Bullets ... **WILLIAM TAYLOR (1901)**, yachting editor of N.Y. Herald-Tribune, later editor of Yachting magazine; first sportswriter to win Pulitzer Prize (1934) for covering the America's Cup. ... **JOHN "HONEY" RUSSELL (1903)**, hall of fame basketball player and later a coach at Seton Hall from 1938 to 1960 (except from 1944 to '49), and led them to the NIT championship in 1953; Russell was the first coach of the Boston Celtics in 1947 ... **CECIL "TINY" THOMPSON (1905)**, Hall of Fame goalie with the Boston Bruins from 1928 to 1938, won the Vezina Trophy four times (1930, '33, '36, and '38) ... **JIM CRAIG (1957)**, another goalie born today, he was in the USA nets when they upset the USSR team at the 1980 Olympics (he was photographed wrapped in the American flag). He later served time for vehicular homicide.

NOTES

■**ALAN "THE HORSE" AMECHE (1933)** —
A great fullback. Born in
Kenosha, Wis., (actor Don
Ameche was also born in Kenosha — I guess they're related), he
played college ball at Wisconsin,
and was drafted by the Indianapolis Colts (when that team was
located in Baltimore) in 1955. He
led the NFL in rushing in his
rookie year and was the clutch
short-yardage guy until he retired
after the 1960 season. He's best
known for scoring the winning TD
in the "greatest game ever," the
sudden death overtime win
against the N.Y. Giants in 1958.

Alan Ameche

■**DEAN CHANCE (1941)** — brilliant 1960s right-
hander. He pitched for the Angels from 1961 to '66,
winning the Cy Young Award in '64 as he led the league
in wins, ERA, innings, complete games, and shutouts. He
was also known for running around Hollywood with
teammate Bo "Bad Boy" Belinsky. After a bout with
tendinitis, Chance was traded to the Twins in '67, where
he went 20-14 and was voted Comeback Player of the
Year. That season he pitched a perfect six-inning game
and, later, a no-hitter. Chance lost all of his money
investing in a 50 percent interest in fighter Earnie
Shavers. He's been working in circuses and state fairs
as a barker on the midway.

■Also born today: auto racer **TOM SNEVA (1948)**, who,
after three second-place finishes ('77, '78, and '80),
finally won the Indy 500 in 1983 ... shot putter **BRIAN
OLDFIELD (1945)**, world indoor record-holder, still
winning track meets ... **JOHNNY MOSTIL
(1896)**, 1920s White Sox outfielder with .301 lifetime
BA; one day made 11 putouts, one under ML record
for outfielders.

NOTES

■ **JOHNNY WEISSMUELLER (1904)** —
Renowned swimmer and actor, born in Windber, Pa., died in 1979. He overcame a bout of polio as a child to become the most successful swimmer of the first half-century. A Chicago high school dropout at age 15, he developed his powerful six-beat crawl stroke (six leg kicks to every two arm strokes) and broke his first world record at age 17. He won five gold medals at the 1924 and '28 Olympics (in the 100 meter, 400 meter, and 800 meter relay), and his record of 36 national titles stood for more than a half-century until recently broken by Tracy Caulkins. One of the first athletes to go Hollywood, Weissmueller became the fourth and most popular "Tarzan" in 1931, appearing in 18 films in the series. In his later years he was plagued by poor investments, income tax troubles, chronic heart ailments, and alimony payments to five ex-wives.

■ **WILBERT ROBINSON (1863)** —
Hall of Fame catcher and long-time manager of the Brooklyn Dodgers, born in Bolton, Mass. He was 5-foot-8½ and a gutsy team-leader of the scrappy Baltimore Orioles in the 1890s, finishing with a .273 lifetime batting average. "Uncle Robbie" took over the Dodger helm in 1914 and managed there until 1931, winning two pennants (in 1916 and 1920). He's the catcher on the all-time all-Robinson team.

■ Also born today: linebacker **JEFF SIEMON (1950)** of Stanford and Minnesota Vikings fame ... Reds righty **JIM MALONEY (1940)**, pitched two no-hitters in 1965, both extra inning games—won one 1-0, lost the other by the same score... **LAWRENCE "DON'T CALL ME LARRY" McCUTCHEON (1950)**, tremendous L.A. Rams running back of the 1970s who ran for 6,578 yards and a 4.3 career average ... **BOB LILLIS (1930)**, Houston Astros manager since The Fall of Bill Virdon (Hey, Bob, you need a clean-up hitter) ... **GARO YEPREMIAN (1944)**, the "left-footed Cypriot" of the Miami Dolphins dynasty of the '70s.

NOTES

■ **JIM GENTILE (1934)** —
Slugging first-baseman mostly with the Orioles. He had a few good years but 1961 stands out. He hit .302 with 46 homers and 141 RBI (on 147 hits). He also hit five grand-slam homers, a feat equalled only once, by Ernie Banks. Two of those slams were not only in the same game but in consecutive at-bats, a major league first. However, Gentile remained a bit in the shadow of Roger Maris and Mickey Mantle that year, finishing third behind them in the MVP balloting. "Diamond Jim" ended his nine-year career with a .260 lifetime BA. He

Jim Gentile

is in a great tradition of San Francisco-born first baseman which includes such luminaries as Dolf Camilli, Keith Hernandez, and let's not forget Babe Dahlgren. Gentile became manager of an automotive center in Mesa, Ariz.

■ Also born today: **BILLY CUNNINGHAM (1943)**, after six seasons as coach of the Philadelphia 76ers, he resigned in the wake of the Celtics' elimination of the Sixers in 1985; as a player, Cunningham spent his nine-year NBA career with the 76ers, averaging 20.8 points per game; as a coach he led Philly to the NBA title in 1982-83 ... **LINDY REMIGINO (1931)**, U.S. sprinter who surprised everyone by winning the 100 meters in the 1952 Olympics; it was a four-way tie (all four were timed in 10.4) but they gave Remigino a one-inch advantage over the Jamaican, Herb McKenley, who thought — and probably still thinks — he won ... two golfers: **HALE IRWIN (1945)**, two-time winner of the U.S. Open ('74 and '79) and **CHARLES SIFFORD (1923)**, the first important black golfer ... **EMMITT THOMAS (1943)**, brilliant ex-defensive back of the K.C. Chiefs.

NOTES

■ **BOB FITZSIMMONS (1862)** — Fitzsimmons, who has a strong claim to being the greatest fighter, pound for pound, of all time, was born in England. He moved to New Zealand as a boy, began fighting in Australia, and later lived in the U.S. "Ruby Robert" was middleweight champion, light-heavyweight champion, and — at 167 pounds — heavyweight champion from 1897 (after KOing James J. Corbett in the 14th round with his "solar plexus" punch) to 1899 (losing to James J. Jeffries in 11 rounds — if it isn't one James J. it's another). Fitzsimmons was not only small but didn't look like an athlete. He was spindly almost, had a smallish head, and was bald except for a bright red ring of hair. He fought until age 55 and died of pneumonia a year later.

Bob Fitzsimmons

■ **TERRY KENNEDY (1956)** —Padres catcher and one of the best in recent years. Born in Euclid, Ohio, he is the son of Bob Kennedy, an outfielder-third baseman with several teams and a longtime baseball executive. Terry is a tremendous performer, perhaps on the verge of greatness. A big (6-4, 220) lefty swinger, he hits for average and power. His 42 doubles in 1982 is a NL record for a catcher.

■ Also born today: golfer **SANDRA HAYNIE (1934)**, Hall of Famer with more than 40 tournament wins, including the 1974 U.S. Open and the LPGA tourney in 1965 and 1974 ... **JOHN MCNAMARA (1932)**, currently managing the Red Sox. Formerly managed the Padres, A's, Reds, and Angels; he's one of the few managers I like ... **BOBBY WANZER (1921)**, basketball guard at Seton Hall and, for 10 seasons (1947-56), with the Rochester Royals ... **ANDREA JAEGER (1965)**, tennis prodigy who was the youngest ever on the pro tour (14 years, 9 months) and youngest ever seeded at Wimbledon (reaching the quarter-final).

NOTES

Sports birthdays / June 5

■**MARION MOTLEY (1920)** —
Tremendous Cleveland Browns fullback during the first eight years of their franchise (1946-53), was born in Leesburg, Ga. He attended U. of Nevada and, because of World War II, had a late start as a 26-year-old rookie. Motley was a 240-pound cannonball that tore up the AAFC and NFL, amassing almost 5,000 yards, 31 TDs, and a phenomenal 5.7 yards per carry. Claims that he was the greatest fullback in pro history receive very little debate.

Marion Motley

■**JACK CHESBRO (1874)** —
Right-handed pitcher who won 41 games in 1904, born in North Adams, Mass. "Happy Jack," one of the great spitballers, had an 11-year career (1899-1909), winning 199 games (not a bad yearly average) with a 2.68 ERA. His 41 wins is a major league season record. That year, pitching for the New York Highlanders (later the Yankees), he completed 48 games in 51 starts and pitched 454 innings. Chesbro is also the only pitcher to lead both leagues in won-loss percentage. He died in 1931.

■Also born today: **BATTLING NELSON (1882)**, lightweight champion, 1908-10, born in Denmark, but grew up in the U.S. Nelson supposedly invented the left hook. He certainly popularized and perfected it ... **ART DONOVAN (1925)**, Hall of Fame defensive tackle for the Baltimore Colts (1950, 1953-61); his father was the boxing referee Arthur Donovan and his grandfather was Mike Donovan, one of the earliest middleweight boxing champions ... **FRANK W. KEANEY (1886)**, famed basketball coach at Rhode Island (1921-48), introduced full-court press from the opening tip...S.F. native **EDDIE JOOST (1916)**, shortstop, mostly with the Philadelphia A's, only a lifetime .239 hitter but walked more than 100 times for six straight years (1947-52) while averaging almost 20 homers a year ... two sprinters: **TOMMIE SMITH (1944)** and **JOHN CARLOS (1945)**, both of whom were involved in the black athlete protest at the 1968 Olympics and who finished first and third, respectively, in their specialty — the 200 meters.

■ BILL DICKEY (1907) —

Hall of Fame catcher for the New York Yankees from 1928 to 1946 (except for '44 and '45 during WW II).

Bill Dickey

Dickey has a strong claim to being the best all-around performer ever to play at his position. A lifetime .313 hitter for 17 seasons, he also had good power and was a good RBI man. He was an excellent all-around receiver and probably the fastest catcher ever. He played on nine pennant-winning Yankee teams that only lost one of those nine World Series. Dickey's last year, 1946, was Yogi Berra's first. When Berra retired after the '63 season, the Yankees ended an era of 26 years of greatness at the catcher's position. Dickey was a Yankee coach from 1949 to 1957 and was Berra's mentor. He transformed Berra from an awkward mess into a solid receiver.

■ Also born today: **HARRY GREB (1894)**, "The Human Windmill," rated No. 3 among all-time middleweights, the only fighter ever to defeat Gene Tunney, died at age 32 ... **BJORN BORG (1956)**, considered by many to be the greatest tennis player of all time, retired at age 27 as one of the richest athletes in the world ... **BOBBY MITCHELL (1935)**, Hall of Fame running back (with Cleveland from 1958 to 1961) and wide receiver (with the Redskins from 1962 to 1968), brilliant as rusher, receiver and returner, he was the Redskins' first black player 16 years after the color barrier was broken ... **BILL ALEXANDER (1889)**, succeeded John Heisman as football coach at Georgia Tech in 1920, retiring in 1944; the first coach to take his team to all four major bowls.

NOTES

■ HERB SCORE (1933) —

One of the all-time hard-luck athletes. A brilliant lefty fastball pitcher who came up with Cleveland, Score led the league in strikeouts as a rookie in 1955 and again in '56. That year he was 20-9 and also led the league in shutouts, but in 1957 a line drive (off the bat of Gil McDougald) hit him in the eye and virtually ended his brief but awesome career at age 23. He struggled through five more seasons with a 19-27 record and finally retired. He became the announcer for Cleveland games, one of the best.

Herb Score

■ RANDY TURPIN (1928) —

Another tragic sports figure, born on this day in England. He shocked the boxing public in 1951 by defeating the great Ray Robinson (on points) to win the middleweight title. But 64 days later he lost it back to Robinson in a rematch, stopped in 10 rounds. That fight (at the Polo Grounds in New York) drew the biggest gate in middleweight history — 61,000-plus fans who paid $750,000. Personal problems and the fact that he had none of the money he won as a fighter caused him to commit suicide at age 37.

■ Also born today: **CAZZIE RUSSELL (1944)**, ex-Michigan All-American and gunner for the Knicks, Warriors and Lakers ... **THURMAN MUNSON (1947)**, the brilliant Yankee catcher and captain and yet another tragic sports figure, died in an airplane crash at age 32 ... **CLARENCE DEMAR (1888)**, born with (and never cured of) a broken foot, he nonetheless became a top marathon runner, winning seven Boston Marathons. and competing with success into his '60s.

NOTES

■**BYRON "WHIZZER" WHITE (1917)** —
Triple - threat running back (and Supreme Court justice). Born in Fort Collins, Colo., he attended the University of Colorado and was an All-American tailback who ran, passed, punted, and place-kicked. He was called the greatest athlete ever from the Rocky Mountain area. He was also a Phi Beta Kappa and went to Oxford as a Rhodes scholar. He played briefly in the NFL with Pittsburgh and Detroit and led the NFL in rushing in 1940 — while attending Yale Law School. White was appointed to the Supreme Court in 1962 by JFK, whom he supported.

Whizzer White

■**HERB ADDERLEY (1939)** —
Hall of Fame cornerback with the Packers and Cowboys, 1961 to 1972. He was a brilliant running back at Michigan State and was the first round draft choice of the Packers, who immediately converted him to defensive back. That helped when he returned his 48 career interceptions. He ran back seven for TDs. Only Ken Houston's nine tops that figure. He was also an outstanding kickoff returner who returned two for TDs and had a 25.7 yard average. Adderley played in the first two Super Bowls with the Packers and with the champion Cowboys in 1972.

■Also born today: **DEL ENNIS (1925)**, outfielder and one of Philadelphia Phillies "Whiz Kids" of 1950, when they won the pennant ... righty **VAN LINGLE MUNGO (1911)**, one of the few baseball players to have a song named after him (pianist-composer David Frishberg's litany of evocative names in baseball history). A 120-115 lifetime pitcher, he won 81 games for the Dodgers, 1932 to 1936 ... **MARK BELANGER (1944)**, Orioles shortstop of the 60s and 70s who owns the best fielding percentage of all time for a shortstop; he's currently president of the Players' Association ... **BERNIE CASEY (1939)**, ex-wide receiver for the 49ers and Rams who became TV and film actor ... **WILLIE DAVENPORT (1943)**, won gold medal at 1968 Olympics in 110-meter hurdles.

■ **EMIL "IRISH" MEUSEL (1893) —**
Solid-hitting outfielder mostly with the New York Giants.
He had some good years with
the Phillies before coming to the
Giants in 1921 and helping them
win four straight pennants (the
only team other than the Yankees
to do so). He was a hitting hero of
the 1922 Series, despite getting
only five hits in 20 trips. He drove
in seven important runs in that
Series as the vaunted Yankees
were swept in four straight. On the
Yankee teams of that era was
Emil's brother, Bob Meusel, slugging outfielder who led the AL in
homers and RBIs in 1925 (and was

Irish Meusel

still in the shadow of teammates Ruth and Gehrig). After
the Waners and the five Delahanty brothers, the Meusels
are the best-hitting brothers in baseball history. Bob was
bigger but only a bit better long-ball hitter. Both had
11-year careers and finished with virtually the same
batting average — .309 for Bob and .310 for "Irish," who
died in 1963 at age 70.

■ Also born today: **BRANCH McCRACKEN (1908)**,
basketball coach at Indiana (1938-65), winning NCAA
titles twice — in 1940 and 1953 ... **FRANK McCORMICK
(1911)**, Cincinnati Reds first baseman (1937-45), MVP in
1940, .299 lifetime hitter,; 40 years ago set NL record by
going 138 straight errorless games, a record that was
broken in 1984 by Steve Garvey ... **DAVE PARKER
(1951)**, another Cincinnati Reds player (also born there —
just as Pete Rose) who won an MVP award (in '78) as a
member of the Pittsburgh Pirates ... **BRIAN TAYLOR
(1951)**, ex-NBA guard, brother of ex-49er defensive back,
Bruce Taylor ... **TOMMY GORMAN (1886)**, Canadian
sports pioneer; co-founded the NHL in 1917 and
managed seven Stanley Cup winners, introduced pro
hockey to New York City in the 1920s; also a pioneer
baseball promoter in Canada ... **ROY SMALLEY (1926)**,
good field-no hit shortstop with the Cubs and Phillies,
father of good hit-no field Twins infielder with same
name ... **BILL VIRDON (1931)**, manager of the Astros
from 1975 to 1982, one run-itis sufferer.

NOTES

■ **BATTLING LEVINSKY (1891)** — Light-heavyweight champion (1916), born Barney Lebrowitz in Philadelphia.

Battling Levinsky

He began his 23-year ring career at age 15 and had an unbelievable 274 fights. In 1914 he had 35 bouts, including nine in January! He outpointed Jack Dillon in 1916 to win the title and lost it four years later to Georges Carpentier via a four-round KO. Levinsky, the sixth-rated light-heavyweight of all time, died in 1949.

■ **JACK GRANEY (1886)** — Outfielder with Cleveland Indians (1910-22) and the first jock-turned-announcer, born in Canada. Graney was only a .250 hitter whose chief claim to fame as a player is that he hit the first home run off Babe Ruth, in 1914. In fact, it was the only homer Graney hit that year. Graney was the Cleveland Indians' radio announcer for 23 years (1932-54) and died in 1978.

■ Also born today: **KEN SINGLETON (1947)**, in 1984 ended 15-year career with the Mets, Expos and the last 10 with the Orioles. His 248 career homers made him the third best home run hitter among switch-hitters (though Eddie Murray passed him in 1985); Mantle, Ripper Collins and Singleton are the only switch-hitters ever to hit 35 home runs in one season ... San Diego Chargers QB **DAN FOUTS (1951)**, S.F.-native, the second QB to throw for 4,000 yards in a season ... **JON McGLOCKLIN (1943)**, dead-eye guard on the Kareem-Robertson Bucks that won title in 1970-71 ... **JIM HICKMAN (1937)**, outfielder with Mets and Cubs, peaked with Cubs in 1970 with .316 average, 32 homers and 115 RBI ... **CHUCK FAIRBANKS (1933)**, football coach with the New England Patriots for several years until Colorado (University, that is) offered him more money... **CHARLIE SAVA (1900)**, San Francisco's legendary swimming teacher, known as "builder of champions," coached swimming greats Ann Curtis, Mark Spitz and Donna de Varona, as well as more than half-million other swimmers, and produced eight women's national championship teams, 1943-48.

NOTES

■ JOE MONTANA (1956) —

Superstar 49er QB. Born in Monongahela, Pa., he played college ball at Notre Dame. Anyone who saw him play in college (except the experts, apparently) knew that he was better than a third-round draft choice when the 49ers picked him in 1979. He and the 49ers put it all together in 1981 and again in 1984, the fulfillment of a dream. His ordinariness endears him to all football fans. He does the routine things perfectly, without having to be big, strong, or fast. His movements are beautiful, classical. Montana can play this game.

Joe Montana

■ VINCE LOMBARDI (1913) —

The great Green Bay Packers coach was born in Brooklyn. A lineman as a player, he was one of the Seven Blocks of Granite at Fordham. He coached under his mentor, Earl Blaik, at West Point (1949-53), then as an assistant with the New York Giants (1954-58). In 1958 he began his years of dynasty at Green Bay, winning five NFL titles in his ten years there (1958-67). He wound up his career coaching the Redskins, giving them their first glimmer of respectability in years.

■ Also born today: ERNIE NEVERS (1903), the great Stanford and Chicago Cardinal fullback, in college and pro hall of fame (also pitched in the major leagues) ... ROGER BRESNAHAN (1879), Christy Mathewson's catcher on the New York Giants (1903 - 08), a lifetime .280 hitter who is given credit for inventing shinguards and chest protector but was only the first to wear them openly; known as "The Duke of Tralee," he liked to pretend he was born in Ireland; his real birthplace was Toledo, Ohio ... "JUMPIN' JACK" McCRACKEN (1911), hall of fame basketball player with such AAU teams as the Denver Nuggets and Phillips 66ers ... BUDDY BAER (1915), brother of Max Baer, he was a big heavyweight (6-foot-6½, 245 pounds) who had an impressive record of 48 wins (43 KOs) and seven losses, two of them to Joe Louis — in the first one, Baer didn't answer the bell for the seventh round because they protested that Louis hit Baer after the bell ended round six and hurt Baer, they wanted Louis disqualified but the ref didn't buy it; in the return match, Louis knocked Baer out in the first round.

NOTES

■JOHNNY BUFF (1888) —
American flyweight and world bantamweight champion
(1921-22),born John Lesky in Perth Amboy, N.J. He began
to box while in the Navy and fought amateur for quite a
while until making his pro debut at age 30. 1921 was a
very good year for Buff. He won his flyweight title and —
at age 33 — decisioned Pete Herman (No. 2 all-time
bantam) for the bantamweight title. 1922 was not a good
year. He lost both of his titles, both by KOs. He fought
long past his prime, losing most of his fights until retiring
at age 38 and re-joining the Navy. Buff was a stylish boxer
who is rated among the top 10 flyweights of all time. He
died in 1955.

■ Also born today: **BILL COWLEY (1912)**, Hockey Hall of
Famer, a center with the Boston Bruins (1935-47),
two-time MVP (1941 and '43) who was first-team all-NHL
four times . . . **DUTCH RENNERT (1934)**, NL ump since
1973 (my kind of ump, he screams out the called strikes)
. . . **HAROLD "BRICK" MULLER (1901)**, the first
All-American football player from Cal; he was an end who
led the legendary Wonder teams of the early 1920s . . .
CARLTON WILLIAMSON (1958), the best strong safety in
the NFL since his rookie season in 1981. Is there a surer
open-field tackler in football?

NOTES

■ MEL PARNELL (1922) —

Brilliant Red Sox lefty pitcher from 1947 to 1956. Parnell had a career 123-75 won-loss record (all with the Bosox), a torrid .621 percent-age. He had it all going in 1949 — a 25-7 record with most wins, complete games (27), innings (295), and a league-leading ERA. Parnell was a Yankee nemesis who shut them out four times in 1953 when he went 21-8, and was locked up in many a big game with Yankee pitchers Reynolds, Raschi and Lopat. He pitched a no-hitter in his final year, 1956, and is the Sox's winningest lefty since Lefty Grove. He later managed in Bos-

Mel Parnell

ton's farm system and was a Red Sox radio announcer. He currently operates a pest control service in New Orleans, his birthplace.

■ DON BUDGE (1915) —

The first tennis player to "Grand Slam." Born in Oakland, Budge was a tall, freckle-faced kid who overcame awkwardness and an initial lack of interest in tennis to become a Hall of Famer. He won the U.S. and British titles in 1937 and '38 and in the latter year won the four "Grand Slam" tournaments: The U.S., British, French, and Australian championships. Only four players have ever accomplished that feat (Maureen Connolly, Margaret Smith Court, and Rod Laver, who did it twice). He competed as a pro until age 40.

■ RED GRANGE (1903) —

Often called the greatest broken-field runner of all time. He was known as "The Galloping Ghost" as well as "The Wheaton Iceman," referring to Wheaton, Ill., where he worked on an ice wagon in summer while attending the Univ. of Illinois (though born in Forksville, Pa.) His college exploits put football on the map. He became a sports idol of the 1920s as prominent as Babe Ruth or Jack Dempsey. He also put pro football on the map. His 1925 signing with the Bears gave credibility to the fledging NFL. (He, Gale Sayers, Walter Payton — all Chicago Bears)

■ Also born today:

Two track and field athletes were born on this day: PAAVO NURMI (1897), "The Flying Finn" won four gold medals at the 1924 Olympics — in the 1,500 meters, 5,000 meters, 10,000 meter steeplechase, and as part of the 3,000 meter relay ... and DALLAS LONG (1940), shotputter who won gold at '64 Olympics and bronze at 60 Olympics.

NOTES

■ DON NEWCOMBE (1926) —

Only pitcher ever to win Rookie-of-the-Year, Cy Young, and MVP awards in a career.

Born in Madison, N.J., "Newk," achieved many milestones: He was the first prominent black pitcher in the big leagues and the first black pitcher to be named rookie of the year (1949), and Cy Young and MVP winner — in 1956, going 27-7. One of the best hitting pitchers of all time, he had a .271 life-time batting average and, in 1955, hit seven homers, a record for a pitcher that is shared by Don Drysdale. That same year, Newcombe (who probably should have been MVP that year, too, going 20-5 and hitting seven homers) stole home (at 6-4, 230 pounds that must've been worth seeing). It was the last time a pitcher has stolen home in the major leagues. Newcombe is a reformed alcoholic. He has worked with the National Institute on Alcohol Abuse and lectures extensively on the dangers of alcohol. He is director of community relations for the L.A. Dodgers.

Don Newcombe

■ ERIC HEIDEN (1958) —

Great speed-skater. Born in La Crosse, Wis., Heiden (whose sister Beth is also a champion skater) won all five men's speed skating events in the 1980 Olympics — 500, 1,000, 1,500, 5,000 and 10,000 meters. An unprecedented feat.

■ Also born today: **TOM MATTE** (1939), all-purpose running back with Colts during the 1960s; in 1965 Western Division playoff game against the Packers, Matte was pressed into service as quarterback when Unitas and his backup were both too hurt to play; Colts lost 13-10 overtime thriller ... KATHERINE RAWLS (1918), won Olympic medals in 1936 in swimming and diving ... Two hockey hall of famers: **JACK ADAMS** (1895), coach (1927-47) and GM (1927-63) of the Detroit Red Wings, and **CLARENCE "HAPPY" DAY** (1901), defenseman (1926-37) and coach (1940-50) of the Toronto Maple Leafs... **BEN DAVIDSON** (1940), ex-Raider defensive tackle and occasional TV actor.

■ BILLY WILLIAMS (1938) —

The A's batting instructor. He spent a 17-year career mostly with the Cubs where he was rookie-of-the-year in 1961, and finished his career with the A's. Williams, a tremendous left-handed hitter with the proverbial sweet swing was a lifetime .295 hitter and finished with 426 homers, 18th on the all-time list. Always in the shadow of Ernie Banks, Williams is just as worthy of the Hall of Fame and should make it in a year or two. It was Steve Garvey who, in 1982, broke Williams' National League record of playing in 1,117 consecutive

Billy Williams

games. Supposedly, Williams' disposition was as sweet as his swing. Read Leo Durocher's "Nice Guys Finish Last" for an interesting portrait of a ballplayer who never got the ink that he deserved.

■ Also born today: **WALLACE WADE** (1892), football coach at Alabama (1922-30) and Duke (1931-41) with a combined record of 171-49-13 ... **DUSTY BAKER** (1949), A's outfielder - 1B - DH clutch performer and team leader (so why did the Dodgers and Giants let him go?) ... **RICCARDO PALETTI** (1958), Italian auto racer who died at age 23 while racing (in his rookie season) in the Canadian Grand Prix ... **BABE DAHLGREN** (1912), played first base for eight teams from 1935 to 1946, including Yankees in 1939 when Lou Gehrig took himself out of the lineup; Dahlgren (born in S.F.) replaced the awesome Gehrig, played in 144 games that season, hitting only .235 but with 15 homers ands 89 RBI; funny that "Babe" (born Ellsworth Tenney Dahlgren) should replace "Larrupin' Lou" ... **JOHN REED KILPATRICK** (1889), All-American end at Yale, (1909-10), later president of Madison Square Garden in N.Y.C. from 1939 until death in 1960 ... **WADE BOGGS** (1958), but can he hit for average? Bosox third baseman came into '85 season with .357 lifetime BA ... **JOHNNY SAMPLE** (1937), ex-DB for N.Y. Jets, author of "Confessions of A Dirty Player."

NOTES

■ **KEN JOHNSON (1933) —**
The only pitcher in major league history to lose a nine-inning, complete game no-hitter. A big (6-4, 210) right-hander, he had a 13-year career (1958-70) with several teams, compiling a 91-106 career won-loss record. Johnson did have three good years with the Braves but one game in his career stands out. In 1964 (while with the Astros versus the Reds), he pitched his unique masterpiece — in defeat — and brought it upon himself. The leadoff batter in the ninth bunted, Johnson fielded it and threw it away, the runner advancing to second. A ground out moved the runner to third and he scored on another ground ball that was booted by the second baseman. No hits, a 1-0 loss.

Ken Johnson

The cast of characters in this Greek tragedy is staggering in itself: Joe Nuxhall, the Reds' winning pitcher (the youngest player ever in the big leagues at 15 was nearly 36, in his twilight years); Nellie Fox (yes, the Hall of Famer from the Chicago White Sox), also in his twilight years with the Astros, the second baseman whose error ended the game; and the leadoff man who bunted and finally scored the only run, Pete Rose, only at the beginning of his career — and he's still playing 21 years later! Ken Johnson lost the game, but that day belongs to him.

■ Also born today: **DARRELL GRIFFITH (1958)**, 1980 college player of the year from Louisville, "Dr. Dunkenstein," a veteran of the Utah Jazz who deserves a better team ... **DEREK SANDERSON (1946)**, roughhouse star of the Boston Bruins who helped them win a couple of Stanley Cups in the early 1970s, but alcohol problems and personality conflicts dragged his career downhill ... **RON LeFLORE (1948)**, after prison term had great years with the Tigers in the late 1970s, dynamite hitter and base-stealer. Hank Luisetti (1916), Stanford hoop phenom... Roberto Duran (1951), one of the greatest lightweights ever.

NOTES

■ **MAURICE STOKES (1933)** —
Tragic basketball star. Born in Pittsburgh, Pa., he went to nearby St. Francis College, a school that Stokes put on the map. He was drafted by the Cincinnati Royals in 1956 and was named rookie of the year. Stokes, at 6-foot-7 and 250 pounds, was a Wes Unseld-type who was considered second only to Bill Russell as a rebounder. In 1958, Stokes suffered a fall on the court that resulted in brain damage and went into a four-month coma. He emerged paralyzed and spent the next 12 years in a wheelchair until he died in 1970. Stokes' friend and teammate, Jack Twyman, who became his guardian, wrote a book about their relationship.

■ **ELROY "CRAZY LEGS" HIRSCH (1923)** —
NFL immortal. Born in Wausau, Wis., Hirsch went to the state university and began his pro career with the Chicago Rockets (1946-48) in the All-America Football Conference. He had a brilliant nine-year career with the Los Angeles Rams (1949-57), equaling, in 1951, the all-time NFL record of 17 TDs for a receiver in one season. Hirsch also set the record in that same year for the most consecutive games (11) catching a TD pass. In 1969, he was named the all-time NFL

"Crazy Legs"

flanker. Hirsch tried an acting career, appearing in the 1955 film "Unchained" (with Unchained Melody the background music, of course).

■ Also born today: **TOMMY BURNS (1881)**, born Noah Brusso in Canada, heavyweight champion, 1906-08, lost crown to Jack Johnson ... **WALTER ECKERSALL (1886)**, one of the all-time great backs, who, at 138 pounds, led the University of Chicago to a 2-0 win over Michigan in 1904, ending its streak of four straight years without a loss... **DAVE CONCEPCION (1948)**, Cincinnati Reds shortstop since 1970, an obscure superstar who deserves to go right into the Hall of Fame; in the great tradition of Venezuelan shortstops (Chico Carrasquel, Luis Aparicio among others)...miler **DEREK IBBOTSON (1932)**, peaked in July 1957, when he set world record of 3:57.2, beating a field of the world's best, including Olympic champion Ron Delany ... **BOBBY BELL (1940)**, All-Pro linebacker on the K.C. Chiefs AFL dynasty of the 1960s.

NOTES

■ LOU BROCK (1939) —

Stole more bases (938) than any other player in major league history. Born in El Dorado, Ark., (as was Goose Tatum and Travis Williams), he came up with the Cubs, struggled for three years and was shipped to the  St. Louis Cardinals (basically, for Ernie Broglio). There he flourished for 15 years, finishing with a .293 lifetime batting average, 3,023 hits, the NL single-season stolen base record (118) and World Series batting average of .391 in 21 games (in 1964, '66 and '67) that is an all-time record. Less known is his 485-foot shot into the center-field bleachers of the Polo Grounds (where the Mets played their home games in 1962), a wasteland that was reached only

Lou Brock

by Brock, Hank Aaron and Joe Adcock. In 1985 Brock was elected to the Hall of Fame, one of only 15 to make it in his first year of eligibility.

■ GEORGE MIKAN (1924) —

The first of the great big men of modern basketball. Born in a suburb of Chicago, he played college ball at DePaul in the mid-1940s (Ray Meyer had just started coaching there) and played nine seasons as a pro with the Minneapolis (now L.A.) Lakers. Many rules, including widening the foul lane from six to 12 feet, were passed to curb the great Mikan who, at 6-feet-10, didn't have to pass and handle the ball as well as he did. His 53 points vs. Rhode Island in the 1945 NIT semifinal set a Madison Square Garden record. Mikan, who earned his law degree, was named the first commissioner of the ABA in 1967.

■ Also born today: **GLENN MORRIS** (1912), won the 1936 Olympic decathlon, setting a record that stood until 1952 ..., another decathlon winner: **PAAVO YRJOLA** (1902), a Finn who won the event in 1928.

NOTES

■ **LEO NOMELLINI (1924) —**
Great lineman. "Nomo" was the first player ever picked by the 49ers (out of Minnesota) in an NFL draft and, like Lou Gehrig, was an iron man who played in every 49er game for 14 seasons (1950-63). He was all-NFL six times —twice on offense, four times on defense — and was named the NFL's all-time defensive tackle. Later a wrestler (he fought the great Lou Thesz three times, drawing twice and winning the third on a disqualification), he has been a long-time wrestling promoter.

Leo Nomellini

■ **LOU GEHRIG (1903) —**
The incomparable "Iron Horse", born in New York City. Gehrig played first base for the Yankees from June 1, 1925 to May 2, 1939, never missing one of those 2,130 games. That is one career record that is safe. His 23 career grand slam homers seems pretty secure, too. He had a .340 lifetime BA and hit 493 home runs. He is third in career RBI (after Aaron and Ruth) and holds the single-season AL record of 184 (in 1931). He was the first to hit four homers in a nine-inning game (in 1932). Gehrig took himself out of the Yankee lineup because he didn't feel well. In 1941, he died at age 37 of ameliotrophic lateral sclerosis.

■ **HELENE MADISON (1913) —**
"The Queen of the Waters", born in Seattle. A 6-footer, Madison held, at age 17, 26 world free-style swimming records from 50 yards to one mile. She won three gold medals at the 1932 Olympics.

■ **EDDIE CICOTTE (1884) —**
One of the "Eight Men Out" who threw the 1919 World Series. Born in Detroit. A righty pitcher, he played mostly with the White Sox in a 13-year career and was 210-147 lifetime with a 2.37 ERA. He led the Chisox to the pennant in 1919 with a 29-7, 1.82 season. Being the ace pitcher, he was in a position to hurt his team most. He had a good shot at the Hall of Fame, but was banned from baseball in 1921 and died in 1969.

■ Also born today: **JERRY REUSS** (1949) lefty pitcher with the Dodgers (formerly with Cardinals, Pirates and Astros) ... **CHARLIE COWAN** (1938), offensive tackle with the L.A. Rams from 1961-69 and from 1970-73.

NOTES

■ **DORIS HART (1925)** —
A tennis star of the 1950s. Born in St. Louis, she won the U.S. Open in 1954 and again in 1955. She and Shirley Fry teamed up to win four consecutive U.S. doubles championships (1951-54). Hart also won singles championships of Australia, France, England, Italy and South Africa.

Doris Hart

■ **GLENNA COLLETT VARE (1903)**—Great golfer of 1920s and '30s, born in New Haven, Conn. Vare dominated women's golf in the '20s, winning the U.S. Amateur title six times. She continued playing good golf in the '30s and represented the U.S. many times in the Curtis Cup, the last time in 1948 at age 45. Vare was known as a class act, a gracious winner or loser. The Vare Trophy, named in her honor, is given each year to the woman pro golfer with the best scoring average.

■ **Also born today: LEEMAN BENNETT (1938)**, ex-Atlanta Falcons coach (1977-83), new coach of the Tampa Bay Buccaneers, second head coach in Bucs' history ... **TEX SCHRAMM (1920)**, president and G.M. of Dallas Cowboys ... **JIM DELAHANTY (1879)**, infielder with several teams in the early 1900s, one of five brothers to play in the major leagues, an all-time record; Big Ed, a Hall of Famer, was the best of them ... **LEN DAWSON (1935)**, quarterback of the K.C. Chiefs dynasty of the late '60s and early '70s; his 19-year career at quarterback is second only to Earl Morrall's 21 years ... **CUMBERLAND POSEY (1891)**, organizer and manager of the Negro Leagues. Dickie Thon (1958), brilliant Astros SS, badly beaned in 1983, trying comeback.

NOTES

■ DUANE THOMAS (1947) —

The controversial running back. Born in Dallas, he played ball at West Texas State and was drafted in the first round by the Cowboys. Thomas had a unique style. Though he was big and fast, it was his wraith-like moves and his ability to slow down to use his blockers that set him apart. He led the Cowboys to Super Bowl glory in 1972 but got shipped to the Redskins because of a "bad attitude" — i.e., he had the guts to criticize Cowboys coaching and management. His career was effectively over. George Allen, the Redskins

Duane Thomas

coach, didn't like his attitude either. Thomas might have been ranked with the all-time greats if he had had his chance to perform.

■ EVERETT N. CASE (1900) —

Great basketball coach. He built North Carolina State into a basketball power, compiling a record of 377 wins and 133 losses from 1947 to 1964. He retired in the middle of the 1964 season because of fatigue and died a year later.

■ ED LOPAT (1918) —

"Steady Eddie," left-hander of the mid '40s to mid '50s, born in New York City. He had some pretty good years with the Chisox (1944-47), but pitched brilliantly for the great Yankee dynasty from 1948 to 1954, his percentage never falling below .600. The stubby breaking-ball artist was 109-51 for seven seasons and formed, with Allie Reynolds and Vic Raschi, one of the best starting trios in baseball history.

■ Also born today:

WILLIAM SHEA (1907), lawyer after whom Shea Stadium was named . . . two Cleveland Browns tackles of the 1950s: BOB GAIN (1929), from Kentucky, played with Browns from '54 to '64, and MIKE McCORMACK (1930), from Kansas, played with Browns from '54 to '62, and later coached the Eagles (1973-75) and Colts (1980-82)... BRIAN STERNBERG (1943), Seattle-born pole vaulter, held world record in 1963 ... BUDDY O'CONNOR (1916), diminutive hockey player with the Canadiens (1941-47) and N.Y. Rangers (1947-1951); a center, he won both the MVP trophy and the Lady Byng Trophy (for ability and sportsmanship) in 1947.

NOTES

■ CARL HUBBELL (1903) —

Carl Hubbell

"King Carl," also "The Meal-ticket," played his entire 16-year career with the New York Giants (1928-43), winning 253 games and losing 154, with a lifetime ERA of 2.97. He was the league's MVP in 1933 and 1936, the only NL pitcher to win that award twice. He is best remembered for striking out Ruth, Gehrig, Foxx, Simmons and Cronin in order in the 1934 All-Star Game — Ruth and Gehrig going down on six screwballs, a pitch Hubbell developed in 1925 and named himself. Among his feats was winning 24 games in a row from 1936 to '37. Hubbell later directed minor league operations for the Giants.

■ PAUL MORPHY (1837) —

Another "king"—of chess, born in New Orleans. Known as "The Pride and the Sorrow of Chess," Morphy was a prodigy who got his law degree at age 18. Against family wishes, he toured Europe and, though an unknown, defeated the best players on the Continent and at age 21 was acknowledged as the best chess player in the world. At age 22 he retired, never to play again, and spent the last 15 years of his life in New Orleans as a paranoid recluse dying in his bathtub of apoplexy at age 47. The novel, "The Chessplayers," by Frances Parkinson Keyes, is about Morphy.

■ Also born today:

PETE MARAVICH (1948), a college phenom at LSU, coached by his father there. In 10 pro seasons with New Orleans (get the Morphy connection?) Jazz, he scored almost 16,000 points for a 24.2 average ... **CORNELIUS WARMERDAM (1915)**, the first to pole vault 15 feet ... **DON JORDAN (1934)**, welterweight champ, 1958-60 ... **FRANK KUDELKA (1925)**, nicknamed "Apples," St. Mary's College's first basketball All-American ... **FAYE THRONEBERRY (1931)**, outfielder with Red Sox and Senators in the 1950s; a lifetime .236 hitter, he is even better known as the older brother of Marvelous Marv Throneberry (a lifetime .237 hitter) ... **BOBBY DOUGLASS (1947)**, strong runner for the Chicago Bears in the early 70s; unfortunately, he was a quarterback (lefty); he was born in Damon Runyan's birthplace — Manhattan, Kan.

NOTES

■ **GEORGE WEISS (1895)** —
New York Yankees empire builder of the 1930s, '40s and '50s, born in New Haven, Conn. Weiss was a hotshot minor league executive when he met Colonel Jake Ruppert, owner of the club, in 1931. Branch Rickey invented the farm system idea with the Cardinals, Ruppert liked the idea and hired Weiss as his farm director. Weiss made sure the post-Ruth Yankees had a steady flow of stars. In his 15 years in that capacity, the Yankees won nine pennants. In 1948, he became general manager and began an entirely new dynasty, hiring Casey Stengel as manager despite general criticism that Stengel had a bad track record and was merely a buffoon. During

George Weiss

that era, the Yanks won 10 pennants (in 13 seasons) and seven World Series, including an unheard-of five in a row (1949-53). Weiss re-emerged as president of the expansion New York Mets and again hired Stengel as manager. Despite record losses during the first years, the Mets outdrew the Yankees. Weiss retired in 1966, but had laid the groundwork for the Mets' pennant in 1969. He was named to the Hall of Fame in 1971 and died a year later.

■ **WILMA RUDOLPH (1940)** — Perhaps the greatest woman short-distance runner of all time. Born in St. Bethlehem, Tenn., she was the 20th of 22 children and had double pneumonia, scarlet fever and polio. She didn't walk without braces until age 11. In 1960 she became the only American woman to win three gold medals in one Olympics.

■ Also born today: two other runners: **GIL DODDS** (1918) (from Kansas, naturally), set indoor mile record (4:05.3) in 1948 which stood for six years; Tanzanian **FILBERT BAYI (1953)**, holds 1500 m and mile records... **LAWSON LITTLE (1910)**, won 1935 Sullivan Award (best amateur athlete), last golfer to win it (Wilma Rudolph also won)... wide receiver **TONY HILL (1956)** of Stanford and Cowboys fame ... **WALTER DUKES (1930)**, basketball star who led Seton Hall to an undefeated season in 1953, later played with the Globetrotters, Knicks, and Lakers ... **TOM HALLER (1937)**, another baseball executive born this day, GM of the S.F. Giants.

NOTES

■ **JACK DEMPSEY (1895)** —

Jack Dempsey

"The Manassa Mauler" (so named after his birthplace — Manassa, Colo.) was heavyweight champion from 1919 to 1926. He lost his title to Gene Tunney, drawing more than 120,000 fans, the biggest crowd in boxing history. His return match with Tunney in 1927 (featuring the famous "long count") grossed more than $2.5 million, the biggest gate in boxing history. The rematch also drew more than 100,000 fans, the only two bouts in history to do so. Dempsey's bout with Georges Carpentier in 1921 was the first $1 million gate. He won 60 fights (49 by KO) and lost seven. He was a tremendous puncher and crowd-pleaser, and more than half of his kayos were in the first round. He later became a successful restaurateur in New York City.

■ Also born today: **BETTY STOVE (1945)**, Dutch tennis player, her forte being doubles and mixed doubles play, she's won five U.S. Opens with men and women; she has been Hana Mandlikova's coach...golfer **BILLY CASPER (1931)**, two-time winner of the U.S. Open (in '59 and '66) ... **LARRY FOUST** (out of LaSalle) for the Fort Wayne Pistons (and Minneapolis Lakers) during the 1950s ... **SAM JONES (1933)**, Celtics guard (1957-68) while they won 10 NBA titles, retired with 15,380 points — an all-time Celtic record ... **CHARLES H. "CHUCK" TAYLOR (1901)**, Hall of Fame basketball ambassador who in 1922 began a traveling basketball clinic spreading the gospel of roundball.... **JUAN MANUEL FANGIO (1911)**, called the greatest auto racer ever, the only driver to win the World Grand Prix championship five times, winning his first at age 40

NOTES

■ **SANDY SADDLER (1926)** —
Featherweight champion (1948-49, 1950 to '56) and one of the greatest ever in that division. The son of a West Indian, Saddler was born in Boston, grew up in Harlem in New York City and began his pro career as a 17-year-old. He got knocked out in his second fight but it never happened again in more than 160 fights. Tall and with a long reach, Saddler shocked the ring world by knocking out the great Willie Pep in the fourth round to win the title in 1948. Pep regained the title via a 15-round decision (though he paid a stiff price physically), but Saddler KO'd Pep again to win the title back for good, and KO'd him

Sandy Saddler

in a fourth match — four classic battles. After a three-year stint in the army during the Korean War, Saddler twice more successfully defended his title. Then tragedy struck in the form of an eye injury in an auto accident. He was forced to give up his title and retire. He won 144 bouts, more than 100 by knockout.

■ Also born today: **WILLIS REED (1942)**, NBA great with the Knicks (won MVP in 1970), coached at Creighton, developing center Benoit Benjamin, NBA draftee ... **KEN HODGE (1944)**, right winger with the Boston Bruins (1967-76) served up many an assist for Phil Esposito ... **PAUL "TANK" YOUNGER (1928)**, L.A. Rams running back (1949-57), an early star out of Grambling (where he was born, in Louisiana) ... **JOE KUHEL (1906)**, first baseman with the Senators and White Sox from 1930 to 1947, a .277 lifetime hitter ... sports birthday compiler **EUGENE LESSER (1936)**, a step or two slower, but happy just to be out there.

NOTES

■ BABE DIDRIKSON ZAHARIAS (1914) —
The greatest woman athlete of all time, born in Port Arthur, Texas. She won two gold medals in the 1932 Olympics in the javelin and 80-meter hurdles

Babe Zaharias

(setting world records in both events). She should have also won the high jump but was disqualified for "diving" over the bar (a technique that was to become legal). She was an All-American basketball player, excelled at swimming, diving, baseball, motorcycling, tennis, and became one of the greatest golfers, winning every major women's golf championship from 1935 to 1950. Her autobiography, "This Life I've Led," was published in 1955. One year later, at age 42, the incomparable "Babe" died of cancer. Her husband, wrestler George Zaharias, died in 1984.

■ ABNER DOUBLEDAY (1819) —
The man who did not invent baseball. Doubleday was a renowned Civil War general who allegedly fired the first shot in defense of Fort Sumter which began the Civil War in 1861. Baseball owners, needing to hype their product and give it a respectable history, formed the A. G. Mills commission (1905-08) to investigate the origins of baseball and concluded that Doubleday (a friend of Mills!) invented the game in Cooperstown, N.Y. in 1839. No way, Hozay.

■ Also born today: **HAL GREER** (1936), guard for the Syracuse Nationals who became the Philadelphia 76ers (1958-71) eighth leading all-time scorer with 21,586 points ... **BABE HERMAN** (1903), yet another "Babe", outfielder with Dodgers and others (1926-37), a .324 lifetime hitter who hit .393 in 1930 and didn't even win the batting title (Bill Terry hit .401); Herman is the only player to hit for the cycle three times ... **THOMAS "OLD TOM" MORRIS** (1821), Scottish golf pioneer ... **FREDDIE MILLS** (1919), light-heavyweight champion (1948-50), born in England. He later became a popular radio and TV personality for many years and opened up a nightclub. But in 1965 at age 46, he died of a mysterious gunshot wound. ... **WILLARD BROWN** (1921), who with Hank Thompson became the first black players to play on the same major league team (St. Louis Browns in 1947); Brown was the first black player in American League history to homer, and it was an inside-the-park one.

NOTES

WILLIE MOSCONI (1913) —
The greatest pool player of all. Born in Philadelphia, he was a prodigy who gave public exhibitions, taking on all comers — at age 7. "The Man With The Golden Arm" was the first to run as many as 310 consecutive balls without a miss and, in 1954, increased that figure to an incredible 525 consecutive balls, playing 35 racks of balls without rest. He was world pocket billiards champion 10 times (1941, 1944-45, 1947-48, 1950-53, 1955).

Gus Zernial

GUS ZERNIAL (1923) —
Power-hitting outfielder with the Philadelphia (and K.C.) A's and others (1949-59). Born in Beaumont, Texas, Zernial led the AL in home runs and RBI in 1951 and hit 237 homers in his career. His ratio of one homer for every 17 at-bats is 22nd on the all-time list. If that isn't enough, his fame is insured as the one who introduced Joe DiMaggio to Marilyn Monroe. Zernial is a born-again Christian who manages real estate investments in Fresno.

Also born today: RICO PETROCELLI (1943), who hit more than 200 homers for the Red Sox (1965-77), including 40 in 1969, an American League record for a shortstop ... DAN CURRIE (1935), Green Bay Packer linebacker, 1958-64. WAYNE TERWILLIGER (1925), "Twig" was a second baseman with the Cubs and Senators, managed in the minor leagues for several years and coaches the Texas Rangers ... ERROL MANN (1941), place-kicker with the Detroit Lions for many years and their all-time leading scorer ... CATHERINE LACOSTE (1945), tennis player, daughter of the great Rene Lacoste ... EDDIE KASKO (1932), shortstop and third baseman, mostly with the Reds (1957-66), played key role in 1961 Reds' pennant race. Kasko managed the Red Sox for awhile, became their director of scouting.

NOTES

■CHUCK HOWLEY (1936) —
Played ball at West Virginia (how many other NFL players came from that school?) and was drafted by the Bears in 1959. In 1960, he went to

the Cowboys and played with them for 15 years, retiring in 1974. A brilliant linebacker, he was probably the most obscure player on a team of highly publicized superstars but by the early 1970s everyone knew his worth — dramatized by being named MVP in the 1972 Super Bowl.

Chuck Howley

■RON LUCIANO (1937) —
Ex-AL umpire. Born in Endicott, N.Y., he went to Syracuse and was an All-American tackle. After two years with the Detroit Lions, Luciano went into umpiring and became the most flamboyant and famous of them all. Personally, I don't cotton to umpires chitchatting with the players during a game, but that was Luciano's trademark — that and pointing at a player as he calls him out on the bases. He retired a few years ago, wrote his autobiography and has been doing some TV sportscasting.

■ Also born today: AL DOWNING (1941), pocket lefty who served up Hank Aaron's 715th home run ... **ISHMAEL LAGUNA (1943)**, Panamanian lightweight champ, 1965 and 1970 ... **KEN WILLIAMS (1890)**, 14-year career, including decade with St. Louis Browns (1918-27), in 1922 led AL in homers (39) and RBI (155); he was the first AL player to hit three homers in one game and also hit two homers in one inning ... **HOWARD DREW (1890)**, the first black world-class sprinter ... two ex-Raiders: **CLARENCE DAVIS (1949)**, whose miracle catch beat Miami for 1974 AFC title, and **RAYMOND CHESTER (1948)**, tight end who later played with Invaders ... **JEAN BALUKAS (1959)**, "The Little Princess," Brooklyn-born pocket billiards ace, won the U.S women's championship at age 13 and then won six more titles in a row ... **CHRISTIAN STEINMETZ (1882)**, "the father of Wisconsin basketball" set scoring records that stood for 50 years; he was the first to score 1,000 points in a single year ... **HAL BREEDEN (1944)**, Expos' first baseman in early 1970s, he and Joe Cronin are the only two players in major league history to hit pinch-hit homers in both games of a double-header

NOTES

■ PAUL"DIZZY" TROUT (1915) —

Righty pitcher with the Detroit Tigers from 1939-1952, born in Sandcut, Ind. Trout won 20 games in 1943, more than anyone in the American League but had his best year in 1944, when he led the AL in earned run average, complete games, shutouts and innings. He also won 27 games (even with teammate Hal Newhouser winning 29, the Tigers still lost the pennant by a game to the St. Louis Browns). By the way, Trout hit .271 that year with five homers. Trout finished with a 170-161 career won-loss record. He later broadcast Tigers games and then

Dizzy Trout

did public relations work with the Chicago White Sox until his death in 1972. His son, Steve Trout, is a Cubs pitcher

■ HARMON KILLEBREW (1936) — One of the great

sluggers in baseball history (with one of its greatest names). "Killer" broke in with the Washington Senators in 1954 as a 17-year-old and played with them (reincarnated as the Minnesota Twins) for two decades. He is fifth on the all-time list in career homers, the No. 1 right-handed home run hitter in AL history, and second only to Babe Ruth in home run percentage. A first baseman, third baseman, and outfielder, he won six home run titles and hit 40 or more eight times. He was voted MVP in 1969 hitting 49 homers, with 140 RBI in 162 games playing mostly at third base. The ex-TV color man for the A's was voted into the Hall of Fame in 1984 — the first Twin in the Hall.

■ Also born today: Scot WILLIE MACFARLANE (1890),

golfer who won the U.S. Open in 1925 ... BOB RULE (1944), high scoring forward with the SuperSonics in the late 1960s ... BOBBY VEACH (1888), outfielder who (like Dizzy Trout) spent most of his career with the Tigers (in the same outfield with Ty Cobb and Sam Crawford), great triples hitter with a .310 lifetime BA ... DAN DIERDORF (1949), long-time Pro Bowl offensive tackle with St. Louis Cardinals (born in Canton, Ohio, home of pro football Hall of Fame, where Dierdorf may one day be honored) ... CLAUDE HUMPHREY (1944), ex-defensive end for the Falcons and Eagles, one of the greats ... ERIK LUNDKVIST (1908), Swedish javelin thrower who won a gold medal at the 1928 Olympics ... GREG MINTON (1951), S.F. Giants' erstwhile relief ace.

NOTES

■ **RON SWOBODA (1944) —**
An unlikely hero on a team of unlikely heroes
(the 1969 Mets). Born in Baltimore, he came up to
the Mets as a 20-year-old outfielder in 1965 and hit a
career-high 19 home runs. Of course, Swoboda is best

known for his 1969 season, especially the World Series against the
Orioles. He went 6-for-15 for a
.400 batting average (he was a
lifetime .242 hitter) and is famous
for his diving catch in Game Four.
With the Mets ahead, 1-0, in the
ninth inning, the Orioles had two
runners on and Brooks Robinson
hit what would have been a triple
but wound up instead in Swobod-
a's glove. The O's did tie it up but
lost it in the 10th inning, putting

Ron Swoboda the Mets ahead, three games to
one. Swoboda later played briefly with the Expos and the
Yankees. Ironically, the once-mighty Yankees of 1973
(Swoboda's last season) were a sub-.500 team, while his
ex-teammates, formerly the laughing stock of New York
City, were winning their second pennant.

■ Also born today: Two tennis stars were born today —
both of them doubles champions: **SHIRLEY FRY (1927),**
born in Akron, Ohio, she and Doris Hart won the U.S.
doubles title four years in a row (1951-54), and **JOHN VAN
RYN (1906),** born in Newport News, Va., he and Wilmer
Allison won the U.S. doubles crown in 1931 and 1935 ...
MATT WINN (1861), known as Colonel Winn, he operated
Churchill Downs for almost a half-century (1902-49) and
witnessed every Kentucky Derby from 1875 until his death
in 1949 ... **EDWARD WACHTER (1833),** basketball Hall of
Famer as one of the first pro stars and as a rules pioneer
... **BILL LENKAITIS (1946),** former center with the New
England Patriots, went through dental school while
playing.

NOTES

■ **BILL STERN (1907) —**
One of the most listened-to sportscasters of his day, was born in Rochester, N.Y. During the 1930s, 40s, and 50s, he covered virtually all major and minor sports, but was best-known for his broad-casts of college football (his vivid style helped popularize the sport) and most of Joe Louis' title fights. He covered the 1936 Olympics in Berlin and the next Olympics in London in 1948. Stern was a controversial sportscaster be-cause of his exaggerated and emotional style. In fact, he often compromised the truth to hype the game. His Colgate Sports Newsreel radio show (1939-51) was very popular, dramatizing famous sports heroes or events, often hammered home with the phrase, "Portrait of a man!" He was famous for closing with "and that's our three-oh mark for tonight."

Bill Stern

■ **NANCY LIEBERMAN (1963) —**
The dominant women's basketball player of the late 1970s. She played for the 1976 Olympic women's team at age 14 — the youngest ever to play on an Olympic basketball team. She played college ball at Old Dominion, leading her school to the NCAA title in her junior and senior years ('79 and '80). Since that time her career has been in limbo in the absence of a viable women's pro league.

■ Also born today: **DANA McLEMORE (1960)**, S.F. 49ers punt returner, among the most exciting returners of all time ... **GLENN "SLATS" HARDIN (1910)**, a hurdler who was way ahead of his time, set the 400-meter hurdles record at 50.6 seconds in 1934 and it stood as a world record until 1953. Hardin won the silver medal in the 400 meters at the '28 Olympics and a gold medal in 1936 (born in Derma, Miss.) ... **CHRISTEL CRANTZ (1914)**, eminent German skier, won 12 World Alpine champion-ships and won a gold medal in combined skiing at the 1936 Olympics ... **SAMUEL D. RIDDLE (1861)**, owner of Man O' War ... **MIKE HAYNES (1953)**, Raider cornerback since coming from the New England Patriots. an All-Pro his whole career ... **SAM RUTIGLIANO (1932)**, coach of the Cleveland Browns from 1978 to '83 ... **JOHN CLARKSON (1861)**, one of baseball's first great pitchers, a moody Hall of Fame curveballer, won 327 games (10th all-time), committed to a mental institution, died 1909.

NOTES

■ **BOB ZUPPKE (1879)** —
Quotable football coach at the Univ. of Illinois (1913-41),
born in Berlin, Germany. He grew up in Milwaukee,

coached high school ball in Michigan and Illinois (one of his warriors in Oak Park, Ill., was Ernest Hemingway), and began at Illinois in 1913 where he coached Red Grange and innovated the huddle, the flea flicker (a pass to a receiver who laterals to half-back trailing the play), and used a T-formation long before it became popular. One of his players, George Halas, learned that from him and was the first to use it in the pros. Zuppke is best remem-

Bob Zuppke

bered as an epigrammatic wit and philosopher. some Zuppke-isms: "Football made the nation college-conscious", "All quitters are good losers,""New York is the cesspool of journalism," "Most games are won or lost before they are played." When a critic carped that all Grange could do was run, Zup retorted, "And all Galli-Curci can do is sing."

■ **CHUCK STOBBS (1929)** — Infamous for giving up, with the Washington Senators in 1953, a 565-foot home run to Mickey Mantle (batting right-handed) that went out of Griffith Stadium, one of the longest home runs in big league history. Another lowlight in Stobbs' career includes a wild pitch he uncorked in 1956 that landed in the seats!

■ **Also born today:** golfer **GENE LITTLER (1930)**, won 1961 U.S. Open, known as "Gene the Machine" for his textbook swing ... **GUS DORAIS (1891)**, Notre Dame quarterback who, in 1913, popularized the forward pass (with end Knute Rockne), putting it and Notre Dame on the map as the team went East and defeated the awesome Army juggernaut ... Tennis player **JEAN RENE LACOSTE (1905)**. He and his two countrymen, Henri Cochet and Jean Borotra, dominated the Davis Cup for six straight years (1927-32); he won two U.S. Opens, two Wimbledon titles and three French titles; later became famous all over again for manufacturing tennis shirts with his famous alligator emblem. ... auto racer **RICHARD PETTY (1937)**, NASCAR's all-time leading driver ... Warrior forward **PURVIS SHORT (1957)** ... **MANUEL ORTIZ (1916)**, bantamweight champ, 1942-46, 1946-50.

NOTES

■ **PETER JACKSON (1861)** —
Some consider this heavyweight fighter the greatest of the late 19th century. He was born in the West Indies. When he became the obvious contender for the world title, John L. Sullivan refused to fight Jackson because he was black. He never did get his chance. In his fight against James J. Corbett (held in San Francisco), Jackson and Corbett fought to a 61-round draw, yet Corbett was given the shot at Sullivan's title because he did so well against the bigger and more experienced Jackson. He suffered only three losses in his career of 41 bouts. Jackson, who later turned to the theatre and toured the U.S. in Uncle Tom's Cabin, died of consumption at age 40.

■ Also born today: **JOHNNIE PARSONS (1918)**, auto racer who won Indy 500 in 1950 after finishing second the year before. He died in 1984 ... Two ex-Dallas Cowboy stars: fullback **WALT GARRISON (1943)** and defensive tackle **JETHRO PUGH (1944)**, a great player with a great name ... **JOHNNY KUNDLA (1916)**, coach of the Minneapolis Lakers during the George Mikan era ... swimmer **MIKE BURTON (1947)**, won 1,500 meter freestyle in 1968 and '72 Olympics, the first in more than 60 years to win that event

Johnnie Parsons

twice in a row... southpaw **FRANK TANANA (1953)**, brilliant w/Angels, 1975-77, can still pitch — he was 15-15 in '84 for the Rangers; must have jumped for joy when the Texas Rangers dealt him to Detroit (where he was born)... **CESAR TOVAR (1940)** outfielder-infielder with Twins and others from 1965 to 1976, only the second player (after Bert Campaneris) to play nine different positions in a nine-inning game, against the '68 Oakland A's. Pitching in the first inning, the first batter Tovar faced was Campaneris himself. Another curio is that Tovar struck out Reggie Jackson in that inning. He also owns the big-league record for breaking up no-hitters — five times Tovar got the only hit for his team.

■ **ABE SAPERSTEIN (1903)** — The founder and coach of the Harlem Globetrotters was born in London, England. When he organized the team in 1926, the 'Trotters

were not the clowns they later became. They played it straight and were as good as the best of the lily-white NBA. The Globetrotters (the "Harlem" designation only indicated that the team was all black — they were from Chicago) truly internationalized basketball as they traveled throughout the U.S. and virtually every country in the world. Their brilliance and their antics helped popularized the game. Saperstein also formed the American Basketball League, a rival league of

Abe Saperstein

the NBA, but it folded in 1963. He died in 1966.

■ **MANOLETE (1917)** — This legendary Spanish bullfighter was the son and grandson of bullfighters also known as "Manolete". He was the top matador in the world from 1940 until fatally gored by a bull at age 29. His autobiography, *My Life As A Matador*, was translated by Barnaby Conrad in 1956.

■ Also born today:

two great defensive backs: **ERICH BARNES (1935)**, w/NY Giants, Browns, etc. and **ROOSEVELT TAYLOR (1938)**, free safety with Bears, Skins, etc . . . two more sports executives: **AL DAVIS (1929)**, the controversial owner of the Raiders; and **GEORGE STEINBRENNER (1930)**, owner of the Yankees, kicker of elevator doors . . . two Hall of Fame basketball coaches: **H. CLIFFORD CARLSON (1894)**, coached Pitt for more than 30 years, winning national titles in 1928 and 1930, originated the "figure 8" play, the first patterned offense; practiced medicine during coaching career, died 1964; and **HOWARD HOBSON (1903)**, whose '39 Oregon team won the first NCAA title; also coached at Yale and became the first basketball coach to win major conference titles on both coasts . . . **MICKEY WELCH (1859)**, a Hall of Fame righty pitcher of the 1880s and '90s, a workhorse who completed almost all his games — 525 of 549 career starts, to be exact. He won 311 games in 12 seasons — an average of about 26 wins a season. Welch struck out nine consecutive batters one day in 1884 and had 17 consecutive wins in 1885.

NOTES

■ **DANIEL MENDOZA (1764) —**
The first Jew to attain fame in the ring, born in London, England. He was heavyweight champion of England (1792-95) and revolutionized and popularized boxing. Fighting at only 168 pounds, he was one of the most scientific bare-knuckle boxers, and was the first man to manage himself and promote his own fights. For one of his big bouts he erected a stage in a barn and, for the first time in boxing history, fans had to pass through a gate and pay admission. After retirement, Mendoza started a school for boxing.

■ **GARY MATTHEWS (1950) —**
The Cubbies' left fielder and 1973 rookie-of-the-year with the Giants, he asked the Giants for a $5,000 raise (giving him a $65,000 salary). They balked and let him become a free agent (an atrocity that still keeps Giant fans waking up in a sweat), Ted Turner and Braves picking him up in a $2 million contract. After four solid seasons, he was sent to the Phillies (for Bob Walk) where he led them to a pennant. In yet a

Gary Matthews

third weird deal, the Phillies offered him to the Cubs and Gary contributed heavily to their renaissance. A tremendous talent, yet he has been unappreciated.

■ **Also born today:** RICH GOSSAGE (1951), Padres' relief ace. Entered '85 season fourth in career saves and will soon be third, behind only Fingers and Sutter ... JOHN McKAY (1923), football coach at USC (1960-75) and Tampa Bay (1976-84) ... PAUL HACKETT (1947), 49er quarterbacks-receiver coach ... tennis player DWIGHT DAVIS (1879), donor of the Davis Cup ... BUMP HADLEY (1904), righty pitcher of the 1920s and '30's with the Washington Senators and Yankees; it was he who threw the pitch (in 1937) that gave Mickey Cochrane a concussion and ended his career ... JAMES LOFTON (1956), tremendous wide receiver for the Green Bay Packers who deserves a better team; played college ball and ran track at Stanford ... "PANAMA AL" BROWN (1902), bantamweight champion (1929-35), one of the all-time top 10 bantams; he was an incredible 5-11 and fought at 118 pounds ... JACK QUINN (1884), righty pitcher for several teams, 247-217 lifetime, one of only six players who played in four decades.

Marcus Dupree (1964), ex-Oklahoma all-American RB w/USFL Breakers in '85.

■ **HAROLD S. VANDERBILT (1884)** — Millionaire financier and sportsman, and the great-

Harold S. Vanderbilt

grandson of Corneluis Vanderbilt and the son of William K. Vanderbilt. Harold S. made his mark as a yachtsman who won the America's Cup three times (1930, 1934, 1937) and as a bridge player, credited with inventing contract bridge.

■ **ADOLF ANDERSSEN (1818)** — Born in Breslau, Germany, universally regarded as the best chess player in the world in the 1860s. Wilhelm Steinitz defeated him in 1866 and was named the first official chess champion of the world. Anderssen created two masterpieces known as The Evergreen Game and The Immortal Game.

■ **DARRELL ROYAL (1924)**–Long-time football coach at Texas where he perfected the Wishbone T, one of the most influential offenses in football history. He was born in Hollis, Okla., and played college football at the Univ. of Oklahoma.

■ **BRAD PARK (1948)** — Brilliant defenseman with the Rangers and Bruins He skated with the Rangers from 1968 to 1975, developing his "submarine bodycheck" which catapulted the unfortunate opponent upside down to the hard ice. Known as a tough customer his whole career, he got in his share of fights, especially against the Boston Bruins, to which he was traded (infamously, some might say) for the great Phil Esposito. He made the switch successfully, nearly filling the shoes of Bobby Orr.

■ **WILLIE RANDOLPH (1954)** — Born in Holly Hill, S.C. Yankee second baseman and leadoff hitter, broke in with the Pirates but was quickly dealt to the Yankees in 1976 and has been a mainstay for them.

Fred Dryer (1946), ex-DE w/ NY Giants and Rams, later a TV actor ("Hunter").

■ SATCHEL PAIGE (1906) —
The legendary black pitcher was born in Mobile, Ala. Because of baseball's segregationist policies, Paige, considered by many to be the greatest pitcher of all-time, did not enter the major leagues until 1948, at age 41 (the fifth black player in the major leagues). He pitched brilliantly in the stretch drive that year, out of the bullpen, to help the Cleveland Indians win the pennant. At age 58, having pitched an estimated 3,000 games, Paige became the oldest player to play in the majors when he pitched three innings for the Kansas City A's (giving up no runs on one hit, one strikeout, and one walk). Among his rules to live by were "Don't look back — someone may be gaining on you" and (a favorite of mine) "avoid running at all times."

■ EZZARD CHARLES (1921) —
Heavyweight champion from 1949 to 1951, born in Lawrenceville, Georgia. After Joe Louis retired and his title was vacant, Charles became the new champ when he outpointed Joe Walcott in their first of four exciting bouts. Charles was a good boxer with a good punch who was overshadowed by Louis before him and Marciano after him. He is the only fighter ever to go 15 rounds against Marciano and, in the rematch, although Charles was stopped in eight rounds, hurt Marciano badly and contributed to Marciano's retirement. Charles won 96 fights (58 by KO) and lost 25. He died in 1975.

■ Also born today: Braves righty **LEN BARKER (1955),** born in Fort Knox, Ky., pitched the major leagues' 12th perfect game in 1981 . . . **FRED BROWN (1948),** ex-Seattle SuperSonics' instant offense off the bench . . . British golfer **TONY JACKLIN (1944),** won the British Open in 1969 and U.S. Open in 1970.

NOTES

■ HARRISON DILLARD (1923) —
The world's best high-hurdler of the late '40s and early

'50s. Born in Cleveland, "Old Bones" was a track star at Baldwin-Wallace and dominated the hurdles a la Edwin Moses, winning 82 consecutive final events — one of the longest streaks in sports history. At the 1948 Olympic games, Dillard — on a rare off day — failed at his specialty but did qualify for the 100-meter dash. A long shot in a field that included Mel Patton and Barney Ewell, Dillard won in record time 10.3 (a mark that wasn't bettered until 1960). In the 1952 Olympics, Dillard won the 110-meter hurdles and became the only man ever to win Olympic gold medals in both sprints and hurdles.

Harrison Dillard

■ Also born today: **HANK O'DAY (1863)**, the umpire who called Fred Merkle out at second after he failed to touch second after an apparent bases loaded single had won the game for the Giants. Cubbie second baseman Johnny Evers picked up neglected baseball, touched second, and O'Day called Merkle out, nullifying run. Cubs went on to win make-up game and a couple of weeks later Cubs beat Giants for 1908 pennant– by one game. O'Day was a former pitcher (who lost 29 games one year) and later managed the Reds (1912) and the Cubs (1914) ... running back **JOHN DAVID CROW (1935)**, won 1957 Heisman Trophy, played w/Cardinals (1958-64) and 49ers (1965-68) ... **TOM CRIBB (1781)**, great English bare-knuckle champion, known as "The Black Diamond" from his trade as coal-porter.

NOTES

■ **O(RENTHAL) J(AMES) SIMPSON (1947)** — The incomparable "Juice", born in San Francisco, went to USC as a junior, and won the Heisman Trophy a year later. In an awesome career begun with the Buffalo Bills (1969-77), and ending with the 49ers (1978-79), O.J. finished with 11,236 yards, second (by 76 yards) only to Jim Brown. Some of Simpson's records — he played 11 seasons — include most yards in a season (2,003 in 1973), most games gaining over 200 yards in a season (6), and most TDs by a

O.J. Simpson

running back in a season (23). O.J.'s singular trait was his propulsion. No one ever picked up speed like he did. After retirement, Simpson pursued an acting and TV career, notably on Monday Night Football, where he surprised and impressed with his candid commentary.

■ Also born today: **WILLIE WILSON (1955)**, reinstated K.C. Royals outfielder who did four months on drug charges; he's the only AL player (Garry Templeton did it in NL) to get 100 hits from either side of the plate in one season (1980) ... **JIM POLLARD (1922)** ex-Stanford basketball great, played with Minneapolis Lakers (1947-54) as second banana to George Mikan ... **RED KELLY (1927)**, Detroit Red Wings defenseman during 1950s; made 1st string all-NHL six times ... another hockey figure: **CLARENCE CAMPBELL (1905)**, NHL pres. from 1946 to 1977, the longest reign in pro sports history; he died in 1984 ... **CLEM DANIELS (1937)**, Raiders running back (1961-68), led AFL in rushing in 1963.

NOTES

■ **JAKE LAMOTTA (1921)** — "The Bronx Bull", middleweight champion, 1949-51. He started as a pro at 19 but didn't get a title shot until 1949, when he knocked out Marcel Cerdan in the 10th round. Cerdan died in an airplane crash later that year en route to a return match with LaMotta, who lost his title in '51 to Ray Robinson by a 13th round KO. LaMotta, a brawler in the ring, won 83 fights (30 by KO) and lost 19. His film biography was "Raging Bull."

Jake LaMotta

■ **ARTHUR ASHE (1943)** — The first black tennis player to reach the top. Born in Richmond, Va., Ashe won the U.S. Open and the Wimbledon title in 1968 and won at Wimbledon again in 1975. He was the first black to make the American Davis Cup team. "Arthur Ashe: An Autobiography," came out in 1970.

■ **BOBBY LOWE (1868)** — "Link" Lowe, first player to hit four HRs in one game, was born in Pittsburgh. He was a 5-foot-10, 150-pound second baseman who played most of his 18-year career with Boston in the NL with a lifetime BA of .273. In 1894 he hit four consecutive homers (two in one inning), the only player to do it until Lou Gehrig did it in 1932. Lowe died in 1951.

■ **GRAHAM McNAMEE (1888)** — McNamee, "The father of sportscasting," was born in Washington, D.C. He pioneered many of the techniques and expressions that became commonplace over the years. He handled the first Rose Bowl broadcast in 1926 and many other famous events. He was also a well-known radio announcer on popular variety shows during the 1930s, such as Ed Wynn's.

■ **ANDRE DAWSON (1954)** — Expos outfielder, a tremendous player with no weakness. He was one of the three or four best all-around performers in the NL.

Roger Craig (1960), 49er RB, all-purpose gem.

Except his knees.

NOTES

■ CARL "BOBO" OLSON (1928) —

Middleweight champ from 1953 to 1955. Olson was popular and why not? A brave brawler, he gave you your money's worth. Born in Honolulu, he began his career with San Francisco as his home base in 1945, and decisioned Randy Turpin for the middleweight title before losing it two years later to Ray Robinson (KO'd in two). He fought Sugar Ray four times, losing all four but providing some thrills in a couple of them. The highlight was lasting 15 rounds against Robinson, losing a decision. He also won 15-round decisions against Kid Gavilan and Rocky Castellani.

Bobo Olson

■ LEON SPINKS (1953) —

Spinks, yet another champion born on this day. He won the light-heavy title in the 1976 Olympics and, in his ninth pro fight, upset Muhammad Ali in a 15-round decision (and I believe it was an injustice to take Ali's title in a split decision while Ali stood toe-to-toe with Spinks, slugging it out for the last 30 seconds of the fight). Spinks, the older brother of light-heavy champ Michael Spinks, has been in the newspapers several times after being stopped by the police on various charges. His career went a bit downhill since he lost his title — but he had seven months as champion, until Ali decisioned him in a rematch to regain the crown.

■ Also born today: **LOU HUDSON (1944)**, Atlanta Hawks guard, 17th all-time scorer (17,940 points) ... **CECIL ISBELL (1915)**, Green Bay QB (1938-42), threw the ball to Don Hutson, led NFL in passing (1941-42).

■ **TONY ARMAS (1953)** —
One of baseball's best power hitters. Venezuela-born, he was one of 14 children. Signed by the Pirates,

Tony Armas

he spent six years in their system until he was dealt (along with Rick Langford, Mitchell Page, et al) to the A's (for Phil Garner, et al). He proceeded to provide Oakland with punch as the cleanup hitter and competently handled right field. Unlike most power hitters, Armas was an excellent outfielder with a great arm. His 11 putouts in a game in 1982 set a major league record. Reluctantly, the A's dealt him to the Bosox for Carney Lansford, a terrible deal for Boston (so what's new?). Armas to the Bosox was coals to Newcastle and while he will hit the long ball, he will never mean to Boston what he meant to the A's. And he will never hit .279 again (as he did for the A's in 1980).

■ Also born today: horse trainer **MAX HIRSCH (1880)**, who trained three Kentucky Derby winners: Bold Venture (1936), Assault (1946), Middleground (1950) ... **PAUL SILAS (1943)**, excellent rebounder and defensive player with the Hawks, Suns and Sonics ... **LASSE VIREN (1949)**, Finnish long-distance whiz, won gold medals in 5,000 meter and 10,000 meter runs in both 1972 and '76 Olympics ... **GLENN DOBBS (1922)**, running back out of Tulsa who was star of late 1940s AAFC with the Brooklyn Dodgers and Los Angeles Dons.

NOTES

■**MICKEY WALKER (1901)** — "The Toy Bulldog," called the "toughest and hardest hitting middleweight of all time," born in Elizabeth, N.J. Walker was both welter-weight (1922-26) and middle-weight (1926-31) champion. Nat Fleischer, boxing authority, rated Walker the No. 4 all-time middleweight. He even fought heavyweights, holding future heavyweight champion Jack Sharkey to a 15-round draw. After retiring from the ring in 1935, Walker opened well-known taverns on both coasts and became known as a painter of primitive art. He died in 1981.

Mickey Walker

■**STAN COVELESKI (1889)** — Hall of Fame right-handed pitcher. In a 14-year career he won 217 games and lost 141 (more than 60 percent) with a 2.88 ERA. He was the pitching star for the Indians in the 1920 World Series against the Dodgers. Coveleski won three games — all of them five-hitters. With the Washington Senators in 1925, he and Walter Johnson led them to a pennant — Coveleski with a 20-5 record (an .800 percentage that led the league) and the league-leading ERA. Inducted into the Hall of Fame in 1969, he died in 1984 at age 93.

■Also born today: **FRANK RAMSEY (1931),** the first great "sixth man" with the Celtics (1954-64) ... **JACK KEMP (1935),** ex-QB with Bills, Chargers, now Republican congressman from N.Y. ... **WILEY PIATT (1884),** the only pitcher in the 20th century to lose two complete games of a double-header.

NOTES

■**ROOSEVELT GRIER (1932) —**
"Rosy," the great defensive tackle who supposedly

Roosevelt Grier

knits in his spare time. Born in Cuthbert, Ga., Grier played college ball at Penn State and was drafted by the N.Y. Giants in 1955 and contributed heavily to five conference titles. He went over to the Rams in 1963 and, for four seasons, was one fourth of the Rams' front-line known as the "Fearsome Foursome." Later an RFK campaign worker, he was near Kennedy when he was assassinated in 1968. He and Rafer Johnson, the decathlon athlete, tackled Sirhan Sirhan.

■**LEE ELDER (1934) —**
The first black to play in the Masters tournament. Born in Dallas, Texas, he turned pro in 1959 and paid his dues, not earning his tour card until 1967, then waiting seven more years before his first tournament victory. Elder, who for over a decade has hosted the Lee Elder Celebrity Pro-Am, made the black man acceptable on the pro golf tour.

■Also born today: **JOHN UELSES (1937)**, the first pole vaulter to break 16 feet, in 1962, shortly after the innovation of the fiberglass pole ... **WALLACE "WAH WAH" JONES (1926)**, All-American forward on great Kentucky teams of latter '40s ... **JOHNNY MURPHY (1908)**, relief specialist with New York Yankees (1934-43); his 73 wins in relief is seventh on the all-time list.

NOTES

■ **ALEX KARRAS (1935)** —
Brilliant defensive tackle and wit. Born in Gary, Ind.
He was All-American at Iowa
(under Forest Evashevski), won
the Outland Trophy and was the
Detroit Lions' first pick in the
draft. He played with the Lions
throughout his career, retiring in
1971. Despite his spheroid
frame, Karras was quick and
beat you with his first shot. In
1963, Karras was suspended
indefinitely (it lasted one year)
for betting on games — despite
betting on the Lions to win.
After his career, he was a hit
replacement (1974-76) for Don

Alex Karras

Meredith on Monday Night Football and appeared in
several films and TV shows. He was also the subject of
two George Plimpton books: "Paper Lion," 1963, and
"Mad Ducks and Bears," 1973. He has even written his
autobiography, "Even Big Guys Cry," 1977.

■ Also born today: first-baseman **DONN CLENDENON**
(1935), started ninth straight season with Pittsburgh in
1969 but got traded to the Mets after 38 games and
wound up hitting some big homers for the Amazin'
Mets ... **FRANK "POP" MORGENWECK (1875)**, "The
Connie Mack of Pro Basketball," he was pioneer,
executive, coach, and promoter ... **GENE UPSHAW**
(1945), Oakland Raider left guard, 1967-82, and bigwig
in Players Association..

NOTES

■ JOE JACKSON (1887) — The legendary "Shoeless Joe," one of baseball's greatest hitters, was born in Brandon Mills, S.C. An outfielder with the Indians (1910-15) and White Sox (1915-20), Jackson owns the third best (after Cobb and Hornsby) lifetime batting average (.356). He hit .408 in 1911 and 395 in 1912 and didn't win the batting title either year. He was rated second only to Cobb. Jackson and seven teammates threw the 1919 World Series to the Reds in the infamous "Black Sox" scandal. This semi-literate farmboy didn't have a lawyer at the hearing

Joe Jackson

and was promised to be taken care of. He wasn't. Despite hitting .375 in the Series, he (and the other seven) were banned from baseball for life. In his last season, 1920 he hit .382. As Jackson was walking into the courthouse during the trial, legend has it that a boy's voice cried out, "Say it ain't so, Joe." Jackson was supposed to have replied, "I'm afraid it is, son." He died in 1951.

■ Also born today: Tennis player **MARGARET SMITH COURT (1942)**, Aussie who won the U.S. Open seven times and was the youngest woman (age 17) to win the Australian singles title ... **MAX McGEE (1932)**, Green Bay Packer wide receiver (1954, 1957-67) and free spirit ... **LARRY JANSEN (1920)**, N.Y. Giants righty who won 96 games in five season (1947-51) roll, including the historic Giant-Dodger playoff game in '51 ... **JOEY GIARDELLO (1930)**, middleweight champion, 1963-65. Jack Fiske (1917), boxing writer w/ S.F. Chronicle since 1950; named to Boxing Hall of Fame in 1985.

NOTES

■ **CONNIE HAWKINS (1942)** — High-scoring forward. Born in Brooklyn, where he developed his schoolyard game, Hawkins went to the University of Iowa and left after a year for the money and glory of the ABA where, as a 19-year-old rookie, Hawkins had a 27.5 average. From 1963 to 1967 Hawkins played for the Harlem Globetrotters. He later sued the NBA for blackballing him for an alleged implication in "fixing" games. The NBA settled out of court and Hawkins was free to join the

Connie Hawkins

Phoenix Suns in 1969, ending his career with them in 1973. Hawkins proved his ability by being an over-20-point scorer in both leagues. His biography, "Foul," written in 1972, is being made into a movie.

■ **LOU BOUDREAU (1917)** — The youngest (age 24) full-time manager in AL history. Cleveland Indians shortstop from 1938 to 1950, he was a .295 lifetime hitter and is second only to Mark Belanger in career fielding percentage. Boudreau was also the last "full-time" player-manager, from 1942 to 1950, leading the Indians to the 1948 pennant and World Series, and named the AL's MVP. A basketball star in his home state of Illinois, Boudreau is the only man ever to play for and manage a major league baseball team and play for and coach a professional basketball team. He coached and played for the Hammond, Ind., team of the NBL (1938-39) with teammate John Wooden. Boudreau, whose daughter married Denny McLain, is the long-time Chicago Cubs announcer.

■ Also born today: QB **DARYLE LAMONICA (1941)**, Raiders' "Mad bomber" of 1960s ... **JERRY LYNCH (1930)**, pinch-hitter deluxe for Cincinnati from 1957 to 1963, fourth in all-time pinch-hits ... **BOB "SLICK" LEONARD (1932)**, another Indiana basketball star, leader of 1953 national championship team, later coach at Indiana and Indiana Pacers.

NOTES

■ **JOE TORRE (1940)** —The Atlanta Braves' manager. Torre had an outstanding 17-year career with the Braves, Cardinals and Mets. A lifetime .299 hitter with 240 career homers, he put his whole game together in 1971 and won the MVP award. A catcher first baseman with a weight problem for a decade, Torre shed 20 pounds, played the whole season at third base and tore up the league. He led the NL in hitting (.363), RBI (137) and hits (230). Torre ended his career with the Mets in 1976 and managed them for five years. Since 1982 he has managed the Braves. As a player, he was versatile, durable and a power hitter who also hit for average. As a manager, I'd rate him average — i.e., not very good.

■ **KIRK COLLINS (1958)** —
Former L.A. Rams cornerback. Drafted out of Baylor in 1983, Collins began the season brilliantly. He had five interceptions in the first four games. It was then discovered that he was stricken with cancer. A few months later, Collins was dead.

■ Also born today: **DENNIS JOHNSON (1954)**, Celtics guard, past his prime but turns it on for the playoffs ... Two great figure skaters: **DICK BUTTON (1929)**, won gold medals in 1948 and 1952, and **TENLEY ALBRIGHT (1935)**, won in 1956 Olympics ... Australian track and field coach **H. ARCHIE RICHARDSON (1879)**, who wrote a book of track records called Archie's Little Black Book.

NOTES

■ **BOB MEUSEL (1896)** —
"Long Bob," one of the "murderers" on the Yankees' "Murderers' Row," born in San Jose. Meusel, a good outfielder with a great arm, was a lifetime .309 hitter who hit for power — home runs, doubles and triples. In 1925 Meusel led the AL in homers (33) and RBI (138) but was destined to be overshadowed throughout his career with the Yanks (1920-29) by Ruth and Gehrig.

■ **ILIE NASTASE (1946)** —
Rumanian tennis star. Known for his temper tantrums on the court, "Nasty" won the U.S. Open in 1972 and has won many doubles titles, including the Wimbledon and U.S. Open titles (both with Jimmy Connors) and the Wimbledon mixed doubles (with Rosie Casals).

■ **PHIL CAVARRETTA (1916)** — Cavarretta, the Chicago Cubs' first baseman for two decades (1934-53), was born on this day — in Chicago. He broke into the majors as an 18-year-old in 1934 and a year later became the second youngest player to appear in a World Series (the youngest was N.Y. Giant Fred Lindstrom in 1924 — curiously, he was a teammate of Cavarretta's in the '35 Series). A lifetime .293 hitter, he won the batting title (.355) in 1945 and led the Cubbies to their last pennant. Only once did he hit as many as 10 home runs in a season but was a clutch hitter and a good RBI man. He also managed the Cubs (1951-53) and is the N.Y. Mets' hitting instructor.

■ Also born today: **J.D. SMITH (1932)**, S.F. 49er running back, 1956-64 ... **ALEX HANNUM (1923)**, basketball All-American at USC, 10-year NBA career as player, coach of Warriors, 76ers and Oakland Oaks ... **LON SIMMONS (1923)**, voice of the 49ers, Giants and A's.

NOTES

■ HEINIE MANUSH (1901) —
Hall of Fame outfielder from 1923 to 1939, born in
Tuscumbia, Ala. Don't hear
Manush's name bandied
about much nowadays but
he had a .330 lifetime BA,
one of the top 20 averages
in baseball history. A big
(6-feet-1, 200 pounds) lefty
swinger, he broke in with
the Tigers in 1923 and
formed one third of the
most awesome hitting out-
field trio ever — joined by
Ty Cobb and Harry Heil-
mann, both of whom had
higher lifetime BAs than
Manush. He won the batting title in 1926 (.378)
and two years later, with the St. Louis Browns, hit
.378 again, though it wasn't good enough to lead
the league this time. Neither were his 20 triples.
His 241 hits that year is one of the top 10 marks.
He died in 1971.

Heinie Manush

■ MIKE GIBBONS (1887) — The "St. Paul Phan-
tom", all-time leading middleweight, was never
champion. Though he laid claim to the middleweight title after Stanley Ketchel's murder left it
vacant, it was never recognized. Nevertheless,
ring authority Nat Fleischer rates Gibbons one of
the top 10 middleweights of all time. He had a
great record: 62 wins (38 KOs), three losses. And
he was never knocked out. His brother, light-
heavyweight Tom Gibbons, was also named by
Fleischer in the top 10 among all-time light-heav-
ies, making the Gibbons boys the greatest brother
duo in boxing history. He died in 1956.

■ Also born today: TONY OLIVA (1940), born in
Cuba, lifetime .307 hitter w/Twins (1964-76), won
three batting titles . . . tennis player **TED
SCHROEDER (1921),** won U.S. Open (1942) and
Wimbledon (1948).

■ **JOHNNY EVERS (1881)** —
One third of the fabled double-play combo of the
Chicago Cubs — Tinker to Evers to Chance — was
born in Troy, N.Y. So many of the great players from
the early baseball years were skinny, scrappy guys
like Evers, who (at 5-feet-9 and about 125 pounds,
that's one-twenty-five) was the best defensive second
baseman in the league, a blur on the bases and in the
field, a fearless performer, and a cunning baseball
mind. In the famous "Merkle's Boner" play in which —
with two on and two out — an apparent single
"scoring" the winning run was nullfield because
Merkle (the runner at first base) failed to touch
second base before he veered off toward the
clubhouse with fans mobbing field, it was Evers who
made the appeal play at second base. Evers played a
few years at the end of his career with the Boston
Braves, including the 1914 "Miracle Team." He and
the equally scrappy and diminutive Rabbit Maranville
formed the Braves' keystone and were the twin
sparkplugs of their incredible comeback to win the
flag and the Series as well. Those two players on the
same team? Take me out to the ballgame.

■ Also born today: **GENE FULLMER (1931)**, in
1957 outpointed Ray Robinson to take his middleweight title, but lost it four months later in rematch.
He regained the title in '59 by beating Carmen Basilio
and kept it until '62, beating Sugar Ray twice in
rematches. But he ran into Dick Tiger, who took
Fullmer's title and forced him into retirement by
fending off Fullmer in two rematches ... **MAX KASE
(1898)**, sportswriter for defunct New York Journal-
American who won Pulitzer for writing about college
basketball fixes in the early 1950s.

NOTES

■ MARCEL CERDAN (1916) —

This great middleweight champion (1948-49) was born in Algeria. Cerdan,

Marcel Cerdan

whose courage, stamina and punching flair made him a national hero, came to the U.S. in 1948 and took the title from the great Tony Zale by a 12th-round KO. He was now an international sensation, fueled by marrying France's national treasure, the singer and patriot Edith Piaf. A year later, in 1949, he was KO'd by Jake LaMotta and lost his title, suffering the only KO of his career. (He won 119 fights and lost only four, two by disqualification). Four months later, Cerdan, en route to the U.S. for his return bout with LaMotta, died in a plane crash at age 33.

■ SPARKY LYLE (1944) —

Lyle, one of the great all-time relief pitchers, was born Albert Walter Lyle in Reynoldsville, Pa., He came up with the Red Sox in 1967 and, in 1972, for the umpteenth time in the last 65 years, a great pitcher was dealt from the Red Sox to the Yankees. Lyle pitched seven years for the Yanks and won the Cy Young Award in 1977. He finished his career with Texas (1979) and the Phillies (1980), retiring with American League records for most games by a reliever, most games won, most games finished and most innings. He wrote a funny book about the Yankees, "The Bronx Zoo."

■ Also born today: **DOC CRAMER (1905)**, outfielder for two decades (1929-28) w/A's, Red Sox and Tigers, .296 lifetime hitter, holds longest streak without a homer — from late 1935 to 1940 with over 2,500 at-bats in between ... **J. V. CAIN (1951)**, St. Louis Cardinals tight end, died on 28th birthday ... **ELY CULBERTSON (1891)**, contract bridge authority (and pacifist).

NOTES

■ DON DRYSDALE (1936) — Big righty workhorse pitcher for the Dodgers (1956-69). He won 209 and lost 166 with a 2.95 ERA, an impressive figure for a power pitcher with a lot of innings. In 1968, he set a major league mark of 58⅔ scoreless innings, breaking Walter Johnson's 45-year-old record. In 1962, he won the Cy Young Award after a 25-9 season. He and Sandy Koufax formed one of the greatest righty-lefty pitching tandems of all time. While Koufax was the impeccable pitching genius, Drysdale was the intimidating,

Don Drysdale

hard-throwing, hard-working righty that every good pitching staff needs. After retirement, Drysdale became a TV announcer on Game-of-the-Week and in the booths of the Angels and Chicago White Sox.

■ PEE WEE REESE (1918) —
Pee Wee, like Drysdale, was a Dodger for his whole career (1940-42, 1946-58). Reese was a lifetime .269 hitter, a slick fielder, clutch performer, and team leader. He lost three peak years by serving in World War II. When Jackie Robinson broke in, it was Reese, a southerner, who helped him by accepting him and inspiring others to do so. Pee Wee is the only man to play in all 44 World Series games between the Dodgers and Yankees from 1941 to 1956. He became a representative of bat makers Hillerich and Bradsby in Louisville, Ky.

■ Also born today: **"SUNNY JIM" FITZSIMMONS (1874),** horse trainer whose famous horses include Nashua and Triple Crown winners Gallant Fox (1930) and Omaha (1935) ... Examiner "jock scribe" **FLOYD "BUCKY" WALTER (1917),** saved from drowning in 1947 by Lefty O'Doul.

NOTES

■ **WALT BELLAMY (1939)** —The ninth-leading scorer in NBA history. Drafted by the Chicago Bulls out of Indiana in 1961, he became an immediate force in the league, averaging 31.6 points and 19 rebounds per game. He was Rookie of the Year and played 13 more years with the Bullets, Knicks, Pistons and Hawks, retiring with 20,941 points and a 20.1 average. Despite his accomplishments, he played in the shadow of Chamberlain and Russell, who were first and second string All-NBA for most of Bellamy's career.

Walt Bellamy

■ **JOE BARRY CARROLL (1958)** —
Another NBA center. The Warriors gave Robert Parish and the pick for Kevin McHale to the Celtics to get this enigmatic 7-foot, 240-pound center. More than anything, Carroll suffers from Warrior-itis, a disease similar to, say, Giant-itis. It's difficult to play for a bad organization. The better the athlete, the more difficult the situation. The good players (Carroll and Jack Clark, for example) are expected to carry the team and make up for the team's overall deficiencies. Also, any athlete who doesn't talk to the press can't be all bad.

■ Also born today: **WILLIE DAVIS (1934)**, defensive end of the 1960s Green Bay Packer dynasty, captain of the 1965-67 teams ... **ALEX CARRASQUEL (1912)**, righty pitcher w/Senators, 1939-45, from Venezuela, the first South American to play major-league baseball (Venezuelan shortstop Chico Carrasquel apparently not related).

In July 1985 the Warriors backed up the truck for J.B. What's up?

NOTES

■ WALTER PAYTON (1954) —

"Sweetness", the Chicago Bears running back who broke Jim Brown's rushing record (12,312 yards) in 1984. Born in Columbia, Miss., he played ball at Jackson State and was drafted by the Bears in 1975. Brown, O.J. Simpson and Payton are the three greatest running backs of all time. At 5-feet-10½ and 202 pounds, Payton has strength, speed, and agility in equal abundance. Payton also owns the record for most yards rushing in a game (275 yards vs. Vikes in '77) and won the MVP award in 1977.

Walter Payton

■ "WHITEY" LOCKMAN (1926) —

Outfielder -first baseman whose best years were with the New York Giants (from 1945 to 1955). He was born Carroll Walter Lockman in Lowell, N.C., and came up as an 18-year-old rookie in 1945, homering in his first at-bat. Lockman was moved to first base in 1951, was brilliant with the glove and one heck of a clutch hitter. It was Whitey who doubled Don Mueller to third in the ninth inning of the 1951 pennant playoff. That drove Don Newcombe out of the game and brought on Ralph Branca to pitch to Bobby Thomson (first base was open, they should've walked him). Lockman became a scout for the Expos.

■ Also born today: **JOHN PENNEL (1940),** the first pole vaulter to attain 17 feet, broke the world record six times... **DAVE SIME (1936),** a one-time "world's fastest human" who shocked everyone by only getting a silver medal in the 100 meters at 1960 Olympics ... **NATE THURMOND (1941),** ex-Warrior center, always gave Kareem fits. *Hall of Fame in '85.*

NOTES

Hoyt Wilhelm

■**HOYT WILHELM (1923)** — One of the greatest relief pitchers of all time. A knuckleballer, he broke in as a 28-year-old Giant rookie in 1952 and led the league in winning percentage, ERA and appearances. He hit a home run in his first at-bat and never hit another one during his 21-year career. He is No. 1 in wins (123), games (1,070) and games finished (651). He later pitched with several teams. With the Orioles, he started about 50 games and pitched a no-hitter in 1958. Wilhelm, currently a Yankee scout, retired at age 49 (that's right, forty-nine). *Hall of Fame in '85*

■**BOB WATERFIELD (1920)** —
This ex-Rams quarterback, who died in 1984 was born in Elmira, N.Y. He moved to Southern California as a child, went to UCLA and led them to the Rose Bowl. A low draft choice, he led the Rams to the NFL title, the first rookie QB to do so in the league's history. A triple-threat star, Waterfield was a spectacular passer who popularized the long bomb and was a tremendous kicker with 60 FGs, 315 PATs and a career 42.4-yard punting average, including an 88-yarder, third longest in NFL history. He was married to actress Jane Russell for 25 years.

■**Also born today: BOB LILLY (1939)**, Hall of Fame defensive tackle w/Cowboys, 1961-76 ... **HENRY WILLIAMS (1869)**, football coach at Minnesota (1900-21), had five undefeated seasons ... **KEN KAISER (1945)**, AL ump.

■**LEO DUROCHER (1905) —**
"Leo the Lip," one of the great baseball managers of all time. He grew up in West Springfield, Mass., where his childhood idol and mentor was Rabbit Maranville, the tough little shortstop. Leo was a worthy disciple, as scrappy as they come — but with a heart of gold. A shortstop with the Yanks, Reds, Dodgers, and the Cardinals' Gas House Gang (1933-37), a lifetime .247 hitter, Durocher's niche was as a manager with Brooklyn (1939), the Giants (1948-55), Chicago (1966-72), and Houston (1972-73). He was fifth in career wins (2,019) and probably got more out of less than any other manager. His teams finished lower than fourth only three times in his 24 years of managing. In 1941 he won with the Dodgers, their second pennant ever and the first in more than 20 years. He also helped develop Pete Reiser. He pulled together the patchwork 1951 Giants, winning again in '54, and was Willie Mays' mentor. Once married to movie star Laraine Day, Durocher's famous alleged quote (which he never said) is the title of his fascinating autobiography, "Nice Guys Finish Last."

■Also born today: figure skater **PEGGY FLEMING** (1948), won gold medal in '68 Olympics, later w/Ice Follies and TV specials ... two more infielders were born on this day: shortstop **JOE TINKER** (1880), as in Tinker to Evers to Chance, and third baseman **RAY "IKE" BOONE** (1923), w/Tigers, Indians, etc.; hit four grand slams in 1953, became Red Sox scout, father of catcher Bob Boone ... **HAVEN MOSES** (1946), wide receiver with Bills and Broncos (love his name) ... **IRV CROSS** (1939), ex-DB w/Eagles, Rams and TV sportcaster.

NOTES

■ **BILL BRADLEY (1943)** – Basketball star turned U.S. Senator. At Princeton he was one of the greatest college players ever. Drafted by the Knicks, he spent his whole career with them (1967-77). From a smooth scoring machine, he became a tough, effective player in every phase of the game. Two years after retirement, Bradley was elected to the U.S. Senate from New Jersey. He may be President in 1988 or '92. He wrote an interesting book called "Life On The Run" while still a player. Also worth a look is John McPhee's portrait of him in "A Sense Of Where You Are."

■ **VIDA BLUE (1949)** —
Lefty pitcher, the American League's MVP at age 22. a rookie w/Oakland in 1971, he was 24-8, won the Cy Young Award, the MVP award, led the AL in ERA with a 1.82 mark and became only the seventh pitcher to strike out 300 or more batters in one season. Traded to the Giants in 1978, he had an excellent 18-10 season and was designated cheerleader. Dealt to the Royals in 1982, he served four months on drug charges. Vida looked impressive in his comeback return to the Giants in 1985.

■ Also born today: **DOUG COLLINS (1951)**, injury-plagued guard w/76ers during 1970s, became assistant coach at Arizona State University ... **TERRY FOX (1958)**, Canadian marathon runner who lost leg to bone cancer but continued to run on artificial leg in "Marathon of Hope" for cancer research ...

NOTES

■**GEORGE DIXON (1870) —**
Dixon, born in Canada, was first black man to hold a world boxing title. Called "Little Chocolate" because of his color and his height (5-foot-3½), he was a great bantamweight, rated No. 1 by ring authority Nat Fleischer. However, he won his title as a featherweight, ruling from 1892 until 1900, when he was KO'd by Terry McGovern (whom Fleischer ranked the No. 1 featherweight). Dixon died at age 38.

■**TIMOTHY J. MARA (1887) —**
The founder of the New York Giants football team was born in New York City. Mara made his money as a bookie and bought the New York franchise in the infant and struggling National Football League. It cost him $2,500 and he named it the Giants because they played their home games in the Polo Grounds. After his death in 1959, his sons, Jack and Wellington, and Jack's son, Timothy, took control of the team.

Timothy Mara

■**TED LINDSAY (1925) —**Considered the greatest left wing in hockey history, Lindsay skated with the Detroit Red Wings from 1944 to 1965 with a four-year period with the Chicago Black Hawks (1957-60). He was "a mean hockey player, a nasty individual on the ice" who is the all-time penalty leader with 1,808 minutes. He was on the famous "Production Line" at Detroit with center Sid Abel and right wing Gordie Howe. Since 1977, Lindsay has been the general manager of the Red Wings.

■ Also born today: bowling titan **DON CARTER (1926)**, the first pro bowler to reach a six-figure annual income and first president of the PBA ... **SCOTT WEDMAN (1952)**, reserve on 1984 and '85 Boston Celtics ... Expos' first baseman **DAN DRIESSEN (1951)**, longtime Reds star ... **GARY THOMASSON (1951)**, outfielder with the Giants, Dodgers, A's, Yankees, and in Japan.

■ **CASEY STENGEL (1890)** — "The Old Perfessor," one of the most colorful figures in baseball history  (and that's saying a lot), was born Charles Dillon Stengel in Kansas City (hence the "Casey"). A lefty outfielder mostly with the Dodgers and Giants from 1912 to 1925, he had a .284 lifetime batting average and played on the pennant-winning 1916 Dodgers and the pennant-winning 1921, 1922 and 1923 Giants under John J. McGraw, from whom he picked up a thing or two. Stengel's career as a manager indicates that having good ballplayers is

Casey Stengel

probably the most important ingredient for success. His Yankees won 10 pennants from 1949 to 1960 — and seven World Series, including five in a row (1949-53). However, his Dodgers (1934-36) and his Boston Braves (1938-43) never finished higher than fifth, and his Mets (1962-65) finished 10th in each of his four years. Perhaps he was overrated as a manager, but at least he didn't sacrifice bunt in the first inning.

■ **JOE NUXHALL (1928)** — Nuxhall, the youngest player ever to appear in a major league game, celebrates his 56th birthday today. Nuxhall pitched two-thirds of an inning for the Reds in 1944 at age 15. It was eight years later that he made his second appearance. Ironically, Nuxhall's best year was in 1963 — at age 35 — when he was 15-8 with a 2.61 ERA. He gave up only 39 walks in 217 innings. He became an announcer and batting practice pitcher for the Reds.

■ Also born today: Slugging catcher **GUS TRIANDOS** (1930), born in San Francisco ... **ARNOLD SCHWARZENEGGER** (1947), bodybuilder and noted for his movie roles ... **BILL CARTWRIGHT** (1957), center with USF and the Knicks since 1979.

Daley Thompson (1958), British Decathalon Champion in '84 Olympics.

NOTES

■ HANK BAUER (1922) —

A leader of men in the World War II trenches and in American League dugouts. Born in East St. Louis, Ill., Bauer was a war hero with the Marines. He broke in with the Yankees in 1948 (I listened to his debut on the radio — he went three for five) and was their right fielder for the entire decade of the 1950s. In his 12 seasons with the Yankees, they won 10 pennants. He was a .277 lifetime hitter who had a line drive swing but hit as many as 26 homers in 1956, averaged 14-15 a year, and hit four of them in the '58

Hank Bauer

series. Bauer spent his last two years with the Kansas City A's in a deal that sent Roger Maris to those damn Yankees. He later managed at K.C. (1961-62), Baltimore (1964-68) and Oakland (1969), winning the 1966 pennant with the Orioles and sweeping the Dodgers four straight, making him the only manager in history to go undefeated in World Series competition. Bauer owned a liquor store near Kansas City for many years; after he retired, he still did some scouting for the Yankees.

■ ARTHUR J. DALEY (1904) —

The late and longtime (1942-74) sports columnist for the New York Times, was born in New York City. He was a beat writer with the Times for 16 years before beginning his column in 1942. In 1956, he won the Pulitzer Prize, one of the few sportswriters to do so. His lead on the Chicago Bears' 73-0 blowout of the Washington Redskins in the 1940 NFL title game: "The weather was perfect. So were the Bears."

■ Also born today: Aussie tennis player **EVONNE GOOLAGONG CAWLEY (1951)**, Wimbledon champ, 1971, 1980, the fifth woman to win $1 million ... Cubbie first baseman **LEON DURHAM (1951)**, came from Cards in Bruce Sutter deal in 1980.

■**PANCHO VILLA (1901)** —Great Filipino flyweight, born Francisco Guilledo. He learned to box at the American base in Manila, adopting the name of the Mexican revolutionary. After beating all of the flyweights and bantamweights in the Orient, he was taken to New York where he became a big favorite. Villa is the No. 2-ranked flyweight of all-time with only five losses until he lost a non-title decision in 1925 to Jimmy McLarnin (the future welterweight great must've had a big weight advantage). Before the McLarnin bout, Villa had a wisdom tooth removed and was suffering from a sore mouth. After a bad beating in the ring, other dental problems followed, including an abcess in his jaw that required surgery. He died on the operating table — 10 days after the McLarnin fight. He was 23.

■**LLOYD MANGRUM (1914)** — The first golfer to fly his own plane on the tournament circuit, born in Trenton, Texas. Mangrum ranked with Ben Hogan and Sam Snead as one of golf's big three in the 1940s and 50s. He won the U.S. Open in 1946 and lost the 1950 Open to Hogan in a historic playoff. Mangrum retired in 1960 and died in 1973.

Lloyd Mangrum

■Also born today: Tennis Player JACK KRAMER (1921), who in 1947 won the U.S. and British singles and doubles titles .. hammer thrower HAROLD CONNOLLY (1931), winner of a gold medal in 1956 Olympics where he met future wife Olga Fikotova, who won gold medal in discus ... diver **SAMMY LEE (1920)**, who won gold in platform diving in 1948 and 1952 Olympics ... **BOB HORNER (1957)**, the Braves' third baseman who hit an NCAA-record 58 career HRs at ASU; a great player plagued with injuries. He made a successful career change in June 1985, switching to first base.

■ **BILLY CANNON (1937)** — A schoolboy football legend in Louisiana, Cannon went to LSU and won the Heisman Trophy in 1959. He became the first player fought over by the NFL and the fledgling AFL (finally signing with the AFL's Houston Oilers) and became the first $100,000 player. Cannon, who later played with the Raiders, studied dentistry during his pro career and after retirement became a prominent orthodontist, making more than $400,000 a year. He was a pillar of the community

Billy Cannon

with five children (including Texas A&M All-American linebacker Billy Cannon Jr.). This respectability was dented somewhat in 1983 when he was sentenced to five years in prison for masterminding a $6 million counterfeiting scheme. Cannon is supposedly a good man whose troubles were in part attempts to help friends.

■ Also born today: **IKE WILLIAMS (1923)**, lightweight champion, 1945-51... **CHARLES CALDWELL (1902)**, football coach at Williams (1928-44) and Princeton (1945-56) ... **JOHN KIERAN (1892)**, journalist, radio personality (panelist on "Information, Please"), first sportswriter for N.Y. Times to have his own bylined column, called "Sports of the Times" (later written by Arthur Daley and Red Smith) ... **MATT HAZELTINE (1933)**, Cal grad, 49er linebacker, 1955-68.

NOTES

Sports birthdays/Aug. 3

■ **HARRY HEILMANN (1894)** — One of the greatest hitters in baseball history, born in San Francisco.

Harry Heilmann

He played for Detroit most of his 17-year career as an outfielder and sometime first baseman. He was a good hitter for a few years but when Ty Cobb began managing the Tigers and tutoring him on how to hit, Heilmann's averages took off. In Cobb's first year at the helm, 1921, Heilmann (known as "Slug") won the batting title — and then won three more titles (in 1923, '25, and '27). All four titles came with averages of .390 or better. Heilmann, a solid (6-foot-1, 200 pounds) righty swinger, once said that he came of age as a hitter when he learned to hit the inside pitch to right field. Ted Williams rates him one of the top five right-handed hitters of all time. He died in 1951.

■ **LANCE ALWORTH (1940)** — perhaps the greatest wide receiver of all time. Born in Houston, Texas, he played college ball at Arkansas and pro ball with the San Diego Chargers and the Dallas Cowboys from 1967 to 1977. Small and quick (nicknamed "Bambi"), Alworth's 18.9 yards per catch is the highest ever. He was ninth in career receptions (542); his 85 TDs are surpassed only by Don Hutson's 99 and Don Maynard's 88; and he is the only receiver outside of Maynard to gain more than 10,000 yards.

■ Also born today: **JIM HEGAN (1920)**, fine defensive catcher for Cleveland in the 1950s; in fact, he's one of only 10 players with less than a .250 lifetime BA who still appeared in more than 1,500 games ... **MAXIE BAUGHAN (1938)**, linebacker in 1960s with Eagles and Rams, later head coach at Cornell ... **LOUIS A. CHIRON (1899)**, the oldest Grand Prix driver, who finished sixth in the Monaco Grand Prix in 1955 at age 55.

NOTES

■ **MAURICE "THE ROCKET" RICHARD (1921)** — The most exciting hockey player of all time, and one of the most exciting athletes of all time. He was with the Montreal Canadiens for his entire career (1942-60) and was the right wing on the famous "Punch Line" with Toe Blake and Elmer Lach. He was named first or second team All-NHL every year from 1944 to 1957. Even in photos, the intensity in his eyes shows through. He has been described as "the epitome of recklessness, of untrammeled fire and fury and abandon on the ice." His 50 goals in 50 games stood as a record for almost forty years until Wayne Gretzky broke it in 1982.

■ **GLENN CUNNINGHAM (1909)** — Greatest indoor miler of all time. Born in Kansas, he was burned as a boy in a schoolhouse fire. He spent a year in bed and six months in a hospital while skin was grafted to his legs before he could walk haltingly. He overcame this adversity to set world records in the outdoor (4:06.7) and indoor (4:04.4) mile in 1934. Father of 12, he and his wife ran ranches for "deprived or wayward" children for 29 years.

Glenn Cunningham

He once said, "Innovative coaches are rare. Most coaches hold back their athletes."

■ Also born today: **DOLF LUQUE (1890)**, Cuban pitcher, won 194 games mostly with Reds in 1920s. "The Pride of Havana" taught Sal Maglie how to throw a curveball when Maglie jumped to the Mexican League in the late 1940s ... **DALLAS GREEN (1934)**, Cubbie GM, managed Phillies to pennant in 1980.

... miler Mary Decker (1958), enfant terrible of women's track.

NOTES

■**TIGER FLOWERS (1895) —**
First black middleweight champ, born Theo Flowers

Tiger Flowers

in Camille, Georgia. Known as "The Georgia Deacon," he won 115 fights (49 by KO) and lost only 13. He won the middleweight title by defeating the great Harry Greb, a brawler like himself, by a 15-round decision in 1926. Later that year he got tricked out of his crown after losing a 10-round decision to Mickey Walker in a controversial bout that was supposed to be a non-title fight. A year later, still active and still a good fighter, Flowers died during an eye operation. He was 32.

■**BILL RICHMOND (1763) —**
The first important black boxer, born into slavery. He was also the first famous American boxer and the first American boxer to fight abroad. In England, Lord Byron became a big fan of his. At around 152 pounds, Richmond fought and beat heavyweights and competed into his fifties.

■Also born today: **BERNIE CARBO (1947)**, one of only two players ever to knock two pinch-hit homers in a World Series (for Bosox vs. Reds in '75) ... **GARY BEBAN (1946)**, UCLA QB, 1967 Heisman Trophy winner ... golfer **FRANK STRANAHAN (1922)** ... **TOMMIE AARON (1939)**, one half of #1 home-run producing brother duo in baseball history, hitting a combined 778 homers — brother Hank hit 755 and Tommie hit 23 ... **ROMAN GABRIEL (1940)**, QB with Rams and Eagles, MVP in 1969. Patrick Ewing (1962 NY Knicks Center-apparent.

The other guy was chuck Essegian (for Dodgers vs. Chisox in '59)

NOTES

■ HENRY IBA (1904) —

Legendary basketball coach at Oklahoma A&M (now Oklahoma State). He developed the first good 7-footer, Bob Kurland, won consecutive NCAA titles in 1945 and '46 with his patented discipline and ball control. His 767 victories is third on the all-time list for college coaches and he is the only coach to guide two U.S. Olympic teams to gold medals (in 1964 and '68). He also coached the 1972 team that lost to the Soviet Union in a controversial game in which the officials turned the clock back to give the Soviets one more chance before the buzzer. Bobby Knight calls Iba one of the two or three greatest innovators in basketball history.

Henry Iba

■ HELEN HULL JACOBS (1908) —

"The Rattlesnake of the West" was born in Globe, Ariz. One of the top 10 women tennis players of all time, Jacobs won the U.S. singles title four straight years (1932-35) and won at Wimbledon in 1936. She also wrote children's books, historical novels and books on tennis.

■ KEN STRONG (1906) —

A football titan who is in the college and pro halls of fame, born in West Haven, Conn. A NYU grad, he had a long pro career, mostly with the New York Giants, playing into his 40s. Strong excelled in every phase of the game — running, passing, blocking, punting, place-kicking and defense.

■ Also born today: **PAULINE BETZ ADDIE (1919),** another great woman tennis player who, like Jacobs, won four U.S. singles titles (1942-44, 1946) and one Wimbledon title (1946) ... golfer **DOUG FORD (1922),** PGA champion (1955) and Masters champion (1957) who, like Ken Strong, was born in West Haven, Conn.

NOTES

■ ALAN PAGE (1945) —

Alan Page

Long-time defensive tackle with the Minnesota Vikings. Born, appropriately, in Canton, Ohio, Page starred at Notre Dame before being drafted by Minnesota in 1967. In 1969 he became the only lineman ever to win the Jim Thorpe Trophy, emblematic of the most valuable player in the NFL. Page was known for his quickness (a Fred Dean-type). In 1981, playing with the Bears in his last years, Page blocked his 28th extra point — a phenomenal record.

■ CARLOS MONZON (1942) —

Great middleweight who held the title longer than anyone in this century. Monzon had a tremendous record in the ring. He won 89 fights (61 by KO) and lost only three, all on decisions, all early in his career. He was never knocked out or stopped and defended his title 15 times against such good fighters as Nino Benvenuti, Emile Griffith, Jose Napoles and Rodrigo Valdez — all champions at one time. He retired undefeated as champion in 1977.

■ DON LARSEN (1929) —

Larsen pitched the only perfect game in a World Series on Oct. 8, 1956: Yankees over Dodgers. Nothing else in his career prepared the world for such an earth-shattering experience. Two years earlier, with the Baltimore Orioles in his first season, he was 3-21. His career won-loss record is 81-91. He did win another World Series game — with the San Francisco Giants in 1962. He won Game 4 in relief of Juan Marichal, pitching one-third of an inning.

■ CHET FORTE (1935) —

Basketball star and TV producer, born Hackensack, N.J. Forte went to college at Columbia and was an All-America high-scoring guard. In 1957, he was the UPI Player of the Year.

■ **FRANK HOWARD (1936)** —

One of the great power hitters in baseball history. At 6-feet-7 and 255 pounds, Howard was among the biggest men ever to play big league baseball. Born in Columbus, Ohio, he went to Ohio State where he was an All Big Ten basketball player who was drafted by the NBA. Instead, he got a huge ($100,000) bonus and signed with Dodgers, and went on to win the 1960 Rookie of the Year award. With the Dodgers and Senators (to whom he was traded in 1965 for Claude Osteen) he became an awesome home run hitter (he hit

Frank Howard

382 in his career) and wound up with a .273 lifetime BA. Howard, later a N.Y. Mets coach, had one of the great home-run streaks of all-time. In May of 1968 he hit 10 homers in 20 at bats during a six-game period.

■ **GERTRUDE "GUSSIE" MORAN (1923)** —

Tennis champion whose lacy underwear was a cause celebre in the early 1950s. She won the U.S. indoor title in 1949, and several doubles and mixed doubles titles. She became famous as "Gorgeous Gussie" because Life magazine showed her frilly underthings beneath her shorts.

■ Also born today: **BILL GADSBY (1927)**, one of the great defensemen in hockey history, who played with the Black Hawks (1946-54), Rangers (1955-60) and Red Wings (1961-65) ... **BRIAN SIPE (1949)**, ex-Cleveland Browns (later went to the USFL) QB whose intercepted pass in waning seconds against the Raiders for the 1980 AFC title will live in infamy ... **VADA PINSON (1938)**, a tremendous offensive player with a .286 lifetime BA, 2,757 hits, 256 homers and 279 stolen bases; went to McClymonds HS in Oakland with Frank Robinson ... **KEN DRYDEN (1947)** five-time Vezina Trophy-winning goalie with Montreal Canadiens.

NOTES

■ BOB COUSY (1929) —

Bob Cousy

Brilliant and innovative Boston Celtics guard for 13 seasons. Born in New York City, he played college ball at Holy Cross (he was a sophomore on the 1947 team that won the NCAA title) and played with the Celtics from 1950 to 1963, helping them win six NBA titles. At 6-feet-1, Cousy was the greatest small player of all time. He was a spectacular ball-handler, dribbler, passer, shooter and clutch player. A 10-time NBA all-star, he scored more than 18,000 points with more than 6,900 assists. Cousy later coached at Boston College (1963-69) and the NBA's Cincinnati Royals (1969-73).

■ ROD LAVER (1938) —

Great Australian tennis star of the 1960s. He won the U.S. Open singles title in 1962 and 1969 and the Wimbledon title in 1961, '62, '68 and '69. In 1962 and 1963, Laver became the first tennis player to win the Grand Slam (U.S., British, Australian and French titles) twice.

■ GENE LIPSCOMB (1932) —

Mammoth football great known as "Big Daddy," born in Detroit. Lipscomb is one of the few to make it big in NFL without playing college ball. He played for the Rams (1953-55), Colts (1956-60) and Steelers (1961-62), his glory years being with the Colts, helping them win NFL titles in '58 and '59. Under mysterious circumstances, the 6-foot-6, 290-pound defensive tackle died at age 31 of a drug overdose, apparently self-inflicted, a claim disputed by many of his friends.

■ Also born today: TED SIMMONS (1949), one of the handful of switch-hitting power-hitters ever to play the game, and current Cards reliever BILL CAMPBELL (1948), both born in Highland Park, Mich. ... PETE KUGLER (1959), 49er defector to the Philadelphia Stars of the USFL who got himself more money, played on a championship team and worked near his hometown.

■ROCKY COLAVITO (1933) —
Clean-up hitter extraordinaire for 14 seasons. He broke in with Cleveland in 1955 and led the league twice in homers. In 1975, Colavito was voted the "Most Memorable Personality" in the team's history. The fans went bananas when he was traded to Detroit in 1960 for Harvey Kuenn. The fans' displeasure was heightened by the recent memory of Colavito's claim to immortality — four homers in a nine-inning game. He had equally good years with Detroit. In 1961, he hit 45 homers and had 140 RBI. He

Rocky Colavito

finished his career with 374 home runs and a .266 lifetime BA. He was also a good outfielder with an excellent arm. In fact, he pitched a few innings and finished with enviable stats — a winning percentage of 1.000 and an ERA of 0.00.

■FRANK MARSHALL (1871) —
Great American chess player, born in New York City. — also the birthplace of Rocky Colavito. Marshall was U.S. chess champion for three decades (1906-36), an unprecedented record. He gave up the title and retired in 1936 to devote his time to helping younger players, organizing chess clubs, and generally promoting the game. The Marshall Chess Club in New York City is the most prominent bastion of chess in the U.S.

■Also born today: jockey **TOD SLOAN (1874),** adopted short stirrups and monkey-crouch style of riding ... **SID FARRAR (1859),** obscure first baseman in NL before turn of century; his claim to fame is as the daddy of soprano Geraldine Farrar.

NOTES

■ **CHARLIE PADDOCK (1900)** —
The first "world's fastest human," born in Gainsville,

Charlie Paddock

Texas. Paddock was the first 'glamorous' figure in track history. He carved his niche in the Golden Age of Sports of the 1920s, winning the 100-meter event in the 1920 Olympics and finishing second in the 200 meters in 1920 and 1924. He also ran for the U.S. at the 1928 Olympics. In 1921, Paddock set the 100-yard standard at 9.6 seconds and the 220 at 21.8. An unorthodox runner, he was also a playwright, poet and was the announcer on the first radio broadcast of the Rose Bowl (1926). At the age of 40, he enlisted in the U.S. Marines in World War II. Captain Paddock was killed in a plane crash at age 42.

■ **BOBO NEWSOM (1907)** —
One of only six major league baseball players to play in four decades. He broke in with Brooklyn in 1929 and pitched 20 seasons, retiring after the 1953 season. He had three straight 20-game seasons (1936-40) and pitched a nine-inning no-hitter, only to give up a hit in the 10th and lose. He pitched with nine different teams (five times with the Senators) and had a career 211-222 won-loss record, one of only two pitchers to win over 200 games yet pitch under .500. He died in 1962.

■ Also born today: **BILL MONBOUQUETTE (1936)**, a 113-112 right-hander, mostly with Red Sox, also pitched no-hitter (in 1962), became a N.Y. Mets scout ... **ERIC HARRIS (1955)**, L.A. Rams cornerback, ex-K.C. Chiefs CB ... **OTIS TAYLOR (1942)**, speaking of ex-Chiefs, their great wide receiver, out of Prairie View ... **CHUCK RAYNOR (1920)**, Hall of Fame goalie with N.Y. Rangers, won Hart Trophy (MVP) in 1950, first time since 1929 that a goalie won the award.

NOTES

■**CHRISTY MATHEWSON (1880)** —
"Matty," the third winningest pitcher in major league
history, born in Factoryville,
Pa. Except for one game, he
won all of his 373 with the N.Y.
Giants from 1900 to 1916. His
career 2.13 ERA is the fifth
best mark and his 83 shutouts
is third (behind Walter Johnson
and Grover Cleveland Alexander). He pitched two no-hitters,
won 20 or more games 12
years in a row and 30 or more
three straight times (1903-05).
He is the only man to pitch
three shutouts in one World

Christy Mathewson

Series (in 1905 v. the A's — in
a span of only six days). Mathewson threw the
"fadeaway," what we now call a screwball, and also
had a "dry spitter" that was probably a sinker. His 37
wins in 1908 is the modern NL record — in fact, no
one's even come close. He wrote a wonderful book in
1912, "Pitching In A Pinch," which is still in print. (He
was also considered an awesome checkers player.) In
the World War I trenches, Matty inhaled poison gas
that weakened his lungs. He developed TB and died at
age 45.

■**ALEX WOJCIECHOWICZ (1915)** —
"Wojie," a member of both the college and pro
Halls of Fame, was born in South River, N.J. A
center, he played college ball at Fordham in the
mid-1930s and was one of the fabled "Seven Blocks
of Granite," which included Vince Lombardi. As a pro,
Wojie played with the Detroit Lions (1938-46) and
Philadelphia Eagles (1946-50). He played linebacker
on defense and was considered equally great in that
role. That's mostly what he played with the Eagles,
helping them win NFL titles in '48 and '49.

■ Also born today: **FRED HUTCHINSON (1919)**, 95-71
righty pitcher with Tigers, managed Tigers, Cardinals,
and Reds (leading Reds to 1961 pennant); he and
Christy Mathewson were both pitchers who died at
age 45 of lung diseases ... **GEORGE BELLOWS
(1882)**, realistic painter of the Ash Can School who
depicted the drama and anguish of boxing in many of
his paintings, notably the incredible Dempsey-Firpo
fight of 1923.

■ BEN HOGAN (1912) —

Ben Hogan

"Bantam Ben," giant of golf. Hogan was riding high at age 26. He had a U.S. Open title and was the biggest money-winner in golf history. In 1949 he was in an auto crash that nearly cost him his life. Doctors said he might never walk again. His road back to the top is one of the greatest comebacks in sports history. Hogan reached new heights by becoming the first golfer since Bobby Jones to win four U.S. Open titles (1948, '50, '51, and '53) and the first golfer in history to win the U.S. Open, the British Open, and the Masters tournament in a single year (1953).

■ TONY CLONINGER (1940) —

A 1960s righty pitcher mostly with the Braves. He had some good years, winning 19 games in 1964 and peaking out the following season with a 24-11 record. His immortality, however, is based on none of the above. On July 3, 1966, in a game at Candlestick Park, Cloninger hit two (count 'em, two) grand slam home runs. He is the only player in National League history — pitcher or non-pitcher — to hit two slams in one game. He also added an RBI single, knocking in nine runs for the day. Oh yeah, he pitched a seven-hitter and coasted to a 17-3 win.

■ Also born today: southpaw **WILMER "VINEGAR BEND" MIZELL** (1930), 90-88 w/Cards and Pirates, later congressman from North Carolina, and then Asst. Sect. of Agriculture for Gov't and Public Affairs ... **ANDRE THORNTON** (1949), DH-1B with Cleveland, tremendous hitter who has spent his whole career in obscurity ... **CHRIS HANBURGER** (1941), Redskins picked this great linebacker in the 18th round out of North Carolina. He went on to play in eight Pro Bowls.

NOTES

■ EARVIN "MAGIC" JOHNSON (1959) —

Magic Johnson

A unique presence on the basketball court. Born in Lansing, MI, he went to nearby Michigan State and, as a 6-foot-9 guard, led them to the NCAA title as a sophomore in 1979. He then turned pro and led the Lakers to the NBA title as a rookie — playing center (!) in the final game for injured Kareem Abdul-Jabbar. Magic was king of the hill at age 20. After six full seasons in the league, he has rewritten the book on dominating a basketball game. Johnson's virtuoso 1985 playoff performance in beating the Celtics quieted critics of some bonehead plays that cost the Lakers in 1984.

■ ROBYN SMITH (1944) —

The first female jockey to win a major stakes race. A San Francisco native, she is also the first female jockey to ride three winners in one day at a major New York track. Smith married Fred Astaire in 1980.

■ EARL WEAVER (1930) —

Weaver is one of only a handful of great managers. A minor league second baseman for 13 years, he is second only to Joe McCarthy in won-loss percentage (for managers with more than five years) and won five pennants (1969-71, 1973, 1979) in his 16 seasons with the Orioles. He is only the fifth manager to win 100 games four times or more. He went back to managing the O's in '85.

■ Also born today: swimmer **DEBBIE MEYER (1952)** — won gold medals at the 1968 Olympics in 400-meter and 800-meter freestyle events . . . **JOHN BRODIE (1935)**, yet another S.F. native, with 49ers 1957-73, threw 214 TD passes, became sports announcer on TV. Mark Fidrych (1954), the incomparable "Bird"

NOTES

■ **CHARLIE COMISKEY (1859)** —
Baseball player, manager and owner of the White Sox, was born in Chicago. In fact, his name is associated with the city of Chicago more than any other figure in baseball history. He was a pioneer first baseman for 13 years who revolutionized the game by ranging far off first base and by teaching his infielders to back up throws, shift according to situation, making the pitcher cover first on balls hit to the first baseman, and other innovations. Known as "The Old Roman," Comiskey was a co-founder of the American League and owner of the Chicago franchise, whose ballpark would bear his name. His tight-fistedness with salaries was blamed for precipitating the 1919 "Black Sox" scandal in which eight players threw the World Series for a few thousand dollars. He died in 1931.

Charlie Comiskey

■ **JOEY JAY (1935)** —
The first Little League baseball player to play in the major leagues. Jay was born in Middleton, Conn. His early physical development helped make him a young star. In fact, attempts were made to bar him from playing in the Little League because he was much bigger than any of the others. When he got to the bigs he was 6-feet-4 and 225 pounds. He won his first game with the Milwaukee Braves at age 18, but came on strong after being traded to the Reds in 1961. He won 21 games (and 21 the following year) and led the Reds to pennant-winning Cincinnati's only victory in the Series against the Yankees. Today Jay is a wealthy man. He owns oil wells, taxicab companies and other businesses.

■ Also born today: **LIONEL TAYLOR (1936)**, brilliant wide receiver w/Broncos (1960-66) and Oilers (1967-69), his 567 receptions is seventh on the all-time list ...**SAM "BAM" CUNNINGHAM (1950)**, mostly used as a blocking back at USC, became tremendous runner in pros with the Patriots.

NOTES

■ **AMOS ALONZO STAGG (1862)** — Winningest football coach of all time, until Bear Bryant eclipsed his 309 wins in 1983, born in West Orange, N.J. As a player, Stagg was picked as an end on Walter Camp's first All-American team and is the only player and coach in the college Hall of Fame. He coached at Chicago U. (1892-1932), College of the Pacific (1933-46), where he was voted Coach of the Year in 1943 at age 81, and Susquehanna U. (1947-52), in collaboration with his son. He retired from coaching at age 91, having originated

Amos Alonzo Stagg

the huddle, man in motion, the tackling dummy, numbers on jerseys, etc. Stagg also helped James Naismith in the early development of basketball when both were students and instructors at Springfield (Mass.) College, and introduced basketball at the Univ. of Chicago. He is in both the football and basketball Hall of Fame. He died in 1965 at age 102.

■ **FRANK GIFFORD (1930)** —
The All-American boy from USC who became the grey eminence of Monday Night Football. A tremendous performer for the New York Giants from 1952 to 1964, he won the MVP award in 1957 and stood out in every phase of the game. He suffered a famous near-fatal tackle by Chuck Bednarik in 1960 that hastened the end of his career. He sat out 1961, returning for three more seasons. His daughter married a son of Robert F. Kennedy.

■ Also born today: **MONTE STICKLES (1938)**, end for Notre Dame and the 49ers (1960-67), radio sportscaster-talk show host and columnist ... tennis player **TONY TRABERT (1930)**, won U.S. singles title in 1953 and '55, and Wimbledon crown in 1955 ... **GENE WOODLING (1922)**, clutch hitter with Yankees and several others, .284 lifetime hitter; raises horses in Ohio and is a part-time scout for the Indians ... relief pitcher **AL HOLLAND (1952)**, one of the best lefty relievers in baseball.

NOTES

■ **BOOG POWELL (1941)** —
Baltimore Orioles (1961-75) first baseman, lefty power-
hitter.

Boog Powell

Boog, born John Wesley Powell in Lakeland, Fla., hit 339 home runs in his career and was a lifetime .265 hitter. At 6-feet-4½ and 230 pounds, Powell was an awesome presence in the middle of the Oriole batting order. He won the MVP award in 1970, hitting .297 with 35 HRs and 114 RBI, appearing in every game. He had a few other years with similar numbers. Yeah, the O's were tough with Frank Robinson batting third and big Boog hitting clean-up.

■ **MIKHAIL BOTVINNIK (1911)** —
Great Soviet chess player known as "The Invincible". Botvinnik was world chess champion from 1948 to 1963, except for two years — an outstanding feat in the modern era. He had a dual career as an eminent electrical engineer.

■ **JACK KEARNS (1882)** —
Jack Dempsey's manager, born in Waterloo, Mich. Dempsey's career was drifting somewhat when he met Kearns, a ring-wise pro who was also a ballyhoo artist. Kearns' connection with promoter Tex Rickard created a trio that ushered in the modern era of boxing, complete with million dollar gates and new levels of media hype. Kearns also managed such boxing greats as Mickey Walker, Benny Leonard, Archie Moore, and Joey Maxim.

■ Also born today: **RUDY YORK (1913)**, hard-hitting first baseman (a la Boog Powell) w/Tigers from 1937 to 1945, playing in '45 World Series in which he singled for only hit off Cub pitcher Claude Passeau; traded to Bosox in '46, he played in World Series again ... **JIM DAVENPORT (1933)**, S.F. Giants manager and Dream Team third baseman; played from 1958 to 1970.

The jury's in [7/85]:
Davvy can't manage.

NOTES

■ ROBERTO CLEMENTE (1934) —
Greatest Latin-American player in ML baseball
history, born in Puerto Rico.
He played his whole 18-year
career with the Pirates, finishing with a .317 career BA and
3000 hits. He won four batting
titles, won the MVP award in
1966, and was a tremendous
right fielder with a cannon arm.
He was also a fine base runner
and had good power. As a
complete player, I rate him
second only to Willie Mays. In
one of baseball's (and life's)
tragic twists of fate, the great
Clemente died New Year's Eve,

Roberto Clemente

1972, in a plane crash while on a humanitarian mission
for Nicaraguan flood victims. He was 38 and, despite
his age, was near — if not at — his peak as a player.

■ RAFER JOHNSON (1935) —
Olympic decathlon champion in 1960. He amassed
a record number of points, in the decathlon, later
became a TV sportscaster, and acted in several films.
Johnson joined Robert F. Kennedy's presidential
campaign in 1968 and, with Roosevelt Grier's help,
grabbed Sirhan Sirhan after he shot RFK. Johnson,
brother of ex-49er defensive back Jimmy Johnson,
carried the torch that lighted the Olympic rings at
the 1984 opening ceremonies in Los Angeles. Born
in Hillsboro, Texas.

■ Also born today: MATT SNELL (1941), 1960s N.Y.
Jets fullback... Swedish swimming twins **ARNE BORG**
and **AKE BORG**, born in 1901, both Olympic medalists
... **BOB KENNEDY (1920)**, 3B-OF Chisox, Indians,
etc.: Houston Astros veep and father of Padre
catcher Terry Kennedy ... **RICKEY GREEN**
(1954), quick point guard w/Utah Jazz.

Joan Joyce (1940), the Cy Young of
women softball pitchers.

■ BILL SHOEMAKER (1931) —

"Shoe," still one of the world's leading jockeys in 1985. Born in Fabens, Texas, he rode his first winner

Willie Shoemaker

(at Golden Gate Fields) four months before his 18th birthday, when they called him Willie Shoemaker. In more than 37,000 races, he finished in the money more than 50 percent of the time, earning almost $100 million. He won over 900 stakes races, including three Kentucky Derbys (1955, '59, and '65) and five Belmont Stakes. In 1979, at age 39, he broke Johnny Longden's record of 6,032 wins. He has since exceeded that by more than two thousand.

■ RENEE RICHARDS (1934) —

Everyone's favorite transsexual tennis player. She was born Richard Raskind, a man and a fine athlete, captain of the Yale tennis team and scouted by the Yankees as a baseball player. He became a leading eye surgeon before having a sex-change operation in the early 1970s. Renee Richards' right to play tennis on the women's tour was challenged but she did play as a woman and became a top player. Her autobiography, "Second Serve," was published in 1983.

■ Also born today:

IZAAK WALTON (1593), born almost 400 years ago, he was a businessman and biographer who wrote The Compleat Angler, 1653, an authoritative classic on fishing ... **BOBBY RICHARDSON (1935)**, N.Y. Yankee second baseman (1955-66), .266 lifetime hitter, caught McCovey's liner to end 1962 Series, long-time coach at Univ. of South Carolina. *Rudy Ortega (1929), boxing referee in over 35 title fights.*

NOTES

■ **GRAIG NETTLES (1944)** —
San Diego Padres' third baseman, one of the best of
the modern era. Nettles, born
in San Diego, has returned
home and has solved the long-
standing Padres' third base
problems. Nettles is a strong
bet for the Hall of Fame. One of
the greatest gloves ever to play
his position, he also holds the
American League record for
homers by a third baseman. His
years of glory with the Yankees
and later disillusionment with
George Steinbrenner are chron-
icled in his book, "Balls." His

Graig Nettles

brother, Jim Nettles, an ex-major leaguer, is a Tacoma
coach in the Oakland organization.

■ **AL LOPEZ (1908)** —
Major league player and manager for 36 years.
born in Tampa, Fla. He managed two teams:
Cleveland (1951-56) and the Chicago White Sox
(1957-69), winning pennants in '54, '59. In 17 seasons
as a manager, his teams finished lower than third only
three times. His teams finished second to the Yankees
nine times. He was a National League catcher from
1928 to 1946 and had a .261 lifetime batting average.

■ Also born today: **QUINN BUCKNER (1954)**, Celtics
(ex-Bucks) guard, on 1976 Indiana team that won NCAA
title ... **GARY COLLINS (1940)**, wide receiver and
punter for the Cleveland Browns in the 1960s.

NOTES

■ **WILT CHAMBERLAIN (1936) —**
Wilt the Stilt owns a truckload of career, season,

Wilt Chamberlain

and game scoring records. Born in Philadelphia, where he was a high school phenomenon at Overbrook HS, he was wooed and won by the Univ. of Kansas. After a stint with the Harlem Globetrotters, Chamberlain entered the NBA in 1959 with the Warriors (first in Philadelphia, then in S.F.), moving to the L.A. Lakers in 1968 and retiring in 1973. His career points record (31,419) was recently eclipsed by Kareem Abdul-Jabbar, making them the only players to reach 30,000 points. On March 2, 1962, Wilt scored 100 points (against the N.Y. Knicks), establishing a mark that no one has even approached. In fact, Wilt's own 78 points is the closest to the record. His career average per game is 30.1. In 1962, it was an incredible 50.4. Chamberlain became a great defensive player in his later years. An index of his dominance: He never fouled out in his NBA career of more than 1,000 games. A tremendous all-around athlete, he would have been a star in several sports — football, track & field, boxing, and volleyball, to name a few. Lately, he's been doing some acting and was recently seen taking on Conan.

■ Also born today: **J. OWEN WILSON (1883),** outfielder with Pirates and Cards from 1908 to 1916, his 36 triples in 1912 is a major league record, a record — like Wilt's 50.4 ppg in '62 — that no one (at least in the 20th Century) has even approached ... **TOE BLAKE (1912),** Montreal Canadiens, 1935-47, one-third of the famous "Punch Line," with Maurice Richard and Elmer Lach ... **CORNELIUS JOHNSON (1913),** won the high jump at the 1936 Olympics (made winning jump in his sweat suit) ... **RINTY MONAGHAN (1920),** flyweight champion, 1947-50, known as the "Singing Irishman," he would sing to the crowd after he won a fight.

■ CARL YASTRZEMSKI (1939) —

"Yaz" played in more American League baseball games than any other player. The Boston Red Sox outfielder-first baseman for 23 seasons retired in 1983 with a .285 lifetime BA, 452 homers, and 3,419 hits. Yaz is the fourth player — and the first American Leaguer — to amass 3,000 hits and 400 home runs. He won three batting titles (1963, 1967 and 1968) and in 1967 was named MVP after a triple crown year, leading the AL in the three main hitting categories as well as hits, runs, total bases and slugging. He went

Carl Yastrzemski

7-for-8 in the last two games in helping the Red Sox to only their third pennant since the live-ball era began in 1920.

■ MEL HEIN (1909) —

One of the great centers in football, born in Redding. California. He played college ball at Washington State and had a brilliant pro career with the N.Y. Giants (1931-45). Hein was big (6-3, 235 pounds), and fast enough to pull after snapping the ball (quite a ways back, remember, to the tailback) and lead the blocking around end. Voted MVP in 1938, Hein was a 60-minute regular (linebacker on defense) for 15 years and never missed a game.

■ Also born today: **URBAN SHOCKER (1890)**, righty pitcher with the St. Louis Browns and N.Y. Yankees (1916-28), 188-117 won-loss record, one of the few pitchers, and one of the last, to hurl two complete-game wins in one day; after great 18-6 season in 1927, he died suddenly of heart disease at age 38 ... Swedish tennis player **MATS WILANDER (1964)**, in '82 became youngest player to win French Open ... **OSCAR "HAPPY" FELSCH (1891)**, Chisox outfielder (1915-20), one of the eight players convicted of throwing the 1919 World Series, banished for life from baseball.

One of the top ten names ever...

NOTES

■**HOWARD H. JONES (1885)** —
Jones, one of the legendary football coaches, born in Excello, Ohio. Jones played college football at Yale with his brother, the great halfback Tad Jones, and began coaching at age 23 at Syracuse. Most of his 29 years as a coach were spent at Iowa (1916-23) and USC (1925-40) with a career record of 193 wins, 63 losses, and 20 ties. Five of his USC teams went to the Rose Bowl, winning each time. Three of his teams (1928, 1931, 1939) were national champions. Jones died in 1941.

Dale Mitchell

■**DALE MITCHELL (1921)** —
Mitchell, a Cleveland Indians outfielder (1946-56) with a .312 lifetime BA. Born in Colony, Okla., Mitchell hit .300 six times, including a .336 season in 1948 that helped the Indians win the pennant. In 1949 he hit 23 triples, more than anyone since Owen Wilson's record 36 in 1912. Unfortunately, his claim to fame is as a Brooklyn Dodger, with whom he played the last 19 season games in 1956. Luckily, he hooked up with a pennant-winner but he was the final out in Don Larsen's perfect game in Game Five. Mitchell took a called third strike. (Dale, I ask you, did you think the umpire was going to give you the call?) Ironically, Mitchell struck out only 119 times in almost 4,000 career at-bats.

■Also born today: **GEORGE KELL (1922)**, Hall of Fame (inducted in 1983) third baseman, mostly with the Tigers. He won the batting title in 1949 to become the first third-baseman in the AL to win the batting title. He became the Tigers announcer ... **SONNY JURGENSON (1934)**, QB with the Eagles (1957-63) and 'Skins (1964-74), third in career yardage and TD passes.

NOTES

■ **CAL RIPKEN, JR. (1960)** —
Wunderkind shortstop of the Baltimore Orioles. Rookie-of-the-year in '82, MVP in '83, Cal is running out of personal goals. He has played in every inning of every game since July 3, 1982 (so why don't they rest him once in a while?), which is the day the Orioles returned him to shortstop after switching him to third base. Yes, some day Ripken will play third but, despite his size, (6-feet-4, 200 pounds) he is a true shortstop — fluid and rangy. That mistake cost the Orioles third-baseman Doug DeCinces, whom they

Cal Ripken Jr.

traded to the Angels for Dan Ford (worst trade in Oriole history). Ripken is impeccable and that's that. His father, Cal, Sr., is the Orioles' third-base coach and his brother Bill is a minor-league infielder, also signed by the Orioles.

■ Also born today: **VIKTO BARNA (1911)**, Hungarian ping-pong player, the greatest of all time ... two auto racers: **ROGER McCLUSKEY (1930)**, national sprint car champion in 1963 and '66, and **HOWARD KAEDING (1932)**, a NorCal legend, active in his early 50s; in '73, he won 14 main events in a row — a record ... **JIMMY COONEY (1894)**, made unassisted triple play as SS for Cubs in 1927, was also caught off second base in 1925 when playing for Cardinals against Pittsburgh and Pirate SS Glenn Wright made an unassisted triple play; thus, Cooney is the only player ever to be involved in two unassisted triple plays; heck, there've only been eight of the darn things and Cooney played in only 448 games.

■ ALTHEA GIBSON (1927) —

Althea Gibson

Broke the color barrier in tennis. Born in Silver, S.C. on a poor cotton farm, she spent her youth in New York City slums. The proverbial gift of a tennis racquet turned her life around. Despite myriad racist obstacles, Gibson persevered to become the first black person to compete in a national tennis tournament. She was the first black to play in the U.S. championship at Forest hills, N.Y. and the first to play in the British championship at Wimbledon, winning both tournaments in 1957 and again in 1958. Her autobiography, written in 1958, is "I Always Wanted To Be Somebody."

■ ROLLIE FINGERS (1946) —

Reliever extraordinaire with A's, Padres and Brewers. Fingers (not a bad handle for a pitcher) holds the all-time record for saves (in '85 about 335 and counting), having soared past Hoyt Wilhelm's mark a few years ago. Despite his age and arm problems, he is still going strong. The 1981 Cy Young Award winner might be around for another decade a la Wilhelm.

■ Also born today: **CHARLIE SANDERS (1946)**, tight end w/Detroit Lions, 1968-78 ... auto racer **GORDON JOHNCOCK (1936)**, won Indy 500 in 1973 ... **DARRELL JOHNSON (1927)**, managed Red Sox to a pennant in 1975 ... **JOHN G. FETROS (1932)**, San Francisco librarian and author of the excellent sports reference book, "This Day in Sports."

NOTES

■ **DUKE KAHANAMOKU** (1890) — Illustrious swimming champion, born in Honolulu. He won the 100 meters for the U.S. at the 1912 Olympics and won it again at the 1920 Olympics (the Games were not held in 1916). In 1924 he finished second to Johnny Weissmuller to win the silver medal. No other swimmer has won Olympic medals twelve years apart. It was Kahanamoku who introduced surfing to California in 1910.

Duke Kahanamoku

■ **TOM HEINSOHN** (1934) — Heinsohn, star forward of the Boston Celtics and later their coach. Born in Newark, N.J., he played college ball at Holy Cross, was drafted by the Celtics and became the 1956 rookie of the year. Heinsohn played nine seasons for the Celtics, averaging 18.6 points a game. The Celts won their division in every year he played and won the NBA title in every year but one. Knee injuries forced his retirement at age 30. He began coaching the Celtics in 1969 and led them to five division titles and two NBA championships. Heinsohn is also a painter whose works have been displayed in galleries and, with Bob Cousy, organized the Players Association.

■ **Also born today:** ALEX KELLNER (1924), lefty pitcher mostly with Philadelphia A's with 101-112 lifetime won-loss record; one of several pitchers to win 20 games one year (1949) and lose 20 the following year ... **DONNIE SHELL** (1952), Pittsburgh Steelers safety ... **JOE JEANNETTE** (1879), one of many fine black heavy-weight boxers who never got a chance at the title.

NOTES

■ **FRANK LEAHY (1908)** —
One of the greatest coaches in college football history born in O'Neill, Nebraska. He played college ball

at Notre Dame under Knute Rockne, who became his mentor. One of Leahy's assistant coaching jobs was at Fordham in the mid-1930s where he developed the famed Seven Blocks of Granite. He began his head coaching at Boston College in 1939, taking B.C. to two bowl games before beginning his tenure at Notre Dame in 1941. He introduced the T-formation at that school and developed two Heisman Trophy

Frank Leahy

quarterbacks, Angelo Bertelli and Johnny Lujack and a Heisman Trophy-winning halfback, Johnny Lattner. From 1946 to 1949, Notre Dame had a fabulous streak of 39 games without a loss. Gastric enteritis forced his retirement in 1953 after a record of 107 wins, 13 losses, and 9 ties, for one of the best percentages of all time. His Notre Dame teams won five national titles.

■ Also born today: **ERNIE BROGLIO (1935)**, won 21 games for Cardinals in 1960 and was 18-8 in '63; he and a couple of others went over to the Cubs for Lou Brock in '64 in one of baseball's infamous deals; Broglio was born in Berkeley ... **BUDDY BELL (1951)**, Texas Rangers third baseman, son of ex-Pirates and Reds outfielder Gus Bell; Buddy is tremendous talent mired in obscurity ... **GEORGE T. HEPBRON (1863)**, basketball pioneer, the first referee in the N.Y. area and author of "How To Play Basketball," 1904, the first handbook on the game.

NOTES

■ **CHARLIE GRIMM (1898)** —
"Jolly Cholly," one of the great names in Chicago
Cubs history, born in St. Louis, Mo. Grimm, a first
baseman, played a few years
with the Pirates before going to
the Cubs in 1925. He played
with them until 1936 and retired
with a .290 lifetime batting
average. He managed the Cubs
from 1932 to 1938 and again
from 1944 to 1949, winning
pennants in 1935 and 1945 (the
Cubs' last flag). He finished in
the first division nine out of 14
seasons. He later managed the
Braves from 1952 to 1956. In 19
seasons managing, his percent-

Charlie Grimm

age was .546. As his nickname suggests, Grimm was a
free spirit and one of the beloved figures in Cubs
history. He died in 1983.

■ **RON GUIDRY (1950)** —
Best Yankee lefty since Whitey Ford. He has a few
team records of his own, including 18 strikeouts in a
game and 13 consecutive wins in 1978 when he won
the Cy Young Award (a unanimous winner for only the
second time). Guidry entered this season with a
132-62 won-loss record for a tremendous .705
percentage. His .893 percentage in '78 (he was 25-3)
is the second best of all time. Guidry doesn't
overwhelm hitters the way he used to, relying more on
pinpoint accuracy, but still has a good fastball.

■ Also born today: **JIM LYNCH (1945)**, linebacker on
K.C. Chiefs dynasty in late 1960s and early '70s ...
ANDY BATHGATE (1932), right wing for N.Y. Rangers
and others, 1953-71, one of the earliest users of the
slapshot. It was his shot off the face of Jacques Plante
that ushered in the era of the goalie mask.

Scott Hamilton (1958), figure skater,
won 1984 Olympics.

NOTES

■ **BOB BEAMON (1946)** —
The long jump record holder. Born in New York City,

of all places, Beamon won the gold medal at the 1968 Olympics. In the rarified air of Mexico City, Beamon broke Jesse Owens' 32-year-old record by more than two feet, leaping 29-2½, one of the greatest track & field achievements in history. Beamon's accomplishment has been the carrot dangling in front of Carl Lewis — a carrot Lewis may some day eat.

Bob Beamon

■ **DOUG DeCINCES (1950)** —
The Angels third baseman. Born in Burbank, California, not too many miles from his current workplace, DeCinces came up with the Orioles, who used him at every position in the infield and the outfield. Rather odd, considering that he is the best defensive third baseman in the league. Then, after the 1981 season, the Orioles went from odd to downright dumb and sent DeCinces to the Angels for Dan Ford. Nagging back injuries have kept him from consistent productivity as well as the recognition he deserves.

■ Also born today: **WYOMIA TYUS (1945)**, won 100 meters in the 1964 and 1968 Olympics ... auto racer **GARY GABELICH (1950)**, in 1970, achieved the highest speed on land — 650 mph ... **BILLY COX (1919)**, Brooklyn Dodgers third baseman of late 1940s and early '50s, among the greatest defensive third basemen of all-time (even better than Doug DeCinces); Cox was one of "The Boys of Summer," Roger Kahn's then-and-now study of the 1950s Brooklyn Dodgers ... **JAMES "ABIE" SOUZA (1898)**, "The Prince of Vendors," at age 87 in 1985, still hawking hot dogs and beer at San Francisco's Candlestick Park and the Oakland Coliseum; he told me he has no intention of retiring.

■ TED WILLIAMS (1918) —

The greatest hitter in baseball history. He is that rare player in the modern era whose lifetime batting average (.344) is comparable, or superior, to those of earlier eras. He hit 521 home runs in a difficult park for left-handed hitters. Williams revolutionized hitting, bringing to it the erudition and dedication of a scientist. And he accomplished everything despite great obstacles: a difficult home park, the "Williams Shift" whereby he swung away facing three infielders on the right side of the diamond, three peak

Ted Williams

years lost to World War II and another one lost to the Korean War, and a rapacious press that was bent (futilely) on ruining a guy who was not in awe of it. Williams' lack of popularity with the press is painfully evident in his "only" two MVP awards. In 1941, he hit .406 but did not win the award. In 1942, he won the Triple Crown again, but did not win the award. Williams hit .388 in 1957 at age 39 (!) and the following year became the oldest player ever to win a batting title. Recommended reading: John Updike's account of Williams' last game, "Hub Fans Bid Kid Adieu" (in which he homers in his last at bat and does not doff his cap to the screaming throng) and Ted's own masterpiece, "The Science of Hitting."

■ Also born today: **ROBERT PARISH (1953)**, Boston Celtics center... auto racer **BRUCE McLAREN (1937)**, at age 22 became the youngest Grand Prix winner ... lefty reliever **TUG McGRAW (1944)**, born in Joe DiMaggio's hometown — Martinez, California.

NOTES

■ FRANK ROBINSON (1935) —

One of the greatest baseball players ever to suit up, his accomplishments are well-known: the only player to win MVP awards in each league, 586 career homers (fourth on all-time list), and many others. As an all-around performer, only Mays and Clemente are on the same level in the modern era. A tad more controversial is Robby's firing as manager (1980 to 1984) of the S.F. Giants. Two points need to be made: One, most managers are bad because they're hired by inept owners with stone-age baseball ideas. Two, Robby was sabotaged by such an owner and a general manager who made some infamous trades.

Frank Robinson

■ EDWIN MOSES (1955) —

For almost a decade the dominant track and field athlete in the world. In more than 90 consecutive final events, Moses has not lost in his specialty, the 400-meter hurdles. He won gold medals at the 1976 Olympics and in 1984 in Los Angeles. Perhaps he will break welterweight Packey McFarland's all-time record of 97 straight wins, a record for an individual or team in any sport.

NOTES

■ ROCKY MARCIANO (1923) —

The only heavyweight who never lost a pro fight and retired as champion, born in Brockton, Mass., (birthplace of another fighter: Al Davis). He is not only the one truly undefeated heavyweight, he is the only boxer in the 20th century never to lose a fight. He held the title from 1952 to 1956 and his incomparable record was 49 and 0, with 43 KOs. Rocky was a rather small heavyweight, under 200 pounds with one of the shortest reaches in the history of the division. His fist

Rocky Marciano

size (11½ inches) didn't compare with, say, Sonny Liston's at 15, but Rocky was a devastating punching machine with an iron chin. Only twice did he ever get knocked down (by Walcott and Archie Moore) and both times arose quickly, winning both bouts by KOs. Marciano died in a plane crash on the eve of his 46th birthday.

■ JAMES J. CORBETT (1866) —

"Gentleman Jim," another great heavyweight champion, born in San Francisco. Interestingly, while Marciano was the incarnate slugger, Corbett was the first scientific boxer. He won the title in 1892 from John L. Sullivan (by a KO, the first ever suffered by the great John L.) with the fighters wearing gloves (which favored Corbett's style) for the first time in a title match. Corbett's emphasis on ring science brought boxing into a new era. He lost his title to Bob Fitzsimmons in 1897. After retirement, Corbett resumed an acting career which he had begun after winning the title.

■ Also born today: **AL GEIBERGER (1937)**, the first golfer to break 60 for 18 holes in a PGA-sponsored tournament ... **JOHNNY MACK BROWN (1904)**, All-American running back at Alabama, leading them to 1926 Rose Bowl win over Washington; later cowboy star in Hollywood.

NOTES

■ ADOLPH RUPP (1901) —

"The Baron," winningest college basketball coach of all time, born in Halstead, Kan., and played college

Adolph Rupp

ball at Kansas under Phog Allen. He coached at Kentucky from 1930 to 1972, winning 874 times and posted an .821 percentage. Kentucky won four national titles (1948, 1949, 1951, 1958), the first to win three, and Rupp made more appearances in the NCAA tournament (20) than any other coach. Rupp, controversial and outspoken, developed a basketball style that was deliberate and based on set offenses — no matter what the opponent did. His bread-and-butter was tough man-to-man defense and he won with rather small teams that were quick and rugged. Rupp was voted Coach of the Year four times, the last time in 1966 — at age 65. He died in 1977.

■ JIMMY CONNORS (1952) —

Great tennis champion of the 1970s. He has won the U.S. Open five times and the U.S. Indoor title five times. Despite his advanced years (for a tennis champion), Connors is still among the top players in the world. He was thought of as the Bobby Fischer of tennis, but has mellowed during the last few years and, having survived the *enfant terrible* stage, is appreciated for his sheer tennis ability more than ever before.

■ Also born today:

QB **TERRY BRADSHAW (1948)**, retired in 1983 after 14 seasons with Steelers; MVP, 1978, led team to four Super Bowl titles (1975, 1976, 1979, 1980) ... **MARV THRONEBERRY (1933)**, symbol of mediocre N.Y. Mets in 1962 and '63; brother of Faye Throneberry. *Peter Ueberroth (1937), Baseball Commissioner (and future Senator?).*

■ STEVE BOROS (1936) —

The former Oakland A's manager, fired in 1984. He was a rarity in sports — a big-league manager who earned a college degree majoring in English, and a serious writer to boot. Boros will probably get various offers as coach, manager, or executive but he is no doubt considering his writing and what he really wants to do.

Steve Boros

■ EDDIE STANKY (1916) —

"The Brat," one of the scrappiest and headiest baseball players ever to play the game. A lifetime .268 hitter, Stanky played second base with three pennant-winning teams: the 1947 Dodgers, the 1948 Boston Braves, and the 1951 N.Y. Giants (in that Series against the Yankees he kicked the ball out of Phil Rizzuto's glove sliding into second). Here's the kind of player he was: In 1945, with Brooklyn, he hit .258 with one home run, and only six stolen bases. But he led the league in two departments — walks (148, setting a NL record) and runs (128). An effective ballplayer. He managed the Cardinals (1952-55), the White Sox (1966-68), and managed the Texas Rangers for one famous day in the summer of 1977 after which he decided he'd rather coach the boys at the Univ. of South Alabama. And, Steve Boros, who can blame him?

NOTES

■EDDIE WAITKUS (1919) —

One of the pennant-winning Philadelphia Phillies "Whiz Kids" of 1950, born in Cambridge, Mass. World War II claimed four lost years from his impressive 11-year career as a slick-fielding, left handed-hitting first-baseman with a .285 lifetime BA. A Chicago Cub rookie in 1941, he didn't return to baseball until 1946, the year after the Cubs won their last pennant. He was traded to the Phillies in 1949. That season, hitting .306 after 54 games, Waitkus was shot in the chest at close range by Ruth Ann Steinhagen, an "admirer" of his who was mentally disturbed. After nine months of rest, he returned in 1950 to play in every game and hit .284. Waitkus died in 1972.

Tom Watson

■TOM WATSON (1949) —

The heir apparent to Jack Nicklaus. After supposedly choking in the 1974 and '75 U.S. Opens, he took his place among the golf greats by winning four British Opens (1975, 1977, 1980, 1982), two Masters (1977, 1981), and the U.S. Open in 1982 In 1980, Watson won three straight tournaments and, through the 12 rounds, never lost the lead — a phenomenal feat.

■ Also born today: Aussie swimmer **DAWN FRASER (1937)**, won 100 meters in three straight Olympics (1956, 1960, 1964) ... tennis player **BILLY TALBERT (1918)**, he and Gardnar Mulloy were U.S. doubles champions in 1942, 1945-46, 1948 ... another golfer: **RAYMOND FLOYD (1942)**, won Masters in 1976 and the PGA in 1969 and 1982, has earned more than $2 million in prize money.

NOTES

■NAPOLEON "LARRY" LAJOIE (1875) —

One of baseball's early immortals, born in Woonsocket.
R.I. A big (6-foot-1, 200 pounds)
second-baseman who played
most of his career with the
Cleveland Indians, Lajoie was
the best player in the American
League in the years before Ty
Cobb. His lifetime BA was .339,
he had 3,251 career hits, and is
fourth on the all-time doubles
list with 657. He won four
batting titles, hitting .422 in
1901 which — after Rogers
Hornsby's .424 in 1924 — is the
highest average in the 20th
century. That year, Lajoie was a

Nap Lajoie

dead-ball era Triple Crown winner, also leading the
league in RBI and homers. He was a master batsman
who could do anything at the plate — bunt, hit to the
opposite field, and hit for power. He was also an agile
second-baseman who still has the AL record of 988
fielding chances in a season and set a record with 11
put-outs in a single game. After retirement in 1916,
Lajoie became a top golfer. He died in 1959.

■BILL MAZEROSKI (1936) —

"Maz," another second- baseman, and also one of
the best ever at his position .   A Pittsburgh Pirate
for his entire career (1956-72), he will always be
remembered for his ninth inning home run in Game
Seven of the 1960 World Series to defeat the N.Y.
Yankees. It was the only World Series ever to end with
a home run. Mazeroski, a .260 lifetime hitter, is
currently owner of a nine-hole golf course and Bill's Bar
in Yorkville, Ohio.

■Also born today: gutsy QB **BILL KILMER (1939)**,
played 1961-78 with 49ers, Redskins, Saints ...
WARREN LAHR (1923), brilliant defensive back with
Cleveland Browns from 1949 to 1959 ... lefty **GENE
BEARDON (1920)**, led Indians to 1948 pennant with
20-7 record and led league in ERA; in six other
seasons he never pitched better than .500.

NOTES

■ VINCE DIMAGGIO (1912) —

Vince DiMaggio

Elder brother of Joe and Dom, and a big-league outfielder for 10 years, he played mostly with the Pirates and the Braves. He was only a lifetime .249 hitter but he had a couple of good years and was, like his brothers, an excellent outfielder. In fact, Vince rates himself better than Joe with the glove. It was Vince, then an outfielder with the San Francisco Seals, who arranged a tryout for his brother Joe with the Seals. Vince, always in his brother Joe's shadow, never became famous or wealthy and has had to scuffle at various jobs. He lives in southern California, a long-time Fuller Brush salesman.

■ MAXIE ROSENBLOOM (1904) — "Slapsie Maxie,"
light-heavyweight champion (1930-34), was born 80 years ago today in New York City. An excellent boxer (who learned to dance from his friend George Raft), Rosenbloom fought in 285 bouts from 1925 to 1939, losing only 35 times. He was a light hitter (he only had 18 KOs) and was called "Slapsie Maxie" because of his penchant for open-handed punches. But he could take a punch. He was knocked out only twice. After retirement, Rosenbloom became an actor and night-club entertainer. He died in 1976.

■ Also born today: FRAN HEALY (1946), catcher
w/S.F. Giants (1971-72), among others, later announcer for Yankees ... URBAN "RED" FABER (1888), righty pitcher (254-212, 3.15), good enough for the Hall of Fame, played entire career (1914-33) with White Sox, one of the few pitchers to play 20 years with one team ... AL SINGER (1930), lightweight champion, 1930, the only case of a world champion winning the title (against Sammy Mandell) and losing the title (against Tony Canzoneri) in a one-round KO.

NOTES

■ AL MCGUIRE (1928) —

A basketball player, coach, and announcer. Born in New York City, he played college ball at St. John's and in the NBA with the N.Y. Knicks — known for his scrappy play. He later coached at Marquette and became famous for his pithy one-liners. He won the NCAA title in his last year as a coach in 1978. His next career was in the broadcasting booth. He was a refreshing presence on the tube for a few years but then became somewhat like a TV comic suffering from overexposure. Al is the younger broth-

Al McGuire

er of Dick McGuire, who also played for St. John's and the Knicks.

■ PAUL BROWN (1908) —

One of the great coaches in football history. Born in Norwalk, Ohio, Brown became a high school coaching legend in Massillon, Ohio, where his teams lost one game in seven years. He coached at Ohio State from 1941 to 1943, then coached at the Great Lakes Naval Training Center team in 1944 and '45. There he developed such greats as Otto Graham, Bill Willis, and others who were to become the nucleus of his greatest monument, the Cleveland Browns, immodestly named after himself. Brown founded the Browns in 1946 and entered the All-American Football Conference, a loop his team dominated. When the Browns entered the NFL in 1950, the skeptics said they wouldn't be able to cut it. They were wrong. The Browns won the NFL title in their first year and were in the championship game seven times in their first eight years in the NFL. Brown was ousted in a 1963 power struggle and re-emerged in 1968 as founder of the Cincinnati Bengals. He coached them until 1978 and has been their general manager since then.

NOTES

■ "DUFFY" DAUGHERTY (1915) —

One of college football's greatest coaches. Daugherty took over at Michigan State in 1954 after the legendary Clarence "Biggie" Munn stepped down to become the full-time athletic director. Daugherty, known as one of football's great humorists, was a master of the split-T. He created a true dynasty in the mid-1960s. In 1965 and '66, his MSU teams were undefeated Big Ten champions and the 1965 team was one of the greatest of all time. Seven players on that squad made All-American squads — a record. They included Bubba Smith, George Webster, Clint Jones and Gene Washington. That team lost to UCLA in the Rose Bowl. In '66, MSU and Notre Dame, both undefeated, played an epic 10-10 tie in which Notre Dame was criticized for running out the clock in the final minute to preserve the tie.

■ WALTER "BUCK" LEONARD (1907) —

One of the great stars of the Negro Leagues. He had .355 lifetime BA but was deprived of his chance at major league fame and fortune because of the odious ban against blacks. When blacks were finally admitted in 1947, Leonard was 40 and out of baseball. He is considered the greatest first baseman in Negro League history and played with Josh Gibson and many other greats. He was elected to the Hall of Fame a few years ago and was last seen at the induction ceremonies for Drysdale, Killebrew, et al.

■ Also born today: **L. C. GREENWOOD (1946)**, great defensive end for Steelers for 14 years, in shadow of Mean Joe Greene...**KOICHI TOHEI (1920)**, founder of aikido in the U.S. .... **ANTHONY DAVIS (1952)**, running back from USC, one of the very few to play in the NFL, CFL., WFL and USFL.

NOTES

■ **FRANKIE FRISCH (1898)** —
A reincarnation of John J. McGraw (one of many), born in New York City. He was a legend at Fordham University (where he got his life-long nickname, "The Fordham Flash"), captain of the baseball, football, and basketball teams. He played second base for the N.Y. Giants (1919-26) under McGraw and became the same kind of scrappy holler-guy player (though a better one) and manager (though not nearly as good). Frisch played in four World Series with them and four more with the Cardinals

Frankie Frisch

(1927-37), had a .316 lifetime BA, and his 2,880 hits for a switch-hitter wasn't equalled until 1978 (that's right, by Pete Rose). He managed the "Gas House Gang" Cardinals from 1933 to 1938 (as a player-manager most of the time), winning a pennant in 1934, and defeating the awesome Tigers in the World Series. Frisch later managed the Pirates (1940-46) and the Cubs (1949-51), and was a radio announcer for the New York Giants during the 1950s with an unforgettable sing-songy W. C. Fields-type delivery. He died in 1973.

■ **CLEM McCARTHY (1882)** —
McCarthy, a man who did one thing very well — announce horse-races on radio — was born in East Bloomfield, N.Y. (also the birthplace of Wavy Gravy — or is that too obscure?). One of the great figures in sports broadcasting, McCarthy announced the Kentucky Derby from 1928 to 1950 and was a household name. He was well-known (and much parodied) for his rapid-style and his growly greeting — "racing fans!"

■ Also born today: pitcher **WAITE HOYT (1899)**, won 237 games with N.Y. Yanks, etc.; long-time (1941-65) voice of the Reds; died in 1984 ...
... three announcers born today.

■ ROGER MARIS (1934) —

One of the most famous North Dakotans in history. The

Man Who Broke Ruth's Record for most homers in a season (61 in 1961) came up with Cleveland in 1957 and was traded to the Kansas City A's the following year. After the '59 season the Yankees pulled the most famous, and the last, of the "heists" that brought the better players on bad teams (A's, Browns, etc.) to New York pinstripes and glory. In Maris' first year with the Yanks he won the MVP award and then won it again the next year, breaking

Roger Maris

Ruth's record. Maris hit 275 home runs in only 12 years with a lifetime .260 BA but was underrated as an all-around performer. He got bad-rapped for not running out ground balls. Maris should be considered for the Hall of Fame for his two MVP years alone. The year he hit 61 he also led the league with 142 RBI — without benefit of a single grand slam. He played in seven World Series — five in a row with the Yankees (1960-64) and two with the Cardinals (1967-68). Maris became a beer distributor in Florida.

■ ARNOLD PALMER (1929) —

One of the titans of golf history. His TV exposure, and that of his fans ("Arnie's Army"), put golf in the multimillion-dollar bracket. In 1963 he became the first golfer to win $100,000 in one year. Palmer won the U.S. Open in 1960, the British Open twice, and the Masters four times. In 1969 he was voted the AP Athlete Of The Decade. Palmer, now a seniors player, has become a TV staple selling oil, manufactured not far from his Latrobe, Pa., home and birthplace.

NOTES

■ **PAUL "BEAR" BRYANT (1913)** —
Winningest major-college coach in football history,
born in Moro Bottoms, Ala. He coached for one
year at Maryland, then at
Kentucky (1946-53) — one of
his QBs was George Blanda
— Texas A&M (1954-57), and
at Alabama (1958-82). His
record was 323 wins, 85
losses, and 17 ties, surpass-
ing Amos Alonzo Stagg's
long-standing mark. Bryant
was a legend at Alabama,
winning five national titles
(1961, 1964, 1965, 1978,
1979), with mythic status a la
John Wayne and George Patton. He once said he'd "croak

Bear Bryant

in a week" if he retired. He died in January 1983,
less than a month after coaching his final game.

■ **TOM LANDRY (1924)** —
Another football coaching legend (pro variety), born
in Mission, Texas, played ball at the University of
Texas. After one year with the AAFC N.Y. Yankees,
he was a fine defensive back with the N.Y. Giants
from 1950 to 1955, and helped develop the famed
"Umbrella Defense." After assistant coaching with
the Giants, Landry became the first, last, and only
coach the Dallas Cowboys have ever had, as of 1985.
His record is impressive: 224-124-6 and, since
1966, the Cowboys have failed to make the playoffs
only three times. Bryant and Landry both will have
coached one team for 25 consecutive years.

■ Also born today: yet a third football coach —
CLARENCE "BIGGIE" MUNN (1908), at Michigan
State (1947-53) ... **STEVE BRODIE (1868)**, the
same guy who "pulled a Steve Brodie" and jumped
off the Brooklyn Bridge (and lived) was a lifetime
.303 hitter with various teams from 1890 to 1902.

NOTES

■ **JESSE OWENS (1913)** — "The supreme physical genius of his age" was born in Danville, Ala. His name was James Cleveland Owens but his initials, J. C., were bent into "Jesse." The son of a sharecropper, Owens picked cotton as a child with his father and other family members until he moved to Cleveland (where he set the 100-yard dash high school record of 9.4 seconds which held up as a record until 1967). Owens, the best-known athlete in track and field history, is famous for his four gold medals in the 1936 Olympics

Jesse Owens

winning the 100 meters, 200 meters, long jump, and as anchor of the 400-meter relay team. (In 1984, Carl Lewis equalled that feat). In the first three events, Owens set records that lasted more than 20 years. In all, Owens set 11 various world records, the last (for 60 meters) not falling until 1974. Despite such glory, there was no money for the track star of that era. Owens returned to the U.S. and worked for years as a janitor and raced in exhibitions against cars and animals (a fate similar to that of Joe Louis, who also had trouble making a living after his retirement). In the late 1970s, Owens finally received official accolades from the White House and even became successful in business. He died of lung cancer in 1980.

■ Also born today: lefty **MICKEY LOLICH (1940)**, dominating strikeout artist with Detroit (1964-74), 217 wins, 2,832 strikeouts, three wins in the 1968 Series; became a doughnut entrepreneur in Rochester, Mich. ... hurdler **GLENN DAVIS (1934)**, the only one to win 400-meter Olympics hurdles twice in row—1956 and '60 (Edwin Moses lost chance to tie that feat in 1980 boycott, and in 1984 became the second to win two golds in that event)... righty **SPUD CHANDLER (1907)**, won MVP with Yanks in '43 with 20-4, 1.64 ERA season; his won-loss record was phenomenal 109-43.

NOTES

■RICK WISE (1945) —

Winner of 188 major league games. 6-foot-3, 195-lb right-hander, Wise pitched with the Phillies, Cardinals, Red Sox, Indians and Padres from 1964 to 1981. He was involved in an infamous deal or two. The Phillies traded him, even up, to the Cardinals for Steve Carlton. The Cardinals traded Wise and Bernie Carbo to the Red Sox for Reggie Smith. Wise, however, was a consistent performer in both leagues. On June 23, 1971, he etched his name on baseball granite. He became the only player to pitch a no-hitter and hit two home runs in the same game.

Rick Wise

■JACK TAYLOR (1873) —

Another right-hand pitcher, born in Straightville, Ohio (my kind of town). He had a 10-year National League career (1898-1907) with Chicago and St. Louis and is one of the great iron-men pitchers of that era in which anything less than a complete game was considered loss of face. In 1904, Taylor set a major league record by pitching 39 consecutive complete games. In fact, for four straight seasons (1902-1905), Taylor started 139 games and completed every one of them. His lifetime figures are 286 starts and 278 complete games. Not too shabby. His won-loss was 150-139 and his lifetime ERA was 2.66. Taylor died in 1938.

■EDDIE ROMMEL (1897) —

Rommel, father of the modern knuckleball, is yet another righty pitcher born on this day. He spent his whole career (1920-32) with the Philadelphia A's, winning 171 and losing 119 as a starter and reliever. He lost 23 games in 1921 and won 27 the next year (19 as a starter and 8 in relief). Rommel, later an AL umpire, died in 1970.

■ Also born today: Always room for one more righty pitcher, **THORNTON LEE (1906).** He and righty pitcher son, Don Lee, are the only father-son combo to give up home runs to Ted Williams.

NOTES

■ **STANLEY KETCHEL (1886)** —
Rated the No. 1 middleweight of all time. Born
Stanislaus Kiecal (son of a Polish immigrant) in

Stanley Ketchel

Grand Rapids, Mich., Ketchel lost
only four bouts in his career. He
won the title in 1907 and, after
defeating everyone in his division,
took on and beat several bigger
opponents. Ketchel even challenged the great (and 35 pounds
heavier) Jack Johnson for the
heavyweight title. Ketchel
decked Johnson in the 12th round
but was KO'd himself later that
round. After a few more knockout
wins and basking in the height of
his fame, Ketchel took a vacation on a ranch in Montana.
There, while eating his breakfast, the world middleweight champion was murdered — shot in the back. The
man known as "The Michigan Assassin" was dead at
age 24.

■ **CHARLES "KID" NICHOLS (1869)** —
Winner of 360 big league games, born in Madison, Wis.
He pitched, mostly for the Boston team in the National
League, from 1890 to 1906 and is fourth in complete
games (533 in 562 starts). Nichols won 30 games or
more — are you ready for this? — seven years in a row.
Only a couple of times in his career did he pitch fewer
than 350 innings in a season. As a 20-year-old rookie
(weighing 135 pounds) "The Kid" won 27 games. He was
inducted into the Hall of Fame in 1949 and died in 1953.

■ Also born today: Golden State Warriors owner
FRANKLIN MIEULI, born in San Jose in an unknown year
(because he doesn't want anyone to know); the Warriors
are the laughing-stock of the NBA, so what else is new?
... **JERRY COLEMAN (1924)**, Yankee second-baseman
and Padre announcer, also born in San Jose.

NOTES

■ **GAYLORD PERRY (1938)** —
Only man to win the Cy Young Award in both leagues.
He played with eight teams,
mostly the Giants, in a 21-year
career, winning 314 games with
an 3.09 ERA. He is one of only
four pitchers to win more than
100 games in each league. He
wound up with more strikeouts
than Walter Johnson (3,534)
and is third behind Ryan and
Carlton. He was involved in two
infamous deals. In each, he won
the Cy Young Award the following year. The first, of course, is
the deal that sent him to
Cleveland for Sam McDowell in

Gaylord Perry

1971 and the other is the deal that sent him to the
Padres (for Dave Tomlin) from the Rangers in 1978. A
tremendous competitor a la George Blanda, Perry was
all guile in his later years and rode his reputation as
the premier spitballer for all it was worth. His
autobiography, "Me and the Spitter," came out in
1974. In 1983, at age 45, Perry announced his retirement and said that it was "time to get back home to
the peanut farm and make a living there." His brother
is ex-pitcher Jim Perry. They are the winningest brothers in baseball history and the only brothers to
win the Cy Young Award.

■ Also born today: **EDDIE GOTTLIEB (1898)**, born in
Russia, an early organizer of pro basketball, coached
famous Philadelphia SPHAS from 1918, co-founder of
the BAA which became the NBA; founder and coach
(from 1946 tro '56) of the Philadelphia Warriors ...
DAN MARINO (1961), Dolphins QB had brilliant rookie
year in '83, and then threw all-time record 55 TD
passes in '84, winning NFL MVP but not the Super
Bowl.... **MERLIN OLSEN (1940)**, defensive tackle
with Rams for whole pro career (1962-77), one of the
"Fearsome Foursome" with Deacon Jones, Rosie
Greer and Lamar Lundy; one of the more enduring of
ex-jock TV announcers.

NOTES

■BATTLING SIKI (1897) —
A Senegalese named Louis Phal, who became light-heavyweight champion of the world (1922-23). He first boxed in a territorial regiment of the French army in Senegal, went to Paris and worked as a dishwasher, ultimately scoring a big upset by mauling the darling of Europe, Georges Carpentier, for the title. Siki was well-known in Paris as a flamboyant character and supposedly walked around town with a lion on a leash. His reign ended quickly. Six months later, his handlers blundered (perhaps intentionally) by arranging a title fight against challenger Mike McTigue. In Dublin. On St. Patrick's Day. You want more? In the arena you could hear Irish rebels outside on the streets. shooting at the British. Siki lost a split decision. He soon went to New York, where he continued to live flamboyantly — and recklessly, a hard drinker with a bad temper. In 1925, at age 28, Battling Siki was shot to death in a street brawl.

Elgin Baylor

■ELGIN BAYLOR (1934) — Perhaps the greatest forward in basketball history. He played his entire career with the Lakers (1958-1972, the first two years in Minneapolis) and finished with more than 23,000 points, seventh on the all-time list. His career average per game is 27.4, the fourth highest. For three straight years (1960-62), Baylor averaged 34 points or better. His 71 points in a game is the most any player — other than Wilt Chamberlain — has scored. Baylor was beautiful to behold on the hardwood. Only 6-foot-5, he was a great leaper and could outrebound bigger forwards. He was strong, agile and had good hands. *Orel Hershiser (1958) Dodgers righty ace.*

■ **GEORGE BLANDA (1927)** —
The leading scorer in football history, born in Young-
wood, Pa. Blanda played college
ball at Kentucky under Bear
Bryant and had a pro career
that spanned 26 years, the
all-time longevity record. He
scored 2,002 points, 600 points
more than the No. 2 all-time
scorer. In 1961, he threw seven
TD passes in one game, a feat
shared by four others (Luckman,
Tittle, Kapp and Adrian Burk).
Blanda really had three separate careers, three incarnations
as hero — with the Chicago
Bears (1949-58), Houston Oilers

George Blanda

(1960-66) and Oakland Raiders (1967-75). He was an
old-style warrior who, when he finally hung them up, at
age 48, just packed up his travelbag and walked off
without fanfare, like John Wayne would've done. Al
Davis was criticized for not making more of a fuss, but
you knew that Blanda was the kind of guy who wouldn't
have wanted any.

■ **MAUREEN CONNOLLY (1934)** —
"Little Mo," the gifted and fated tennis champion,
born in San Diego, Calif. She won the U.S. women's
singles title in 1951 at age 16, becoming the youngest
tennis champion in history — then won it again the next
two years, a three-time champion at age 19. That third
year, 1953, she won the Grand Slam (U.S., British,
Australian and French titles) — the first woman tennis
player to do so. A few months later, Connolly suffered
a horseback riding accident that ended her career
at age 20. She died in 1969 at age 35.

■ Also born today: auto racer **STIRLING MOSS (1929)**,
retired after near fatal crash in '72 ... **HAROLD
SOLOMON (1952)**, another tennis player; Vitas Ger-
ulaitis said Martina Navratilova couldn't beat Solomon (or the 100th best male player).

NOTES

■ HARVEY HADDIX (1925) —

Famous for giving *the* hard-luck pitching performance in major league history. Haddix came up with the Cardinals in 1952, at the tail end of the Cards' Harry "The Cat" Brecheen's career. Brecheen became Haddix's mentor and because they resembled each other (both were smallish lefties with similar bone structure) Haddix was tagged "The Kitten." He pitched for four more teams until 1965, finishing with a 136-113 record. Haddix's claim to immortality occurred on May 26, 1959 while pitching for

Harvey Haddix

the Pirates against the Braves in Milwaukee County Stadium. Haddix pitched 12 perfect innings — 36 batters retired in a row — with the score 0-0 at the end of 12th. In the 13th, Felix Mantilla led off with a ground ball that Pirate third-baseman Don Hoak threw away for an error, sending Mantilla to second where he finally scored on a hit by Joe Adcock. The 1-0 game was won by Lew Burdette, who went all the way, giving up 12 hits (all singles). The following year Haddix won two games in the series against the Yankees — the fifth game and the dramatic seventh game, relieving in the top of the ninth. Mazeroski hit the game (and Series) winner, a homer, in the bottom half. Haddix became the Pirates' pitching coach.

■ DARRYL STINGLEY (1951) —

Another athlete known for his hard luck. Stingley, a fine wide receiver, was the Patriots' first draft choice in 1972. In 1977, in a game against the Oakland Raiders, Stingley was tackled hard by Jack Tatum, a hit which paralyzed him from the neck down and ended his career. Eight years later, Stingley is still paralyzed after showing some early improvement. The Patriots hired him as executive director of player personnel.

NOTES

■ EDWIN "DUKE" SNIDER (1926) —

The Duke of Flatbush, Dodger centerfielder from 1947 to 1962. A .295 lifetime hitter with 407 career homers, Snider was beloved in Brooklyn (1947-57) and was a big part of one of baseball's greatest dynasties. He was the one great lefty stick, batting third in an otherwise righty lineup. Known as "The Silver Fox" because of his prematurely gray hair, Snider, Babe Ruth and Ralph Kiner are the only players to hit 40 or more home runs in five consecutive seasons. During

Duke Snider

the decade of the 1950s, Snider hit more home runs (326) than any player. His last two seasons ('63 and '64) were spent first with the Mets and, although it's hard to believe it, the San Francisco Giants. He has been a minor league manager, a scout, and a hitting instructor, and has been an announcer for the Padres and Expos. The Duke's uniform No. 4 (after his idol, Lou Gehrig) is a lasting memory to every Brooklyn Dodger fan.

■ JOE MORGAN (1943) —

"Little Joe," the greatest second baseman of his era. Morgan broke in with the Astros in 1963 and was part of an infamous deal that sent him to the Reds where he helped them win three pennants. He won two straight MVP awards in 1975 and '76, leading Cincinnati to two straight World Series triumphs. He later led the Astros to a division title in 1980, led the Giants to respectability in 1982, led the Phillies to the pennant in 1983, and with the A's in 1984 decided to call it a career. Morgan has expressed no desire to manage. They're dusting off a seat in the Hall of Fame for the first player to steal 600 bases and hit 200 home runs, the man who broke Rogers Hornsby's record for career home runs for a second baseman. Al Oerter (1936), discus great, won four straight Olympics - '56, '60, '64, '68.

NOTES

■ **ARNOLD "RED" AUERBACH (1917) —**
The most successful coach in professional basketball
history. Born in Brooklyn, he
began his pro coaching career in
the newly formed NBA in 1946. He
led the Washington Capitols to
two Eastern Division titles in his
three years there and then began
his awesome era at the helm of
the Boston Celtics (1951-1966), a
team that won eight straight NBA
titles (from '59 to '66). After
retiring from coaching with 1,037
wins (the only coach to win more
than 1,000 games), Auerbach
became the Celtics' general manager and has had a successful
reign in that capacity. Like Al Davis in the NFL, Auerbach
seems to know more than the other guys. He announced
his retirement in 1983. No longer can we turn to him,
sitting in the stands in the waning minutes of the fourth
quarter, and watch him light up his "victory cigar." He
smoked a lot of them.

Red Auerbach

■ **JIM TAYLOR (1935) —**
Great fullback of the Green Bay Packers dynasty
(from 1958 to 1966). Taylor played college ball at LSU in
the shadow of Billy Cannon and was only a second-round
draft choice but finished with 8,597 yards (currently
seventh on the list) and 83 TDs (fourth after Jim Brown,
Franco Harris and John Riggins), and a 4.4-yard average
per carry. He is tied with Earl Campbell and Chuck
Muncie for most rushing TDs in a season (19), back
when they played fewer games. The Packers won four
NFL titles while he was with them. After a salary
dispute, Taylor finished his career in 1967 with the
Saints.

■ Also born today: **GUY LEFLEUR (1951)**, great hockey
player with Montreal Canadiens, MVP in '77, led NHL
scoring, 1974-77 ... **CHARLIE DRESSEN (1898)**, who
managed Brooklyn Dodgers to two straight pennants in
1952 and 1953, and also managed the Reds, Senators,
Braves and Tigers; in 1951 uttered the immortal (and
incorrect) words, "the Giants is dead."

■ **HOWIE MORENZ (1902)** —
Hockey great with the Montreal Canadiens (1923-1934, and 1936-1937). Like a great back in football, he was almost impossible to stop one-on-one. He had raw speed, great moves and was dedicated to the game — and he prepared Canadiens fans for Maurice Richard, a similar performer who began his career a few years later. Twice he won the Hart Trophy (MVP), 1931 and 1932, and twice won the Art Ross Trophy (most points), 1928 and 1931. In 1937, Morenz suffered a badly broken leg. In the hospital, he became morose, suffered a nervous breakdown, then suddenly developed heart trouble. Six weeks after Morenz's last hockey game, he was dead at age 34. His funeral service was held at center ice of the Forum, home of the Canadiens in Montreal and the rink that Howie Morenz made famous.

■ Also born today: **"SUDDEN SAM" McDOWELL (1942)**, lefty strikeout pitcher mostly with Cleveland, infamously traded to the Giants in 1971 (after a 13-17 season) for Gaylord Perry (after 16-12, 2.76 ERA season, helping the Giants win their last division title), not that it still bothers me or anything ... **ARTIS GILMORE (1949)**, 7-2 center with the San Antonio Spurs, formerly with the Chicago Bulls ... **HUGH "SHORTY" RAY (1884)**, Hall of Fame football referee, supervisor of NFL officials from 1938 to 1952 ...
ELMER SMITH (1892), Cleveland outfielder who, in 1920, hit the first grand slam homer in a World Series game; in that same game, Bill Wambsganss made the only unassisted triple play in World Series history; Smith died in 1983.

NOTES

■ **INGEMAR JOHANSSON (1932)** — Swedish boxer, heavyweight champion of the world (1959-60). Johansson reached the Olympic finals in 1952, but was disqualified for "not giving his best." After turning pro, he won 20 straight fights before facing Eddie Machen, No. 1 contender for Floyd Patterson's title. When he KOd Machen in the first round, he world took notice and he won a shot at the title. Johansson stunned everyone, especially Patterson, knocking him down seven times and scoring a three-round KO. He held the title only nine months, losing to Patterson in a rematch. In their third title fight, Johansson twice decked Patterson but got knocked out again and lost his bid to regain the title. He fought a few more fights and retired at age 31, entering the trucking business. Johansson's two losses to Patterson were the only ones of his 28-fight career.

■ Also born today: **HAROLD CARMICHAEL (1949)**, the tallest (6′8″) wide receiver ever to play (or, at least star) in the NFL; in his 13-year career with the Eagles, he set an NFL record for catching a pass in 127 consecutive games – from 1971 to 1980! He retired after '84 season, among the all-time top ten in receptions, TDs, and yardage...**TOM LASORDA (1922)**, Dodger manager since 1976, great eater; his auto-biography *Artful Dodger* came out in '85...**BOB LEMON (1920)**, great righty pitcher for Cleveland (1946-58) with 207-128 won-loss record, won 20 or more games seven times in only 13 seasons, struck out 200 or more nine consecutive times, equaled by Tom Seaver...**VINCE COLEMAN (1961)**, Cardinal rookie base-stealing phenom in '85 (both Coleman and Carmichael born in Jacksonville, Fla.).

NOTES

Since no famous figures in the world of sport were born today, let us now praise obscure ones: What could be more obscure than an offensive tackle? Here are two: **BOB VOGEL (1942)**, with the Colts from 1963 to 1972, an All-Pro out of Ohio State, and **TUNCH ILKIN (1957)**, with the Steelers since 1980, vaults into the pantheon of great sports names ... here's three obscure lefty pitchers: **JIM ROOKER (1942)**, had a couple of good years with the Pirates in the early 1970s; **MARCELINE LOPEZ (1943)**, Cuban-born, best year was 1965 with Angels, posting 14-13 mark and 2.93 ERA; **LEFTY**

Jim Rooker

STEWART (1900), his two best years were 1930 with the Cardinals (20-12) and 1933 with the Washington Senators (15-6) ... running back **CLARENCE PEAKS (1935)**, with the Philadelphia Eagles (1957-63), out of Michigan State ... how about an obscure utility infielder, good field/no hit (naturally); **WOODY WOODWARD (1942)**, with Braves ('63-'68) and Reds ('68-71), peaked in 1966 with Braves, playing in 144 games and hitting .264 ... golfer **FORREST FEZLER (1949)**, who was probably also called "Woody" ... here's the big ending; **LOUIS RUBENSTEIN (1861)**, the father of figure skating in North America and the first figure skater in North America; he was a Canadian who learned the balletic approach to figure skating in Europe; it passed through Canada before it emerged a few years later in the U.S. (in the 1880s).

NOTES

■ **JOE GREENE (1946)** —

"Mean Joe," the greatest defensive lineman of his era (the 1970s). Born in Temple, Texas, played college ball at North Texas State (where he picked up "Mean Joe" tag, as one of The Mean Green defense), and was drafted by the Steelers (the fourth player chosen), who then went from cellardom to becoming one of the great NFL dynasties. Pittsburgh was a team of defensive heavies, but Greene stood out — 275 pounds and quick. He could dominate a game — back when a defensive tackle could still do that (back when there were defensive tackles).

Joe Greene

■ **TOMMY ARMOUR (1895)** —

Legendary golfer and golf teacher. He won the U.S. Open (1927), the PGA (1930), and the British Open (1931). He later became a noted author and teacher who, in the '40s and '50s, commanded the highest teaching fees. And he was quotable: Asked who the greatest golf teacher was, Armour said, "How can there be any 'greatest' or even 'great' golf teachers when the task itself is too great to permit greatness?" (thank you, Professor Irwin Corey). Another Armour-ism: "It takes great 'learners' to make great reputations for teachers, in golf and other studious fields."

■ Also born today: English tennis player **CHARLOTTE DOD (1871)**, the first tennis prodigy ... **JIM McKAY (1921)**, longtime host of TV's Wide World of Sports and Olympic Games anchorman. He was the first sportscaster to win an Emmy, for his coverage of the 1972 Olympics; at the '84 games supposedly talked too much while the divers were diving ... **FRED "DIXIE" WALKER (1910)**, "The People's Cherce," outfielder with Brooklyn Dodgers (1940-47) and others; .306 lifetime hitter, won batting title in 1944 (.357). Brother of Harry "The Hat" Walker.

NOTES

■ RED SMITH (1905) —

Considered by many to be the greatest of all sports-writers, born Walter Wellesley Smith in Green Bay, Wis.

Red Smith

He was a newspaperman for 54 years with the Philadelphia Record, N.Y. Herald Tribune, and N.Y. Times — syndicated in 500 newspapers, worldwide. In 1976, he won the Pulitzer Prize, the first sportswriter to win a Pulitzer for commentary. Two of his best-known collections are "Out of the Red" and "Views of Sport." He was also an avid fisherman and wrote extensively on the outdoors. He was best on the three sports that interested him most — horse racing, boxing and baseball. He died in 1982.

■ JOHNNY SAIN (1917) —

Sain, renowned as pitcher and pitching coach, was born in Havana (Arkansas, that is). Sain pitched for the Braves and won 20 or more games four times from 1946 to 1950 as righty ace of the Braves' rotation, "Spahn and Sain, and pray for rain." He spent some golden days with the Yankees from 1951 to '55 as a starter and reliever, and finished with a 139-116 won-loss record. Sain (like Spahn) was an excellent hitting pitcher. He hit .346 in 1947 (while winning 21 games) and is the only pitcher ever to lead the league in sacrifice hits — 16 in 1948 (while winning 24 games). He has been a respected pitching coach for several clubs, currently the Braves.

■ PHIL RIZZUTO (1918) —

The beloved "Scooter," Yankee shortstop for 13 years. This man belongs in the Hall of Fame and, now that Pee Wee Reese is in, will soon follow. Born in New York City, he spent his entire career with the Yanks, losing three peak years to World War II. A lifetime .273 hitter, winner of the MVP award in 1950, Rizzuto was the glue that kept the big chunks together. Excellent glove, base runner, bunter. He could do all the little things that the big guys couldn't. He's the long-time Yankee announcer.

NOTES

■ BOBBY SHANTZ (1925) —

Pocket lefty pitcher with the Philadelphia A's, Yankees, and others. He came up with the A's in 1949 and had two fine years with them. One good and one, in 1952, great. He went 24-7, 2.48 ERA, and 27 complete games, winning the MVP. At 5-feet-6, 139 pounds, Shantz was the smallest player ever to win the MVP. Late in that season he had the bad luck to get hit on the wrist by a pitch (pitchers used to hit in the American League) and never came near those heights again. He did enjoy a new life as a starter and reliever with the Yankees (1957-60), helping the Yanks to three pennants and posting a combined 30-18 record. Shantz was also one of the best fielding pitchers ever to play the game. He won eight Gold Gloves. Shantz became manager of a dairy bar in Chalfont, Pa.

Bobby Shantz

■ JOHN BUNN (1898) —

Basketball coach and pioneer, born in Wellston, Ohio. He became the first University of Kansas athlete to earn 10 varsity letters and, for nine years, was Phog Allen's assistant. Bunn coached at Stanford in the 1930s and helped develop the great Hank Luisetti and the one-hand shot concept. Bunn unveiled both in New York City and defeated the awesome LIU team, breaking their 43-game consecutive win streak. That single game influenced the evolution of basketball, as the one-hand shot became the rage and teams became offense-minded. Bunn, once a student of James Naismith (inventor of basketball), later coached at Springfield and Colorado State. He also wrote several books on the game, edited The Basketball Guide, and, from 1949 to 1964, was chairman of the Basketball Hall of Fame Committee.

■ Also born today: **TOM BROWN** (1922), S.F. tennis luminary; a high-ranking senior player, "probably the best (at age 62) in the history of tennis" ... goalie FRANK BRIMSEK (1915), with Bruins in 1940s, called "Mister Zero," he set record for 231 minutes, 54 seconds of shutout goal tending ... **LUCIUS ALLEN** (1947), guard with Kareem at UCLA, the Bucks, and Lakers, one of the first athletes popped for drugs ... **MARTY ROBBINS** (1925), country singer, also auto racer.

NOTES

■ **MIKE SCHMIDT (1949)** —
Voted by Philadelphia fans the greatest Phillies player in the history of the franchise. He has been the best National League third baseman for a decade and one of the greatest of all time — if not the greatest. Don't bet against him hitting 500. He's passed the 400 home run career mark, and won the home run title seven times (only Ruth has won it more — nine times). He won the MVP award two years in a row (1980 and '81). A perennial Gold Glove and a good base runner, Schmidt is one of the best complete players in baseball history.

Mike Schmidt

■ Also born today: **PAUL LOWE (1936)**, running back for the San Diego Chargers (out of Oregon State) in the mid-1960s, led AFL in rushing in 1965 ... **JOHNNY PESKY (1919)**, Red Sox shortstop of 1940s and early '50s, .307 lifetime hitter, his hesitation on throw to the plate from shallow left field allowed Enos Slaughter to score from first on Harry "The Hat" Walker's single (to left!) ... **KATHY WHITWORTH (1939)**, called the greatest woman golfer of the modern era and the first to earn $1 million, in 1984 won 86th tournament, a record for men and women ... **HARRY STEINFELDT (1876)**, third baseman with Cincinnati for eight years but better known for his five seasons with the Cubs (1906-10) as the fourth man in the Tinker-to-Evers-to-Chance infield.

Those same fans now boo Schmidt's every move...

NOTES

■ **TOM HARMON (1919)** —

Great Michigan running back. Born in Gary, Ind., he starred

Tom Harmon

for Michigan from 1938 to 1940 under Fritz Crisler and won the Heisman Trophy as a senior. He was the most exciting player to come out of the Big Ten after Red Grange and was known as "Old Ninety-Eight," the number on his jersey (usually in tatters from would-be tacklers). In the final game of his college career, Harmon scored three TDs for a total of 33, breaking Red Grange's record of 31 (in four fewer games). World War II interrupted a pro career that started in 1941 but didn't resume until 1946 with the L.A. Rams. He was then 27, with too long a layoff. He played one more year. After retirement he became a long-time football announcer on radio and TV.

■ **ALICE MARBLE (1913)** —

Hall of Fame tennis player. From a family of athletes, she learned her strokes in S.F.'s Golden Gate Park. Her promising career seemed to be ended when she was stricken with pleurisy but in one of sport's great comebacks she returned to tennis and won four U.S. National singles titles (1936, '38, '39, 1940). She is the only woman to win all six major tournaments in one year (1939).

■ Also born today: **CHARLEY TAYLOR (1942)**, Redskins wide receiver (1964-77), No. 2 in career receptions (649) with 79 TDs (fifth-best mark) ... **MAX SCHMELING (1905)**, German fighter who was heavyweight champion from 1930 (winning vacant title on a foul by Jack Sharkey) to 1932 (losing a 15-round decision to Sharkey in a rematch); best known for knocking out Joe Louis in 1936 and being KO'd in first round by Louis two years later in title bout.

■ **SEBASTIAN COE (1956)** —
British runner whose 3:47.33 mile has been a record
since 1981. In the L.A. '84 Olympics, Coe won the gold
medal in the 1500 meters, still holds records in the 800
and 1000 meters. Only Jim Ryun has dominated
middle-distance running for as long a time as Coe, who
set a world record in 1979, fought off Steve Ovett's
challenge to his supremacy, and is currently all by
himself in his field. His coach, since his days as a
schoolboy runner in England, is his father, Peter Coe.

■ **BUM PHILLIPS (1923)** —
The popular "Bum," coach of the New Orleans Saints.
Born Oail Andrew Phillips in Orange, Texas, he is
yet another throwback to the John Wayne School of
coaching and is seen on the sidelines in cowboy boots,
10-gallon hat, and obligatory though diminishing gut.
After many years as an assistant, Phillips began
coaching the pros in 1975 with the Houston Oilers and
eventually took a solid team and maimed them with an
unimaginative offense. Fired in 1980, he has been
coach of the Saints since 1981. Bum is probably great
to play for and is no doubt an outstanding defensive
coach but most critics feel (with reason) that he will
never create a viable offense.

■ Also born today: **FIDEL LA BARBA (1905)**, flyweight
champion, 1927, won gold medal at 1924 Olympics in
Paris, retired to go to school at Stanford but returned
to the ring, twice trying to win featherweight title; finally
retired in 1933 and finished up at Stanford ... **GENE
AUTRY (1907)**, singing cowboy in Hollywood (1934-54),
owner of the California Angels since 1962.

NOTES

■ ROBIN ROBERTS (1926) —

Righty ace of the Phillies "Whiz Kids," he came up with

Robin Roberts

the Phillies as a 21-year-old in 1948. Two years later he was 20-11 and led the Phils to the pennant. He won 20 games or more six times in a row (1950-55), winning 19 in 1956, and won 286 in his 19-year career, including some years with the Orioles and others. A workhorse-type pitcher, with seven straight years of about 300 innings or more, he pitched 28 straight complete games from August, 1952, to July, 1953. In fact, he completed half of the games he started, an impressive record for a pitcher in the modern era. Roberts also set records for giving up home runs in a season (46) and career (502). He is currently baseball coach at the University of South Florida.

■ JOHNNY PODRES (1932) —

Southpaw mainstay of the (Brooklyn and L.A.) Dodgers from 1953 to 1966. In the 1955 World Series against the Yankees, Podres was the pitching hero, winning game three and game seven, a brilliant 2-0 shutout that sealed the Dodgers' first-ever Series victory (he also won Series games in 1959 and 1966). After his great triumph, Podres had to spend the following year in the service. When he returned in 1957, he led the league in ERA. In 1961 he had the league's best percentage, going 18-5. Podres has been a pitching coach with the Padres and Red Sox, and is currently with the Twins. Part of the Twins' recent success is attributed to Podres, who has taught his staff how to throw the changeup, a pitch he mastered in the big leagues.

NOTES

■ ROD CAREW (1945) —

One of baseball's greatest batsman of any era. Born in Panama, raised in N.Y.C., Carew broke into the bigs as a second baseman with the Twins in 1967 and was rookie of the year. Carew's lifetime batting average (.322) is one of the few that compares with the old-time greats. He hit .300 for 15 straight seasons, a feat surpassed only by Ty Cobb (23), Honus Wagner (17), and Stan Musial (16). He has won seven batting titles, outgunned (again) only by Cobb's 12 and Wagner's

Rod Carew

eight. He was also one of the best base runners in the game and stole home 16 times in his career. He has been with the Angels since 1979 as a first baseman and DH. Carew handles the bat like a wand and is master of it. He has influenced hitting by making batters think more, by adapting their swing and even stance to the pitcher, the count, the defense, the ballpark, and the situation. He remains unique — a bat for all seasons.

■ HERMAN HICKMAN (1911) —

One of the greatest offensive guards in college football, born in Johnson City, Tennessee. He played at Tennessee and is selected as one of the all-time guards in virtually every all-time college team. He was Earl Blaik's line coach at West Point in the post-WW II dynasty, the Blanchard-Davis era, and head-coached at Yale from 1948 to 1952. Hickman was a colorful character in his playing and coaching days. Known as "The Bard of the Great Smokies," he could — and would — recite poetry by the hour. He resigned at Yale in 1952 to become a sports commentator on radio and TV.

■ Also born today: golfer **GEORGE ARCHER (1939)**, S.F. native, won the 1969 Masters, and the $350,000 Bank of Boston Classic in 1984 by 6 strokes, the biggest margin of victory on the PGA Tour that year.

■ MAURY WILLS (1932) —

First player to steal 100 bases in a season, broke Ty Cobb's record. A long-time Dodger shortstop (1959-1966, 1969-72), he had an impressive .281 lifetime batting average to go with 586 stolen bases and the National League record — six straight seasons leading the league in stolen bases. He won the MVP award in 1962 for breaking Cobb's record and remains one of only three (with Lou Brock and Rickey Henderson) to steal 100 in a season. Wills'

Maury Wills

managerial career, after a long wait and much expectation, was a bomb. He alienated players, was caught altering the batter's box, and was fired about two months into his rookie year managing in the bigs. He is the father of the ex-Ranger infielder, Bump Wills.

■ Also born today: **DICK BARNETT (1936)**, guard with Lakers and Knicks in '60s and early '70s; a lefty, he tucked his legs in on jump shot ... **H. V. PORTER (1891)**, Hall of Fame basketball pioneer, high school coach, author, executive, invented the "molded" basketball, the fan-shaped backboard, and the 29½-inch ball ... righty pitcher **FRANK "SPEC" SHEA (1920)**, "The Naugatuck (Conn.) Nugget," was 14-5 as rookie in 1947 with Yankees, then became one of only three rookies to start and win a World Series opener (he also won Game Five), currently a rec director and superintendent of parks in his native Naugatuck ... **GARY GREEN (1955)**, defensive back w/KC Chiefs until dealt to Rams in 1984.

NOTES

■ **DAVE WINFIELD (1951)** — Your basic superstar Yankee outfielder. He went to the University of Minnesota (born in St. Paul) where he pitched and hit his way to the College World Series MVP award as a senior and was drafted by pro teams in baseball, football, and basketball. He played his first eight seasons with the Padres and went to the Yanks as a free agent in 1981, signing a humongous 25-year contract. He's worth it. He hits, throws, and runs with the best who ever played. Despite his gifts (because of them?), he is not a

Dave Winfield

popular player. Big guys aren't supposed to be cocky. Big guys are supposed to be humble like Dale Murphy. When's the last time a power hitter hit .340? On the same day Winfield was born (at the same moment, for all I know), Bobby Thomson hit the home run that won the 1951 pennant for the N.Y. Giants.

■ Also born today: **JACK G. KIRK (1906)**, June '85 marked his 50th consecutive run in the Dipsea race in Marin County, California, considered the toughest race in the world (he's won it twice) ... **LYNN "PAPPY" WALDORF (1902)**, won first college football coach of the year award in 1935 at Northwestern, later coached at Cal, taking them to four straight Rose Bowls (1948-51) ... **JOHN MACLEOD (1937)**, coach of the Phoenix Suns since 1973 ... **JIM PERRY (1936)**, righty pitcher with Indians and Twins, won 215 games and Cy Young Award in 1970. Gaylord's brother.

NOTES

■ SAM HUFF (1934) —

Hall of Fame middle linebacker with the Giants and Redskins.

Sam Huff

Born in Morgantown, W.V., he played college ball at the University of West Virginia and had great years with the Giants from 1956 to 1963, helping them win six division titles and one NFL title (1956). In 1959, Huff was featured in a pioneer TV documentary called The Violent World of Sam Huff. Microphones were rigged around his neck and the real raw world of pro football came through. It was probably the first intimate, documentary approach to the sport. Huff is currently vice-president of Marriott hotels, and a radio analyst in Washington for the Redskins.

■ JOHN B. KELLY (1889) —

Olympics sculls champion and father of Grace Kelly, born in Philadelphia, Pa. In 1919, he formed a bricklaying company that became one of the biggest in the U.S. and made him rich. In 1920 and 1924 he won the Olympic singles and doubles in sculling, the only one to perform this feat. His son, John B. Kelly, Jr., was also a sculls champion.

■ Also born today:

FRANKIE CROSETTI (1910), N.Y. Yankee shortstop (full-time in the 1930s and part-time until 1948) after which he became a longtime Yankee coach and wound up with more World Series appearances (as player and coach) than anyone ... ROY BLOUNT, JR. (1941), Sports Illustrated sportswriter and author ... JERREL WILSON (1941), punter with K.C. Chiefs for more than 15 years, No. 1 in number of punts.

NOTES

■ **BILL WILLIS (1921)** —
The first black football player in the modern NFL. Born in Columbus, Ohio, Willis was an All-American at Ohio State and played under Paul Brown on the 1942 national championship team. Willis later was head coach and athletic director at Kentucky State when Brown summoned him in 1946 to join him and the Cleveland Browns in the newly formed AAFC (All-America Football Conference). Willis gave up his coaching career to become one of the greatest lineman of all time. His forte was defense. At 6-foot-3, 215 pounds, Willis was exceptionally fast and catlike. In fact, he was known as "The Cat." He was a middle guard on the old five-man defensive line and was known to leap over offensive lineman. This seven-time All-Pro was inducted into the Hall of Fame in 1977.

■ Also born today:
righty pitcher **JIM BAGBY JR. (1887)**, led Cleveland Indians (more Cleveland) to 1920 pennant with a 31-12 record, then became the first pitcher to hit a home run in a World Series game (Game Five, the same game in which Elmer Smith hit the first Series grand slam and Bill Wambsganss made the first — and only — Series unassisted triple play) ... **RAY KROC**

Jim Bagby Jr.

(1902), founder of McDonald's (and the innovative Hamburger University) and owner of the San Diego Padres from 1974 until his death in 1984 ... jockey **MERLIN VOLZKE (1925),** active into his 50s.

NOTES

■ HELEN WILLS ROARK (1906) —

Roark (as Helen Wills), great tennis champion of the 1920s and 30s. Nicknamed

Helen Wills Roark

"Little Miss Poker Face," Wills ruled tennis for a decade, winning seven U.S. national titles (1923-25, 1927-29, 1931) and eight Wimbledon titles (1927-30, 1932-33, 1935, 1938). Her classic beauty attracted the attention of Charlie Chaplin ("The most beautiful thing I have ever seen is Helen Wills playing tennis") and muralist Diego Rivera. She was the first woman to receive an athletic letter at the University of California, where she was also a Phi Beta Kappa. Many, including tennis champion Jack Kramer, consider her the greatest woman player of all time.

■ HENRY CHADWICK (1833) —

This baseball pioneer was born in England. Chadwick came to the U.S. and settled in New York City. He was one of the earliest sportswriters and probably the first to cover baseball exclusively, writing for the New York Clipper for 30 years (1858-88) and the Brooklyn Eagle. He compiled the first baseball rule book in 1859 and achieved immortality by inventing the box score. Chadwick had a strong influence on the game.

■ Also born today: **LES RICHTER (1930)**, great linebacker with the Rams (1954-62), All-American at Cal ... **JACK SHARKEY (1902)**, heavyweight champion (1932-33), won title by outpointing Max Schmeling but lost title the following year on a six-round KO by Primo Carnera. Dennis "Oil-Can" Boyd (1959), Sensational 145 lb. Bosox righty.

NOTES

■ ALEX GROZA (1926) —

The All-America center from Kentucky in the late 1940s, born in Martins Ferry, Ohio. His brother was the great Cleveland Browns kicker and lineman Lou Groza. Alex, along with Ralph Beard and Wah Wah Jones, led Kentucky to consecutive NCAA titles in 1948 and '49. He was named the MVP in both tournaments. Groza and Beard played pro ball with the newly formed Indianapolis Olympians and Groza became an immediate star, named first string All-Pro in his first two seasons. However, the point-shaving scandal in college basketball shocked the nation in 1951. Groza (and Beard) were among the many big names indicted. The beginning of a tremendous pro career ended abruptly.

Alex Groza

■ CHUCK KLEIN (1904) —

Hard-hitting outfielder of the 1930s, born in Indianapolis. Klein, a lefty swinger, spent most of his career with the Phillies, finishing with a .320 lifetime BA and 300 home runs. He was named MVP in 1932 and won the triple crown the following year, but his best year was probably 1930 when he hit .386 with 40 homers, 170 RBIs, and 250 hits — none of which led the league. In 1932 he led the league in homers and stolen bases. Ty Cobb is the only other player to do that. Klein, one of the few to hit four home runs in a game (his was in 10 innings), was the only player to win the MVP award and be traded after the season. He died in 1958.

■ Also born today:

ANDY KERR (1878), football coach at Colgate (1929-46) ... **RUBY GOLDSTEIN (1907)**, boxing ref, did Louis-Walcott, Louis-Marciano, Patterson-Johansson, many others ... **FRANKIE BAUMHOLTZ (1918)**, Reds and Cubs outfielder of late 40s and early 50s; basketball star, was MVP in 1940-41 NIT with Ohio U.

NOTES

■ BILLY CONN (1917) —

Light-heavyweight champion (1939-41). "The Pittsburgh Kid," a handsome devil, was quick and clever, though no puncher (only 14 KOs in 74 fights). He decisioned Melio Bettina in 15 rounds to become world champion — at age 21. One year later he vacated that title to pursue Joe Louis' heavyweight title. After seven straight wins against the big boys, Conn was ready for the awesome "Brown Bomber." For 12 rounds, he outpointed Louis and was winning the fight when he made one tactical blunder — in the 13th round he decided to duke it out with the hard-hitting Louis and was knocked out in that same round. Five years later, including a two-year stint in World War II, Conn was given a rematch but his inactivity and waning interest in boxing led to an eighth round KO for Louis which caused Conn's semi-retirement.

Billy Conn

■ DANNY MURTAUGH (1917) —

Ex-Pirate manager, born on the same day and year as Billy Conn, and also born in Pennsylvania (Chester), and wound up managing in Conn's birthplace. Murtaugh was a utility infielder with the Phillies and Pirates in the 1940s. He did lead the league in stolen bases (18) in his rookie season despite playing in only 85 games. He is best remembered as the Pirates' manager, on and off, from 1957 to 1975, winning two pennants along the way (1960 and 1971). Murtaugh was of the laid-back school of managing. He would just sit there, cross his legs and watch the game, the only movement being his jaws working over some sunflower seeds. He died in 1976.

NOTES

■ JOE SEWELL (1898) —

Shortstop with the Indians (1920-30) and Yankees (1931-33), born in Titus, Ala. Few ballplayers were as effective as Sewell yet remain so obscure. A .312 lifetime hitter, a fine gloveman, and an iron-man, he made few mistakes on the field. He was the most difficult man to strike out in baseball history, fanning once every 63 at bats. No one is even near that record, nor this one for a single season: four strikeouts in more than 600 at bats in 1925. That's one strikeout in every 150 at bats! He also played in more than 1,100 consecutive games — one

Joe Sewell

of only five players to play in more than 1,000 consecutive games. He was also one of only 13 sets of three brothers to play major league baseball. One, Tommy, played for only one season. The other, Luke Sewell, was a long-time catcher, mostly with Cleveland, where they played together in the 1920s.

■ RUBE MARQUARD (1889) —

Hall of Fame left-hander mostly with the N.Y. Giants and Brooklyn Dodgers, born in Cleveland, Ohio. In 1912, Marquard set the modern major league single-season record of 19 consecutive wins. He also set the record for most wins (24) at age 21, a record destined to be broken by Dwight Gooden of the Mets. He won 204 games and lost 177 (with a 3.08 ERA) in an up-and-down career in which he had brilliant 20-win seasons along with such records as 5-13, 12-22, and 9-18. Marquard was married for three years to Blossom Seeley, actress and singer, who performed a popular song called "The Marquard Glide."

■ Also born today: **WALTER O'MALLEY (1903),** long-time owner of the Brooklyn (later L.A.) Dodgers, died in 1979 ... **AL ROLLINS (1926),** goalie with Maple Leafs, Black Hawks, and Rangers, won Vezina Trophy in 1951 and Hart Trophy (MVP) in 1954.

Joe Pepitone (1940), Yankee, etc. first baseman. Introduced the blow-dryer into big-league clubhouses.

■ **WALLY BERGER (1905) —**
Hard-hitting 1930s outfielder with Boston Braves and others, born in Chicago. He hit exactly .300 for his career with 242 home runs, an impressive figure considering his career amounted to about nine full seasons. Berger holds two major league records that should make him better known than he is. He set a rookie record by hitting 38 home runs in 1930, a feat equalled by Frank Robinson in 1956. He also holds the record for driving in the highest percentage of his team's runs in a season — 22.6 percent. In 1935, Berger drove in 130 (leading the league) of his team's 575 runs.

Wally Berger

■ **GUS WILLIAMS (1953) —**
One of the great fast-break guards in basketball history. Born in Mt. Vernon, New York, he played college ball at USC and was drafted in 1975 by the Warriors in the second round. Williams proved to be a find and was brilliant in his rookie year, despite being infamously benched during the playoffs by Al Attles. The Warriors let Williams go to free agency. The Supersonics outbid the others and won the NBA title with him a year later. In 1984, he was dealt to the Washington Bullets.

■ Also born today: **FURY GENE TENACE (1946)**, ex-A's (and Padres) catcher, World Series MVP in 1972 when he hit four homers against Reds ... **OMAR SHARIF (1932)** actor and expert bridge player, co-writes syndicated bridge column with the venerable Charles Goren

■ **WILLIE HOPPE (1887)** —

The man who popularized and became synonymous with billiards, born in Cornwall, N.Y. In 1906, at age 18, Hoppe, "The Boy Wonder," caused a sensation by traveling to Paris and winning the world billiards championship. He won his last tournament in 1952 at age 64 and retired that year, having won 51 world titles in 46 years of competition. In the 1920s, Hoppe was a household name and was even invited to the White House to give an exhibition.

Willie Hoppe

■ **LUIS FIRPO (1896)** —

Argentinian heavyweight (and almost champion), "The Wild Bull of the Pampas." He is famous for his dramatic two-round bout with Jack Dempsey in 1923. Firpo had an undefeated string of about 20 straight wins, almost all of them by KO. In the first round Firpo caught the great Dempsey with a punch that drove him out of the ring and into the seats. Witnesses claim that Dempsey never would've made it back into the ring before the count of 10 if he hadn't gotten a lot of help from his friends. He held on until the bell and re-grouped between rounds. In round two, Dempsey tore into Firpo and, this time, drove Firpo out of the ring. Firpo, with not as many ringside fans around him, never made it back into the ring.

■ Also born today: **DUTCH CLARK (1906)**, tailback with Detroit Lions in late 1930s; great runner, passer and kicker. Of him, Clark Shaughnessy said, "If Clark stepped on the field with Grange, Thorpe and Gipp, Dutch would be the general" ... tennis champion **MARIA BUENO (1939)**, born in Brazil, won U.S. title in 1959, '63, '64, and '66; rated by Alice Marble as the No. 2 all-time woman player.

NOTES

■ **JOE CRONIN (1906)** —
Hall of Fame shortstop with Senators (1928-34) and Red Sox (1935-45), born in San Francisco — in the same year as The Earthquake. Cronin's baseball history includes a 20-year Hall of Fame career as player (with .302 lifetime BA), as manager from 1933 to 1947 (most of those years as player-manager), as Red Sox general manager from 1947 to 1959, and as AL president (1959-75). How many players win the MVP award and manage teams to pennants (he won with the Senators in 1933 and the Red Sox in 1946)? In 1983 at

Joe Cronin

Fenway Park, Cronin's uniform (No. 4) was retired along with Ted Williams' (No. 9). When Williams spoke he looked up to Cronin (in a wheelchair and unable to go on the field) and said, "...No one respects you more than I do, Joe. I love you. In my book, you're a great man." Cronin, the "boy wonder" who managed the Senators to a pennant at age 26 (while hitting .309), died of cancer in 1984.

■ Also born today: **RICK FERRELL (1905)**, catcher mostly with the Senators and Red Sox (like Cronin), caught more games than any other AL catcher and had a .281 lifetime BA, inducted into Hall of Fame in 1984 (brother of pitcher Wes Ferrell) ... **T. TRUXTON HARE (1878)**, made Walter Camp's All-America teams four years in a row in late 1890s, college hall of famer from Pennsylvania.

NOTES

■ **EDDIE MATHEWS (1931) —**
The only Boston, Milwaukee and Atlanta Brave player.
Mathews broke in as a 20-year-old rookie in 1952, the Braves' last year in Boston. He retired in 1968 with 512 home runs, one of only 14 players to hit 500 or more, and a .271 lifetime BA. For more than a decade, Mathews and Henry Aaron formed a duo in the middle of the batting order that has been equalled only by Ruth / Gehrig, Mays / McCovey, and Maris / Mantle. Mathews holds the National League record of nine consecutive seasons hitting 30 homers or more. Mathews,

Eddie Mathews

McCovey and Mel Ott are the greatest lefty power-hitters in NL history. Inducted into the Hall of Fame in 1978, Mathews is currently an Oakland A's scout.

■ Also born today: **NAT "SWEETWATER" CLIFTON (1922)**, ex-Harlem Globetrotter, in 1950 he became one of the first blacks to play in the NBA, with the N.Y. Knicks until 1957 ... Southpaw **RUBE WADDELL (1876)**, won 191 games mostly with the Philadelphia A's, zany character, died of TB at age 37 ... **KID McCOY (1872)**, middleweight champion, 1897, inspired the phrase "the real McCoy" because of his penchant for not always giving his best ... **SWEDE RISBERG (1894)**, one of the eight White Sox players banned for life for throwing the 1919 World Series. He was the shortstop, born in San Francisco.

NOTES

■ **JOHN WOODEN (1910) —**
Coach of the greatest dynasty in college basket-

ball history. His UCLA teams won 10 NCAA championships, including seven in a row (1967-73), during his reign from 1948 to 1975. Wooden was voted Coach of the Year six times and is credited with developing the zone-press defense. He was also an All-American player at Purdue in the early 1930s under legendary coach Ward "Piggy" Lambert. Wooden is the only man elected to the college basketball hall of fame as player and coach.

John Wooden

■ **LANCE RENTZEL (1943) —**
NFL receiver whose career ended abruptly at its peak. A running back out of Oklahoma, he was drafted by the Vikings and turned into a wide receiver but was traded after morals charges were brought against him. Later, with the Dallas Cowboys in 1970, he was again charged with making sexual advances toward children, and retired soon thereafter. Rentzel wrote about the whole sordid mess in the 1972 opus, "When All the Laughter Died In Sorrow." By the time his book came out, his marriage to actress-dancer Joey Heatherton had ended.

■ Also born today: speed skater **SHEILA YOUNG** (1950), the first American, male or female, to win three medals in a single Winter Olympics (1976) — gold in 500m, silver in 1500m and bronze in 1000m; also a bicycle racer and the only athlete ever to become a world champion in two sports ... **CHARLIE JOINER** (1947), wide receiver with Oilers, Bengals and (currently) Chargers, who in '84 became No. 1 in receptions, passing Raymond Berry, Don Maynard and Charley Taylor.

NOTES

■ **JOHN L. SULLIVAN (1858) —**
"The Great John L.," the last bare-knuckle heavyweight champion, 1882-92. Sullivan was the first ring idol in the U.S., admired alike by novelists, clergymen, and the working class. At the peak of his fame he offered $1,000 to anyone who could stay four rounds with him. He was in 42 fights and lost only one, his most famous match. When he fought James J. Corbett, most of the population felt that Sullivan was invincible, but this bout was to be the first title fight in which the boxers used gloves. The era of sheer brawn had ended and the rise of the scientific boxer, represented by Corbett, took its place. Corbett knocked Sullivan out, effectively ending the career of "The Boston Strong Boy." Sullivan was a big hit on stage, touring in melodramas, and — after he had become a teetotaler — lectured extensively on the evils of drink. He died in 1918.

■ **JIM PALMER (1945) —**
Long-time righty pitcher with the Orioles and later TV commentator. He was released in 1983 after 18 years with the Orioles, winding up with 268 wins and 152 losses, making him one of the top percentage pitchers of all time. He won the Cy Young Award three times (1973, '75, and '76), won 20 or more games eight times in nine years (1970-78), and never — great craftsman that he

Jim Palmer

was — gave up a grand slam. Palmer is a refreshing voice in the broadcasting booth. He is knowledgeable, relaxed, and unafraid to be irreverent.

■ Also born today: sprinter **BOBBY MORROW (1935)**, won gold medals in 100m. and 200m. at 1956 Olympics ... **HUNTINGTON "TACK" HARDWICK (1892)**, college Hall of Fame end from Harvard.

NOTES

■ DAVE DeBUSSCHERE (1940) —

Dave DeBusschere

Perhaps the greatest defensive forward in basketball . Born in Detroit, he went to the University of Detroit and starred in basketball and baseball. He played both sports on the pro level. In two seasons (1962-63), he was a 3-4 pitcher with the White Sox. He began his NBA career with the Detroit Pistons in 1962. For seven years he labored in obscurity, despite playing well, and was player-coach at age 25, the youngest coach in pro sports. He was traded to the N.Y. Knicks in 1968 for Walt Bellamy and Howard Komives, a move that turned the Knicks around and ushered in great years for them. Every night DeBusschere gave his team 15 points, 11 rebounds, and tremendous defense. One of the great fundamental players, he rarely made a mistake. He became the Knicks' general manager.

■ LEON "GOOSE" GOSLIN (1900) —

Hall of Fame outfielder from 1921 to 1938, born in Salem, N.J. He played most of his career with the Washington Senators, leading them to two straight pennants in 1924 and '25 (hitting three home runs in each of those World Series) and again in 1933 — the only man to play in every one of the Washington Senators' 19 World Series games. He is one of the few players to hit safely in at least 30 consecutive games and was the first major league player to hit three home runs in a game three times. Goslin, playing for Detroit (1934-37), appeared in the 1934 and '35 World Series. A .316 lifetime hitter who drove in 100 runs or more 11 times, Goslin was one of the first Jewish baseball stars. He died in 1971.

■ Also born today: **WALT MICHAELS (1929)**, offensive guard for Cleveland Browns from 1952 to 1961, later coached the N.Y. Jets, USFL N.J. Generals ... **TIM McCARVER (1941)**, Steve Carlton's designated catcher with Cardinals and Phillies, later became TV sportscaster.

NOTES

■ **JIM "JUNIOR" GILLIAM (1928)** —
Dodger second baseman, third baseman and outfielder. 1953 to 1966, born in Nashville, Tenn. Gilliam led the league in triples (17) in his rookie season and was named Rookie-of-the-Year. He played on seven pennant-winning Dodger teams (four of which won the World Series). Gilliam was an all-around gem — a versatile performer who could play most positions well, run the bases, and handle a bat. His .265 lifetime average includes a lot of clutch singles. He is the only player to appear in both a regular season perfect game (Koufax's in

Jim Gilliam

1965) and a World Series perfect game (Larsen's in 1956). Gilliam died in 1978 after coaching the Dodgers for many years. He spent more than a quarter of a century in a Dodger uniform.

■ **REINHOLD MESSNER (1944)** —
Climbed Mt. Everest alone, without oxygen, transforming the sport of mountain-climbing. His asceticism (disdaining most modern equipment) and his penchant for solitary climbing "has given climbing a new purity." He produces films, writes books, and lectures on climbing. He also runs a climbing school. See the 1982 biography by Ronald Faux, "High Ambition."

■ Also born today: weightlifter **PAUL ANDERSON (1932)**, "world's strongest man," won gold medal in 1956 Olympics; in 1955, lifted 6,270 pounds, more than anyone in history ... pole vaulter **BOB SEAGREN (1946)**, gold medal in 1968 Olympics ... **WILLIAM "CANDY" CUMMINGS (1848)**, righty pitcher, allegedly invented the curve ball in 1864 ... **DON CORYELL (1924)**, football coach at San Diego State (1961-72), St. Louis Cardinals (1973-77), with the San Diego Chargers since 1978.

NOTES

■**MARTINA NAVRATILOVA (1956)** —
The best woman tennis player in the world since 1978.

She was born in Prague, Czechoslovakia, and was that country's top player until she defected to the U.S. in 1975. In 1984 she defeated Chris Evert Lloyd in the U.S. Open and broke Lloyd's record of winning 56 consecutive tournaments. Navratilova, who once was coached by Renee Richards, the transsexual tennis player, caused a mild sensation in 1981 when the break-up of her affair with author Rita Mae Brown was revealed.

Martina Navratilova

■**NAT HOLMAN (1896)** —
Renowned basketball player and coach, born in New York City. Holman was the sparkplug guard on the original Celtics from 1920 to 1928. He later coached at CCNY for more than 40 years, peaking in 1950 as his freshman and sophomore-dominated team won both the NIT and NCAA tournaments, the first and only "grand slam." A year later the basketball world was shocked by the point-shaving scandals and Holman's entire squad was among the indicted.

■**THOMAS HEARNS (1958)** —
The "hit-man" from Detroit and junior middleweight champion since 1982. Hearns' first defeat was by Sugar Ray Leonard in 1982, although he proved his ability to box in that fight, something the public was unaware of. In 1984 he forced the great Roberto Duran's retirement with a devastating second-round KO. His hand injury and long layoff fooled a lot of people. After Duran, Hearns took out Fred Hutchings in one round. Though he was KO'd in round three by Marvin Hagler (Hearns' only other loss, in 1985), Hearns is still the best middleweight in the world outside of Marvy Marv.

NOTES

Martina won her sixth
US open in '85.

■ **MORDECAI "THREE-FINGER" BROWN (1876)** — Brown, one of the greatest pitchers in major league history, was born in Nyesville, Ind. Mordecai Peter Centennial (it was the United States' centennial year) Brown lost his right index finger as a boy while feeding corn into a chopper. Very few predicted a career as a pitcher, yet Brown became a great one because of that accident. The action of his thumb, the three remaining fingers and the stump that used to be his index finger produced a kind of sinker and knuckleball that helped him win 239 games and lose only 135,

'Three-Finger' Brown

making him one of the top percentage pitchers in baseball history. His phenomenal lifetime ERA was 2.06, the third best mark. He had six straight 20-game seasons and had an ERA of less than 2.00 for five straight seasons (1906-10). Brown had his big years with the Chicago Cubs and led them to their pennant in 1908. He also won two games in that World Series against the Tigers, the only World Series the Cubbies have ever won. Brown died in 1948.

■ Also born today: **ANNIE SMITH PECK (1850)**, mountain climber, explorer and author; she climbed Mt. Coropuna in Peru (21,250 feet) at age 61; also climbed the Matterhorn and many other peaks ... Lefty pitcher **ALPHA BRAZLE (1914)**, because he has a great name and because of his 97-64 record as starter and reliever with the Cardinals (1943, 1946-54), died in 1973 ... **RICHARD C. HARLOW (1889)**, football coach for 36 years at Penn State (1914-17), Colgate (1922-25), Western Maryland (1926-34) and, most notably, Harvard (1935-42, 1945-47); died 1962.

NOTES

Mickey Mantle

■ **MICKEY MANTLE (1931)** — Alone as *the* power-hitting switch-hitter in baseball history. He played his entire career (1951-68) with the N.Y. Yankees, finishing with a .298 lifetime BA, 536 career homers (6th on the list) and three MVP awards (1956, 1957, 1962). In 1956, he won the Triple Crown with 52 home runs, 130 RBIs and a .353 BA. Mantle was the greatest combination of power and speed the game has ever produced. When he broke in as a 19-year-old rookie, he was the fastest runner in baseball and was already hitting tape-measure homers. Of his 2,400 career games, he spent more than 2000 of them plagued by recurring leg ailments. His entire right leg was tightly taped before almost every game he played, and he played hurt every day. Even his home run trot was painful to watch. Despite his impressive career stats, they were probably only the tip of the iceberg. It's awesome to consider what he might have done if he spent a career as healthy as, say, Willie Mays.

■ Also born today: **AARON PRYOR (1955)**, the great juniorwelterweight champion (WBA), retired in 1983 (after his TKO of Alexis Arguello in 1983) with a record of 34-0 with 32 KOs ... good lefty stick and golden glover **KEITH HERNANDEZ (1953)**, in the great tradition of S.F.-born first basemen; he's the best Mets player ever ... sprinter **VALERI BORZOV (1949)**, in 1972 Olympics, he won the 100 meters and 200., the first Soviet sprinter ever to win an Olympic individual medal, and the only European ever to win the Olympic sprint double for men.

NOTES

■ WHITEY FORD (1928) —

Winningest pitcher in New York Yankee history. Ford came up to the Yanks in the middle of the 1950 season as a 21-year-old rookie and went 9-1. He finished in 1967 with a 236-106 record, a .690 percentage — the highest of all time. Known as "the chairman of the board," Ford was the Yankees' meal-ticket, helping them win 10 pennants and seven World Series. His Series records include most games pitched, most games won, most innings, strikeouts and consecutive scoreless innings. He was 25-4 in 1961 and

Whitey Ford

won the Cy Young Award. Ford is also renowned as Mickey Mantle's drinking buddy and co-reveler. Whitey, elected to the Hall of Fame in 1974, currently runs a baseball camp and is a spring training coach for the Yankees.

■ Also born today: **AL WEILL (1891)**, manager of Rocky Marciano, also matchmaker of the IBC in the late 1940s and early '50s, an organization run by underworld figure Frankie Carbo ... **VERN MIKKELSEN (1928)**, Minneapolis Laker forward (1949-58), a good scorer and rebounder who played in the shadow of George Mikan ... **BRIAN PICCOLO (1943)**, running back with the Chicago Bears (1966-69), died of leukemia in 1970 and was the subject of the film, "Brian's Song," and Gale Sayers' book, "I Am Third" ... Golfer **BOB ROSBURG (1926)**, San Francisco native, won the 1959 PGA tournament.

NOTES

■ **JIMMIE FOXX (1907)** — "Double X," awesome slugger with the A's (1925-35) and Red Sox (1936-42), was born in Sudlersville, Md. Only Harmon Killebrew (573) has hit more right-handed home runs than Foxx (534) in AL history. In fact, no other righty AL hitter has ever hit 400. Foxx (6-feet, 195 pounds) was also a great average hitter with a .325 lifetime BA and two batting titles (1933, winning the triple crown, and 1938). He won three MVP awards — in 1932 and 1933 with the A's and 1938 with the Bosox (the only player to win MVPs with two teams in the same league). He holds the record for hitting 30 or more homers for 12 straight years, and hit 100 RBI or more for 13 straight years. First baseman Foxx, also known as "The Beast," died in 1967.

Jimmie Foxx

■ Also born today: **JOSEPH CARR (1880)**, co-founder (1919) of the NFL and its first president (1921-39) ... **DARRYL RAY BEARDALL (1936)**, one of the greatest long-distance runners in NorCal history ... **JOHNNY BECKMAN (1895)**, captain of the Original Celtics, the best foul-shooter of his era ... **KEENA TURNER (1958)**, S.F. 49er linebacker, drafted obscurely out of Purdue in 1980, a true gem, one of the quickest linebackers in the NFL ... **HARRY "THE HAT" WALKER (1916)**, .296 lifetime hitter with 10 homers in 2,651 at bats, won batting title in 1947 with Phillies (though he started with the Cardinals — the first player to win a batting title for two teams); his brother was Fred "Dixie" Walker (who also won an NL batting title).

NOTES

■ PELE (1940) —

Regarded as the greatest soccer player of all time, Pele (accent on the second syllable), was born Edson Arantes de Nascimento in Tres Coracoes, Brazil. He began as a 17-year-old on the Brazilian national team and led them to three World Cup titles (1958, 1962, and 1970), scoring a record 1,281 goals. In 1974, he signed a 3-year, $4.7 million contract with the New York Cosmos and single-handedly established soccer as a viable sport in the U.S. He retired in 1977.

Pele

■ GERTRUDE EDERLE (1906) —

The first woman to swim the English Channel (1926), born in New York City. Not only was she the first woman to accomplish the feat (from France to England) but she did it in a faster time (14 hours, 31 minutes) than any man had ever done it. She instantly became the most famous woman in the world and synonymous with woman athletes. Though there had been some women tennis players and others, Ederle was the first internationally famous and admired woman athlete.

■ Also born today: **JIM BUNNING** (1931), righty sidearmer with Tigers and Phillies, won 224 games; one of only three pitchers to win 100 games in each league; also threw no-hitters in each league, including 1964 perfect game ... **CHI CHI RODRIGUEZ** (1935), Puerto Rican-born golfer, won the Lucky Invitational and Western Open in 1964.

NOTES

■ **JUAN MARICHAL (1937) —**
One of the distinguished mound artists in baseball history. He was born in the Dominican Republic and was discovered there by big-league scouts. A rookie with the Giants in 1960, he pitched a one-hitter in his debut and never looked back, compiling a brilliant 243-142 won-loss record (including his combined 5-2 record with the Bosox and — incredibly — the Dodgers). Marichal probably had more stuff than any pitcher who ever lived, including fastball, curve, screwball and a couple of trick pitches that he threw at various speeds and with various motions — from over the top to sidearm. Among modern pitchers, only Bob Gibson had Marichal's competitive fire. In 1965, the year Marichal threw his no-hitter, he was suspended for nine days and fined $1,750 when he hit Dodger catcher John Roseboro over the head with a baseball bat (he was at bat at the time). That incident probably delayed Marichal's eventual induction into the Hall of Fame in 1983.

Juan Marichal

■ **Y. A. TITTLE (1926) —**
"The Bald Eagle," one of the great late-bloomers in NFL history. Born Yelberton Abraham Tittle in Marshall, Texas, he had three separate (and impressive) careers with three teams a la George Blanda. He was Rookie of the Year with the Colts in the old AAFC, then played with the 49ers (1951-60) and was named UPI Player of the Year in 1957, then, considered washed up, was dealt to the N.Y. Giants where he achieved his greatest fame. He was named MVP in his first year with the Giants, 1961, and again in 1963 when (at age 37) he set an NFL record with 36 TD passes. That year he also became one of six QBs to pass for seven TDs in a single game.

Marichal has been a Latin American scout for the A's (not the Giants, of course).

NOTES

■ **JOHN HEISMAN (1869)** —
"The Father of the Forward Pass" born in Cleveland, Oh.
He coached at many colleges in his 39-year career, but

is best known for his years at
Georgia Tech (1904-19). In 1895
(as coach of Auburn), Heisman
attended a North Carolina-Geor-
gia game in which a desperate
punter, scrambling away from the
rush, ran out of room and just
heaved the darn thing downfield
end over end. His teammate
caught it and ran for the only
score of the day. Heisman saw
the light. For years he cam-
paigned to legalize the forward
pass but the idea was too radical.

The Heisman Trophy

Finally, in 1906, "Heisman's forward pass" was adopted
and football entered the 20th century. Heisman, a
well-educated man, gave up a law career to coach.
During the off-season, he was a Shakespearean actor
and was known to utter his footballisms in theatrical
style. He was fond of saying "thrust your projections into
their cavities." He first described a football as "a
prolate spheroid" and added, "better to have died as a
small boy than to fumble this football." The man who
originated the hidden-ball play, the center-snap,
"quarterback as safety" defense, and much more was
also a dictator whose later years in coaching were
marred by his irritability, impatience, and inability to
communicate. The Heisman Trophy, given yearly to the
best college football player, is his monument. He died of
pneumonia in 1936.

■ Also born today: **BOBBY THOMSON (1923)**, hit homer
"Heard 'round the world" to beat Dodgers in 1951; with
Braves in 1954, broke leg which forced them to bring up
rookie Hank Aaron ... **DAVE COWENS (1948)**, Celtics
center (1969-79), MVP, 1973 ... **JACK KENT COOKE
(1912)**, ex-owner of L.A. Lakers; built The Forum in
Inglewood.

NOTES

■ **PRIMO CARNERA (1906)**–"The Ambling Alp," heavyweight champion (1933-34), born in Italy. He weighed 22 pounds at birth. Carnera was the heaviest champion in history at about 265 pounds and he stood 6-feet-5¾. Curiously, he was a pretty good boxer and not much of a puncher. He KO'd Jack Sharkey in the sixth round to win the title and lost it a year later to Max Baer, who knocked Carnera down 11 times en route to an 11th-round KO. His career was virtually over, although he fought a few more times. Budd Schulberg wrote a novel, "The Harder They Fall," a fictionalized account of Carnera's career that was made into a movie in 1957 (Humphrey Bogart's last). Many of Carnera's fights were set-ups, possibly even his title fight against Sharkey. His promoters made a lot of money on his fights and toured the U.S. with him. His innocence and difficulty with English were exploited by everyone around him. He wound up with virtually nothing. After WW II, Carnera toured the world as a wrestler, appeared in several movies, became a U.S. citizen and settled in L.A. where he owned a liquor store. He died in 1967.

■ Also born today: **"JUMPIN' JOE" FULKS (1921)**, high-scoring forward with Philadelphia Warriors (1946-54), the first great scoring forward of the post-WW II era; his running two-handed jump shot was something to behold...**CHUCK FOREMAN (1950)**, brilliant running back/receiver with the Vikings in the mid-1970s...**RICHARD DUDLEY SEARS (1861)**, winner of the first U.S. singles tennis championship in 1892 and winner of seven consecutive titles...**KID GLEASON (1866)**, unwitting but suspicious manager of the 1919 Chicago "Black Sox," the team that threw the 1919 World Series.

NOTES

■ RALPH KINER (1922) —

One of the great sluggers in baseball history. He hit 369 home runs in only a 10-year career. With the Pirates from 1946 to 1952, he led the league in homers every one of those years — seven straight seasons, a major league record. Kiner also had an impressive .279 lifetime BA. Back injuries forced his retirement at age 32 but he had Hall of Fame credentials already and was inducted in 1975. Kiner, who married ex-tennis player Nancy Chafee, is the long-time N.Y. Mets announcer and one of the best.

Ralph Kiner

■ KYLE ROTE (1928) —

A college football legend who later made it big in New York. An All-American at Texas, he was a versatile back and later a tight end during the N.Y. Giants' glory years of the late 1950s. He retired in 1961 and became one of the best TV football announcers ever. His cousin, Tobin Rote, was an NFL quarterback and his son, Kyle Rote Jr., was an outstanding soccer player.

■ Also born today: **PUMPSIE GREEN (1933)**, the first black baseball player to play for the Boston Red Sox, he was a rookie in 1959, 12 years after Jackie Robinson broke the color barrier; of course, the Red Sox selected a black player who wasn't very good and didn't play much ... Expos shortstop **U.L. WASHINGTON (1953)**, who likes playing with a toothpick in his mouth ..., **MATT CAVANAUGH (1956)**, 49ers second-string QB.

Brother of ex-Cowboy CB Cornell Green.

■ LENNY WILKENS (1937) —

Coach of the Seattle SuperSonics and one of the best coaches in the NBA. Born in Brooklyn, he played college ball at Providence and was drafted in the first round by the St. Louis Hawks in 1960. After eight seasons, he spent four years with Seattle and also had brief stints with the Cavs and the Blazers. Wilkens was one of the top all-around guards in NBA history. Among the top 10 scoring guards, he was also a great assist man, and is one of only 10 players to appear in more than 1,000 games. He started as a player-coach with Portland and has been coaching the SuperSonics since 1979. In 1984 he became the youngest NBA coach to win 500 games. The Sonics have been on a slow decline. It's Wilkens (and such teams as the Warriors) who keeps them from bottoming out.

Lenny Wilkens

■ JOE PAGE (1917) —

Great relief pitcher for N. Y. Yankees in the late 1940s, born in Cherry Valley, Pa. Page won a lot of games for a reliever, 57 in seven seasons (1944-50), including 14 in 1947 and 13 in 1949, but he also lost 49 games, far too many, and had too high of a career ERA (3.53). After all, he did pitch for the dominant team in major league baseball. Page's greatness was in his stamina and durability. A big (6-foot-3, 200 pounds) left-hander, he was probably the first reliever to appear in 50 games in a season. He also turned it on in the World Series. In 1947, he made four appearances, including the seventh game, pitching five innings of one-hit relief to thwart the Brooklyn Dodgers. In 1949, he made three appearances (in a five-game series), winning game three (against Brooklyn again) with another five-inning relief stint. Page died in 1980.

Wilkens Update: Became Sonics' GM in '85

NOTES

■ **JIM BIBBY (1944) —**
Big right-handed pitcher of the 1970s with the Cards, Rangers, Indians and Pirates. He won 19 games for the Rangers in 1974, was 13-7 with the Indians, and then after a couple of .500-ish seasons, pitched the best baseball of his career, going 12-4 with the 1979 Pirates and then (blossoming at age 36) had his big 19-6 season in 1980, leading the NL in percentage for the second straight year. His brother is the former UCLA and NBA basketball star Henry Bibby.

Jim Bibby

■ **DENIS POTVIN (1953) —**
Longtime defenseman with the New York Islanders. He was Rookie of the Year in 1974 and won the Norris Trophy (for best defenseman) three times (1976, '78 and '79). He and Bobby Orr are the only defensemen to score 100 points and 30 goals in a season. Potvin, always in Orr's shadow, has carved his own Hall of Fame niche.

■ Also born today: **CHARLIE EBBETS (1859)**, middle name Hercules, early owner of the Brooklyn Dodgers; Ebbets Field (built in 1913), the Dodgers' intimate and beloved bandbox, was named after him ... **FRANK SEDGMAN (1927)**, Australian tennis player, won the U.S. singles title in 1951 and '52, and the British title in 1952 ... **JOHN DEWITT (1881)**, great Princeton lineman in the College Hall of Fame who also won the college hammer throw title four straight years and won the silver medal at the 1904 Olympics ... **DICK GARMAKER (1932)**, basketball All-American from Minnesota, played pro ball with Minnesota Lakers and N.Y. Knicks from 1955 to 1961; in 1957, he scored 26 points in a quarter, an NBA record at the time.

NOTES

■ BILL TERRY (1898) —

The great New York Giants player and manager, born in Atlanta, Ga., (though he was known as "Memphis Bill").

Bill Terry

A big lefty first baseman, he played his entire career with the Giants (1923-36), and had a lifetime BA of .341. He is the last NL player to hit .400. (In 1930 he hit .401 on 254 hits — an NL hit record — including 23 home runs and 15 triples). He also managed his entire career (1932-41) with the NY Giants, a player-manager for the first five years. It was Terry who was annointed to receive the managerial mantle from John J. McGraw (after his 32-year reign) and he led them to three pennants (in 1933, after finishing last the year before, 1936, and 1937). Terry was inducted into the Hall of Fame in 1954 — 13 years after he was eligible. The baseball writers (who hold the key to the Hall) didn't cotton to his no-nonsense aloofness. Terry just came to play but the writers wanted more.

■ ED DELAHANTY (1867) —

"Big Ed," one of five brothers to play in the major leagues — and the best of them— born in Cleveland. He was an outfielder, mostly with the Philadelphia Nationals from 1888 to 1903. His .345 lifetime BA is the fourth highest of all time after Cobb's, Hornsby's, and Joe Jackson's. In 1896, Delahanty became the first major league player to hit four consecutive home runs in a game. Curiously, he hit all four of them off a pitcher named Bill Terry. Delahanty was an alcoholic, and this flaw led to his premature death in 1903. Frustrated by contract disputes with the team owner and with changing rules on jumping leagues, he went on a drinking binge. Traveling on a train, he became so rowdy he was thrown off at Niagara Falls station. In a rage, he ran after the departing train, on the railway ties that spanned the Falls, and slipped, falling into the icy waters. He was 35.

NOTES

■ CAL HUBBARD (1900) —

The only man ever inducted into both the baseball and pro football Halls of Fame, born in Keytesville, Md. Hubbard was a tackle who also played end and would occasionally drop back a few feet and roam the area like a modern-day linebacker. He has been called the greatest tackle ever to play football. Bo McMillan, Hubbard's coach at Centenary College of Louisiana, called him the greatest football player of all time. He played for the N.Y. Giants and the Green Bay Packers from 1927 to 1936. Hubbard

Cal Hubbard

began umpiring baseball games during the off-season after his rookie year and he continued throughout his NFL career. He went big league in 1936 and umpired until 1951 when a hunting accident affected his vision. He stepped down but was named supervisor of American League umpires. Hubbard died in 1977.

■ DAVE McNALLY (1942) —

Baltimore Oriole lefty, 1962 to 1974. He won 20 or more games four straight years (1968-71), leading them to three pennants during that period. McNally is the only pitcher to hit a grand slam home run in the World Series. It was game three, 1970. The O's won the game and the Series. After the 1974 season, McNally was traded with two others to the Expos for Ken Singleton and Mike Torrez. It was a coup for the O's — McNally was already known to have arm problems. He won three more games and retired with 184 career wins.

■ Also born today: marathon man **FRANK SHORTER** (1947), gold medal winner in 1972 Olympics ... auto racer **WILBUR SHAW** (1902), three-time winner of Indy 500 ... **MICKEY RIVERS** (1948), Texas Rangers of-dh, had worst arm in majors.

NOTES

■ FERNANDO VALENZUELA (1960) —

Fernando Valenzuela

Brilliant Dodger left-hander. Born in Mexico, he came up as a 19-year-old rookie in September, 1980, and pitched two shutouts. The next year he won the Cy Young Award and led the Dodgers to the pennant. At age 20, he vaulted into the top echelon of pitchers in all of baseball. Since that time, the Dodgers have declined. Unfortunately, so has Fernando. Though he has the best stuff of any pitcher in the league, he overpitches (e.g., starts, say, Johnnie LeMaster off with a hellacious screwball — "just misses, ball one" — and winds up walking him on sweeping curveballs. Oh, yeah, then four or five obligatory throws to first, "gotta keep the runner close"). Valenzuela changed his diet and has trimmed down considerably. If he could do the same thing to his pitching philosophy, no one would touch him.

■ GRANTLAND RICE (1880) —

The original Dean of American Sportswriters, born in Murfreesboro, Tenn. He wrote for The New York Herald Tribune, among others, and had a syndicated column called "The Sportlight" from 1930 until his death in 1954. Rice gave the 1924 Notre Dame backfield a celebrated nickname in what is the most famous lead in sportswriting history: "Outlined against a blue-gray October sky, the Four Horsemen rode again ..."

■ Also born today: Golfer GARY PLAYER (1935), won U.S. Open in 1965, also won PGA twice, the Masters three times, and the British Open three times; only the third man ever to win all four major tournaments ... DAVE MEGGYSEY (1941), ex-NFL linebacker-turned sports activist and educator, wrote "Out of Their League," a denunciation of pro football.

■ **JOHNNY VANDER MEER (1914)** —
The only major leaguer to throw two consecutive
no - hitters. A lefty strikeout
pitcher (led NL, 1941-43) who
spent most of his career with the
Cincinnati Reds, Vander Meer had
a lifetime 119-121 won-loss record. He had his double no-no in
1938, first against Boston (then
known as the Bees) and four days
later, on June 15 (the day Lou
Brock was born), against the
Dodgers in Ebbets Field, the first
night game ever played there (the
Dodger hitters must have loved it
— facing a fastball pitcher, under
lights for the first time ever, who

Johnny Vander Meer

threw a no-hitter in his last start). Less known is a game
he pitched in 1946, going 15 scoreless innings in the
longest scoreless game in major-league history (19
innings).

■ **LEON HART (1928)** —
One of only two linemen ever to win the Heisman
Trophy. Hart was a great All-American on the
Notre Dame teams of the late 1940s, among the
greatest college football teams of all time. He doubled
as end and fullback and was a 60-minute tower of
strength. He played pro ball with the Detroit Lions from
1950 to 1957. In 1951, Hart was named first team All-Pro
on offense and defense, the only player ever to achieve
such an honor.

■ Also born today: Tennis player **WILLIAM "LITTLE
BILL" JOHNSTON (1894)**, S.F. native, won U.S. singles
title in 1915 and 1919 ... another tennis player, **KEN
ROSEWALL (1934)**, who also won two U.S. singles titles
(1956 and 1970, 14 years apart).

NOTES

■ **BOB FELLER (1918)** —

A great pitcher and a Great American Hero— a farm boy from Iowa whose father encouraged him and helped him develop into a great athlete. The Cleveland Indians signed Feller while he was still in high school and he burst upon the scene like a meteor, striking out 15 batters in his major league debut (at age 17, shortly after his high school graduation) and, three weeks later, striking out 17 in a nine-inning game, equalling the record. He later became the first to strike out 18. By 1939, at age 20, Feller was fully mature and dominated the American League with most wins and most strikeouts in that year and the two following it. At that apex, Feller's career was tragically interrupted by World War II and he missed almost four seasons. He won 266 games, and would probably have been the winningest right-handed pitcher of the live ball era. He pitched three no-hitters and, even more impressive , 12 one-hitters. After the loss of Feller's fastball he emphasized his curveball (he always had a good one) and a slider. In 1954, at age 35, he won thirteen, lost three, and helped Cleveland win its last pennant.

■ Also born today: **LARRY HERNDON (1953)**, Detroit Tigers outfielder (and, need I say, ex-Giant?), born in Sunflower, Miss. ... **LARRY HOLMES (1949)**, heavyweight champ since 1978, and that's a long time — too long; if Rocky Marciano were alive, he could accuse Holmes of running out of bounds. *Bronko Nagurski (1908), Hall of Fame Chicago Bears fullback of 1930's.*

NOTES

■**DICK GROAT (1930)** —One of America's greatest two-sport athletes. There have been many who were outstanding at basketball and baseball, but Groat is the only one to be a first-string All-American in basketball (at Duke) and win the MVP award in baseball (with the Pittsburgh Pirates). Born in Swissvale, Pennsylvania, he grew up in a sports family. His older brothers went to nearby Pitt, but he decided to carve his own niche at Duke. In his junior year, Groat led the nation in scoring (25.2 ppg) and his 831 points set an NCAA single-season scoring record. A 6-3 guard who was an offensive machine, he also led the Duke team in assists. Groat's first love was baseball. In 1952, he played a partial season in the NBA and began his

Dick Groat

rookie season as the Pittsburgh Pirates' shortstop. Unfortunately, Groat spent the next two years in the Army. In '54, he resumed his career with the Pirates, playing eight seasons with them, peaking out in 1960 when he led the NL in hitting, won the MVP award and led the Pirates to the pennant — and beyond. He was dealt to the Cardinals in 1963 and had two very good years, another trip to the World Series in 1964 — his second, both times a winner in dramatic seven-game Series, both times against the awesome NY Yankees. Since retirement (with a .286 lifetime BA), Groat has been active in business, as an analyst for Pitt basketball games on radio and TV, and as an operator (with ex-teammate Jerry Lynch, pinch-hit specialist) of an 18-hole golf course in Ligonier, Pa.

■Also born today: **BOB DOUGLAS (1884)**, was the first black elected to the basketball Hall of Fame, organized the New York Rens (as in Renaissance) ... sportswriter **FURMAN BISHER (1918)**, with the Atlanta Constitution and The Sporting News.

Sports birthdays/Nov. 5

■ BILL WALTON (1952) —
One of the greatest centers in basketball history. A

Bill Walton

high school phenomenon in his birthplace, La Mesa, (a suburb of San Diego), Walton kept right on going at UCLA, where he was a three-time All-American and three-time College Player of the Year, an honor shared only by Oscar Robertson and Ralph Sampson. In 1977, Walton's third year with the Portland Trail Blazers (former doormat of the league), the 6-foot-11 redhead led them to the NBA title and won the MVP award. He averaged 18.6 points per game and was No. 1 in rebounds and blocked shots. Walton was probably the greatest passing center of all time and is equalled only by Bill Russell as a tenacious and enthusiastic performer. And no 6-11 center ever ran the fast break like Bill Walton. Unfortunately, his pro career has been sparse because he has been plagued with injuries to the back, legs, and feet. He has never played a complete season (by far the closest was his MVP year when he missed only 12 games) in his career. Walton's been with the San Diego (now L.A.) Clippers since 1979. He became a radical at UCLA and went public against war, abuse of the environment, and other topics. His concern over a wide range of non-sports issues had a tremendous influence on young athletes. For most of his pro years, however, he has kept a mighty low profile, no doubt distracted by difficulties in his own career.

■ Also born today: **KELLEN WINSLOW (1957)** phenomenal tight end for S.D. Chargers ... **EARLE "GREASY" NEALE (1891),** coached Philadelphia Eagles (1941-50), won NFL titles in 1948 and '49, died 1973.

■ **WALTER JOHNSON (1887)** — "Big Train," great right-handed fireballer who spent his entire 21-year career with the Washington Senators, born in Humboldt, Kan., (somebody must have called him the Humboldt Thunderbolt). Only Cy Young won more games than Johnson (416), who won 20 or more games 12 times, including ten years in a row (1910-19), leading the Senators to two pennants (1924 and '25). Johnson's 113 shutouts is the all-time record and his 3,508 career strikeouts stood as the record for more than a half century. Unlike many power pitchers, he was a low ERA pitcher

Walter Johnson

with a lifetime figure of 2.17 (with 11 seasons under 2.00!) and a control pitcher with an incredible two walks for every nine innings. He supposedly never threw at a batter. He was nearly unhittable anyway. Old films reveal Johnson as a sidearmer who had absolutely no follow-through despite being one of the hardest throwers ever. His right foot never left the rubber! Johnson had especially long arms and fingers that gave his fastball more pop and more movement. He died in 1946.

■ **JAMES NAISMITH (1861)** — The inventor of basketball, born in Canada. He went to McGill University there and after three years of studying for the ministry, switched to physical education, which he began teaching at Springfield (Mass.) College. In 1891, the department head gave Naismith the task of devising an indoor game during the cold winter months. Thus, basketball was born. Though Naismith's game was played with a soccer ball (I guess there weren't basketballs yet) and two peach baskets, 12 of his original 13 rules are still basic to the game. Naismith, who was later physical education director at the University of Kansas for 40 years, died in 1939.

NOTES

■ JIM KAAT (1938) —

The sixth baseball player to play in four decades. He

Jim Kaat

was a 20-year-old rookie with the Washington Senators in 1959 (they became the Minnesota Twins in 1961) and peaked in 1966, winning 25 games. Kaat was picked up on waivers at age 35 by the White Sox and had two straight 20-game seasons with them (in '74 and '75). He pitched for a few more teams until he finally retired in the middle of the 1983 season — his 25th year in the bigs, an all-time record for a pitcher. Kaat's longevity is attributable to more than talent. He was the kind of guy who shagged fly balls even when it was his turn to pitch. He loved the game and stayed in top physical condition. He was also a smart fundamental player, and one of the best fielding pitchers ever, earning 16 Gold Gloves. Although Kaat's name is never mentioned when discussing the great pitchers, his 283 career wins make him the fourth winningest lefty of all time, after Spahn, Carlton and Lefty Grove.

■ AL ATTLES (1936) —

S.F. Warriors player, coach, and executive. His 11-year career with the Warriors (first in Philadelphia, then in S.F.) is the longest ever in the history of the Warrior franchise. He was a tough, physical guard who averaged nine points a game from 1960 to 1971. He began as a player-coach in 1969 and was the longest tenured NBA coach when he retired in 1982. Attles worked well with over-achievers like himself and he got a lot out of a Warrior team in 1975 that consisted of 11 no-names and Rick Barry, winning the NBA title. After that, Attles' record is poor. Brilliant players, like Gus Williams and Jamaal Wilkes, were under-appreciated and allowed to leave as free agents. Attles couldn't develop a big man and actually played Clifford Ray over Robert Parish. During Attles' last six years, the Warriors failed to make the playoffs. Joe Niekro (1944)

Astros righty who achieved the 200-win plateau while brother Phil closes in on 300

■ **LOU AMBERS (1913)** — Ambers, lightweight champion of the world (1936-37, 1939-40), born Louis D'Ambrosio in Herkimer, N.Y., was known as the "Herkimer Hurricane." He fought Tony Canzoneri for the vacated lightweight title after Barney Ross stepped up to the welterweight division. Ambers, a former sparring partner of Canzoneri's, lost a 15-round decision but won the title a year later in a rematch (in another 15-round decision). Ambers is best known for his two title fights against Henry Armstrong, both of which also went 15 rounds. In the first one,

Lou Ambers

Armstrong took Ambers' title from him but Ambers won it back a year later. Both fights took their toll on the fighters. Neither would be the same again. The ring world was shocked when Ambers lost his title in 1940 to Lew Jenkins via a third-round KO. It was the first time Ambers had been knocked out. He tried a rematch a year later, got KO'd again, and retired — at age 27 — to join the U.S. Coast Guard. Ambers, managed by Al Weill, who later managed Rocky Marciano, was known as a clean liver who didn't smoke or drink and was a crowd pleaser. Though he lacked a knockout punch (only 28 KOs in his 88 wins), he was an aggressive and gallant performer.

■ **BUCKY HARRIS (1896)** —
A major league baseball manager for 29 years, born in Port Jervis, N.Y. (sounds like it's not too far from Herkimer). Harris caused a sensation by leading his Washington Senators to a pennant in 1924 and then defeating John J. McGraw's vaunted New York Giants in the Series. Harris, only 28, was a rookie manager. For the rest of his career he would be known as the "boy manager." He won his second pennant the very next year. During the next three decades, Harris finished in the first division twice — leading the Yankees to the 1947 pennant and then finishing third the following year — for which he was fired. He also managed the Tigers, Red Sox and Phillies.

NOTES

■ **BOB GIBSON (1935)** — The great St. Louis Cardinal right-hander and one of the fiercest competitors ever to suit up. Before he began his baseball career, Gibson was a star basketball player at Creighton University, averaged more than 20 points a game and played a year with the Harlem Globetrotters. He pitched from 1959 to 1974, finished with 251 wins, 3,117 strikeouts, two Cy Young Awards, and an MVP award in 1968 for dominating the National League with a 22-9 record that featured a stingy 1.12 ERA, the lowest in the 20th

Bob Gibson

century. He also led the league in strikeouts (268, with only 62 walks in more than 300 innings), shutouts (13), and had 28 complete games in 34 starts. In the World Series against Detroit, he set Series records with 17 strikeouts in a game and 35 in a Series. A year earlier, 1967, Gibson pitched the Cardinals to a World Series triumph against the Red Sox. He was 3-0, all complete games, throwing a six-hitter in Game One, a five-hitter in Game Four, and a three-hitter in Game Seven. Gibson homered in that seventh game and again in the '68 Series, making him the first pitcher (Dave McNally later did it) to hit two home runs in World Series competition. Somewhat like Juan Marichal, Gibson was a menacing figure on the mound who featured a big kick, a scowl, and a contempt for hitters.

■ Also born today: golfer **TOM WEISKOPF (1942)**, one of six to win $2 million, supposedly has one of the shortest fuses on a golf course ... **WHITEY HERZOG (1931)**, Cardinals manager and GM ... swimmer **FLORENCE CHADWICK (1918)**, the first woman to swim the English Channel both ways.

NOTES

■ **JACK CLARK (1955) —**
A great player kept back by an awful organization, the San Francisco Giants. Clark was much maligned (by management, press and fans alike) in the NL — despite being one of the best. His burden has been — because of his great ability — to have to play the role of savior for an organization that has too many flaws for one man to compensate for. He has always been the scapegoat — an unusual role for the best player on the Giants. Anyway, in '85 Clark got lucky and was traded to the Cardinals — the rest is history as he looks to win the MVP, and have a great World Series.

Jack Clark

■ **CLYDE "BULLDOG" TURNER (1919) —**
Hall of Fame center for the Chicago Bears (1940-52) Turner got his nickname when he showed up at the Chicago Bears camp as first-round draft choice out of Hardin-Simmons wearing chaps, boots and a 10-gallon hat — looking ready to "bulldog" steers. That 20-year old made an immediate impression in the NFL. He became a link in the chain of dominating centers, beginning with George Trafton in the '20s, Mel Hein in the '30s, Turner in the '40s, and Chuck Bednarik in the '50s. He had halfback speed at 235 pounds. Also a gifted linebacker, he led the league in interceptions in 1942. In 1947, he returned a Sammy Baugh pass 96 yards for a TD (Baugh caught him at the 'Skins 12-yard line but couldn't bring him down). Born in Sweetwater, Texas.

NOTES

Sports birthdays/Nov. 11

■ PIE TRAYNOR (1899) —
The all-time third baseman, born Harold Joseph Traynor on this date in Framingham, Mass. He played his

Pie Traynor

whole 17-year career (1920-35, 1937) with the Pittsburgh Pirates (compiling a .320 lifetime BA), managing them for six years (1934-39), and later becoming the Pirates announcer. Traynor was the best defensive third baseman of his era — quick, rangy, and with a great arm. And along with his high average hitting, he was a solid RBI hitter, knocking in 100 runs or more seven times. The Pirates retired his No. 20 jersey. He died in 1972.

■ RABBIT MARANVILLE (1891) —
The tiny Rabbit (5-5, 155 pounds), Leo Durocher's mentor, was born Walter James Vincent Maranville in Springfield, Mass. Leo, who wrote a glowing portrait of him in his autobiography, "Nice Guys Finish Last," learned never-say-die hardball from Maranville, a shortstop who survived 23 years in the major leagues (mostly with the Boston Braves) with a slick glove, quick mind, and just plain guts. Rabbit was the sparkplug of the Braves' "Miracle Team" of 1914 — in last place on July 4th, they won the pennant (by 10½ games), then swept Connie Mack's vaunted A's in the first World Series four-game sweep. Maranville and Traynor were both born in Massachusetts and played together at Pittsburgh, forming the left side of the infield from 1922 to 1924. They also both had cute nicknames.

■ Also born today: **AL SCHACHT (1892)**, "The Clown Prince of Baseball" ... golfer **FUZZY ZOELLER (1951)**, won the U.S. Open, but developed a serious back ailment. *Great comeback in '85, winning Bay Hill Classic.*

■CARL MAYS (1891) —

Right-hander with the Red Sox and Yankees, born in Liberty, Ky. Mays and a southpaw named Ruth were pitching mainstays for the Red Sox in the late 1910s. Both were traded to the Yankees, Mays in 1919, a year before Ruth. In 1920, Mays, a stocky submarine specialist, struck Ray Chapman, Cleveland shortstop, with a pitch to the temple. Chapman died hours later, the only fatality to occur in a major league game. Mays was not a popular player (and Chapman was). A petition circulated to ban him for life was signed by many players, includ-

Carl Mays

ing Ty Cobb. Though the petition was unsuccessful, enough bad feeling toward him persists to this day, denying his induction into the Hall of Fame despite strong credentials: A brilliant 207-126 won-loss record, a 2.92 lifetime ERA, and five 20-game seasons (including two other 19-game seasons). Curiously, Mays and Chapman were both born in Kentucky in 1891. Mays died a half-century after Chapman, in 1971.

■NADIA COMANECI (1961) —

This Romanian-born gymnast was 14 when she captivated the world (and the judges)at the 1976 Olympics, not only winning the gold medal in the combined exercises but, for the first time in history, scoring a perfect 10 in each event — the beam, asymmetrical bars, floor exercises, and the vaulting horse.

■R. C. OWENS (1933) — R. C. (the "R" is for Raleigh), best known for his years as a receiver with the 49ers (1957-61). R. C. (out of tiny College of Idaho) and Y. A. (Tittle, that is) formed an exciting duo with their patented "alley-oop" pass plays featuring Owens' dynamic leaping ability.

NOTES

■ EARL SANDE (1898) —

Beloved jockey who helped define the Golden Age of Sports in the 1920s — along with Ruth, Grange, Dempsey, Tilden, and Bobby Jones — was born in Groton, S.D. Curiously, Sande almost got killed in his very first race because of a freak accident. He survived that to ride two Kentucky Derby winners (Zev in 1923 and Flying Ebony in 1925) and earn a small fortune before retiring while still in his 20s. He lost that fortune in the stock market crash of 1929, came out of retirement, and won his third Kentucky Derby, riding Gallant Fox to Triple Crown glory

Earl Sande

in 1930. Sportswriter Damon Runyon immortalized him in verse, a paean to "that handy/Guy named Sande/bootin' a winner in!"

■ EDDIE ANDERSON (1900) —

Great football coach at DePaul (1926-32) and especially at Holy Cross (1933-38, 1950-64) and Iowa (1939-43, 1946-49), born in Oskaloosa, Iowa. Anderson played end at Notre Dame under Knute Rockne (1918-21), and later took Holy Cross and Iowa teams that were in the doldrums and made them powerhouses. He won 201 games overall, one of only a handful of college football coaches to win more than 200 games. Anderson was also an M.D. and maintained a practice through the 1930s and '40s.

■ Also born today: **OLGA CONNOLLY (1932)**, represented Czechoslovakia as Olga Fikotova at the 1956 Olympics, won gold medal in the discus; met American hammer-thrower Harold Connolly there in Melbourne, Australia (he also won gold medal) and they soon married (and later divorced) ... **JIM DELSING (1925)**, light-hitting outfielder with several AL teams, achieved trivia status in 1951 when St. Louis Browns owner Bill Veeck sent up 4-foot-3 midget Eddie Gaedel to pinch-hit; after walking promptly on four pitches, Gaedel was taken out of the game for a pinch runner — that was Jim Delsing.

NOTES

■ **WILLIE HERNANDEZ (1955)** —
Winner of 1984 Cy Young Award and also 1984 MVP.
A lefty reliever with a good
screwball, Hernandez had an
up-and-down career until a couple of years ago. He spent six
erratic years with the Cubs
(1977-82), going 8-2 in 1978 and
1-9 in 1980. Going to contending
teams did a lot for his consistency. In 1983, he was dealt to the
Phillies (who won the pennant)
and was 9-4. In 1984 he was
dealt to the Tigers (who won the
pennant) and was 9-3 with 32
saves and a league-leading 1.92
ERA. Yes, he had a great year.
But I would've given the Cy
Young Award to Jack Morris.

Willie Hernandez

■ **JIM PIERSALL (1929)** — Born in Waterbury, Conn.,
one of the great defensive outfielders of all time. He
played 17 years mostly with the Boston Red Sox
(1950, 1952-67), finished with a .272 lifetime BA, and
was a mainstay in center field between Ted Williams in
left and Jackie Jensen in right. He is the only player in
Red Sox history to go 6-for-6 in a nine-inning game. His
1955 autobiography, "Fear Strikes Out," (made into a
movie with Tony Perkins), tells of his early erratic years
with the Sox and his "nervous breakdown." A baseball
announcer in Chicago, Oakland and elsewhere, Piersall
has remained controversial.

■ Also born today: **MORIHEI UYESHIBA (1883)**, Japanese founder of aikido, a non-violent martial art which
literally means "way of spiritual harmony" He said
"winning means winning over the discord in yourself" ...
JAMES "TED" MEREDITH (1892), set records in 440-
yard and 800-meter runs that stood for 15 years ...
JACK SIKMA (1955), Seattle Supersonics center since
1977.

NOTES

■ **FRANK THOMAS (1898)** —
Hall of Fame football coach at Alabama, 1931 to 1946,

Frank Thomas

born in Munice, Ind. He was a quarterback at Notre Dame under Knute Rockne. Thomas succeeded Wallace Wade at Alabama (Wade went over to Duke) and had a long reign, amassing one of the 10 best winning percentages in college football history. He won 141 games, lost 32 and tied 8, and from 1935 to 1945 had the best coaching record in the country (90-17-7). He was the 2nd coach to send teams to four major bowls, including two Rose Bowl appearances in 1935 (beating Stanford, 29-13) and 1938 (losing to Cal, 13-0). "The Top Sergeant" was an arch conservative coach who stayed with the Notre Dame box formation that he learned from Rockne throughout his career and who argued against two-platoon football. He retired because of ill health (he had a bad heart) at age 48 while still one of the top coaches (only a year before, Alabama had its fourth unbeaten season under Thomas). He died in 1954.

■ Also born today: **FRED BREINING (1955)**, probably the only S.F. native ever to pitch for the S. F. Giants; traded in 1983 to Expos ... **GUS BELL (1928)**, Reds/Pirates outfielder of the 1950s, father of Buddy Bell; currently manages a temporary employment agency in Cincinnati ... **I.A. HOROWITZ (1907)**, chess writer and editor of Chess Review ... '76 Olympic discus champ **MAC WILKENS (1950)** ... and two literary figures: **MARIANNE MOORE (1887)**, poet and rabid Brooklyn Dodgers fan, and **FRANKLIN PIERCE ADAMS (1881)**, NYC columnist who wrote the famous poem, *"Baseball's Sad Lexicon"* (*Tinker To Evers To Chance*), that many feel got Joe Tinker into the Hall of Fame without his meriting it.

NOTES

Bobby Cruickshank

■ **BOBBY CRUICKSHANK (1894)** "Wee Bobby," a great golfer, born in Scotland. A diminutive man with a compact swing, he is probably best known for a match he lost. It was the U.S. Open in 1923. He tied the great Bobby Jones (only to lose in a playoff) on a long iron shot that buffs still talk about. For most of his life, Cruickshank lived in Florida, serving for most of that time as a golf pro at a local club. He died in 1975.

■ Also born today: **JO JO WHITE (1946)**, Celtics guard of the 1970s, averaged 17 points per game and played in more than 500 consecutive games. Drafted out of college (Kansas) in the three major sports (a la Dave Winfield) — the Celts, the Dallas Cowboys, and the Cincinnati Reds ... Righty pitcher **PAUL FOYTACK (1930)**, in 1963, pitching for the Angels, he gave up four consecutive home runs (probably a unique distinction); so how come the manager (Bill Rigney) didn't take him out after the third homer? ... **HARVEY MARTIN (1950)**, a mainstay in the Cowboys' Doomsday Defense for a decade ... **MEL PATTON (1924)**, the sprinter who set 100-yard standard at 9.3 and won 200-meter gold in '48 Olympics ... and another sprinter, **HERB WASHINGTON (1951)**, the trackman hired by Charlie Finley for A's as baseball's first "designated runner." Dwight Gooden (1964), the best pitcher in baseball and the youngest player in the NL.

NOTES

■ **TOM SEAVER (1944)** — "Tom Terrific".
He shocked the baseball world in 1983 by going 15-11 and being the Chicago White Sox's best pitcher. He

still has that classic form. His right knee is dirty after the first inning. Among his many monuments are the most consecutive 200-plus strikeout seasons (9), the most consecutive strikeouts (10), and the highest career percentage compared to his team's percentage (more than 120 points). Of course, he will always be identified with That Championship Season, 1969, when he was 25-7, won the Cy

Tom Seaver

Young Award, and carried the Amazin' Mets to World Series glory. *Going for the 300-win club in '85.*

■ **ELVIN HAYES (1945)** —
" The Big E," an NBA great for 15 seasons. Hayes was the college Player of the Year in 1968 with the University of Houston, played most of his career with the Washington Bullets, finishing up in 1983 with the Rockets. Hayes is No. 1 in games played (1,303) and minutes played (50,000 even), the third-leading all-time scorer (after Kareem and Wilt), and the third all-time rebounder (after Wilt and Bill Russell). It's true that Hayes was a gunner, disdained defense, and often sulked, but the aforementioned stats balance out the picture and can't be denied.

■ Also born today: **BOB MATHIAS (1930)**, won the decathlon at the 1948 Olympics at age 17, the youngest ever to win that event (or any other Olympic track and field event), and won it again in the 1952 Games (the only man ever to win it twice until Daley Thompson — '80-'84) ... **GEORGE STALLINGS (1867)**, managed the "Miracle Team," the 1914 Boston Braves; in last place on July 4th, they won pennant, then beat Connie Mack's heavily favored A's in four straight, the first World Series sweep.

NOTES

■ **FORREST "PHOG" ALLEN (1885)** —
Second winningest coach in college basketball history,
born in Jamesport, Mo. Allen
began coaching in 1908, replac-
ing the venerable James Naismith, the inventor of basketball,
at the University of Kansas. Allen
coached for 39 seasons, winning
24 conference championships,
an NCAA title in 1952, and won
771 games, second only to
Adolph Rupp's 874 (Rupp played
college ball at Kansas and was a
protege of Allen's). Allen's
teams (like Rupp's) specialized
in defense and ball-control. Allen
founded the National Association

Phog Allen

of Basketball Coaches in 1927 and later worked hard to
include basketball on the Olympics program. Incidental-
ly, Allen grew in Independence, Mo., on the same street
as future President, Harry Truman.

■ **JACK TATUM (1948)** —
The Oakland Raiders free safety of the 1970s.
Born in Cherryville, N.C., he was an All-American
at Ohio State and was the Raiders' first draft choice in
1971. He became one of the hardest-hitting defensive
backs in NFL history and set the tone for the Raiders'
rowdy style. Tatum holds the NFL record of 104 yards
on a fumble recovery. He is best known, however, for
his infamous hit on Darryl Stingley in 1979 that ended
the wide receiver's career — and almost his life —
paralyzing his body from the neck down. Tatum defends
himself in his book, "They Call Me Assassin."

■ Also born today: **MARJORIE GESTRING (1922)**,
youngest ever to win an Olympic gold medal—at age
13, in springboard diving ... golfer **CRAIG WOOD
(1901)**, won the U.S. Open and Masters in 1941 ... **DON
LOFGRAN (1928)**, USF basketball All-American, led
team to 1949 NIT title... **ROY SIEVERS (1926)**, AL rookie
of the year in 1949, hit 318 career HRs, mostly with the
Senators ... **PAUL WIGGIN (1934)**, ex Stanford coach, Pro
Bowl defensive end for the Cleveland Browns from 1957 to
1967. Come to think of it, how many great coaches have
been down linemen?

NOTES

■ ROY CAMPANELLA (1921) —

"Campy," the great Brooklyn Dodgers catcher. Born

in Philadelphia, he was a star in the Negro Leagues before breaking in with the Dodgers in 1948 — one of the first black players to enter the majors after Jackie Robinson broke down the barrier a year earlier. He and Stan Musial are the only National League players ever to win three MVP awards. In only ten seasons (averaging about 120 games a season), Campy hit 242 home runs. Johnny Bench (in a much longer career) is the only NL catcher to hit more. Campanella

Roy Campanella

is considered by many to be the best defensive catcher ever. He had a cannon arm and, despite his stocky build (5'9½", 190 lbs.), pounced on everything hit in front of the plate. In 1958, tragedy struck Campanella in the form of an auto accident that rendered him paralyzed from the waist down. He was a beloved and inspiring figure, and his autobiography, "It's Great To Be Alive," was made into a TV movie. He has owned a liquor store for many years and does public relations work for the Dodgers.

■ Also born today: **TED TURNER (1938)**, "The Mouth of the South," owner of the Atlanta Braves, Atlanta Hawks, and Turner Broadcasting System, not to mention leading yachtsman; his releasing Phil Niekro in 1983 was unforgivable ... **FRANK X. SHIELDS (1910)**, tennis player, uncle of Brooke Shields ... **JOSE CAPABLANCA (1888)**, Cuban chess genius, world champion, 1920-27; from 1916 to 1924 he never lost a game ... **AHMAD RASHAD (1949)**, brilliant WR, U. of Oregon All-American as Bobby Moore... **BOB BOONE (1947)**, Angels catcher, son of Ray "Ike" Boone.

NOTES

■ **CLARK GRIFFITH (1869)** — "The Old Fox."
Baseball player, manager, and owner, born in Stringtown, Mo. Griffith won 239 games and lost 148 as a small (5-foot-6½, 156 pounds) righthander with several teams in the 1890s and early 1900s. He managed from 1901 to 1920, a player-manager for a few years (the only pitcher I can think of to also manage at the same time), notably in 1901 when he managed the Chicago White Sox to the first ever American League pennant and pitched them there, too, with a league-leading 24-7 won-loss record. Griffith, a co-organizer of the American League

Clark Griffith

before its initial season in 1901, took over ownership of the Washington Senators in 1923 and held it until his death in 1955. The Senators (later the Twins) continued to be owned by the Griffith family until they sold the club in 1983.

■ **LEON CADORE (1891)** —
A 68-72 lifetime pitcher with the Brooklyn Dodgers (1915-23) who has one big claim to fame, was born in Chicago. Cadore achieved immortality on May 1, 1920 when he and Joe Oeschger (born in the same year) of the Boston Braves hooked up in the longest game ever played in major league history— a 26-inning 1-1 tie. Unbelievably, both pitchers went all the way.

■ Also born today: **MARK GASTINEAU (1956)**, N.Y. Jets hotdog defensive end, earns $850,000 and is probably the best pass-rusher in the NFL (when Fred Dean isn't playing) ... **KENESAW MOUNTAIN LANDIS (1866)**, achieved fame as judge in 1907 when he fined Standard Oil a record $29 million; in 1921 became the first commissioner of baseball in wake of Chicago "Black Sox" scandal; reigned until his death in 1944. .... **JAY JOHNSTONE** and **RICK MONDAY**, both born on this date in 1945, both left-hand-hitting outfielders, and both ex-Dodgers.

■ **STAN MUSIAL (1920)** —
"Stan the Man," the greatest left-handed hitter in N. L. history.

Stan Musial

A 20-year-old rookie in 1941, Musial played his entire career with the St. Louis Cardinals, retiring after the 1963 season with a lifetime .331 batting average, 475 home runs, seven batting titles and three MVP awards. Consistency was his hallmark. Of his 3,630 hits (an NL record until Pete Rose broke it last year), 1,815 were at home and 1,815 were on the road. He didn't hit under .300 until his 18th season in the major leagues. And he was durable. At age 41, he hit .330 with 19 homers and 82 RBIs. An iron-man, he is one of only three players to appear in more than 3,000 games. Musial also is famous for torturing Brooklyn Dodger pitching throughout his career. He has been a restaurateur in St. Louis and is currently a vice president of the Cardinals.

■ **SID LUCKMAN (1916)** —
The first great pro football T-formation quarterback. Born in Brooklyn, a star at Columbia, he spent a brilliant NFL career with the Chicago Bears from 1939 to 1950, leading them to four NFL titles, including the 73-0 drubbing of the Redskins in the 1940 title game. Luckman is one of only five QBs to throw seven TDs in a game. He is second in average yards per completion (8.42) and still holds the record for most TDs (5) in a playoff game.

■ Also born today: **FRED LINDSTROM (1905)**, N.Y. Giants third baseman (1924-32), the youngest player ever to appear in a World Series — six weeks shy of 19; Senators beat Giants in Series, winning seventh game on routine grounder that hit a pebble and bounced over Lindstrom's head ... **EARL MONROE (1944)**, the "Pearl" of many moves with the Bullets and Knicks... Celtics forward **CEDRIC MAXWELL (1955)** ... rodeo star **LARRY MAHAN (1943)** ... Lombardi's great center, **JIM RINGO (1932)**.

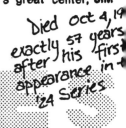

Died Oct 4, 19 exactly 57 years after his first appearance in '24 Series

NOTES

■ **LEW BURDETTE (1926)** —
Braves right-hander (in Boston and Milwaukee) who tamed the N.Y. Yankees in the 1957 World Series. Born Selva Lewis Burdette in Nitro, W.V., he came up with the Yankees, who reluctantly gave him up to the Braves for Johnny Sain. Sain helped the Yanks in his twilight years but Burdette became the righty mainstay of a great Braves team for a decade, averaging about 17 wins a year. Burdette won three complete games against the Yankees in the '57 Series — a 4-2 seven-hitter in Game Two, a 1-0 gem against Whitey Ford (only the best World Series pitcher ever) in Game Five, and his second straight shutout, 5-0, in Game Seven to wrap up the Series right in Yankee Stadium. Burdette also deserves a niche in the Hall of Obscurity, being the winning pitcher in Harvey Haddix's heartbraking 1-0 loss in 13 innings after Haddix pitched 12 perfect innings. Burdette's 13-inning shutout was a 12-hitter (all singles). His lifetime won-loss record was 203-144 and among his various pitches was a spitter. Burdette became a public relations man for a cable TV company in Georgia.

Billie Jean King

■ Also born today:
BILLIE JEAN KING (1943), tennis player, pioneer in women's sports as athlete and promoter; the first woman in three decades to win the singles, doubles and mixed doubles championships at both Wimbledon and the U.S. Open. She's the sister of ex-Giants reliever Randy Moffitt.... "Hacksaw" **JACK REYNOLDS (1947)**, 49ers' linebacker, got one more Super Bowl ring and a Hall of Fame shot, too ... **GARDNAR MULLOY (1914)**, another tennis player, best known, with partner Billy Talbert, for their four national doubles titles in the 1940s ... **LYMAN BOSTOCK (1950)**, a lifetime .318 hitter, killed at age 27 by a shotgun fired by the irate husband of a woman sitting next to Bostock in a car... **HARRY EDWARDS (1942)**, sociologist, sports activist, author, teacher at Cal, a leader of the black athlete revolt in the 1960s ... "The Bull," **GREG LUZINSKI (1950)**, for whom the DH was invented, retired with 307 home runs ...

■ SHANE GOULD (1956) —

"queen of the pool"

Shane Gould

at 1972 Summer Olympics. Born in Australia, she won three gold medals, two silver medals and one bronze. She waved a toy kangaroo after winning each of her three gold medals, which were for the 200m individual medley, the 400m freestyle and the 1500m freestyle — all won in world record time. She appeared in 12 heats and final races, more than any other female swimmer in Olympic history. At age 15 she became the only champion ever to hold all of the women's freestyle swimming titles.

■ LUIS TIANT (1940) —

"El Tiante," winning pitcher of 225 major league games. Born in Havana, Cuba, where his father was a baseball great, Tiant broke in with Cleveland in 1964 (he was 21-9 in 1968 and 9-20 in 1969), went briefly to Minnesota, then spent eight seasons with the Red Sox, where he had three 20-game seasons, and finished up with the Yankees, retiring in 1981. Tiant was something to watch. His delivery had every piece of deception known to his profession — the fluttering glove, the head fakes, the turn to second before delivery, and the wide assortment of stuff often thrown sidearm. A true craftsman, complete with big post-game cigars.

■ Also born today: **DICK KAZMAIER (1930)**, triple-threat tailback for Princeton, won Heisman Trophy in 1951 ... **OSWALD TOWER (1883)**, basketball pioneer, official rules interpreter from 1915 to 1959, longtime editor of The Basketball Guide, and a referee for 35 years ... Tennis player **LEW HOAD (1934)**, from Australia (like Shane Gould), won Wimbledon in '56 and '57 ... **KEN KAVANAUGH (1916)**, Chicago Bears end of the 1940s . .

Sports birthdays/Nov. 24

■ **OSCAR ROBERTSON (1938)** — "The Big O," revolutionized the NBA as the first dominating big guard. Born in Charlotte, Tenn., Robertson was a high school legend in Indianapolis and then a great All-American at the University of Cincinnati, where he led the nation in scoring for three years. He was drafted in 1960 by the Cincinnati Royals and caused an immediate sensation, averaging 30.5 points per game (making him the highest scoring guard in NBA history) and leading the league in assists with a record-setting 9.7 per game average. After a decade

Oscar Robertson

with the lowly Royals, Robertson joined Kareem Abdul-Jabbar on the Milwaukee Bucks, a combo that resulted in an NBA title in 1970-71. Robertson ended his 14-year career with more than 26,000 points and ranks fourth behind Kareem, Wilt Chamberlain and Elvin Hayes. He is also the all-time assist leader. Many regard Robertson as the greatest guard of all-time — and even the greatest all-around basketball player.

■ Also born today: **JOE "DUCKY" MEDWICK (1911)**, outfielder with Gas House Gang Cardinals in the 1930s; lifetime .324 hitter, MVP in 1937, the year he won the Triple Crown ... **JOHN HENRY JOHNSON (1929)**, great running back with the Steelers, Lions and 49ers from 1954 to 1966, rushed for 6,574 yards, one of the top marks before the expansion era, had a lifetime 4.4 yards per carry (born in Waterproof, La.) ... **BOB FRIEND (1930)**, righty pitcher with 197-230 won-loss record in 16-year career (15 with the Pirates) who almost joined Bobo Newsom and Jake Powell as the only pitchers to win more than 200 games and still have more losses. ... **RUDY TOMJANOVICH (1948)**, high-scoring NBA forward whose career virtually ended when his face was re-arranged by Kermit Washington ... pole vaulter **STEVE SMITH (1951)**, the first to go over 18 feet indoors ... Dodger catcher **STEVE YEAGER (1948)**, World Series MVP of 1981.

NOTES

■ **JOE DIMAGGIO (1914)** — "The Yankee Clipper," "Joltin' Joe," one of the reverberating names in human history.

Joe DiMaggio

Though he was born in Martinez, California, San Francisco claims DiMaggio as its own. He learned the game on S.F. diamonds and played for the beloved Seals until breaking in with the Yankees in 1936, leading the AL in triples and hitting .323 with 29 HRs and 125 RBI. He went on to win three MVP awards (1939, 1941, 1947) and two batting titles (1939, 1940), amass a .325 lifetime BA and 361 homers (despite losing three peak years to World War II), and set (and still holds, four decades later) the most famous and impressive baseball record — hitting safely in 56 consecutive games. You'd expect a singles hitter such as Pete Rose to have that record, not a power-hitter who didn't once bunt during the streak. DiMaggio had no weakness. He hit for power and average, was a tremendous outfielder with a great arm, and an excellent baserunner. And he was much more — an inspiring performer who was a genuine hero of millions, personifying quiet dignity and classic grace. No one who watched him play will ever forget him.

■ Also born today: **JOE GANS (1874)**, lightweight champion, considered by many to be the greatest lightweight ever, lost only eight times in 156 fights, died of TB at age 35 ... **LENNY MOORE (1933)**, brilliant running back and flanker with the Baltimore Colts from 1956 to 1967 (the closest thing to Lenny Moore today is Marcus Allen) ... **EDDIE SHORE (1902)**, Boston Bruins hockey immortal in 1920s and '30s; seven-time first-team All-NHL, four-time winner of the Hart Trophy (for MVP); he and Bobby Orr are considered the greatest defensemen ever.

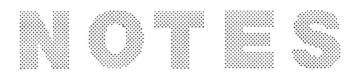

NOTES

■ **VERNON "LEFTY" GOMEZ (1909)** —
Yankee lefty pitcher of the 1930s, and the man who gave flaky southpaws a good name. Gomez, born in Rodeo, California, was a 20-year-old rookie with the Yankees in 1930. The following year he won 21 games and was their ace for a decade. He was an incredible 26-5 in 1934 and led the league in ERA, strikeouts, complete games, and shutouts. He won 189 career games, losing only 102 for a .649 percentage, among the top 10 figures in the 20th century. He had a perfect

Lefty Gomez

6-0 World Series record in five Series. Gomez was also known as "Goofy" because of his zany humor and quotable quotes. My favorite story about him is the time, during a tense World Series game, when he stood on the mound and suddenly looked up and slowly followed the flight of birds passing overhead. Talk about smelling the flowers along the way!

■ Also born today: **SAMUEL RESHEVSKY (1911)**, U.S. chess champion (1936-44, 1946, 1969-71), the most famous of chess prodigies, he began at age 4 and could play blindfolded at 8 ... **JAN STENERUD (1942)**, has kicked more field goals than anyone, breaking George Blanda's record in 1983 ... **MIKE McTIGUE (1892)**, light-heavyweight champion 1923-25, won title from an African, "Battling Siki," taking a 20-round decision in Dublin on St. Patrick's Day!...**BOB ELLIOTT (1916)**, 1948 NL MVP third baseman with Boston Braves ... **"INDIAN JOE" GUYON (1892)**, born on the White Earth Indian Reservation in Minnesota. Guyon, a running back, is a member of the college and pro Hall of Fame. He played college ball at Carlisle with Jim Thorpe and at Georgia Tech under coach John Heisman, and played pro ball with the Canton Bulldogs (again with Thorpe).

■ **JOE BUSH (1892)** — "Bullet Joe," righty pitcher who won 196 games with the A's (1912-17), Red Sox (1918-21), Yankees (1922-24), and others, was born Leslie Ambrose Bush in Brainerd, Minn. Bush had some good years with the A's. Even when he was 15-22 and 12-17, in 1916 and 1917, his ERA was 2.57 and 2.47. He had three good years with the Red Sox before he joined the long list of Bosox pitchers who were dealt to the Yankees — Babe Ruth, Carl Mays, Herb Pennock, down to Sparky Lyle in recent times. And there he had winning seasons with his third straight team. He led the AL in percentage with a 26-7 season in 1922, and thereby became the only pitcher in modern major league history to win 25 or more games in a season without pitching a shutout. After appearing in a World Series with his first three teams, Bush's career declined with the St. Louis Browns, Senators and Pirates.

Bruce Lee

■ **BRUCE LEE (1940)** — Martial artist and actor, was born in San Francisco. He was baptised Liu Yuen Kam, which means "protector of San Francisco." Lee went to Hollywood but couldn't make it there. He did play "Kato" in 30 segments of "The Green Hornet" on TV in 1966-67. He then went to Hong Kong and became an immediate sensation in such films as "Fist of Fury,""Enter The Dragon," and "The Chinese Connection." Lee was a spectacular artist, a kung-fu and karate master who studied with his father and other masters. He died mysteriously ("of apoplexy") at age 32.

■ Also born today: **TED HUSING (1910)**, considered in a class by himself as a sports announcer on radio in 1930s and 40s; retired in 1954 because of failing eyesight, wrote autobiography, "My Eyes Are In My Heart" ... **JOHNNY BLOOD (1903)**, born John McNally, great running back with the Packers (1925-39), took alias from Rudolph Valentino film, "Blood and Sand"... **WILLIE PASTRANO (1935)**, the light-heavy champ 1963-65 ... and three Miami Dolphins: **DON STROCK (1950), DURIEL HARRIS (1954)** and **A.J. DUHE (1955)**.

■**PAUL WARFIELD (1942)** — Brilliant wide receiver for the Cleveland Browns (1964-69, 1976-77) and Miami Dolphins (1970-74). An excellent all-around high school athlete in Warren, Ohio (his birthplace), Warfield went to Ohio State where he was a two-way halfback and an All-American in 1963. He was the Browns' No. 1 draft choice and they won five conference titles in his six years with them. He played on the 17-0 Dolphins team in 1972 and picked up two Super Bowl rings with them. Warfield caught 85 TD passes. Only Don Hutson (99)

Paul Warfield

and Don Maynard (88) caught more. His 20.1-yards-per-catch average is an NFL record and his ratio of a TD for every fifth catch has been equalled only by Hutson. Warfield was inducted into the Hall of Fame in 1983.

■Also born today: **CECIL HART (1883)**, hockey pioneer, manager and coach of the Montreal Canadiens; the Hart Memorial Trophy, emblematic of the league's MVP, was named after him ... **SIXTO LEZCANO (1953)**, a good all-around baseball player; Sixto can play for me anytime ... **WES WESTRUM (1922)**, N.Y. Giants catcher, 1947-57, excellent receiver, .217 lifetime hitter, managed Giants 1974-75. **FRANCIE LARRIEU (1952)**, America's top woman miler and two-miler of the 1970s, born in Palo Alto ... **PRESTON DENNARD (1955)**, L.A. Rams wide receiver and 49er nemesis.

NOTES

■DAVE BING (1943) —

One of the high-scoring guards in basketball history.

Dave Bing

Born in Washington, D.C., Bing played college ball at Syracuse and was the Detroit Pistons' first draft choice in 1966. He retired in 1978 (after three seasons with the Washington Bullets) with 18,327 points, fifth among guards in NBA history (behind Oscar Robertson, Jerry West, Hal Greer and Gail Goodrich). Bing was a scoring machine. Twice he averaged 27 ppg and had a 20.3 career average. After playing nearly-full seasons for a decade, leg injuries forced his retirement. He's past his five-year waiting period of Hall of Fame induction. Hopefully, that bit of business will be taken care of soon.

■MINNIE MINOSO (1922) —

Born in Havana, Saturnino Orestes Arrieta Armas Minoso was a 28-year-old rookie in 1951 and people are still saying he was robbed of the rookie-of- the-year award (which went to Gil McDougald). A .299 lifetime hitter, mostly with the White Sox, Minoso became the oldest player to appear in a major league game when, in 1980, as the Chisox hitting coach, he pinch-hit.

■TOMMY LOUGHRAN (1902) —

Loughran, light-heavyweight champion (1927-29) and one of the all-time master boxers, was born in Philadelphia. He vacated his title in 1929 to fight as a heavyweight and got his title shot against Primo Carnera in 1934, losing a 15-round decision. Carnera had the biggest weight advantage in boxing history — he was 270 pounds while Loughran weighed 186.

■Also born today: DAVE RIGHETTI (1958), lefty starter-reliever with the N.Y. Yankees since 1981, son of Leo Righetti, a second baseman in the Yankee system. He pitched a no-hitter in his first full season, the first for a Yankee pitcher since Don Larsen's perfect game in '56, and was named AL Rookie of the Year ... VIN SCULLY (1927), "The Voice of the Dodgers" ... DWAINE BOARD (1956), The 49ers tend to win when this defensive end is in the lineup ... and FUZZY THURSTON (1933), great Packers guard of the 1960s.

NOTES

■ **BILL WALSH (1931)** —
49er coach since 1979. He coached at Stanford in 1977 and 1978 after spending eight years with the Cincinnati Bengals as Paul Brown's chief offensive assistant and a year as Tommy Prothro's offensive coordinator with the Chargers. Walsh inherited a 49er team that had won seven of its last 30 games and was still in shock from the Joe Thomas regime. In two years, the 49ers won the NFL title and, three years after that, made it No. 2. Let's face it,

Bill Walsh

Walsh *is* a genius — impeccable theoretically and organizationally. Offensively, he's way ahead of everybody. He made All-Americans out of Guy Benjamin and Steve Dils while at Stanford, developed Ken Anderson, Dan Fouts and — one who ranks with the greatest of all time — Joe Montana. He has drafted boldly, creating an instant dynasty with Montana, Clark, Lott, Turner, Craig, et al. He sure *looks* the part of genius with that silver mane and white V-neck sweater. Starring Jimmy Stewart. Walsh has created not only one of the best teams in recent years but one of the most interesting of all time.

■ Also born today: **FIRPO MARBERRY (1898)**, the first relief specialist, pitched with Washington Senators (1923-32) and Detroit (1933-35); in 1925, he served up the first of Lou Gehrig's 23 grand slams ... **WILLIAM H. LEWIS (1868)**, son of ex-slaves, football All-American center from Harvard, the first black All-American and probably the first black to captain a college team; later a lawyer, in 1911 he became the first black admitted to the American Bar Association ... horse trainer **MICHAEL "BUSTER" MILLERICK (1905)**, whose horses include Native Diver and Nasrullah ... **COTTON DAVIDSON (1931)**, Oakland Raiders QB of early 1960s, who threw six interceptions in one game (only tying the AFL record).

NOTES

◼ LEE TREVINO (1939) —

Great golfer, winner of the 1984 PGA tournament. Born

of Mexican parents in Dallas, Trevino, who has earned more than $3 million, grew up in poverty, learned his golf in the U.S. Marines, and paid his dues for years until shocking the golf world by winning the U.S. Open in 1968. Three years later, he became the first golfer to win the U.S. Open (again), the Canadian Open, and the British Open in the same year — in fact, within 20 days! In 1975, Trevino and two other golfers (Jerry Heard and Bobby Nicholls) were struck by lightning during the Western Open. All three survived but Trevino needed a disc removed surgically and has had back problems ever since. He had not won a major tournament in a decade until his PGA triumph. Trevino scorched the Birmingham, Ala., course for a 15 under-par 273, a PGA record, and shot four consecutive sub-70 rounds; the first golfer to accomplish that feat.

Lee Trevino

◼ Also born today: **WALTER ALSTON (1911)**, the Brooklyn and L.A. Dodgers manager from 1954 to 1976, all under standard one-year contracts ... **COOKIE LAVAGETTO (1912)**, who pinch-hit the ninth-inning double for the Dodgers to win a 1947 Series game against the Yankees and at same time spoil Floyd Bevans' no-hitter ... **MARTY "SLATS" MARION (1917)**, greatest defensive shortstop ever as well as answer to good trivia question (Who was manager of the last St. Louis Browns team in 1953?). ... **GEORGE FOSTER (1948)**, currently with the Mets, won the MVP award in 1977, led the NL in RBI three straight years, 1976-78, a feat accomplished only by Babe Ruth, Ty Cobb and Joe Medwick. ... **ED REULBACH (1882)**, righty pitcher mostly with the Cubs, owns a record that will never be broken and has only a slightly better chance of being equalled — he is the only pitcher in major-league history to throw shutouts in both games of a double-header.

■ BOB PETTIT (1932) —

One of the elite forwards in basketball history. Born Robert E. Lee Pettit in Baton Rogue, La., he was an All-American at LSU. In an 11-year pro career with the St. Louis Hawks (in his first year — 1954 — they were the Milwaukee Hawks), Pettit was named first-team All-NBA for 10 straight years. At 6-foot-9 and about 215 pounds, Pettit was considered too skinny by many when he graduated from LSU, but he proved to be an excellent rebounder, strong and able to finesse an opponent as well. Pettit was a scoring ma-

Bob Pettit

chine. He had a great jump shot and was difficult to stop around the basket. He was the first NBA player to score 20,000 points and he retired in 1965 as the highest scorer in NBA history (and the third best rebounder). His career average of 26.4 ppg is exceeded only by Wilt Chamberlain's, Elgin Baylor's and Jerry West's.

■ Also born today: **JAMES SULLIVAN (1903)**, Welsh rugby player; the sport's most famous kicker, he kicked 100 or more goals for 19 years ... **DAN JENKINS (1929)**, sports writer for Sports Illustrated and author of the football novel, "Semi-Tough" ... Two football players named Brown who were born on this day in the same year: **WILLIE BROWN (1940)**, all-time defensive back with the Raiders and currently a DB coach for them, and **BILL BROWN (1940)**, Viking fullback, 1962-75, still holds team career records for rushing (5,757 yards) and TDs (73) ... High-jumper **CHARLEY DUMAS (1937)**, in 1956 became the first to break seven feet ... **ANDRE RODGERS (1934)**, OK hit-no field shortstop with the Giants, Cubs and Pirates; a cricket star in the Bahamas where he was born.

■ **TOM FEARS (1923)** —
Brilliant wide receiver with the L.A. Rams, 1948 to

Tom Fears

1956. Born in Los Angeles, he played college ball at UCLA but was only an 11th round draft choice — and projected as a defensive back. Instead, he became an instant star as an end and led the NFL in receptions in his first three seasons (1948-50), a feat accomplished only by Don Hutson. In 1949 he set the receptions record with 77 and broke it again the next year with 84. No one caught 80 again for 14 years. Fears still holds the record for most receptions (18) in a single game (it occurred on his birthday in 1950). He and Elroy "Crazy Legs" Hirsch formed one of the best receiving tandems in NFL history. At 6-feet-2 and 215 pounds, Fears was known as a glue-fingered speedster who ran precise patterns. He was All-NFL in '49 and '50, and played on the Rams' only NFL championship team (in 1951).

■ **ALBERTO JUANTORENA (1951)** — This great Cuban runner, star of the 1976 Olympics in Montreal, is the only man ever to win the 400 and 800 meter races in the same Olympics. He broke an Olympic record in the 400 (44.26) and set a world record in the 800 (1:43.5), an event he never seriously attempted until that year. A former basketball player, he began running at age 20. Rather big and muscular, and called "El Caballo," the Horse, Juantorena was known for his long stride and graceful style.

■ Also born today: stock car racer **BOBBY ALLISON** (1937) ... two ex-NBA forwards, both born in 1951, both 6-9 and 220 pounds — **MIKE BANTOM** and **JIM BREWER** ... **HARRY "SUITCASE" SIMPSON (1925)**, one of the first black players in the American League, broke in with Cleveland in 1951 and played for several teams (the Yankees got him to be Elston Howard's roommate on the road), including three teams in his final season — true to his nickname.

■ **LEW JENKINS (1916)** –Jenkins, lightweight champion (1940-41), a brawler in and out of the ring, was born Verlin Jenks in Milburn, Texas.
He is considered one of the hardest hitting lightweights ever despite his thin frame and his undistinguished overall record (65-39-5), including "only" 47 KOs. He KO'd Lou Ambers, the 'Herkimer Hurricane," in the third round to win the title in 1940, KO'd him again in a rematch, but lost the title to Sammy Angott on a 15-round decision in 1941. Jenkins, managed for a while by his wife, was a hell-raiser known for his drunken sprees—usually

Lew Jenkins

on a motorcycle. He often showed up for fights drunk and that is why he lost so many of them.   Jenkins served in the Korean War and was a hero, winning the Silver Star. He died in 1981.

■ Also born today: **RANDY VATAHA (1948),**   pint-sized receiver Jim Plunkett used to play catch with at Stanford ... **ALEX DELVECCHIO (1931),** only Gordie Howe played in more NHL games... **BERNARD KING (1956),** drives the base line with ferocity like no one else in the NBA.   Bay Area basketball fans are still shaken by the Warriors' failure to sign the best thing to happen to their franchise in years. The former Tennessee star, Brooklyn-born, is back home with the NY Knicks ...   **HARVEY KUENN (1930)** rookie-of-the-year with the Tigers in 1953, winner of the 1959 batting title a lifetime .303 hitter — and a SF Giants outfielder in the early 1960s... **ADAM WALSH (1901),** center on the Notre Dame offensive line of the early 1920s called "The Seven Mules," beasts of burden for "The Four Horsemen." Known for his guttiness, he once played an entire game with two broken hands. ... **LUTHER H. GULICK (1865),** as "chairman of training" at Springfield College, he achieved immortality by asking his friend and colleague James Naismith to make up an indoor game for the cold winter months between football and baseball. Thus basketball was born. Gulick later influenced its development as the game's first booster. He died in 1918.

■ **PHILIP K. WRIGLEY (1894)** — The long-time owner of the Chicago Cubs (he died in 1981) was president of the Wrigley chewing gum company founded by his father, William Wrigley. P.K. was a community-oriented owner who disdained lights in Wrigley Field because he didn't want night games disturbing the neighbors —who have been disturbed by only one pennant in 45 years.

Jim Plunkett

■ **JIM PLUNKETT (1947)** — Celebrating his 36th today, the San Jose-born Heisman Trophy Award winner from Stanford has had an up-and-down career with the NE Patriots, 49ers and the Raiders, including Super Bowl glory in 1980. Not the prettiest QB of all-time, he is one of the guttiest and a great team leader.

■ **DAVE "BOO" FERRISS (1921)** — A right-handed pitcher with the Boston Red Sox, he won the first eight games of his rookie season in 1945, a record that stood until rookie Fernando Valenzuela equalled in 1981. Ferriss won 21 games that year and in 1946, when the Red Sox won the pennant, he was 25-6 with 26 complete games. Like Fernando, he was also a good hitter.

■ Also born today: chess player **HARRY PILLSBURY (1872)**, U.S. champion from 1897 until his death in 1906 at age 33 ... KC Chiefs DE **ART STILL (1955)**... **BRUCE DRAKE (1905)**, basketball All-American at Oklahoma in 1929, later coach there for 17 years ... golfer **LANNY WADKINS (1949)**, won U.S. Amateur in 1970, turned pro in '71, won the 1977 PGA tournament at the third extra hole after a tie with Gene Littler, finished second behind Trevino in 1984 PGA.

NOTES

■ **OTTO GRAHAM (1921)** —
Great Cleveland Browns quarterback for a decade (1946-55). Born in Waukegan, Ill., Graham went to college at Northwestern, starred in football and was one of the top basketball players in the country. After dominating the AAFC (All America Football Conference) from 1946 to 1949, Graham and the Browns were met with skepticism when they merged with the NFL. Graham proved the skeptics wrong by leading the Browns to the NFL title in their first year in the league, throwing four TD passes in the title game. Paul

Otto Graham

Brown said, "The test of a quarterback is where his team finishes. By that standard, Otto was the best of them all." In Graham's 10 years, the Browns won their division 10 times and played in every NFL title game from 1950 to 1955, winning three titles. Graham began on top, stayed on top and finished on top.

■ Also born today: **TONY LAZZERI (1903)**, S.F. native, second baseman for N.Y. Yankees (1926-37), .292 lifetime hitter, great RBI man, holds AL record for most RBI (11) in a nine-inning game, died in S.F. at age 42 ... **JIMMY BRADDOCK (1905)**, won heavyweight championship in 1935 after stunning world and Max Baer with 15-round decision, didn't defend title for two years and lost it to Joe Louis in 1937 via eighth-round KO ... Two Cubbie infielders born on this day in Sacramento: **STAN HACK (1909)** and **LARRY BOWA (1945)** ... **RAY PERKINS (1941)**, Baltimore Colts wide receiver (1967-71) and coach of the N.Y. Giants, and later at Alabama.... high-jumper **DWIGHT STONES (1953)**... **LOU LITTLE (1893)**, Columbia football coach, 1930-56... **ANDY ROBUSTELLI (1930)**, defensive end with the New York Giants during the glory years, 1956-64 (he missed only one game in his 14-year career)... **ELEANOR HOLM (1913)**, gold medal swimmer in 1928 and '32 Olympics, married showman Billy Rose, who featured her in his watery extravaganzas called Aquacades.

■ **LARRY BIRD (1956)** —
The premier forward in the NBA, and the pride of French Lick Ind., was a college great at

Larry Bird

Indiana State (which lost to Magic Johnson and Mich. State in the 1979 NCAA final). As a rookie, he invited comparison with the greatest forwards in basketball history. Now he seems the equal of any of them and is only halfway through his career. Bird's talent and his basketball sense are supreme but, even among superstars, his physicality — an aggressive 6-feet-9, 225 pounds — sets him apart.

■ Also born today: **JOHNNY BENCH (1947)**, MVP in 1970 and 1972, hit more home runs than any other catcher in one season (45 in 1970) or in a career (389, breaking Berra's mark) ... **LLOYD LEITH (1902)**, S.F.-born basketball coach and official who was elected to the Naismith Basketball Hall of Fame in 1983 ... **HAMILTON FISH (1888)**, college Hall of Fame tackle from Harvard, later arch-conservative congressman from New York ... **MAX ZASLOFSKY (1925)**, guard out of St. John's, played with Chicago Stags (1946-49), N.Y. Knicks (1950-52) and others; a star of the early NBA ... **BO BELINSKY (1936)**, "Joe Hollywood" pitched a no-hitter as a rookie in 1962 (though only a 28-51 career record), ran around with Mamie Van Doren, et al. ... **ALEX JOHNSON (1942)**, won AL batting title in 1970 (like Belinsky, an individualist and a California Angel).

NOTES

■ **HANK THOMPSON (1925)** — The first black player on two different major league teams, born in Oklahoma City. He was the second black player in the American League (after Larry Doby), coming up with the St. Louis Browns in 1947. He didn't play in 1948, then in 1949 became the N.Y. Giants' first black player. In eight seasons Thompson hit 129 homers, including three in a game in 1954, the year he hit 26. A left-swinging third baseman, he hit .302 in 1953 with 24 homers and retired after the 1956 season with a .267 lifetime BA. He played on

Hank Thompson

two pennant-winning Giants teams (1951 and '54) and hit .364 in the four-game sweep of the Indians in the World Series, including a four-game record of seven walks. After retirement, Thompson served time in prison for robbery. Later, working with youngsters in Fresno, he died of a heart attack at age 43.

■ Also born today: **GEORGE ROGERS (1958)**, Heisman Trophy Award winner in 1980 from South Carolina, NFL Rookie of the Year with New Orleans Saints after rushing for 1,674 yards, an NFL record for a rookie (broken in 1983 by Eric Dickerson) ... **WILMER LAWSON ALLISON (1904)**, tennis Hall of Famer, won U.S. Open in 1935 ... **RED BERENSON (1939)**, hockey player with Canadiens, St. Louis Blues, etc. In 1969, skating for the Blues, he scored four goals in a single period and six goals in the game, tying a modern record ... **EDDIE BRINKMAN (1941)**, great field-no hit shortstop mostly with Senators (1961-70) and Tigers (1971-74), set records for the best fielding percentage in a season of 150 games or more (.990 in 1972) and the fewest errors (7, also in 1972) ... offensive tackle **BOB BROWN (1941)**, all-pro with Eagles, Rams and Raiders, 1964-75 ... **BOB LOVE (1942)**, high-scoring forward for the Chicago Bulls in the early 1970s. ... financier **AUGUST BELMONT (1816)**, horse breeder and turf official, Belmont Park named after him.

Traded to Redskins in '85

NOTES

■ DICK BUTKUS (1942) —

Perhaps the greatest middle linebacker in football history. Born in Chicago, he was an All-American at Illinois and was the first of three first-round draft choices that the Chicago Bears had in 1965 (their second choice was Gale Sayers — not a bad draft so far). Butkus retired after the 1973 season, his career shortened by a severe knee injury. Butkus was an absolute terror from sideline to sideline. He intercepted 22 passes in his time and pounced on 25 fumbles. He played in eight straight Pro Bowls. Butkus

Dick Butkus

looked tough — and was. That demeanor achieved new fame in the many beer ads he has been in — usually as second banana to Bubba Smith. Butkus was inducted into the Hall of Fame in 1979.

■ WORLD B. FREE (1953) —

One of the greatest shooting guards ever to play basketball. Born Lloyd Free in Atlanta, he legally changed his name in 1981. He played college ball at tiny Guilford College (one of his teammates was John Drew) and was drafted in 1975 by the Philadelphia 76ers. He has since played with the Clippers, Warriors, and — recently — the Cavaliers.

■ BILL HARTACK (1932) —

One of the greatest jockeys of all time. He equalled Eddie Arcaro's record of five Kentucky Derby winners; Iron Leige (1957), Venetian Way (1960), Decidedly (1962), Northern Dancer (1964), and Majestic Prince (1969).

■ DEACON JONES (1938) —

Jones, like Butkus, was a Hall of Fame defensive star who later did Lite Beer commercials. A defensive end with the Rams from 1961 to 1971, he was known for his quickness and his (now illegal) head-slap.

■ Also born today: **DEL UNSER (1944)**, ex-NL outfielder, holds record for three consecutive pinch-hit homers ... Spanish bullfighter **LUIS MIGUEL DOMINGUIN (1926)** ... golfer **ORVILLE MOODY (1933)** ... basketball player **CLIFF HAGAN (1931)** of Kentucky and the St. Louis Hawks.

■ **CHARLIE CONACHER (1909) —**
One of five brothers, all hockey players (none as good as Charlie), born in Toronto. He broke in as a 19-year-old rookie with the Toronto Maple Leafs in 1929 and skated with them for 10 years. He won the Art Ross Trophy (for most points) twice and was all-NHL five straight years (1932-36). He was one-third of the famous KidLine, with Busher Jackson and Joe Primeau. Charlie's older brother Lionel played hockey and almost every other sport and was named Canada's Athlete of the Half-Century (1900-1950). Charlie's younger brother Roy was a star for the Boston Bruins, Red Wings and Black Hawks. Charlie died of cancer in 1967, which led to the formation of the Charlie Conacher Cancer Fund.

■ **JAMES NORRIS (1878) —**
Sports promoter and executive, born in Montreal. Our second Canadian of the day was also involved in hockey — as owner of the Detroit Red Wings (he named them the Red Wings). He also owned arenas in several cities and had interests in boxing and horse racing. The James Norris Memorial Trophy, given annually to the NHL's top defenseman, is named for him. He died in 1952. His son, James D. Norris, owned the Chicago Black Hawks for a while and formed the International Boxing Club which ushered in boxing's TV era.

■ **RAGNHILD HVEGER (1920) —**
Danish swimmer, known as "The Golden Tornado." She held 42 world records from 1936 to 1942, the most for a woman. She is often called the greatest swimmer who never won an Olympic title (the Games weren't held in 1940).

■ **JOSEPH BLACKBURNE (1841) —** Known as "the Black Death," he was the greatest chess player England ever produced. A great popularizer of the game, he gave simultaneous exhibitions —shabbily dressed, drinking whisky, and bantering all the while.

NOTES

FRED TONEY (1887) —

Pitched in major league baseball's only "double no-hitter." Born in Nashville, Tenn. Toney had a 12-year career (1911-13, 1915-23), most-

Fred Toney

ly with the Reds and Giants, with an impressive 137-102 won-loss record and 2.69 ERA. A 6-foot-1, 195-pound right-hander, Toney (then with the Reds) achieved immortality on May 2, 1917, hooking up with Jim "Hippo" Vaughn of the Cubs in a game that was tied, 0-0, after nine innings — with no hits in the ballgame. Vaughn gave up the game's first hit in the 10th, a one-out single. That base runner moved to third on an error by the center fielder on a fly ball. The stage was set for Jim Thorpe, football great and Olympic decathlon winner. Thorpe swung and just topped the ball, a swinging bunt that dribbled onto the infield grass. The runner scored and Toney had his incredible win.

CHARLES "OLD HOSS" RADBOURN (1854) — Another

right-handed pitcher born today (who also pitched a no-hitter), Radbourn won 308 games (in 11 seasons!) and was the workhorse pitcher of all time— hence his nickname. In 1884, he won 60 games, the major-league record. Radbourn died at age 42, of, among other things, syphilis.

Also born today: FRED COX (1938), ex-Viking kicker

who set an NFL record by kicking field goals in 31 straight games from 1968 to 1970 ...
FELIX "DOC" BLANCHARD (1924), "Mr. Inside," All-American Army fullback (1944-46) who teamed with "Mr. Outside," Glenn Davis, one of the most famous backfield tandems in college football history, and ... twins JOHNNY and EDDIE O'BRIEN (1930), both basketball stars at Seattle U. (especially Johnny), then Pittsburgh Pirate infielders for the same six years (1953-58).... actor VICTOR MCLAGLEN (1886), an ex-pug who fought Jack Johnson and Jess Willard.

NOTES

HENRY ARMSTRONG (1912) — Feather- weight, lightweight and welterweight champion (1937- 41). Born Henry Jackson in Columbus, Miss., he grew up in St. Louis and lived in poverty. As a teen-ager, he hitch-hiked to Los Angeles and began fighting as a pro, handled by managers who allegedly fixed many of his bouts. Fortunately, Al Jolson took an interest in Armstrong and found a new manager for him. He also stopped fighting as Henry Jackson (to cover up his earlier record) and emerged in New York City in 1937, a perpetual motion machine in the

Henry Armstrong

ring who won his three titles within 10 months. Known as "Homicide Hank," he is one of only six boxers to hold three world titles (the other five are Bob Fitzsimmons, Barney Ross, Tony Canzoneri, Alexis Arguello and Wilfred Benitez) and the only one to hold them simultaneously. In 175 bouts, Armstrong lost only 22 times, and except for the first fight of his pro career as an 18-year-old, was knocked out only once — by Fritzie Zivic in 1941 to take away Armstrong's welter title. Though he earned millions in the ring, he had nothing when he retired in 1945 and suddenly was back on the streets. Armstrong's religious beliefs pulled him out of his downward spiral and he has been an ordained Baptist minister for more than 30 years.

Also born today: Tennis player **TRACY AUSTIN (1962)**, U.S. champion in 1979, the youngest ever; she also became the youngest millionaire in sports history ... Two great basketball guards: **RANDY SMITH (1948)**, all-time NBA leader in steals and in consecutive games played (906), and **RALPH BEARD (1927)**, three-time (1947-49) All-American at Kentucky, two-time college Player of the Year...gymnast **CATHY RIGBY (1952)**... outfielder **RALPH GARR (1945)**, won 1974 NL batting title, hitting .353... **WILLIAM VANDERBILT (1849)**, yachtsman, horseman and auto racing pioneer... **GORMAN THOMAS (1950)**, Seattle outfielder.

NOTES

■ **LARRY DOBY (1923)** —
The first black baseball player in the American League.

Born in Camden, S.C., Doby broke in with the Cleveland Indians at the tail end of the 1947 season, a few months after Jackie Robinson broke the color barrier in the National League. Doby retired after the 1959 season with a lifetime .283 batting average and 253 home runs, averaging about 20 a season. In 1952, he led the AL in homers, runs and slugging percentage. In 1954, he led the AL in homers and RBI. He managed the Chicago White Sox in 1978,

Larry Doby

becoming only the second black manager in big league history. Doby later became the director of community relations for the New Jersey Nets basketball team.

■ **ARCHIE MOORE (1916)** —
Light - heavyweight champion from 1952-62 and one of the great figures in boxing history. Born Archibald Lee Wright in Benoit, Miss., Moore had 234 professional fights in 26 years — a staggering career — and lost only 26 times. His 138 knockouts is an all-time ring record. It took him 16 years before he got a crack at the title but he won it — at age 36 — and kept it for a decade. He also fought as a heavyweight until age 40.

■ Also born today: auto racer **BILL VUKOVICH (1918)**, won Indy 500 in 1953 and 1954 (in record time); he died in a crash in 1955, going for an unprecedented third straight win; his son is auto racer Billy Vukovich ... **HANK MAJESKI (1916)**, AL third baseman mostly with the Philadelphia A's; .279 lifetime hitter who still holds major-league fielding record for third baseman in one season (.988 in 1947) ... two Dodger "Boys of Summer" — pitcher **CARL ERSKINE (1926)** and outfielder **GEORGE "SHOTGUN" SHUBA (1924)** ... Cubs righty **FERGUSON JENKINS (1943)**, who has 284 victories ... **BILL RING (1956)** clutch 49er running back.

NOTES

■ **ERNIE DAVIS (1939)** —
The first black football player to win the Heisman Trophy (in 1961). Born in New Salem, Pa., Davis followed in Jim Brown's footsteps at Syracuse, and then some, breaking Brown's school records in TDs, points, rushing yardage and total yardage. Davis was, like Brown, a big running back with speed and power. The Cleveland Browns drafted the Heisman Trophy winner, wanting to team up the two ex-Syracuse greats in the pros, and signed Davis to a then-huge $80,000 contract. Shortly afterward, Davis was stricken with leukemia. A year

Ernie Davis

later, 1963, before he had ever played a single game in the NFL, he died. He was 23.

■ **CHARLEY TRIPPI (1922)** —
Another great running back born on this day, in Pittston, Pa. He was an All-American at Georgia where he led them to the Rose Bowl (beating UCLA 9-0 in 1943) and Sugar Bowl (beating North Carolina in 1947). Trippi played his entire pro career (1947-55) with the Chicago Cardinals. He was a halfback, quarterback and defensive back. He was also a fine receiver, kicker and punt returner. Trippi formed one-fourth of the famous "$100,000 Backfield" which included Marshall Goldberg, Pat Harder and Paul Christman. In 1955, Trippi suffered a severe collision with running back John Henry Johnson that rendered him unconscious for several hours and ended his career. He was elected to both the college and pro football Halls of Fame.

■ Also born today: **SAM JONES (1925)**, "Toothpick Sam" with the S.F. Giants in 1959, led the league in wins (21) and ERA (2.83) ... two tennis players: **STAN SMITH (1946)**, who won the U.S. Open in 1971 and **HENRI COCHET (1901)**, who won the U.S. Open in 1928.... **BILL BUCKNER (1949)**, a clutch .294 lifetime hitter, a Dodger from 1970 to '76, traded to the Cubs in 1977, currently with Red Sox.

NOTES

Sports birthdays/Dec. 15

■ **NICK BUONICONTI (1940)** Buoniconti was the middle linebacker and field general of the Miami dynasty of the early 1970s He is one of the all-time leaders in interceptions for a linebacker. A lawyer since his retirement in 1975, he is on the legal staff of the NFL Players' Association.

Nick Buoniconti

■ **JACK "THE NONPAREIL" DEMPSEY (1862)** — Middleweight champion, 1884 to 1891, born in Ireland. He earned his nickname (meaning peerless) by defeating all comers in over 60 fights before finally losing his first one (except for a bout he lost because of an illegal blow) and his middleweight title to the great Bob Fitzsimmons. They fought for the biggest purse ever in a boxing match — $12,000. His backers lost a lot of money on that one and Dempsey fought only three more times, suffering the only other loss of his career. After an illness, Dempsey died at age 33, only a few months after his last fight. The more famous Jack Dempsey, the heavyweight, was born William Harrison Dempsey but assumed the name "Jack" in homage to this great middleweight.

■ **HAROLD ABRAHAMS (1899)** — English sprinter depicted in film, "Chariots of Fire." He won the 100-meter title in the 1924 Olympic Games, the first European — and the only Englishman — ever to win that event. He also was a long jumper and set an English mark that stood for 32 years. It was in that event that he broke his leg in 1925, ending his track career. He later became a distinguished lawyer, sportswriter, broadcaster and longtime official — and later president — of the British Amateur Athletic Board. He died in 1978.

■ Also born today: **CHARLIE SCOTT** (1948), ABA superstar, his 34.5 average in 1972 was the highest in ABA history . . . **RUDY BUKICH** (1932), QB from USC (leading them to 7-0 Rose bowl win over Wisconsin), later with Chicago Bears (led NFL in passing, 1965), and others . . . **JOE WALTON** (1935), N.Y. Giants head coach.

■ RAYMOND "BUDDY" PARKER (1913) —
Coach of the last Detroit Lions team to win an NFL title.

He was a running back for the Lions on their 1935 championship team but spent most of his playing career with the Chicago Cardinals (1937-43). Parker took over the coaching job with the Lions in 1951. In his first year, Parker took the Lions to a second-place finish. The following year, 1952, the Lions won their division and defeated the awesome Cleveland Browns for the NFL title. In 1953, they

Raymond Parker

did it again — two consecutive championships — again beating the Browns in the title game, 17-16. In 1954, the Lions won their conference for the third straight year and went for their third straight NFL title — yet again battling the Cleveland Browns. This time the Browns prevailed. Parker, an innovative coach, was the first to develop the "two minute drill" at the end of each half. He resigned in 1956.

■ Also born today: **MIKE FLANAGAN (1951)**, veteran Oriole lefty pitcher; in 1982, his wife Kathy gave birth to the fourth test-tube baby born in the U.S. and the first not delivered by Caesarean section ... **JOHN HOBBS (1882)**, "Jack" Hobbs was the most famous British cricket player and in 1953 became the first cricketer to be knighted ... **VINCE MATTHEWS (1948)**, 400-meter Olympic champion in 1972.

■ **JIMMY McLARNIN (1907)** —
One of the greatest welterweight champions. Born in Ireland, McLarnin moved to Canada (Vancouver) as a child, and began his pro career as a 17-year-old. The nickname, "Babyface," stuck with him. He won the title in 1933 via a one-round KO of Young Corbett III. McLarnin's next fight — one year later — was against the great Barney Ross, the first of three famous bouts in which McLarnin lost his title, regained it, and lost it finally to Ross — all 15-round decisions. In 77 fights, McLarnin lost only 11 times (KO'd once).

Jimmy McLarnin

McLarnin's last few fights were big money-makers for him. He retired at age 29, invested his ring earnings and lived a comfortable life.

■ Also born today: **PETER SNELL (1938)**, New Zealand-born miler, one of the greatest of all time; broke Herb Elliott's world mark with a 3:54.4 mile in 1962; won gold in the 800 meters in the 1960 Olympics, then in 1964 won the 800 again as well as the 1,500 meters, the first double at those events in 44 years ... **JERRY ADAIR (1936)**, Oklahoma-born second baseman with the Orioles and others in the 1960s; great glove, set AL mark of 89 straight games and 458 chances without an error (in 1964-65); he holds the all-time single season fielding average (.994) for a second baseman; played college basketball at Oklahoma State under Hank Iba and later with the Phillips 76ers, one of the top AAU teams ... **LEO CARDENAS (1938)**, Cuban-born shortstop mostly with the Reds ... **GERALD L. PATTERSON (1895)**, one of the earliest Australian tennis greats, in 1919 he was the No. 1 ranked player in the world.

NOTES

■ **TY COBB** (1886) —

Among the most ferocious competitors in sports , born in Narrows, Ga. He was the greatest baseball player of the dead ball era (i.e., before 1920) and holds the highest lifetime batting average in major league history — .367, a record that no one will take away from him, though others of his have fallen in recent years: most games, most at bats, most stolen bases, and —(tho it will be Pete Rose's someday) most hits. Cobb is still No. 1 in runs scored (2,244) and the world is waiting for the guy to equal his 12 batting titles — nine in a row!

Ty Cobb

And those records that fell did so a half century after Cobb retired. "The Georgia Peach" (nicknamed by Grantland Rice) was probably the meanest son of a gun ever to don cleats (which Cobb filed to a razor's edge). His childhood was scarred by family tragedies, which made him a loner and difficult to understand even by most of his teammates. Cobb and Rusty Staub (their names almost rhyme) are the only players to hit home runs before their 20th and after their 40th birthdays. He died in 1961.

■ Also born today: golfer **HUBERT GREEN** (1946), winner of the 1977 U.S. Open ... **FREDDIE STEELE** (1912), middleweight champion, 1936-38, lost only six fights out of 139; had nine pro fights by age 13 with the largest purse at $12.50, died in 1984 ... **GENE SHUE** (1931), coach of the Washington Bullets, one of the best in the NBA, set record in 1983 with 2,000th win as player and coach ... **ZOILO "ZORRO" VERSALLES** (1939), Cuban-born, only a .242 lifetime hitter, won MVP award in 1965, leading the league in doubles, triples, runs and at-bats for the pennant-winning Twins.... **BOBBY JONES** (1951), the premier sixth man in the NBA since coming to the 76ers in '79 ... **GREG LANDRY** (1946), best passing-running QB in early 1970s.

NOTES

■ AL KALINE (1934) —

The youngest player ever to win a batting title. Born in Baltimore, Kaline went to the

Al Kaline

Detroit Tigers at age 18 without any minor league experience and played with the Tigers throughout his career, retiring after the 1974 season with a .297 lifetime batting average and membership in the elite 3,000-hit club. He also hit 399 home runs. If he had hit one more homer, he would join Carl Yastrzemski as the only two American League players to amass 3,000 hits and 400 homers. Kaline was only 20 years old when he won the 1955 batting title. Ty Cobb (another Tiger) also won a batting title at age 20, but turned 21 on Dec. 18, one day before Kaline. A smooth, consistent, and versatile performer, Kaline was an excellent outfielder and fine base runner. He supposedly tutored Kirk Gibson and aided his development. Kaline, inducted into the Hall of Fame in 1980, became the Tigers' announcer.

■ BOBBY LAYNE (1926) —

One of the guttiest quarterbacks in football history. An All-American at Texas, Layne played with four NFL teams but his glory years were spent with the Lions from 1950 to 1958, leading them to three NFL titles (in 1952, '53, and '57). He still holds the Detroit Lions' record for most TDs in a game, season and career. Layne was a hellraiser on and off the field. His partying is legendary. When he retired in 1962, he was the only player in the NFL not to wear a face mask.

■ DOUG HARVEY (1924) —

Hall of Famer for the Montreal Canadiens, won the James Norris Trophy for the league's best defenseman seven of eight years, from 1954 to 1961. Harvey was first-string all-NHL every year but one from 1952 to 1962.

■ Also born today: **REX BARNEY (1924)**, Brooklyn Dodgers righty of the late 1940s, pitched a no-hitter in 1948, became Baltimore Orioles PA announcer ... **FORD FRICK (1894)**, NL president, 1934-50, and commissioner of baseball, 1951-65 ... **TONY HINKLE (1899)**, pioneer basketball coach at Butler, 1924-63.

NOTES

■**GABBY HARTNETT (1900)** — catcher with the Chicago Cubs born Charles Leo Hartnett in Woonsocket, R.I. He played aggressively and with a confident flair, talking with fans, umpires, and players of both teams. Hartnett was a power hitter who also hit for average (a .297 lifetime BA). He was MVP in 1935, but 1938 is the year that will always be associated with Gabby Hartnett. With 25 games left in the season, he was named manager, while still an active player and took the Cubbies from 6½ games out to the N L

Hall of Fame from 1922 to 1940,

Gabby Hartnett

pennant, as they won 21 games of their remaining 25. Hartnett himself won the decisive game against the Pirates with a two-out, two-strike home run — the historic "home run in the gloaming." He died on his birthday in 1972.

■**HAZEL HOTCHKISS WIGHTMAN (1886)** — "The Queen Mother of American tennis", born in Healdsburg, Ca. She won 43 national titles and competed into her 70s. In 1923 she donated the trophy (Wightman Cup), awarded to women's tennis teams.

■**BRANCH RICKEY (1881)** — Pioneer baseball exec, invented the farm system as GM of St. Louis Cardinals, 1917-41, and, as president of the Brooklyn Dodgers, 1942-49, racially integrated the major leagues by signing Jackie Robinson in 1946.

■**PUDGE HEFFELFINGER (1867)** — A three-time All-American at Yale, 1889-91. In 1892, he became the first professional football player and played into his late 40s.

■**BOB HAYES (1942)** — The first—and the best—world class sprinter to play pro football. In the 1964 Olympics he won the 100-meter dash in the record time of 10 seconds flat. The following year, Hayes began his distinguished 11-year career with the Dallas Cowboys as their deep threat.

■Also born today: Brewer first baseman **CECIL COOPER** (1949) ... **JACK CHRISTIANSEN (1928)**, Detroit Lions defensive back, 1951-58, the second defensive back (after Emlen Tunnell) to be inducted into the Hall of Fame ... **FRED MERKLE (1888)**, N.Y. Giants first baseman, of "Merkle's Boner" fame in 1908.

NOTES

■ WALTER HAGEN (1892) —

Golf immortal and a true man of the world, born in Rochester, N.Y. He showed major league potential as a

baseball player but chose golf instead and gave reasonable proof that he made the right choice by winning the U.S. Open at age 21. He won the U.S. Open again in 1919, then won four British Opens in the 1920s and five PGA championships in that same decade (he was the first American-born golfer to win the PGA). He won more than 65 major tournaments and was the first golfer to win more than $1 million. Considered without peer

Walter Hagen

in the short game, Hagen is considered by many the greatest golfer ever. He overwhelmed Bobby Jones in their one "private" 36-hole match in 1926. "The Haig," a friend of royalty and movie stars, and an international figure, elevated the status of golf, revolutionized the style of dress and manners, and inspired countless human beings to "smell the roses as you go." He died in 1969.

■ JOSH GIBSON (1911) —

"The Black Babe Ruth" was a legendary slugger who even stole some of the Babe's thunder by being the only player to hit a home run out of Yankee Stadium. He was also a great catcher (Roy Campanella called him the greatest) who caught Satchel Paige with the Pittsburgh Crawfords of the black major leagues. Troubled by brain tumors for four years, Gibson died of a stroke at age 35.

■ Also born today:

DAVE KINGMAN (1948), who in 1984 became the Comeback Player of the Year for the Oakland A's, hitting 35 homers and tying Reggie Jackson's A's RBI record (118) ... **CHRIS EVERT LLOYD (1954)**, U.S. Open champion four years in a row (1975-78) and again in 1980 and '82 ... **JOE PATERNO (1926)**, Penn State football coach since 1966 ... **CHARLIE GOLDMAN (1887)**, Rocky Marciano's trainer, also handled Lou Ambers, Al McCoy, Marty Servo, and others ... **NORMAN "RED" STRADER (1904)**, great running back with St. Mary's College and the Chicago Cardinals.

Joaquin Andujar (1952), Cardinals ace righty

NOTES

Funny his name wasn't on the '85 All-Star ballot

■ **STEVE GARVEY (1948)** —
Holder of the National League record for consecutive games (1,207). Born in Tampa, Fla., he was a Dodger batboy at their Vero Beach spring training ballpark and his father drove the team bus. Garvey was signed by the Dodgers and he struggled at third base offensively and defensively for three years until he was moved to first base in 1973, liberating one of the greatest ever to play that position. After a brilliant career with the Dodgers, in which he won the MVP award in 1974 and batted more than .300 seven times, Garvey, un-

Steve Garvey

wanted by the Dodgers because of his high price and because of their emerging phenom, Greg Brock, went free agent and signed with the Padres for $6.6 million over five years. In 1984, Garvey gave the Padres their money's worth in full (all $6.6 million) and he led the Padres to their first pennant ever — while the Dodgers fell to fourth place, under .500, a poor defensive team with no center. Meanwhile, Garvey hit .284 and drove in 86 runs on only eight home runs, the best ratio in the league. On the defensive side, has anyone ever played every game and made zero errors? Garvey did that in 1984. Another embarrassment suffered by the Dodgers was Garvey breaking Billy Williams' NL consecutive-game record of 1,117 in a Padre uniform.

■ Also born today: **STEVE CARLTON (1944)**, another Steve, also born in Florida, also Hall of Fame-bound ... **RAY GUY (1949)**, Raiders punter since 1972 when he became the only punter ever drafted by an NFL team in the first round ... Aussie golfer **JAN STEPHENSON (1951)**... **MATTY ALOU** (1938), .309 lifetime hitter, brother of Felipe and Jesus ... **BILLY BRUTON (1929)**, left- handed hitting outfielder with Milwaukee and Detroit. ... auto racer **DAVID PEARSON (1934)**, NASCAR champ in 1966, '68 and '69.

■ **BARNEY ROSS (1909)** —
One of only three boxers (also Henry Armstrong and Roberto Duran) to

Barney Ross

hold both the lightweight and welterweight titles simultaneously, born Barnet Rosofsky in Manhattan's Lower East Side but grew up in the slums of Chicago. His father was a Talmudic scholar from Russia who operated a small grocery. Young Barnet also studied the Talmud and thought of becoming a Hebrew teacher when he grew up, which he did quickly — at age 14 — when his father was murdered by hoods trying to rob his store. The whole family was traumatized — his mother suffered a nervous breakdown and his two brothers were sent to an orphanage. He was taken in by a cousin and, bitter and rebellious, gave up his religious life and became a street-fighter and petty criminal. To make money, he started boxing as an amateur (and selling his medals to eat), turned pro at 18, beginning a phenomenal career in which he lost only four fights out of 81 and was never knocked out or even knocked down. He won the lightweight title in 1933, then won the welter title in the first of three classic 15-round decisions with Jimmy McLarnin in which Ross won, lost, and regained the title. He finally lost that title to Henry Armstrong in yet another 15-round decision. After retirement, Ross joined the Marines and fought at Guadalcanal, winning the Silver Star. Stricken with malaria, he became dependent on morphine and began years of addiction until taking the cure at Lexington, Ky. He later crusaded against narcotics dealers and wrote his autobiography, "No Man Stands Alone." He died in 1967.

■ Also born today: Two immortal Green Bay Packers: **PAUL HORNUNG (1935)**, the 176 points he scored in 1960, running and kicking, is still a record, and **WILLIE WOOD (1936)**, only the sixth defensive back selected for the Hall of Fame, he became the first black head coach in pro football — with CFL's Toronto Argonauts ... **BOB KURLAND (1924)**, basketball's first dominating 7-footer ... marathon runner **BILL RODGERS (1947)** ... **KEN HUBBS (1941)**, 1962 rookie-of-the-year with Cubs, who died in an airplane crash the following year, age 22.

NOTES

■ **BILL DUDLEY (1921)** — "Bullet Bill," a member of the college and pro football Hall of Fame and one of the best all-purpose backs in NFL history, born in Bluefield, Va. Dudley was a triple-threat back from the University of Virginia (1939-41) and Virginia's first All-American, leading the nation in rushing in 1941. In 1942 he was the Pittsburgh Steelers' first-round draft choice (and tore off a 55-yard TD run in his first pro game), spent the next two years in the army, returning to the Steelers for two more seasons. In 1946, Dudley won the MVP

Bill Dudley

award and a rare triple crown — first in the NFL in rushing, punt returns and interceptions. A personality clash with Steeler coach Jock Sutherland resulted in a trade to Detroit immediately after his MVP season. With the Lions, Dudley signed the biggest contract in the league — $25,000. He finished his career with the Redskins, retiring in 1953 with more than 8,000 combined yards, 484 points, and 23 interceptions. Dudley was rather small (175 pounds), slow (despite his nickname) and awkward. He was also a tremendous football player.

■ Also born today: **CLARENCE "WOODY" DUMART (1916)**, left wing with Boston Bruins (1936-54), one-third of the famous "Kraut Line" with Milt Schmidt and Bobby Bauer, the top three scorers in the 1939-40 season ... **EMMANUEL LASKER (1868)**, German-born chess champion of the world from 1894 to 1921, by far the longest tenure of any champion; also wrote books on chess (as well as bridge and philosophy) ... **CAS BANASZEK (1945)**, ex-49ers offensive tackle.

NOTES

■ RICKEY HENDERSON (1958) —

One of the most exciting performers in baseball history. He grew up in S.F.'s East Bay and went to Berkeley High where he was a tremendous running back (not difficult to imagine) as well as a baseball player. He was only 20 when he broke into the major leagues in 1979 with the Oakland A's. A year later he hit .303 and stole 100 bases. He has been that kind of player ever since and is poised to reach a new plateau, capable of winning the batting title and/or MVP award. He is the only player ever to steal 100

Rickey Henderson

bases three times — in only five and a half seasons! In 1983, he led the league in stolen bases (66) and hit 16 homers. Can anyone else do that? Henderson became the first victim in the Mieuli-ization of the Oakland A's. In a rather blatant commitment to losing, the A's dealt the awesome Henderson to the New York Yankees (Steinbrenner, whatever else you say about him, does want to win) for five *prospects*. Gag me with a spoon. If you can't afford a great player, you're in the wrong business. Henderson immediately became the scapegoat (a la Jack Clark and the Giants and J.B. Carroll and the Warriors — it's always the best player on the team) for the A's failures, and the local sporting press queued up to take their parting shots at Rickey, a *guy the fans adore*.

■ Also born today: **KEN STABLER (1945)**, retired in mid-'84 ripping Bum Phillips (which was justified); he's the greatest QB ever to throw more interceptions than TDs ... Atlanta Falcons fullback **WILLIAM ANDREWS (1955)** ... **KYLE ROTE JR. (1950)**, the first American-born soccer star in the U.S. ... two brilliant second basemen — **NELLIE FOX (1927)**, .288 lifetime BA, 1959 MVP, and **MANNY TRILLO (1950)**, Giants second baseman, in 1982 he broke Rich Dauer's record of 426 consecutive chances without an error ... **LARRY CSONKA (1946)**, comes from a long tradition of running backs from Syracuse, led the Dolphins to two straight Super Bowl triumphs in '72 and '73.

NOTES

■ **STU MILLER (1927)** —
Ace reliever in both leagues from 1952 to 1968. Born
in Northampton, Mass., he was
a starter and reliever for several
years with the Cardinals and
Giants. After 1960, he never
started a game again. In 1961,
Miller was a brilliant 14-5 for the
Giants, led the NL in saves and
gained lasting fame by being
blown off the rubber by a gust of
wind at Candlestick Park during
the All-Star game. Less
well-known is the fact that he
was the winning pitcher in that
game. He also won the "Fireman
of the Year" award that year,

Stu Miller

and he won that award again four years later with the
Baltimore Orioles to become the only reliever to win it
in both leagues. Miller is one of the all-time leaders
in both wins (79) and saves (154). He became
owner of a liquor store in San Carlos, California.

■ **GLENN DAVIS (1924)** — Great running back for
Army during the mid-1940s. "Mr. Outside" teamed with
Doc Blanchard, "Mr. Inside," to form perhaps the most
famous backfield tandem in college football history.
Davis won the Heisman Trophy in 1946 and Blanchard
won it the year before. After serving three years as an
army officer, Davis played briefly with the Los Angeles
Rams (1950-51) and was one of football's first "glamour
boys." He dated Elizabeth Taylor, was briefly married
to Terry Moore (longtime companion of Howard Hughes).

■ Also born today: **STORM DAVIS (1961)**, the Orioles'
gifted young right-hander ... **OZZIE SMITH (1954)**,
Cardinal shortstop ... two college football coaches, both
Wishbone-T innovators, both in the Southwestern
Conference — **FRANK BROYLES (1924)** of Arkansas (now
AD since 1977) and **BILL YEOMAN (1927)** of Houston ...
CHRIS CHAMBLISS (1948), Atlanta Braves first
baseman ... **CARLTON FISK (1947)**, pride of Bellows
Falls, Vt., Rookie of the Year with the BoSox in 1972,
with the White Sox since 1979.

■ **ARCH WARD (1896)** — As sports editor of the Chicago Tribune, Ward originated the idea of a football charity game and was the main force behind establishing the annual College All-Star game against the pro champs of the previous year, beginning in 1934

(with the All-Stars and the Chicago Bears playing to a scoreless tie). Ward also promoted the first Golden Gloves matches in 1926, also in Chicago. He died in 1955.

■ **ROY WHITE (1943)** — White came up to the Yankees in 1965 and spent a decade learning humility with the rest of his teammates. He was the only survivor of that era

Arch Ward

and could truly savor the Yankee renaissance that began in 1976. After the 1979 season, he finished his career playing Japanese baseball.

■ **JIM TOBIN (1912)** — This right-hand pitcher won most of his 105 games with the Boston Braves during the World War II years. His claim to fame is a no-hitter that he pitched against Brooklyn in 1944. He also hit three home runs in a single game in 1942 and how many pitchers (or non-pitchers) have done that? Tobin was born in Oakland and died there in 1969.

■ Also born today: **JERRY LAMBERT (1940)**, a leading jockey of the 1960s and the regular jockey of Native Diver ... **PAUL V. COSTELLO (1899)**, one of only four to win three Olympic gold medals in sculls — in 1920 and 1924, with John Kelly, father of Grace Kelly, and in 1928 in a record time that still stands.

NOTES

■ BILL LEE (1946) —

Boston Red Sox lefty ace of the mid-1970s and one of the most quotable athletes ever, Lee went to USC. He came up with the BoSox in 1969 and won 17 games with them three years in a row (1973-75). By this time, Lee had been radicalized by the upheaval of the Vietnam War and spoke out, usually humorously, on social issues. He clashed with manager Don Zimmer (likening him to a gerbil)) and, after a while in Zimmer's doghouse, was traded to the Expos in 1979. Just to

Bill Lee

show up the Red Sox and Zimmer, Lee had a good year, going 16-10 with an ERA of 3.04, his lowest in six years. Lee retired in 1981 and has spent his time playing some semi-pro ball (because he loves the game, a la Jim Bouton) and writing his long-awaited book, "The Wrong Stuff," published in 1984.

■ TERRY SAWCHUK (1929) —

Considered by many to be the greatest goalie in hockey history, born in Winnipeg, Manitoba, Canada. His career spanned two decades (1950-70), mostly with the Detroit Red Wings. His goals-against average was an incredible two or less per game during his first five years in the NHL and he wound up with a record 103 career shutouts. Sawchuk felt his own greatest season was in 1966-67 when he dramatically led the underdog Toronto Maple Leafs to Stanley Cup glory. This "enigmatic, brooding" man died in 1970 (while still an active player) from injuries during horseplay with his teammate, Ron Stewart, on the lawn of a house they shared.

■ Also born today: **RAY KNIGHT** (1952), Mets third baseman and husband of golfer Nancy Lopez ... **TED LYONS** (1900), who won 260 games in 21 years with the Chicago White Sox — only Walter Johnson pitched that many years for the same team ... **STEVE VAN BUREN** (1920), power runner with the Philadelphia Eagles, 1944 to 1951. His 68 career TDs is the eighth best mark in NFL history. Born in Honduras.

NOTES

■ **RAY NITSCHKE (1936)** —
Named in 1969 the best linebacker in the first half-century of the NFL. A running back at Illinois with a 6.5-yard average, he was switched to middle linebacker and spearheaded the Vince Lombardi-led Green Bay Packers from 1958 to 1972, earning his niche in the Hall of Fame.

Jess Willard

■ **JESS WILLARD (1883)** — Born in Pattawatomie Co., Okla. At 6-feet-6 and 240 pounds, he was the first "giant" of the ring. In 1915, the long hunt for the "great white hope" ended when he won the title from Jack Johnson (who was 37 and well past his prime). Willard lost his title four years later, brutalized by Jack Dempsey in three rounds, including seven knockdowns in Round One.

■ Also born today: Panamanian jockey **LAFFIT PINCAY JR. (1946)**, leading money-winning jockey five years in a row, 1971-74, and again in 1979 ... hockey immortal **NELS STEWART (1902)**, the first player to score 300 goals in a career and twice MVP (1926 and 1930) ... **CHARLEY GOGOLAK (1944)**, field goal kicker for the Redskins in the late 1960s, brother of Pete Gogolak, the first soccer-style kicker ... two track and field stars, **FRED HANSEN (1940)**, who won the pole vault gold medal in 1964, and **ANDY STANFIELD (1927)**, who won the 200-meter event in the 1952 Olympics, equaling Jesse Owens' mark of 20.7 in the 1936 Olympics... **BOBB McKITTRICK (1935)**, 49ers offensive line coach.

NOTES

■ **SANDY KOUFAX (1935)** — The most dominating pitcher of the modern era. Born in Brooklyn, he came up with the Dodgers as a wild 19-year-old and stayed with that team until his premature retirement after the 1966 season. Koufax pitched four no-hitters, including a perfect game against the Cubs in 1965 (curiously, the Cubs' pitcher, Bob Hendley, threw a one-hitter and lost, 1-0). That year, Koufax set the record for most strikeouts in a season (382), which has since been eclipsed (by a single strikeout) by Nolan

Sandy Koufax

Ryan. His career won-loss record was 165-87 for a .655 percentage, one of the top ten marks. Tragically, a serious arm ailment forced him to retire after the '66 season, in which he won 27 games. He led the league in ERA in his last five seasons (1962-66) and he was under 2.00 three times. At age 30, Koufax was finished. He married the daughter of actor Richard Widmark and worked as a baseball announcer on TV. At age 36, he became the youngest ever elected to the Hall of Fame.

■ **JIM MARSHALL (1937)** — A defensive end for the Minnesota Vikings for 19 years, he is the Lou Gehrig of pro football, holding the record for starting 282 consecutive games — every game played by the Vikings during his career.

■ **MEL RENFRO (1941)** — The All-American running back from Oregon who became the right cornerback for the Dallas Cowboys from 1964 to 1978. Renfro is only the second player (after Merlin Olsen) to be selected for the Pro Bowl in each of his first 10 seasons.

■ Also born today: **LESTER PATRICK (1883)**, the George Halas of hockey — player, coach, club owner and league founder ... high jumper **FRANKLIN JACOBS (1957)**, only 5-feet-8, but who jumped 7'7¼" — an unbelievable 23¼ inches over his head.

NOTES

■ **HUGH MCELHENNY (1928)** — Hall of Fame running back with the 49ers from 1952 to 1960. When he was 11 he stepped on a broken milk bottle and severed all the tendons in his right foot. It was feared he might never walk again. After more than a year on crutches, McElhenny did walk again. In fact, he ran. At the University of Washington, he ran all over the place and became the 49ers' first draft choice in 1952. He is credited with saving a faltering franchise by causing an immediate sensation in the NFL.

Hugh McElhenny

The first time he touched the ball (against the Bears), McElhenny returned a punt 94 yards. Forty Niners quarterback Frankie Albert instantly dubbed him "The King." His versatility (rushing, receiving and returning) earned him six Pro Bowl selections. His 8.0 rushing average in 1954 is the third highest of all-time. His other records include the three longest touchdown runs from scrimmage— 89, 86 and 82 yards — all in his rookie season. McElhenny became dispensable when 49ers coach Red Hickey installed the shotgun formation in 1960. He finished his career with short stints at Minnesota, New York and Detroit. When he retired in 1964, he was the eighth leading rusher in NFL history. He later became a vending market manager for a Seattle bottling company.

■ Also born today: **BEN A. JONES (1882)**, one of the illustrious horse trainers, he made Calumet Farms one of the great racing stables, training no less than six Kentucky Derby winners — Lawrin (1938), Whirlaway (1941), Pensive (1944), Citation (1948), Ponder (1949), and Hill Gail (1952) ... **TOM CONNOLLY (1870)**, baseball ump for 34 years, umpired first American League game in 1901, born in England... Swedish miler **GUNDER HAGG (1918)**, whose 4:01.4 mark in 1945 stood for almost a decade until Roger Bannister broke it *and* the four-minute barrier ... **DON JAMES (1932)**, head football coach at Washington (McElhenny's alma mater!)... and **MICHAEL "KING" KELLY (1857)**, today's other "King" born in Troy, N.Y., baseball star. His daring and innovative baserunning inspired the cry (and song of the same name), "Slide, Kelly, Slide." He invented the "fade-away slide" and "cutting the bases."

NOTES

NOTES

NOTES

NOTES

NOTES

NOTES

NOTES

NOTES

Index / 7

NOTES

NOTES

NOTES

NOTES

S

NOTES

NOTES

NOTES

NOTES

Order Form
-Autographed Copies-

Eugene Lesser's **SPORTS BIRTHDAYS**

* A unique biographical almanac with thousands of
  sportsworld names.
* A pocket encyclopedia for sports-nuts and novices alike,
  compiled from the author's feisty columns in the
  San Francisco Examiner.
* Complete index of names and birthdays.
* Space on each page for reader's notes.

4¼ x 8½, 400 pp, $9.95

Ed Buryn's **VAGABONDING IN THE U.S.A.**

* The "why-to" as well as "how-to" of travel-adventure
  in North America
* Complete coverage of camping, car-camping,
  backpacking, bicycling, motorcycling, hitchhiking,
  lots more.
* Also with cost-cutting strategies, how to meet people,
  making money on the road, sports and adventure activities, plus 50-page Travel Resource Directory.
* Latest (fourth) edition, profusely illustrated.

5⅜ x 8½, 432 pp, $10.95

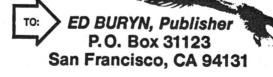

TO: ⟩ ***ED BURYN, Publisher***
P.O. Box 31123
San Francisco, CA 94131

Dear Ed: Date:_____

Yes, I want the following autographed book(s):

_____ SPORTS BIRTHDAYS @ 9.95 $_____

_____ VAGABONDING IN THE U.S.A. @ 10.95 $_____

_____ $_____

6½% Sales Tax (Calif. Residents Only) $_____

Shipping (For either or both books) $1.00

I'm enclosing a total of $_____

*(Send payment in cash or money order or check
made out to "Ed Buryn")*

My Name and Address   *Mailing Address, If Different*

_____   _____

_____   _____

_____   _____

Reader's Memo

To: Eugene Lesser
P.O. Box 410132
San Francisco, CA 94141

Date: _____

Message: Dear Eugene,

From:

Order Form
-Autographed Copies-

Eugene Lesser's **SPORTS BIRTHDAYS**

* A unique biographical almanac with thousands of sportsworld names.
* A pocket encyclopedia for sports-nuts and novices alike, compiled from the author's feisty columns in the *San Francisco Examiner.*
* Complete index of names and birthdays.
* Space on each page for reader's notes.

4¼ x 8½, 400 pp, $9.95

Ed Buryn's **VAGABONDING IN THE U.S.A.**

* The "why-to" as well as "how-to" of travel-adventure in North America
* Complete coverage of camping, car-camping, backpacking, bicycling, motorcycling, hitchhiking, lots more.
* Also with cost-cutting strategies, how to meet people, making money on the road, sports and adventure activities, plus 50-page Travel Resource Directory.
* Latest (fourth) edition, profusely illustrated.

5⅜ x 8½, 432 pp, $10.95

TO: **ED BURYN, Publisher**
P.O. Box 31123
San Francisco, CA 94131

Dear Ed: Date:_____

Yes, I want the following autographed book(s):

_____ SPORTS BIRTHDAYS @ 9.95 $_____

_____ VAGABONDING IN THE U.S.A. @ 10.95 $_____

_____ $_____

     6½% Sales Tax (Calif. Residents Only) $_____

     Shipping (For either or both books) $1.00

         I'm enclosing a total of $_____

(Send payment in cash or money order or check
made out to "Ed Buryn")

My Name and Address   *Mailing Address, If Different*

_____   _____

_____   _____

_____   _____

Reader's Memo

To: Eugene Lesser
P.O. Box 410132
San Francisco, CA 94141

Date: _____

Message: Dear Eugene,

From: